Beginning Drupal 8

Todd Tomlinson

Beginning Drupal 8

ISBN-13 (pbk): 978-1-4302-6580-1

ISBN-13 (electronic): 978-1-4302-6581-8

Trademarked names, logos, and images may appear in this book. Rather than use a trademark symbol with every occurrence of a trademarked name, logo, or image we use the names, logos, and images only in an editorial fashion and to the benefit of the trademark owner, with no intention of infringement of the trademark.

The use in this publication of trade names, trademarks, service marks, and similar terms, even if they are not identified as such, is not to be taken as an expression of opinion as to whether or not they are subject to proprietary rights.

While the advice and information in this book are believed to be true and accurate at the date of publication, neither the authors nor the editors nor the publisher can accept any legal responsibility for any errors or omissions that may be made. The publisher makes no warranty, express or implied, with respect to the material contained herein.

Managing Director: Welmoed Spahr
Lead Editor: Ben Renow-Clarke
Technical Reviewer: Clive Linsell
Editorial Board: Steve Anglin, Louise Corrigan, Jim DeWolf, Jonathan Gennick, Robert Hutchinson, Michelle Lowman, James Markham, Susan McDermott, Matthew Moodie, Jeffrey Pepper, Douglas Pundick, Ben Renow-Clarke, Gwenan Spearing, Matt Wade, Steve Weiss
Coordinating Editor: Mark Powers and Christine Ricketts
Copy Editor: William McManus
Compositor: SPi Global
Indexer: SPi Global
Artist: SPi Global

Distributed to the book trade worldwide by Springer Science+Business Media New York, 233 Spring Street, 6th Floor, New York, NY 10013. Phone 1-800-SPRINGER, fax (201) 348-4505, e-mail orders-ny@springer-sbm.com, or visit www.springeronline.com. Apress Media, LLC is a California LLC and the sole member (owner) is Springer Science + Business Media Finance Inc (SSBM Finance Inc). SSBM Finance Inc is a Delaware corporation.

For information on translations, please e-mail rights@apress.com, or visit www.apress.com.

Apress and friends of ED books may be purchased in bulk for academic, corporate, or promotional use. eBook versions and licenses are also available for most titles. For more information, reference our Special Bulk Sales–eBook Licensing web page at www.apress.com/bulk-sales.

Any source code or other supplementary material referenced by the author in this text is available to readers at www.apress.com. For additional information about how to locate and download your book's source code, go to www.apress.com/source-code/. Readers can also access source code at SpringerLink in the Supplementary Material section for each chapter.

There are so many people to thank for making this book possible, including seven very special people who had a huge influence on my life and my desire to write. This book is dedicated to them.

To my wife Misty, who proved that dreams do come true, who is always there to support me and cheer me on.

I want to thank my 102-year-old grandmother, Gladys Tomlinson, who at 96 published her first book. Thank you, Grandma, for all you've done for me over the years, and for the influence that you have had on my life, and for inspiring me to write. My grandmother passed away as I was writing this book and continues to inspire me to achieve great things even in her absence here on Earth.

I also want to thank my parents for giving me so many opportunities to explore my dreams and desires. Without your support and encouragement none of this would be possible. And to my wife Misty and my daughters Anna, Alissa, and Emma for sacrificing so much while I have pursued the future of technology.

Joseph Bell, who I had the honor of working with for several months on a large Drupal project. We became best friends even though we were on opposite sides of the United States. Joseph passed away while I was writing this book, way too young. His inspiration and friendship were priceless.

Contents at a Glance

Contents

About the Author

Todd Tomlinson is the Senior Enterprise Drupal Architect at Unicon in Gilbert, Arizona. Todd's focus over the past 20 years has been on designing, developing, deploying, and supporting complex web solutions for public- and private-sector clients all around the world. He has been using Drupal as the primary platform for creating beautiful and feature-rich sites since Drupal 4.

About the Technical Reviewer

Clive Linsell is a senior developer with iSOS (www.isos.com). He has planned, developed, and delivered dozens of commercial-grade solutions, covering a wide range of industries. He works extensively with PHP (Drupal, Symfony, CodeIgniter, etc.), C#, Ruby, and (more recently) Swift. He plays the guitar and piano, and is an avid supporter of Liverpool Football Club. Much of the time he can be found on Drupal Answers (http://drupal.stackexchange.com), where he helps out as a moderator.

Acknowledgments

I would like to thank the following people:

My wife Misty for inspiring me each and every day to be all that I can be.

My parents for giving me the encouragement to explore new opportunities.

My sisters for putting up with a geeky brother, before geeky was cool.

My daughters Anna, Alissa, and Emma for giving Dad the time to write this book when they really would have rather gone to a movie or the park.

My awesome team: John Blakely, Chris Franz, John Lewis, Eric Goldman, Lasbrey Nwachukwu, Chuck Crandall, Robert Nield, Drew Wills, Jim Layne, Jason Lacy, David Lipari, Jesus Cabanillas, Dan Barber, Jillian Fenton, Lisa Di Pietro, Patty Wolfe, Chris Lawson, and Patience Breinholt. You make work more than just a place to hang my hat; each of you makes it feel like home and family.

John, Justin, Abby, Todd P., Todd M., Jason, Nick, Troy, Daniel, Darren, and Jon for standing beside me over the past two years and walking through life as true brothers. I look forward to the journey ahead with each of you.

Dries for having the vision and passion for creating Drupal.

The Drupal community for your dedication to making the platform the best CMS on the planet.

The Apress team for leading me through the jungle of authoring a book. Without your passion for publishing the best books on the planet, I wouldn't have had the opportunity to cross the "author a book" item off my bucket list.

Introduction

In its relatively short life, Drupal has had a tremendous impact on the landscape of the Internet. As a web content management system (CMS), Drupal has enabled the creation of feature- and content-rich websites for organizations large and small. As a web application framework, Drupal is changing the way that people think about web application development. When I experienced the power of the Drupal platform for the first time, I knew that it was something more than just another content management solution. When I saw how easily and quickly I could build feature-rich websites, I shifted gears and focused my entire career around Drupal. While working with clients, I was often asked, "Where can I go to find information for someone who is new to Drupal?" Unfortunately there wasn't a comprehensive resource that I could point them to, and thus began my journey of writing *Beginning Drupal 7*, *Pro Drupal 7 Development*, and now *Beginning Drupal 8*.

I'm also often asked, "What is Drupal?" The short answer is, "Drupal is an open source web content management system that allows you to quickly and easily create simple to complex sites that span everything from a simple blog to a corporate site, a social networking site, or virtually anything you can dream up." What you can build with Drupal is only limited by your imagination and the time you have to spend with the platform.

As an open source platform, Drupal's community is constantly improving the platform and extending the functionality of the core platform by creating new and exciting add-on modules. If there's a new concept created on the Web, it's likely that there will be a new Drupal module that enables that concept in a matter of days. It's the community behind the platform that makes Drupal what it is today, and what it will become in the future. I'll show you how to leverage the features contributed by the community, making it easy for you to build incredible solutions with minimal effort.

The very act of picking up this book is the first step in your journey down the path of learning how to use Drupal. If you will walk with me through the entire book, you'll have the knowledge and experience to build complex and powerful Drupal-based websites. You'll also have the foundation necessary to move beyond the basics, expanding on the concepts I cover in this book.

Learning Drupal is like learning any new technology. There will be bumps and hurdles that cause you to step back and scratch your head. I hope the book helps smooth the bumps and provides you with enough information to easily jump over those hurdles. I look forward to seeing your works on the Web and hope to meet you at an upcoming DrupalCon.

CHAPTER 1

■ ■ ■

Introduction to Drupal

This chapter provides a basic overview of what a content management system (CMS) is, how Drupal fills the role as a CMS, the major building blocks of Drupal, and how to create content on your new Drupal website.

Content Management Systems

In its simplest form, a CMS is a software package that provides tools for authoring, publishing, and managing content on a website. "Content" includes anything from a news story, a blog post, a video, or a photograph, to a podcast, an article, or a description of a product that you are selling. In more general terms, content is any combination of text, graphics, photographs, audio, and video that represents something that visitors to your site will read, watch, and hear.

A CMS typically provides a number of features that simplify the process of building, deploying, and managing websites, including the following:

- an administrative interface
- a database repository for content
- a mechanism for associating information that is stored in the database with a physical page on the website
- a toolset for authoring, publishing, and managing content
- a component for creating and managing menus and navigational elements
- the tools required to define and apply themes
- user management
- a security framework
- Social networking capabilities such as forums, blogs, wikis, and surveys
- taxonomy and tagging
- online forms
- e-commerce capabilities

There are hundreds of CMSes available (check out www.cmsmatrix.org). They range from simple blogging-centric platforms, such as WordPress, to complex enterprise-class content management solutions, such as Drupal.

1

Drupal

Drupal is a free and open source CMS written in PHP and distributed under the GNU General Public License. Drupal stems from a project by a Dutch university student, Dries Buytaert. The goal of the project was to provide a mechanism for Buytaert and his friends to share news and events. Buytaert turned Drupal into an open source project in 2001, and the community readily embraced the concept and has expanded on its humble beginnings, creating what is now one of the most powerful and feature-rich CMS platforms on the Web. Individuals, teams, and communities leverage Drupal's features to easily publish, manage, and organize content on a variety of websites, ranging from personal blogs to large corporate and government sites.

The standard release of Drupal, known as Drupal core, contains basic features that can be used to create a classic brochure website, a single- or multi-user blog, an Internet forum, or a community website with user-generated content. Features found in Drupal core include the ability to author and publish content; to create and manage users, menus, and forums; and to manage your site through a web browser–based administrative interface.

Drupal was designed to be enhanced with new features and custom behavior by downloading and enabling add-on modules. There are thousands of additional modules (known as contributed or "contrib" modules) that extend Drupal core's functionality, covering a broad spectrum of capabilities, including e-commerce, social networking, integration with third-party applications, and multimedia.

Drupal can run on any computing platform that supports both a web server capable of running PHP version 5.4.5+ (including Apache, IIS, lighttpd, and nginx) and a database (such as MySQL, SQLite, or PostgreSQL) to store content and settings.

Drupal Core

When you download and install Drupal, you are installing what is commonly called Drupal core. Core represents the "engine" that powers a Drupal-based website, along with a number of out-of-the-box features that enable the creation of a relatively full-featured website. The primary components of Drupal core include capabilities to create and manage

- content
- file uploads/downloads
- menus
- user accounts
- roles and permissions
- taxonomy
- discussion forums
- views to extract and display content in various forms such as lists and tables
- WYSIWYG-based content editor

Drupal core also includes a feature-rich search engine, multilingual capabilities, and logging and error reporting.

Contributed Modules

Although Drupal core can be used to build feature-rich websites, there are likely situations where core lacks the functionality needed to address specific requirements. In such cases, the first step is to search through the thousands of custom modules, contributed by developers from all around the world to the Drupal project, for a solution that meets your needs. It's very likely that someone else has had the same functional requirement and has developed a solution to extend Drupal core to provide the functionality that you need.

To find a contributed module, visit the Drupal.org website at www.drupal.org/project/project_module. You will find a general list of categories and the current number of contributed modules (for all versions of Drupal) contained within each. Here is a short sampling of the types of categories and the number of modules you can find in each (modules are added to the list on a daily basis, and the number of modules in each category will have grown considerably since the time of this writing):

- Administration (1145)

- Community (614)

- Content (1981)

- Content Display (1612)

- Content Construction Kit (CCK) (673)

- Developer (960)

- E-commerce (892)

- Media (778)

- Third-party Integration (1908)

- Utility (1959)

To find modules that are supported on Drupal 8, select 8.x for the "Core compatibility" search filter.

A few of the most popular contributed modules, and the ones that you will likely want to install, include the following (also check out the "Most installed" list to the right of the search filters):

- *Commerce*: A full-featured web storefront module that provides all of the mechanisms required to sell products (physical as well as electronic downloads), collect credit card payments, and manage shipments. If you want to sell something on your website, this is the module you will want to use.

- *Display Suite*: Allows you to take full control of how your content is displayed using a drag-and-drop interface.

- *Calendar*: Provides the ability to create and render a list of events on a calendar.

- *Backup and Migrate*: Handles scheduled backups of content in your Drupal database, with the ability to restore the database to a previous state based on one of the backup files created by this module. This is a must-have module for any production website.

- *Google Analytics*: Provides a simple to use form for setting up Google Analytics on your site. Google Analytics is a free service that tracks the number of visitors to your website, where those visitors came from, what search terms they used to find your site, the pages they visited while on your site, how long they spent on your site, and many other useful metrics that will help you view and understand the usage of your website. For more information on Google Analytics, please visit www.google.com/analytics.

- *Pathauto*: Creates search engine–friendly URLs by automatically generating a "pretty" URL that is based on the page's title (such as www.example.com/examples instead of the default Drupal URL of www.example.com?node=1234).

- *Scheduler*: Provides the ability to specify the date that a node will become published on the site, and the date when a node will no longer be published. This allows a content author to create a node now and have it not appear on the site until some date in the future.

Drupal Themes

A *theme* is the Drupal component that defines how the pages on your website are structured and the visual aspects of those pages. A Drupal theme defines attributes of your website such as:

- How many columns of information will be presented on a page (a three-column layout with a left, center, and right column; a two-column layout with a narrow left column and a wide right column for content; a one-column layout, and the like).

- Whether a page has a banner at the top.

- Whether a page has a footer.

- Where navigational menus appear (at the top of the page, under the banner, in the right column, and so on).

- The colors used on the page.

- The font and font size used for various elements on a page (such as headings, titles, and body text).

- Graphical elements, such as logos.

Drupal core includes a number of off-the-shelf themes that you can use for your new website. You may also download one or more of the hundreds of free themes that are available at www.drupal.org/project/project_theme, or create your own theme by following the directions found at www.drupal.org/documentation/theme.

Creating Content

A website without content would be like a book without words, a newspaper without news, and a magazine without articles: hardly worth the effort of looking at. Drupal makes it easy to create, publish, and manage content on your new website. Let's look at how simple it is by creating our first piece of content. If you haven't installed Drupal yet, please visit the Appendix and follow the step-by-step process for installing and configuring Drupal core.

There are multiple paths for getting to the content-authoring screens in Drupal. I'll focus on the simplest first, and then discuss other methods in Chapter 2.

On the front page of your new website, you will see an "Add content" link beneath the no front page content has been created yet message on your home page. In the left-hand column, you will also see an "Add content" link in the Tools menu (see Figure 1-1). Click either of the links: they both take you to the content editing form where you will create your first piece of content.

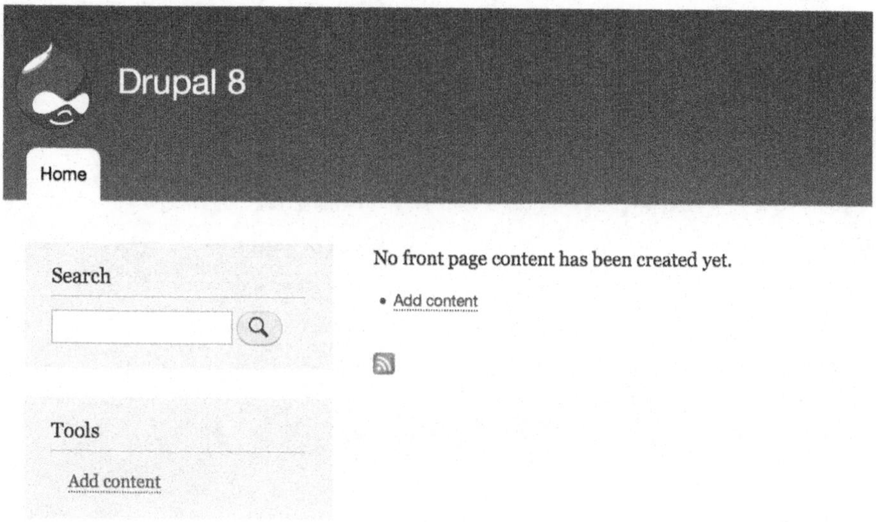

Figure 1-1. *Click either "Add content" link to get started*

Next you'll see a listing of the content types that you can use (see Figure 1-2). Drupal 8 comes with two basic content types: an article and a basic page. Both content types provide you, the author, with a text field for entering the title of the content item, and a body text area where you can write. Different content types provide additional elements. In the case of an article, you have the ability to enter "tags" for categorizing your content and an image. I will cover tagging and several other content types later in the book, as well as the capability for creating your own custom content types.

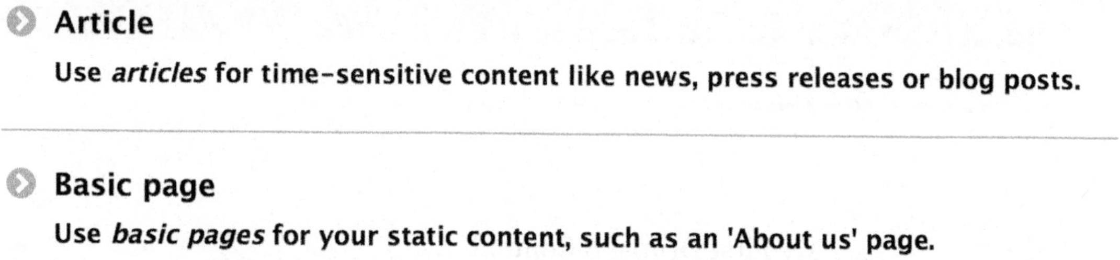

❯ Article

Use *articles* for time-sensitive content like news, press releases or blog posts.

❯ Basic page

Use *basic pages* for your static content, such as an 'About us' page.

Figure 1-2. *Selecting your content type*

Start with the simplest content type, a page, as the basis for your first content item on your new website. Click the "Basic page" link, which opens the content creation form for creating that content type (see Figure 1-3). On this form, enter the title of your first article and some text into the body area. After you have entered the title and body of your article, click the "Promotion Options" link in the right sidebar, and from the list of options presented, notice the "Promoted to front page" check box. When this option is checked, it tells Drupal to display this article on the front page of your site. If it is not checked, please click on the checkbox. Finally, scroll down to the bottom of the page and click the "Save and publish" button (I will cover the other options in Chapter 2).

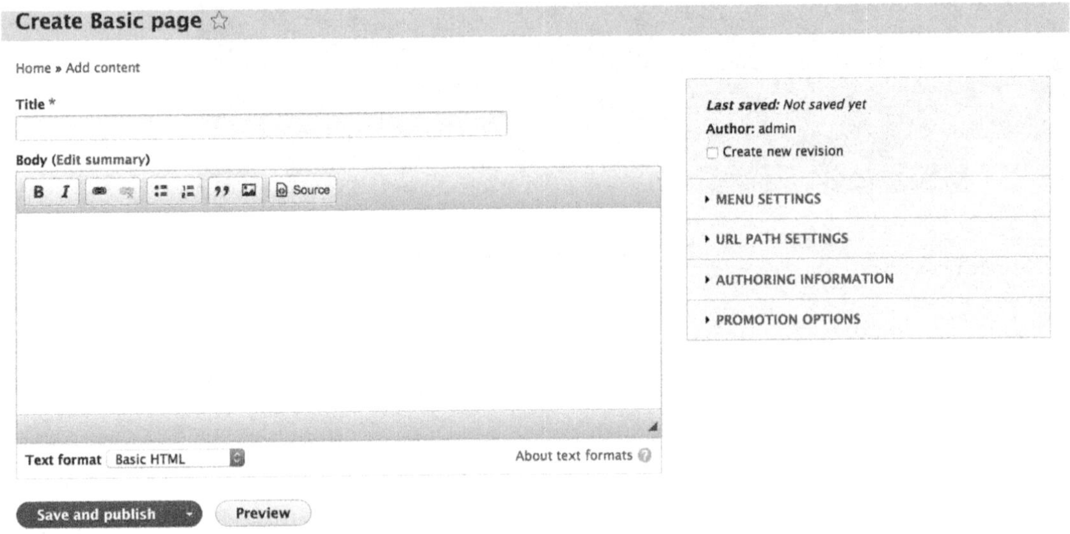

Figure 1-3. *Creating a basic page*

By clicking the "Save and publish" button, the content you just authored will be immediately displayed on the front page of your website (see Figure 1-4).

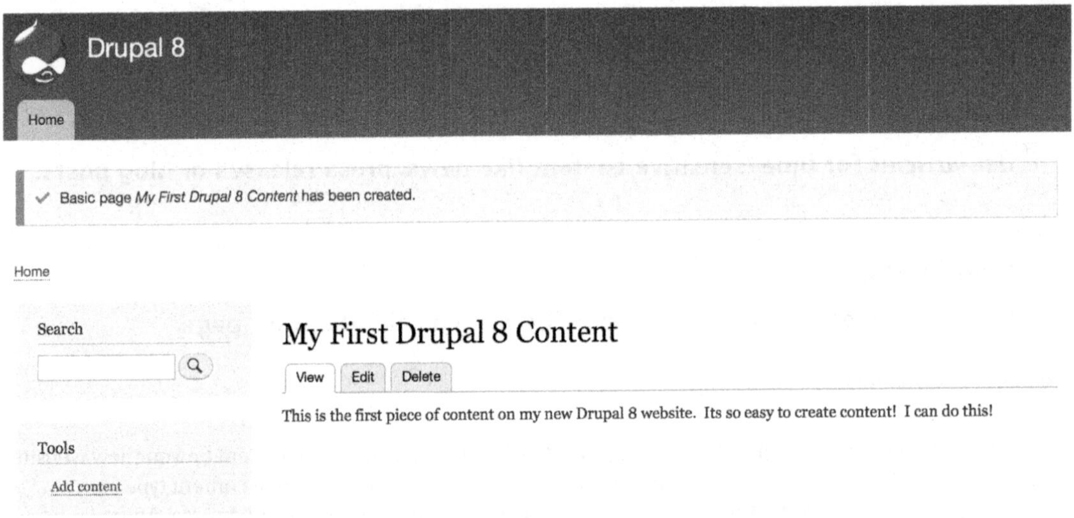

Figure 1-4. *Voila, you are published!*

Congratulations! You've authored and published content on your new Drupal website. There are many other content authoring, publishing, and management features that I will cover throughout the remainder of this book. You are well on your way to building incredible websites on Drupal.

Summary

This chapter focused on the basics of what a CMS is, the base functionality available in Drupal core, how to extend the functional footprint of Drupal core by adding contributed modules, Drupal themes, and creating your first content item in Drupal. Chapter 2 will dive deeper into the content creation, publishing, and management capabilities of Drupal 8.

CHAPTER 2

■ ■ ■

Creating and Managing Content

Remember, a website without content is as interesting and informative as a book without words. In this chapter, I focus on Drupal's content creating, publishing, editing, and management features, providing you with the knowledge necessary to venture out and create, publish, and manage a wide variety of content on your new Drupal website. You started that process in the previous chapter; now let's see what you can add.

Understanding the Basics

Content is the primary building block of any website, whether it is constructed using Drupal or any other tool in the marketplace. Content is what visitors come to a website to find, and a lack of content is often the reason visitors fail to return to a website after the first time. In its most basic form, content is any combination of text, pictures, video, audio, and graphics. An individual piece of content may take a variety of different forms:

- news story
- blog post
- product description
- company overview
- forum post
- photograph
- wiki entry

Content on a Drupal-based website often starts with a title followed by body text. In Chapter 1, we created a basic page, which consisted of content with just a title and body. Drupal provides the ability to expand on this with a custom content type. A custom content type enables you to create additional fields that can be used to capture other relevant and related information. A common example is a calendar event. An event includes a title and body text (the description of the event), as well as other pertinent information, such as the date and time, the location, and possibly a map or photo. I'll cover creating custom content types in Chapter 5.

Creating Content in Drupal

In Chapter 1, I introduced Drupal's content creation capabilities by showing you how to create your first content item and publish it to your website. The content type that you used in Chapter 1 was the basic page. Drupal 8 includes a second content type: – an article.

An article is identical to a basic page, with the single exception that an article has an image upload feature and an additional field where the author can enter what are called tags. Tags are simply words that help classify, organize, and search for related content on your site. They are a powerful Drupal feature that I will cover in detail in Chapter 4.

To create and publish your new article, click one of the "Add content" links on your website and select Article from the list of content types. The form that is used to create an article looks identical to the form used to author a basic page, with the exception of the image upload and tags fields. Proceed with the content creation process by entering a title. Next, upload a picture by clicking the Browse button and finding a picture on your computer to upload and include in the article (see Figure 2-1).

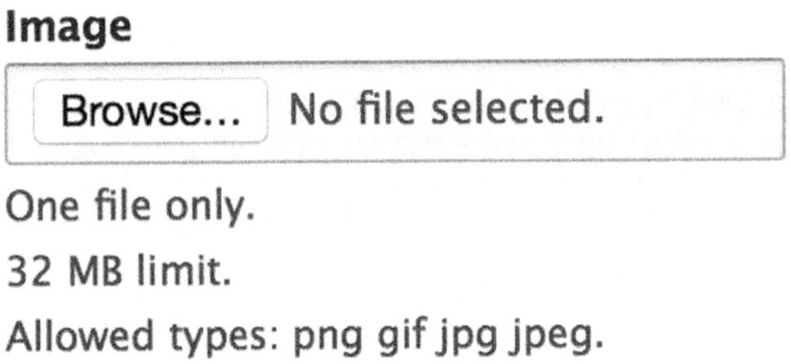

Image

Browse...   No file selected.

One file only.

32 MB limit.

Allowed types: png gif jpg jpeg.

Figure 2-1. *Browse your computer for the image you wish to add to your article*

After you locate and upload an image, your content creation form should display a miniature version of the image on the form (see Figure 2-2), along with an alternate text field. It is a good idea to enter text into this field, especially if you expect to have visitors with visual disabilities.

Image

Alternative text *

A line drawing of a boat|

This text will be used by screen readers, search engines, or when the image cannot be loaded.

   boat.gif (10.47 KB)   (**Remove**)

Figure 2-2. *The image you wish to upload appears, and you are given the chance to add descriptive text*

The next step is to create the body text and the tags associated with your article (see Figure 2-3). Tags can be any list of words or phrases, separated by commas, that describe the general concepts covered in your article. I'll discuss tags in more detail in Chapter 4.

Create Article ☆

Home ▸ Add content

Title *

Boats

Body (Edit summary)

B I ⚭ ⬚ ⁝≡ ⁝≡ ❞ ⊡ ⧉ Source

A **boat** is a watercraft of any size designed to float or plane, to work or travel on water. Small boats are typically found on inland (lakes) or in protected coastal areas. However, boats such as the whaleboat were designed for operation from a ship in an offshore environment. In naval terms, a boat is a vessel small enough to be carried aboard another vessel (a ship). Another less restrictive definition is a vessel that can be lifted out of the water. Some definitions do not make a distinction in size, as bulk freighters 1,000 feet (300 m) long on the Great Lakes are called orebolats. For reasons of naval tradition, submarines are usually referred to as 'boats' rather than 'ships', regardless of their size and shape. Boats have a wide variety of shapes and sizes and construction methods due to their intended purpose, available materials or local traditions. Canoe type boats have a long history and various versions are used throughout the world for transportation, fishing or sport. Fishing boats vary widely in style partly to match local conditions. Pleasure boats include ski boats, pontoon boats, and sailboats. House boats may be used for vacationing or long-term housing. Small boats can provide transport or convey cargo (lightering) to and from large ships. Lifeboats have rescue and safety functions.

body p

Text format   Basic HTML ▾   About text formats ⃠

Tags

boat, ship, sailboat, pontoon boat, house boat, fishing boat, ski boat   ○

Enter a comma-separated list. For example: Amsterdam, Mexico City, "Cleveland, Ohio"

Image

Alternative text *

A line drawing of a boat

This text will be used by screen readers, search engines, or when the image cannot be loaded.

🖻 boat.gif (10.47 KB)   [Remove]

[Save and publish   ➕]   [Preview]

Last saved: Not saved yet
Author: admin
⬚ Create new revision

▸ MENU SETTINGS

▸ COMMENT SETTINGS

▸ URL PATH SETTINGS

▸ AUTHORING INFORMATION

▸ PROMOTION OPTIONS

Figure 2-3. *Creating article body text and adding tags*

Next, click the "Save and publish" button at the bottom of the page. Return to your site's homepage by clicking the Home tab. The results of your actions should be an updated homepage that displays your new article (see Figure 2-4).

Figure 2-4. *Your updated homepage appears*

As you can see in Figure 2-4, an article displays the image that was uploaded as well as the list of tags entered. I will cover tagging and taxonomy in detail in Chapter 4, but as a preview, clicking one of the tags automatically renders a list of all articles that were tagged with that same term.

Teasers and Full Nodes

One of Drupal's key content-related features is the ability to automatically display a content item in either "teaser" mode or "full-node" view mode. A teaser is a shortened version of the article, typically the first 600 characters, whereas "full node" refers to the entire length of the content. In Figure 2-4, you'll notice a "Read more" link at the bottom of both articles. This tells you that Drupal is automatically rendering the content items in teaser mode. You can modify the length of the teaser as well as several other aspects of a view mode. I'll cover the details in Chapter 10.

Editing Content

At some point you will need to change something about a piece of content that you've posted on your site. The process for editing content is nearly identical to the process for creating it, the only difference being the need to find the content that you want to change. To find content, click the Content link in the menu at the top of the page. The Content page lists all of the content that appears on the site and is filterable by published status, type of content, language, and a title search feature. To edit a content item from the list presented on the Content page, simply click the Edit button for that item and Drupal will display the content editing form for that item. If you are on the page where the content you need to change resides, and you are logged in as a user who has the correct permissions (see Chapter 6), you will see View, Edit, and Delete tabs (see Figure 2-5).

Boats

View | Edit | Delete

Submitted by admin on Sun, 07/05/2015 - 16:57

A **boat** is a watercraft of any size designed to float or plane, to work or travel on water. Small boats are typically found on inland (lakes) or in protected coastal areas. However, boats such as the whaleboat were designed for operation from a ship in an offshore environment. In naval terms, a boat is a vessel small enough to be carried aboard another vessel (a ship). Another less restrictive definition is a vessel that can be lifted out of the water. Some definitions do not make a distinction in size, as bulk freighters 1,000 feet (300 m) long on the Great Lakes are called oreboats. For reasons of naval tradition, submarines are usually referred to as 'boats' rather than 'ships', regardless of their size and shape. Boats have a wide variety of shapes and sizes and construction methods due to their intended purpose, available materials or local traditions. Canoe type boats have a long history and various versions are used throughout the world for transportation, fishing or sport. Fishing boats vary widely in style partly to match local conditions. Pleasure boats include ski boats, pontoon boats, and sailboats. House boats may be used for vacationing or long-term housing. Small boats can provide transport or convey cargo (lightering) to and from large ships. Lifeboats have rescue and safety functions.

Tags
boat   ship   sailboat   pontoon boat   house boat   fishing boat   ski boat

Figure 2-5. *You can edit the content of your own site by clicking Edit*

By default, Drupal allows the author of a content item to edit, update, and delete that item. Only site administrators or users with roles that permit them to edit, update, and delete other authors' content may make changes to your content. If you do not see Edit next to the title of a content item, then you are not logged in with an account with the proper permissions to make changes to that item.

To change a content item, click the Edit tab. Drupal will display that content item in editing mode, where you can change or delete the item (see Figure 2-6).

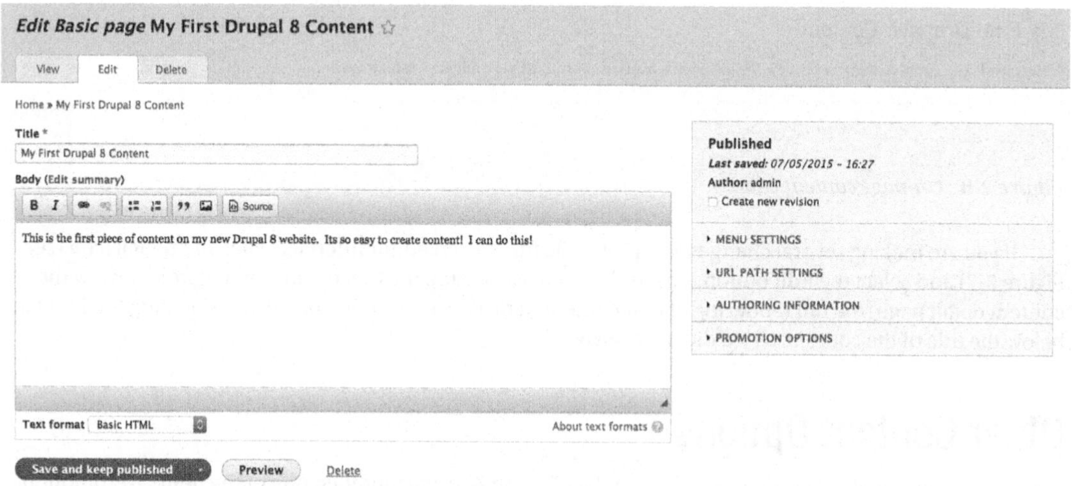

Figure 2-6. *Content is displayed in editing mode*

There's also another way to edit your articles. Try updating the article you created in the previous step by navigating back to your homepage. To navigate back to the homepage, click the "Back to site" button located at the top left of the page. On the homepage, hover over the article you wish to change. You'll notice a pencil icon appear to the right of the title as you hover (see Figure 2-7). Click the pencil icon, select the "quick edit" option, and then click the content body.

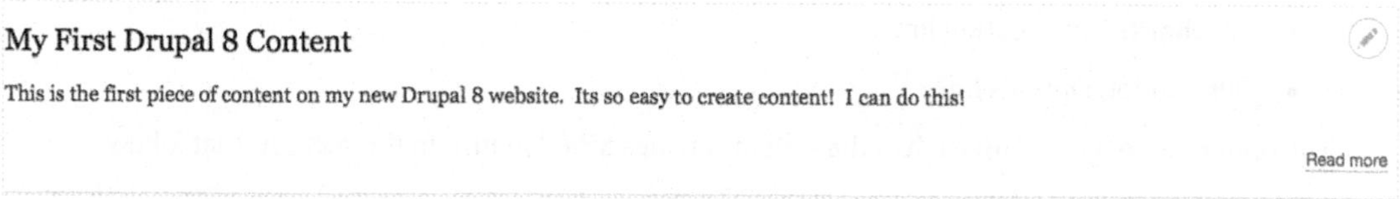

Figure 2-7. *Pencil icon*

■ **Note** If the article you wish to edit is the first article in a list, then hovering over that article will cause two pencil icons to appear. The top icon provides the ability to edit the view that generates the list of content that appears on that page, while the second pencil icon will take you to the editing form for that article.

A pop-up window will appear in which you can update the text without leaving the homepage (see Figure 2-8). Make changes to the text in the editor and click the Save button. The new version automatically appears on the homepage after you've saved it. This is a great way of performing quick text touch-ups or fixing errors that you've spotted.

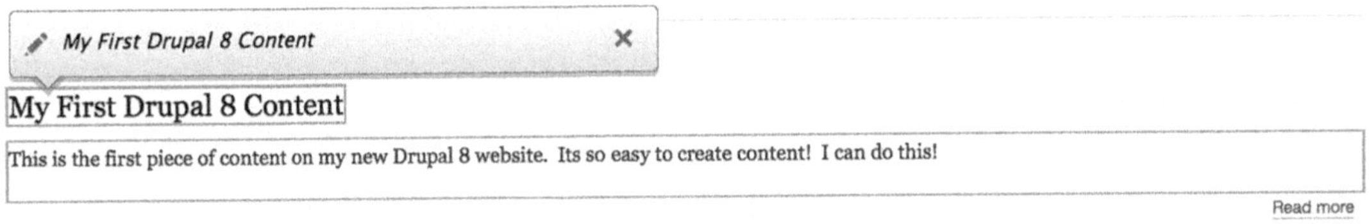

| ✎ My First Drupal 8 Content | ✕ |

My First Drupal 8 Content

This is the first piece of content on my new Drupal 8 website. Its so easy to create content! I can do this!

Read more

Figure 2-8. *On-page content editor*

If you are making several changes and prefer the full-screen editor interface, click the pencil icon (see Figure 2-7) and select the Edit option. This is the same as clicking the title of any content item to view the content detail page (the full rendering of that content item as a stand-alone page) and selecting the Edit tab below the title of the content, as we did previously.

Other Content Options

In the right column of the content editing form (see Figure 2-6), we modified one of the items—Promotion Options—before we saved our new content item. Let's look at this and the other options associated with a content item before moving on to more advanced content topics.

Click the Edit tab next to the title of the content item you just updated and examine the items in the right column:

- "Create new revision" check box
- Menu Settings link
- Comment Settings link
- URL Path Settings link
- Authoring Information link
- Promotion Options link

The options associated with each of these items are described in turn in the sections that follow.

Revision Information

Have you ever made a change to a document, saved those changes, and then realized that you made a mistake and need to "undo" the changes you made? Have you ever realized this *after* closing Microsoft Word, when it's too late to revert to the document in its pre-changed state?

There will come a time when you or someone else makes changes to a content item, and you'll wish you had a copy of the content before it was changed. Drupal solves this problem by providing the ability to create a new version (copy) of your content when that content item is changed. Edit the sample article you created in previous steps and check the "Create new revision" check box in the right column. Enter a description of the changes that you made (see Figure 2-9) in the "Revision log message" field.

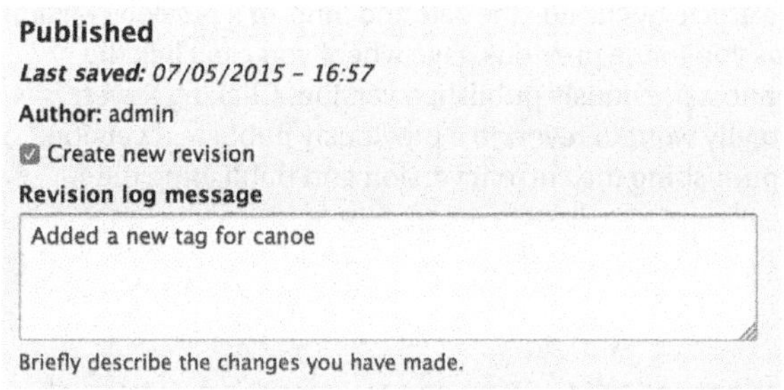

Published
Last saved: 07/05/2015 – 16:57
Author: admin
☑ Create new revision
Revision log message

Added a new tag for canoe

Briefly describe the changes you have made.

Figure 2-9. *Enter an explanation of the changes you made*

Once you have entered the description of what you changed, click the "Save and keep published" button. Drupal then displays your content with a Revisions tab (see Figure 2-10).

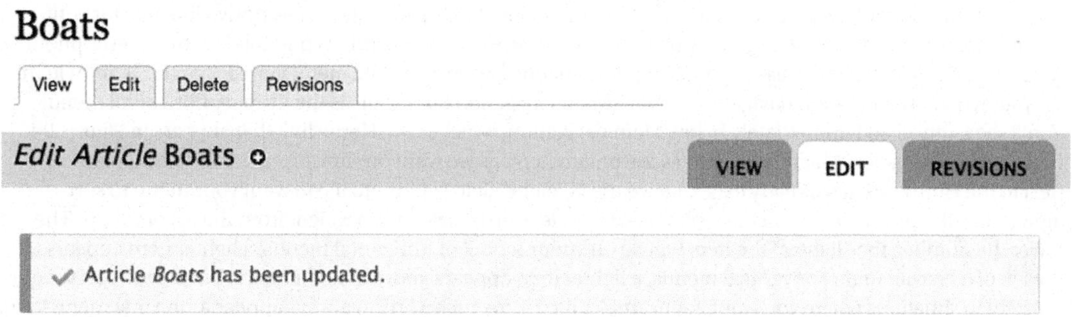

Boats

| View | Edit | Delete | Revisions |

Edit Article Boats ○   VIEW | EDIT | REVISIONS

✓ Article *Boats* has been updated.

Figure 2-10. *Your item now includes a Revisions tab*

Clicking the Revisions tab takes you to a page that lists the current version and all previous versions of that content item (see Figure 2-11).

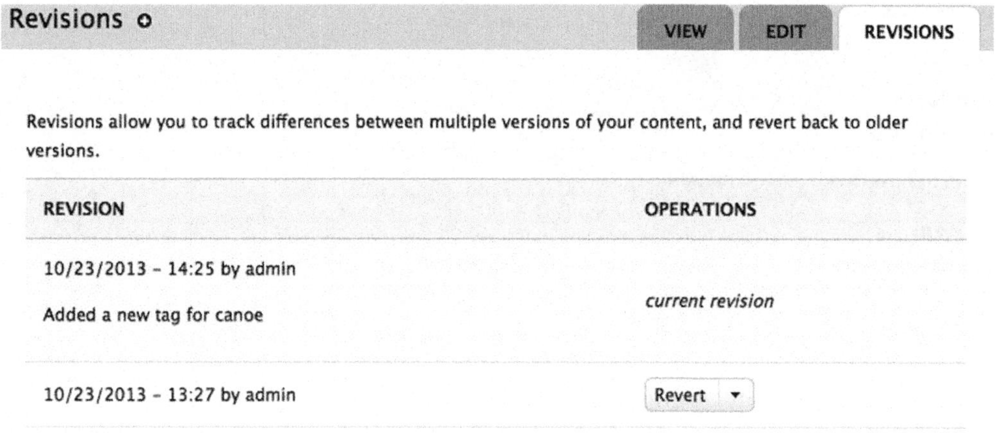

Revisions ○   VIEW | EDIT | REVISIONS

Revisions allow you to track differences between multiple versions of your content, and revert back to older versions.

REVISION	OPERATIONS
10/23/2013 – 14:25 by admin Added a new tag for canoe	*current revision*
10/23/2013 – 13:27 by admin	Revert ▾

Figure 2-11. *All the revisions to an item appear on this screen*

You can view a previously published version of the article by clicking the date and time for a previous version.

Clicking the Back button in your browser returns you to the previous page where you can click the Revert link, changing the currently published version to a previously published version. Clicking Revert causes Drupal to display a page that asks you if you really want to revert to a previously published version.

Clicking the Revert button results in Drupal unpublishing the current version and publishing the selected version.

Menu Settings

There may be instances when a content item is important enough to list on one of your site's navigational menus. By default Drupal creates a "Main navigation" menu. The Main navigation menu is typically displayed at or near the top of the page. I'll cover menus in detail in Chapter 5, but for now I'll show you how to assign your test content item to the Main navigation menu.

While on the homepage of your site, hover over one of the content items you have created, click the pencil icon, and select the Edit link. Click the Menu Settings link (see Figure 2-6). The Menu Settings panel will appear. Check the "Provide a menu link" check box, and you will see four fields (see Figure 2-12): "Menu link title," "Description," "Parent item," and "Weight." In the "Menu link title" field, enter a descriptive link title for your content item (remember that this will appear in a menu, so use as few words as possible). In the "Description" field, enter the text that you wish to appear when someone hovers over that menu item. From the "Parent item" drop-down list, select "Main navigation," where Main navigation on our site is the primary horizontal menu. You'll see Home listed immediately below Main navigation, which is the Home link that appears in Figure 2-4. For our example, select Main navigation as the parent item, as we want our link to appear as another tab next to the Home tab that already exists. Leave the "Weight" field set to zero if you want your menu to sort alphabetically. You can override the alphabetical sort feature by selecting a weight from the list of values. The lower the number, the "lighter" the item will be on your menu. For horizontal menus, a lighter item appears to the left of a heavier item. For vertical menus, a lighter item appears above a heavier item. Setting the sort weight is useful in situations where you want, for example, the Home menu link to always appear as the first menu item. To force the Home link to the front of the list, select the lowest number from the drop-down list of values.

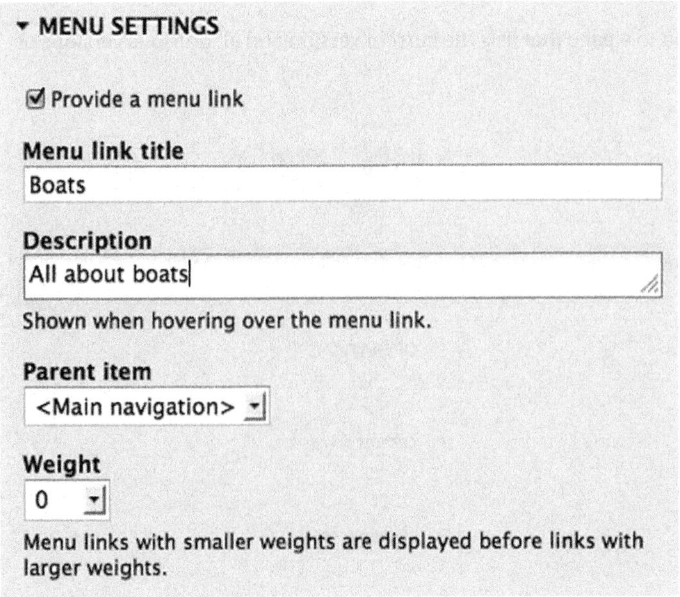

▼ MENU SETTINGS

☑ Provide a menu link

Menu link title

Boats

Description

All about boats|

Shown when hovering over the menu link.

Parent item

\<Main navigation\> ▾

Weight

0 ▾

Menu links with smaller weights are displayed before links with larger weights.

Figure 2-12. *Click the Menu Settings link and set your preferences*

Click the "Save and keep published" button. Drupal will save your content item, and the item will now appear on the Main navigation menu, with the menu items sorted alphabetically. By default, menu items are sorted alphabetically; you may change the sort order through the menu administration tools which are discussed in Chapter 8. In this scenario we're linking a single piece of content to a menu item. In cases where you wish to link multiple content items to a single menu item you'll need to create a landing page (see Chapter 7) or a View (see Chapter 10). If you are using the standard Bartik theme (which is the default theme in Drupal 8), you should see a new tab near the top of your page with the value you entered in the "Menu link title" field. Clicking that tab will take you to that content item (see Figure 2-13).

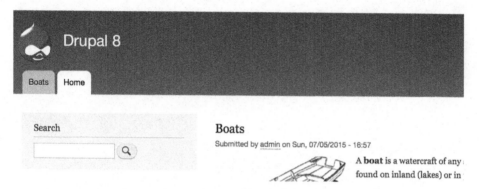

Figure 2-13. *Click the new menu tab to see the content item*

If you delete the related content item, the menu item will automatically disappear.

Comment Settings

Drupal provides the capability for visitors to your website to post comments about your site's content. To try it, click the Edit tab next to the title of your content item, or hover over your content item and click the pencil icon and select Edit. In the right column of the content editing form, click Comment Settings. Clicking the link reveals the screen shown in Figure 2-14.

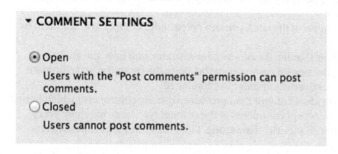

Figure 2-14. *Setting your comments preferences*

Two options are presented: Open, the default option (see Figure 2-15), which allows site visitors to post comments to a content item created with this content type, and Closed, which precludes visitors from posting comments. There may be cases where you don't want visitors to have the ability to post comments. Try both options to see the difference in how the content appears on your site. Leave the Open option selected and click the "Save and keep published" button. You'll see your content with the Add new comment form displayed immediately beneath the content. Edit the content and select the Closed option and click the "Save and keep published" button. You'll notice a significant change in how your content item is displayed, because comments will no longer appear.

Comments

Add new comment

| Your name | admin |

| Subject | |

Comment *

| B *I* ∞ ⬚ ⋮≡ ≔ „ 🖼 🅰 Source |

Text format   Basic HTML ▾   About text formats ⑦

Save   Preview

Figure 2-15. With the default settings of Open, users can now post comments on your site

With the default settings of Open, visitors to your site can now write and publish comments in response to your content item (assuming you have set the permissions to allow anonymous users to post comments, which I will cover in Chapter 6). Try entering a Subject and Comment and then clicking Save. Your comment should now appear in the Comments section.

As the content author (or as an administrator of the site), you can delete, edit, or reply to a comment by clicking the links under each comment.

Comments typically appear in chronological order. As the site administrator, you have the ability to specify how comments are displayed: either the newest comment at the top of the list or the first comment posted at the top of the list. I'll cover how to set the default order in Chapter 10.

Turning comments on and off at the individual content item provides absolute control over which items accept comments. You can also set whether to accept comments at the content type level, meaning every content item created using that content type will "inherit" that setting. I'll cover setting global parameters, such as accepting comments, in Chapter 10.

URL Path Settings

You may have noticed while working with the revisions feature that the URL that was shown in your browser's address bar looked something like `http://localhost/node/1`, where "node" in the URL tells us that Drupal is displaying a single piece of content (a node) and "1" represents the unique ID of the node that is being displayed. In this case, it's the first node that we created in the system, so the ID is 1. That number will increase by 1 for each node we add. Although http://localhost/node/1 gets us to the content that we wanted, the URL is not very people- or search-engine-friendly. Fortunately, Drupal lets us override the URL to something that is more understandable and representative of the content on the page being displayed.

Click the Edit tab or hover over your content item and click the pencil icon and select Edit. In the right column, click URL Path Settings. Drupal lets you create an alias, or an alternative URL, to the same content item as http://localhost/node/1. In the "URL alias" field, enter a more descriptive link than node/1. For example, if the article describes recreational boating, you might enter "recreational-boating" in the "URL alias" field. Note that you only enter the URL portion after the base URL of your site; for example, if your site's URL is http://example.com, there is no need to enter http://example.com in the "URL alias" field, only the descriptive portion of the URL (see Figure 2-16).

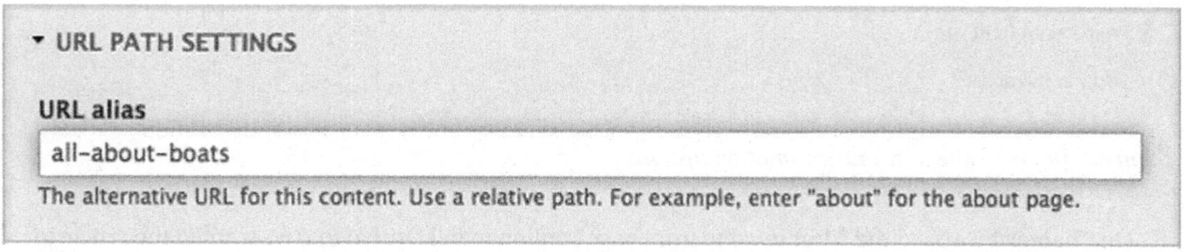

Figure 2-16. *Changing your content's URL to a more descriptive one*

■ **Caution**   You must use hyphens, underscores, periods, or other characters to separate the words in your URL. Spaces between words will not work.

After entering the new URL alias, click the "Save and keep published" button at the bottom of the form. Drupal will redisplay the page using the new alias URL that you created. In our example, the new URL is http://localhost/all-about-boats. The new URL is easy for a human to understand and, more important, easy for a search engine to pick up: the URL better indicates the content that the page provides.

Creating alias URLs is an important aspect of creating content on your website. However, manually creating an alias for every content item is tedious. Fortunately, there is a Drupal module that automatically creates a URL alias for every content item saved on your site after the module is installed and enabled. That module is called Pathauto and was introduced in Chapter 1. I'll cover the installation of modules like Pathauto in Chapter 8.

Authoring Information

Once again, click the Edit tab or use the pencil icon to edit a content item. Click Authoring Information in the right column, and you'll see the screen shown in Figure 2-17.

Figure 2-17. *Enter author information here*

19

This screen provides information about the user who created the content and the date that the content was authored. It's unlikely that you'll want to change this information, but you can if you need to.

Promotion Options

The final item on the vertical menu is Promotion Options. Click the Edit tab or use the pencil icon to edit a content item. Click the Promotion Options link to see the screen shown in Figure 2-18.

Figure 2-18. *Checking out your promotion options*

In Chapter 1 we used the "Promoted to front page" option to tell Drupal that we wanted the article to show up on the front page of our website. If we uncheck this box, our article will be removed from the front page, but will still be available through the URL that we set up in the previous steps, or directly through the `http://localhost/node/X` link, where *X* is the node ID of the content that we are seeking. I will cover alternative methods for having content show up on the front page in later chapters when I talk about advanced Drupal features.

The "Sticky at top of lists" option provides a mechanism for ensuring that this content item always appears at the top of lists. I will cover lists in detail in Chapter 10. This is a helpful feature when you have content that you want to highlight, such as an article on the rules for posting content on your site.

Deleting Content

I've covered how to create and edit content, but I haven't covered how to delete content. There may be cases where you have a piece of content that is no longer relevant to your site, and you want to delete it. The process for deleting a content item is fairly simple. First create a new article following the steps covered earlier in the chapter. The title and content aren't important, as you're going to immediately delete the article after you've created it. Once finished, click the "Save and publish" button. If you are viewing that piece of content, you may:

- Click the Delete tab (see Figure 2-10)
- Hover over the article and click the pencil icon to reveal a Delete link
- From the Content listing page (click Content on the menu) you may click the Delete button in the Actions column
- If you're editing the content you may click the Delete link at the bottom of the content editing form

All of these methods permanently remove the content item from the Drupal database. If you created a menu link for that content item, that menu item will also be removed.

There may be cases where you simply don't want a content item to appear on the site but you wish to retain that article for future reference, or cases where you're working on a long article and need to finish it at a later time. In those situations, to effectively hide that content item from visitors to your site, simply edit the article and click the arrow next to the "Save and keep published" button to reveal a "Save and unpublish" link. Clicking that link retains the content but hides the content from visitors to your site.

Previewing Content

Another activity that you may wish to perform as you are authoring content on your site is to preview how that item will look when it's saved and published on your site. The Preview link at the bottom of the content editing form does just that, displaying your content as it will appear in teaser mode as well as in the full content mode.

Finding Content

It is likely that your site will have dozens to hundreds of content items, and at some point you'll need the capability to look for an item that you want to view, change, or delete. To find that content item, you could do any of the following:

- Navigate to the page where that item resides, and click the Edit button next to the title.

- Enter the URL for that item in the address bar of your web browser.

- Search for that item using your site's search feature.

- Use the content listing page.

Any of the methods would work, but using the content listing page is probably the most common method. To view this page, choose Manage ➤ Content. You'll see the screen shown in Figure 2-19.

Figure 2-19. *Viewing the content listing page*

On this page you can sort the list by clicking the Title, Content Type, Author, Status, or Updated column headings and then clicking the up and down triangle to sort in ascending or descending order. You can also filter the results (limit what is shown) by selecting the status from the top drop-down menu (for example, Published or Unpublished) and/or the content type drop-down menu (such as Article or Basic page). Clicking the Filter button will refresh the list to show only those items that meet the criteria you selected.

From any item in the list, you can click the title of the article to view that article, or you can click the arrow to the right of the Operations button to reveal Edit or Delete options. You may also save, publish, unpublish, delete, promote to the front page, unpromote to the front page, make sticky and remove stickiness on multiple content items at the same time. Just click the check box to the left of each content item, select from the "With selection" drop-down menu the option that you want to apply to all items you checked, and then click Apply.

Summary

This chapter focused on creating content, setting the various options that are available when creating a content item, and updating and deleting content. You learned how to place a content item on a menu so users can easily find and view that content, and how to create search-engine- and user-friendly URLs. At this point, you have the basic skills and understanding necessary to create a basic Drupal website, but stopping now means that you would miss out on all of the other rich and powerful features that Drupal has to offer. In the chapters that follow, I will describe the processes for creating complex page layouts, rendering lists of content, and controlling who has access to various features and functions on your website, and I will share tips and tricks for managing your new site.

■ ■ ■

## CHAPTER 3

Creating and Managing Users

Now that your site is up and running, you have a couple of decisions to make. First, will you have any administrators on the site other than yourself? Second, will your site be open to everyone, or will users need to log in to view content and other features? In this chapter, I cover how Drupal treats visitors to your site, and how you as a site administrator can configure Drupal's user account features to restrict the capabilities of those who have user accounts on your system.

Users, Roles, and Permissions

Controlling who has the ability to do what on your website is performed through Drupal's security features. Drupal's security features provide the ability to define who has the ability to view, create, update, delete, and participate through a combination of individual user accounts, user roles, and permissions.

Users (or site visitors) in Drupal 8 are divided into two general categories: anonymous users and authenticated users. Anonymous users are individuals who visit your website and do not log in using a user ID and password. If you visit www.cnn.com and don't log in, you're classified as an anonymous user. With Drupal, you have the ability to support anonymous users, and you also have the ability to restrict what an anonymous user can do on your site. Authenticated users are visitors to your site who log in using a unique user ID and password. I'll cover how user IDs and passwords are created shortly, but understanding the difference between the two categories of users is important.

Roles are a Drupal mechanism that allow you, the site administrator, to define categories of authenticated users of your website. You may define roles on your website that are department specific (e.g., a role each for human resources, purchasing, sales, marketing, and customer service), roles that are functionally oriented (e.g., content authors, content reviewers, content publishers), roles that are associated with a specific section of your website (e.g., products, support, sales, homepage), or any other definition that you can dream up. Roles are simply a way of putting authenticated users into categories, where categories are associated with specific permissions. Any authenticated user of your website may be assigned to none, one, or more than one role (e.g., you may have a user who is assigned roles of sales department, content author, and products).

Permissions in Drupal are a mechanism for controlling what a user assigned to a specific role can do. There are dozens of permissions that you can enable or revoke for each user role you have defined. Examples of permissions that you might set for a specific role include: the ability to create a new page, the ability to create a new article, the ability to edit any article regardless of who authored it, the ability to search content on the website, and the ability to add a new user account. The combination of permissions that you set for each role defines the capabilities that a user assigned to that role can do on your website once they have successfully logged in.

When you combine user roles with permissions and individual user accounts, you end up with a highly configurable solution for securing access to key features and content on your website.

User Accounts

All Drupal websites have at least one user account: the system administrator. This account is created automatically during the installation process, and is the account that you will use to administer your site. For sites where the site owner is the only one who creates content and administers the site, having just the site administrator's account is all that is required. If you anticipate having others who will administer or create content, then you'll need to decide which Drupal mechanism to use to create user accounts. Drupal provides three alternatives for you to pick from:

- Only administrators can create user accounts.
- Visitors can create their own accounts without an administrator approving their account.
- Visitors can request a new account, but an administrator has to approve the account before it is activated.

Which approach you should take depends on how you anticipate visitors using your website. If your site is informational in nature and visitors don't need to log in to see content or participate in site features (e.g., posting comments), then the first option is the best approach, as it doesn't confuse visitors to the site by making them think that you have to log in to your site to see content. If your site has content or features that are considered "not for public consumption" and require a user account, then you will want to pick an approach that works for you depending on whether you want visitors to be able to create their own accounts without verifying their credentials (second option), or you want an administrator to perform some form of verification before the users account is activated (third option).

Setting the approach that you wish to use is part of the process of setting up the various settings for user accounts on your system.

Configuring User Account Settings

Before creating your first user account, it is advisable that you visit the user account settings page and review or modify the general user account configuration settings, of which there are many (see Figure 3-1).

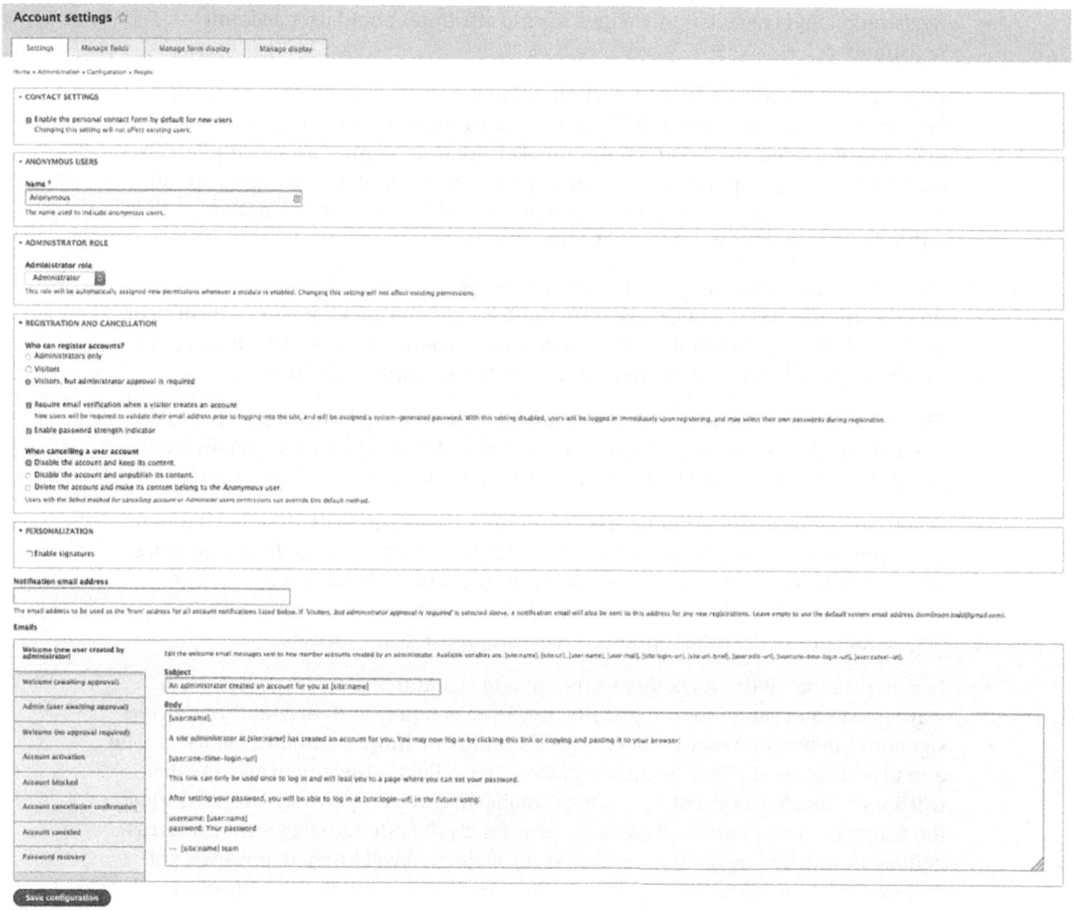

Figure 3-1. *Account settings page*

To access the settings page choose Manage ➤ Configuration (assuming you are logged in as the administrator), and, on the Configuration page, locate the section titled "People." Click the Account Settings link, which will take you to the page that you will use to set various configuration parameters for user accounts:

- *Contact settings*: you may enable individual users on the site to have a personal contact form. This feature is enabled by default; to disable it, simply uncheck the box.

- *Anonymous users: the name used to identify anonymous users*: In most cases, leaving the default value is appropriate, which is "Anonymous."

- *Administrator role: what role to associate with administrator capabilities*: The role selected becomes the default role assigned as the administrator of new modules that you install on the system. Using the default value "administrator" is an appropriate action. (I will cover creating roles later in this chapter.)

- Registration and cancellation: defines several attributes about user account registration:

    Who can register accounts: if only administrators can create accounts, select the first option "Administrators only." If any visitor to your website can create their own account, select the "Visitors" option. If visitors can request an account but an administrator must approve that request before the account is active. This option is selected by default. For demonstration purposes I'll select the first option, so that only administrators may create user accounts.

    "Require e-mail verification," is a good option to leave checked. This option requires that the user responds to a Drupal-generated e-mail that asks them to confirm their account. This helps to avoid "bot"-created user accounts, as most bots do not have the intelligence or capabilities to respond to user account verification e-mails.

    The password strength indicator is a helpful tool to indicate how strong a person's password is. A weak password may be easily hacked, whereas a strong password is harder to crack. It's a good tool to enable to help keep your Drupal site secure.

    When cancelling a user account: a set of options allows you to define what happens to content on your site that was created by this user when you disable that person's account in the future. In most cases the default option, "Disable the account and keep all content," meets the needs of a majority of websites. You may, however, decide that one of the other options is more appropriate for your site.

- Personalization: defines whether users can add signatures to their profiles. I will leave the default values for our test site; however, you may wish to enable or disable signatures depending on whether you wish to provide those capabilities to users. The e-mail address in the "Notification e-mail address" field is the e-mail address that will appear on all user account–centric e-mails that are generated by Drupal during the registration and password recovery process. By default, the site's e-mail address defined during the installation process is the value that will be used; however, you may override the default by entering a valid e-mail address in the "Notification e-mail address" field.

The remaining options at the bottom of the page define the format of e-mails generated by the system to inform users of their new account, and the content that is included in each of the e-mails generated by the system. You may modify the content of the e-mails to address your individual preferences. Simply click through each of the tabs in the vertical menu to view each of the e-mails generated by the system and sent to users. If you examine the default content, you will see values such as "[user:name]"; these are tokens used by Drupal to place dynamic content into the body of the generated e-mails. For example, [user:name] will insert the person's username that was entered on the registration form into the specific spot where that token appears in the e-mail.

Now that you have the definition of user accounts completed, you are ready to define roles and set permissions.

Creating Roles

User roles are a mechanism for categorizing groups of users with similar responsibilities and capabilities on your website. If your website is for an elementary school, you might have roles for teachers, students, and staff. If your website is a community website, you might have roles for content authors, content reviewers, publishers, and forum administrators.

The hardest part about creating user roles is deciding what roles you'll need for your site. In general terms, it is easier to administer a site that has fewer roles than one that has lots of roles, as you must set the permissions for each individual role. However, fewer roles means less flexibility, so it is a balancing act, and often one that you have to adjust over time as you become more familiar with the types of users on your site. Unfortunately, there isn't a formula you can use to determine how many roles you'll need, but fortunately there isn't a right or wrong answer as to how many you will need. For our example, we'll create two general-purpose roles:

> A role for users who are part of our organization and who will have responsibility for authoring, publishing, and managing content and menus on our site.

> A role for site visitors who are provided access to "non-public" content that is intended only for authenticated users (visitors who have been assigned a user ID and password). These users can view content and add comments to content, but cannot author, edit, or delete content.

To create a new user role, assuming you are logged in with the administrator account, click the Manage link in the menu at the top of the page and then the People link in the submenu. On the People page, click the Roles tab to view the page where you view, create, edit, and delete roles. On this page there is a blank text box titled "Role name", which is where you will enter the name of your new role. For demonstration purposes, enter "company user" as the name of the new role (see Figure 3-2).

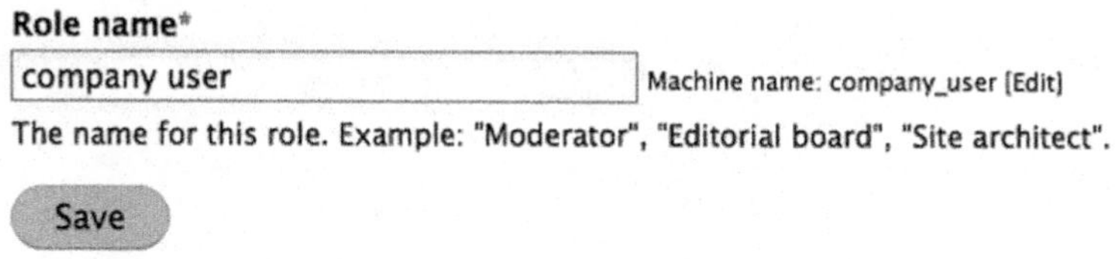

Role name*

| company user | Machine name: company_user [Edit] |

The name for this role. Example: "Moderator", "Editorial board", "Site architect".

Save

***Figure 3-2.** Working with roles in the People page*

Click the Save button. This results in the creation of the company user role, as shown in the list of defined user roles in Figure 3-3.

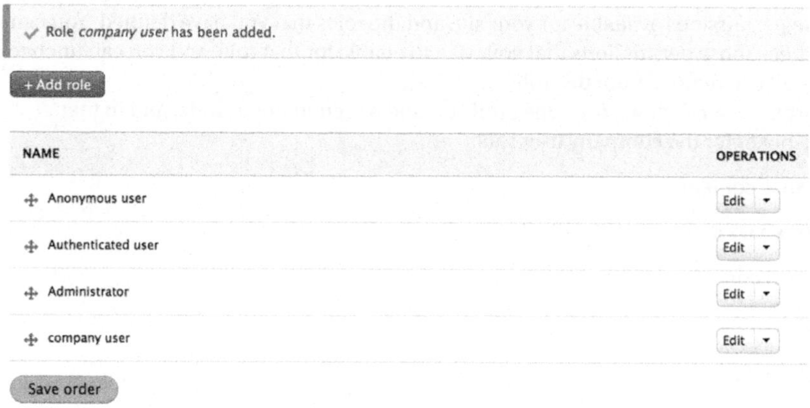

✓ Role *company user* has been added.

+ Add role

NAME	OPERATIONS
✛ Anonymous user	Edit ▾
✛ Authenticated user	Edit ▾
✛ Administrator	Edit ▾
✛ company user	Edit ▾

Save order

***Figure 3-3.** The list of defined roles*

For your second example user role, enter "restricted user." A restricted user is any user who has an account on the website and who can view restricted content and post comments to that content, but cannot create, edit, or delete content or perform any administration functions on our website. Click the "Add role" button, enter the value "restricted user" in the text box, and click the Save button to continue.

With both of your new roles defined, you're ready to assign permissions to the roles that you have created.

Assigning Permissions

Permissions provide a mechanism for controlling what users assigned to specific roles on the website can and cannot do. Drupal core and each contributed module provides a set of predefined permissions that you must either enable or disable on a role-by-role basis.

To assign permissions to a role, click the Manage link at the top of the page and the People link in the submenu (assuming you are logged in as the site administrator). On the People page, click the Permission tab, which reveals the page that you will use to set permissions for each of the roles that you have defined (see Figure 3-4).

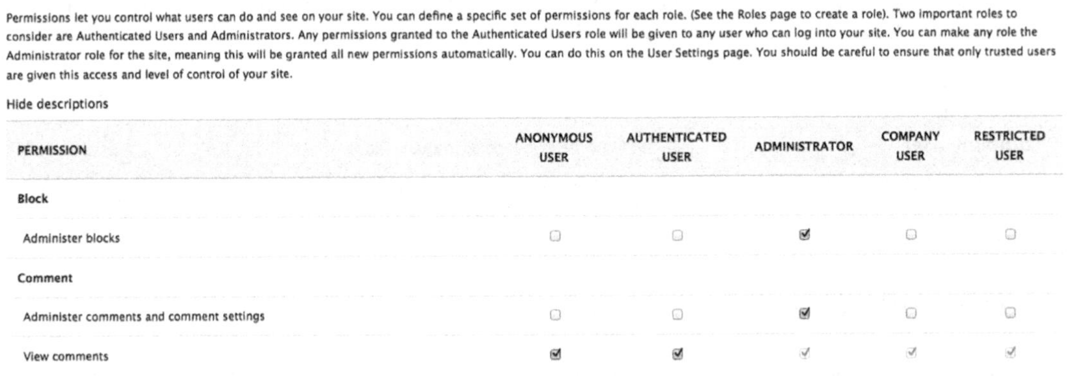

Permissions let you control what users can do and see on your site. You can define a specific set of permissions for each role. (See the Roles page to create a role). Two important roles to consider are Authenticated Users and Administrators. Any permissions granted to the Authenticated Users role will be given to any user who can log into your site. You can make any role the Administrator role for the site, meaning this will be granted all new permissions automatically. You can do this on the User Settings page. You should be careful to ensure that only trusted users are given this access and level of control of your site.

Hide descriptions

PERMISSION	ANONYMOUS USER	AUTHENTICATED USER	ADMINISTRATOR	COMPANY USER	RESTRICTED USER
Block					
Administer blocks	☐	☐	☑	☐	☐
Comment					
Administer comments and comment settings	☐	☐	☑	☐	☐
View comments	☑	☑	☑	☑	☑

Figure 3-4. *Setting permissions for each role*

This page lists all of the permissions available for your site and the roles that you have defined. You can scroll down the page and check those permissions that you wish to enable for that role, and you can uncheck permissions that you would like to remove from this role.

For demonstration purposes, scroll down the page until you find a section titled Node, and in that section check the following boxes for the company user role:

- *Article*: Create new content

- *Article*: Delete own content

- *Article*: Delete revisions

- *Article*: Revert revisions

- *Article*: View revisions

- *Basic page*: Create new content

- *Basic page*: Delete own content

- *Basic page*: Delete revisions

- *Basic page*: Edit own content

- *Basic page*: Revert revisions

- *Basic page*: View revisions

- *Access the Content overview page*

- *Administer content*

- *View published content*

For the restricted user role, scroll up to the Comment section and ensure that the following permissions are checked:

- View comments

- Skip comment approval

- Edit own comments

Once you have checked the boxes for the required permissions, scroll to the bottom of the page and click the "Save permissions" button. At this point, you have created roles and assigned permissions to those roles. You are now ready to create user accounts.

Creating User Accounts

You now have user roles defined, appropriate permissions set, and are ready to create user accounts. The process for creating a new user account is accomplished by first clicking the Manage link in the menu at the top of the page, followed by clicking the People link in the submenu. Clicking this link reveals the page shown in Figure 3-5.

Figure 3-5. *Creating user accounts*

This screen lists all existing user accounts. At this point, the only account that is listed is the admin account, which was created when we performed the installation process. To add a new user, click the "Add user" button at the top of this page, which reveals the "Add user" form (see Figure 3-6).

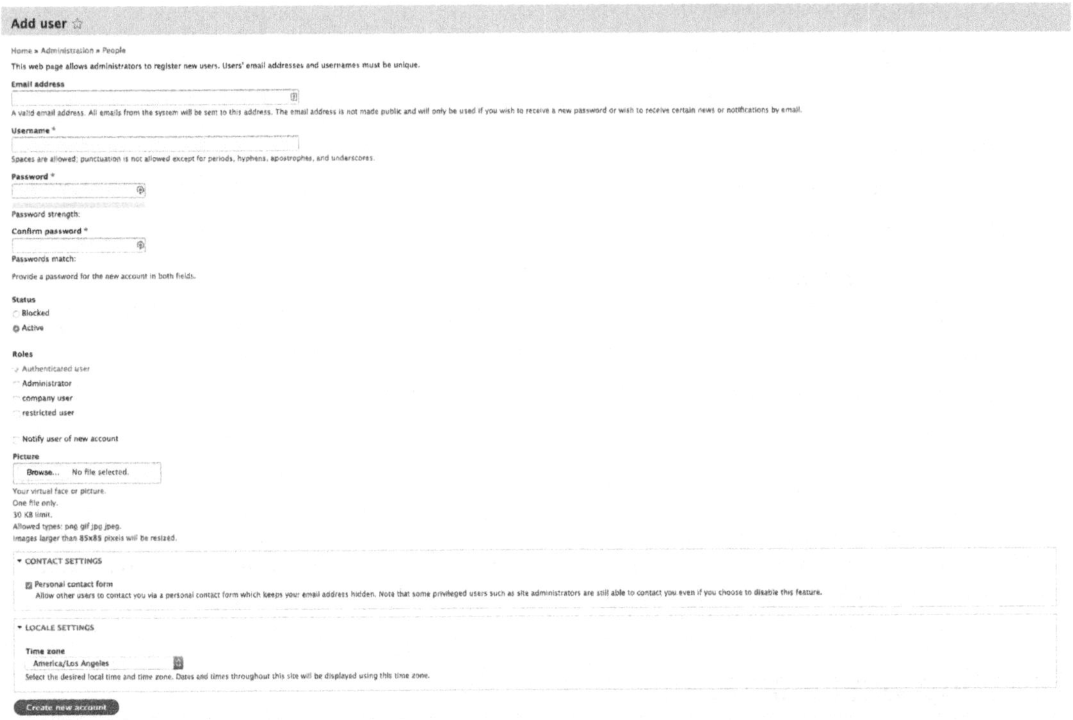

Figure 3-6. *The "Add user" form*

For demonstration purposes, we will create a new user account by entering the following values:

- In the E-mail address field enter: johnsmith@example.com.

- In the Username field enter: johnsmith.

- In the Password field enter: 12johnsmith34.

- In the Confirm password field enter: 12johnsmith34.

- For Status make sure that Active is selected.

- For Roles check the "company user" box.

- Check the "Notify user of new account" box (clicking this option causes Drupal to send an e-mail to the user notifying them of their new account).

- You may optionally upload a user picture (avatar), enable the personal contact form for this person by checking the "Personal contact form" check box, and set the time zone to the value where the person resides. For demonstration purposes, we'll leave those fields at their default values.

- Click the "Create new account" button to save the account.

- Click the People link in the administrators menu to see the complete list of user accounts on your site (see Figure 3-7), including the account that you just created.

Figure 3-7. *All the user accounts of your site*

John Smith can now log in to your site and perform all the tasks associated with the company user role.

There may be instances where you need to update a user account. For example, you may need to reset a user's password, change his or her e-mail address, update his or her assigned roles, or disable the account. You can perform all of these actions by clicking the Edit link associated with the user's account on the People page.

User-Generated Accounts

If you configured your site so that visitors can create their own accounts, requiring that a site administrator review and approve their account, the process is slightly different than that of an administrator creating the users' accounts. If you selected the user account option where a visitor can create their account but requires administrator approval, or the option where visitors can create their account without an administrator approving their account, the login form on the homepage has an additional option under the "Log in" button: "Create new account." See Figure 3-8.

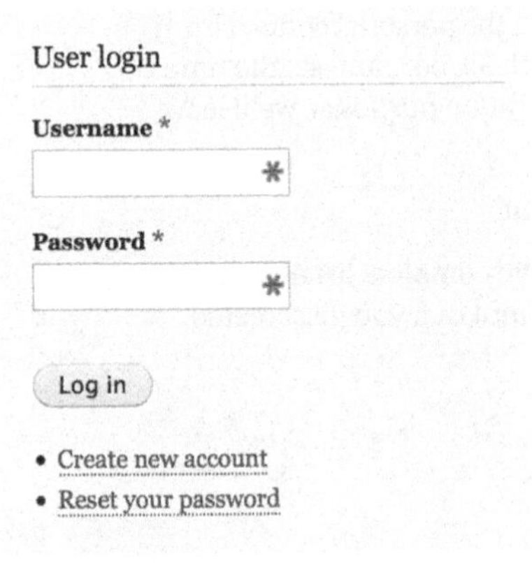

User login

Username *

[✳]

Password *

[✳]

[Log in]

• Create new account
• Reset your password

Figure 3-8. *The "Create new account" option*

Clicking this link (while not logged in to the site) brings you to a screen where a visitor can enter their requested username and their e-mail address (see Figure 3-9). For this example, enter a username and an e-mail address for the new account and click "Create new account." (Note: Drupal only allows you to use an e-mail address once across your entire site. Attempting to reuse an e-mail address that is already assigned to an account on your system will result in an error message.)

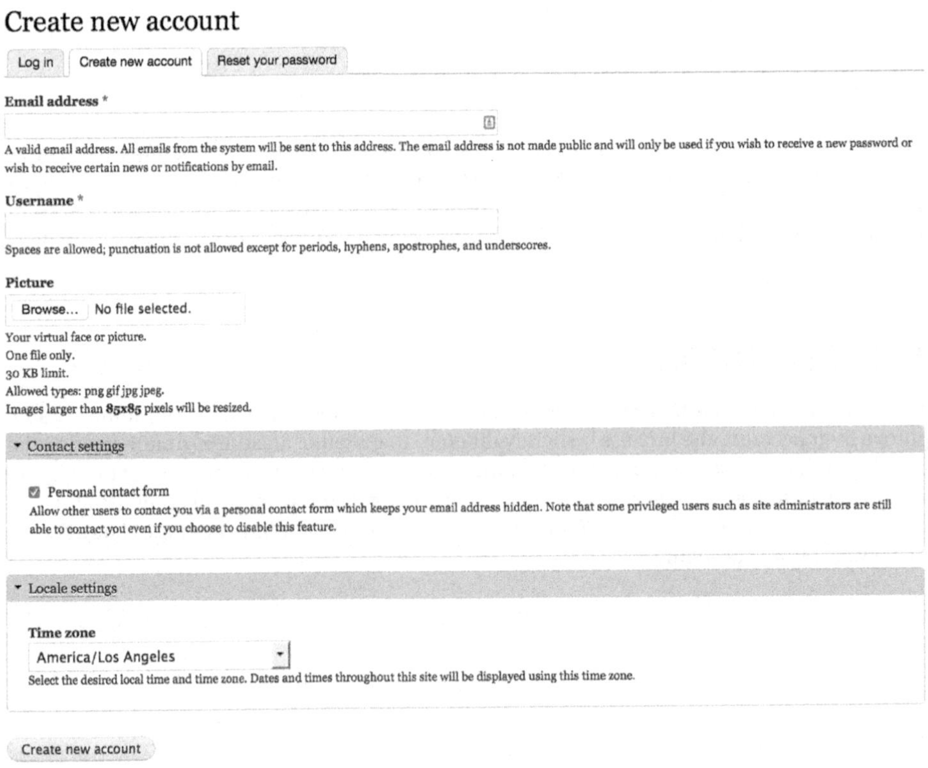

Create new account

[Log in] [Create new account] [Reset your password]

Email address *

[🔒]

A valid email address. All emails from the system will be sent to this address. The email address is not made public and will only be used if you wish to receive a new password or wish to receive certain news or notifications by email.

Username *

[   ]

Spaces are allowed; punctuation is not allowed except for periods, hyphens, apostrophes, and underscores.

Picture

[Browse...] No file selected.

Your virtual face or picture.
One file only.
30 KB limit.
Allowed types: png gif jpg jpeg.
Images larger than **85x85** pixels will be resized.

▼ Contact settings

☑ Personal contact form
Allow other users to contact you via a personal contact form which keeps your email address hidden. Note that some privileged users such as site administrators are still able to contact you even if you choose to disable this feature.

▼ Locale settings

Time zone

[America/Los Angeles   ▾]
Select the desired local time and time zone. Dates and times throughout this site will be displayed using this time zone.

[Create new account]

Figure 3-9. *Entering new account information*

As soon as the account is created, Drupal sends an e-mail to the e-mail address entered by the user and displays a success message displayed on the screen: "Thank you for applying for an account. Your account is currently pending approval by the site administrator. In the meantime, a welcome message with further instructions has been sent to your e-mail address."

If you configured your system to allow users to create an account but an administrator must manually approve that account, you'll need to visit the People page and edit that user's account, changing the user's status from Blocked to Active. Until the user's status has been changed, they will be unable to log in to your site with their user ID and password. If you selected the option where users can create an account and the account does not require administrator approval, the user will be able to log in to your site immediately.

Resetting Users' Passwords

One of Drupal's features that saves site administrators hours of work a year is the ability for users to reset their passwords without having to e-mail a site administrator asking someone to reset their password for them. If you log out of your site (clicking the logout link at the top right of the page), you'll note that in the right column, under the "Log in" button, there is a link for resetting your password (refer to Figure 3-8).

Clicking this link reveals a page where the visitor can enter either their user ID or their e-mail address.

Entering either a valid username or a valid e-mail address (where "valid" means that it exists as either a valid user ID on your site or a valid e-mail address associated with a user account on your site) results in Drupal generating an e-mail that is sent to the user with a "one-time login" link that allows them to reset their password.

Summary

In this chapter, I covered the process for configuring how Drupal handles user accounts and the approach for creating user roles and assigning permissions to those roles. I discussed the decisions that you as the site owner must make when setting up your site, including whether you will be the only person who has the ability to administer the site and create content, or whether you will have others who will be responsible for those areas.

If there will be others assigned to tasks of creating content or managing the site, then you'll want to configure the base settings for user accounts, create roles for those who will be performing activities on your site, and set the appropriate permissions. You'll also want to define whether only administrators can create accounts, visitors can create their own accounts without an administrator approving their accounts, or visitors can create an account but an administrator must approve it. Once you've made those decisions and set the parameters discussed in this chapter, you're ready to start adding users to your site.

You can have all the visitors you can handle, but they probably won't stick around long if they can't find the content they're interested in on your site. That's where taxonomy comes in, which is what we'll talk about next.

CHAPTER 4

■ ■ ■

Taxonomy

One of the Drupal features new Drupal users underuse and misunderstand is taxonomy. New Drupal users are overwhelmed with all of the other features and functions provided by the platform, and they bypass what may be one of the most powerful and useful features that Drupal has to offer. In this chapter you will create and use taxonomy terms to categorize content so that visitors can easily find information related to a specific topic.

Taxonomy Overview

While many of us may not be able to define the word "taxonomy," the reality is that we use taxonomy on a daily basis as a means for categorizing "things" in our lives. If you open the doors to your kitchen pantry, you might find an orderly assemblage of food items: all of your spices on the top shelf, canned food on the second shelf, pastas and other boxed foods on the third shelf, and cereal boxes on the fourth. Categorizing your food items and putting things away in an orderly fashion so that you can easily find food items when you need them to prepare a meal is in its simplest form the use of taxonomy. Without this "kitchen taxonomy system," you may have everything you need to make dinner jammed randomly in the pantry, but finding it may be a challenge, leading to frustration and a phone call to the local pizza delivery restaurant when you're not able to find the ingredients you need to make a meal.

In Drupal, taxonomy is divided into two general capabilities: tagging and structured taxonomy. Both are powerful solutions and can be used simultaneously on your site. *Tagging* is a simplified yet powerful use of the taxonomy system, enabling content authors to enter keywords that describe the content in a text field on the content editing form. As an example of tagging content, an author who writes an article about alternative energy could use keywords, or *tags*, such as "solar," "wind," and "geothermal" to categorize the article. The keywords created by the author are typically displayed as hyperlinks at the end of the article and can be used by site visitors to locate other content tagged with the same keywords.

Tagging is freeform, meaning it's up to the author to define what words they want to use to classify their content. A common issue with using tagging as an approach to categorize content is that different people use different words to refer to the same concept. For example, an article about rain might be tagged with the word "rain" by one author, "precipitation" by another author, and "drizzle" by a third. Site visitors trying to find articles about the general concept of rain would have a difficult time finding the ones tagged with words other than "rain." Another common problem is misspellings. If an author tags an article about rain with "reign," then site visitors are going to have a hard time, using taxonomy, to find that article using the word "rain."

The second approach for using taxonomy to categorize content in Drupal is *structured taxonomy*. In this approach, a site administrator creates all the words that can be used to categorize content, and content authors simply select from the list of words to categorize their content. A benefit of structured taxonomy is that it can be hierarchical, meaning terms may be put into groups to categorize content. An example of a hierarchy could be taxonomy for sports. The first level of terms could be "team sports" and "individual sports." Under team sports you might see football, basketball, baseball, hockey, volleyball, and other team sports. Under individual sports, you might see golf, swimming, track and field, and motor sports. You could continue to build out the hierarchy of sports until you have a representation of every sport on the planet. As an author writing an article about a sporting event, I could choose one or more predefined terms to categorize my article.

A big benefit of structured taxonomy over simplified tagging is the ability to select articles by individual terms, or by categories of terms. In the previous example, you could look for articles specifically about football, or you could take a more generalized approach and look for all articles within the category of team sports.

Determining whether to use tagging or structured taxonomy is a matter of deciding how ridged you want the categorization of content to appear on your site. And the great news is that you can use both approaches simultaneously to provide authors with a high level of flexibility.

Let's take a look at a real-world example. Let's say we are creating a website that is focused on sports news. Our targeted audience is people who like to follow what is happening with their favorite teams. If we think about how people might want to search and navigate content on our site, we might think of organizing the content by the type of sport, for example:

- Football

- Baseball

- Basketball

- Hockey

- Soccer

People may also want to find sports news by team:

- Ravens

- Trailblazers

- Lakers

- Raiders

- Yankees

In this example we would follow our previous example and create a structured taxonomy. We would first create a *vocabulary*, which is the highest level in a hierarchical structure. For this example we would create a vocabulary called "type of sport." The terms that we would create within that vocabulary are football, baseball, basketball, hockey, and soccer. We would then create a second level in our hierarchy where we assign the terms for the team names; for example, beneath the term football we would assign the terms Ravens and Raiders. Beneath the term basketball we would assign the terms Trailblazers and Lakers. Beneath the baseball term we would assign the term Yankees. We could continue adding team names until every team in every sport is assigned to their appropriate spot. For the purposes of our demonstration, we'll stick with the simplified list.

Creating Vocabularies

The first step in using taxonomy is to identify and create the vocabularies that you will use to categorize content on your website. Depending on the focus of your site and the breadth of subjects that you cover, you may only need a single vocabulary or you may need several vocabularies. There isn't a "correct" answer, nor is there a formula that you can use to determine how many vocabularies your site will need. The best approach is to think about the content that you will include and the subjects that the content will cover. If the subjects are all related (for example, types of sports), then a single vocabulary is likely all that you will need. If the subjects are not related (for example, a book-related website where books may be categorized by author, subject, publisher, and targeted audience), then the use of several vocabularies may be necessary. It's up to you, the site creator, to define the structure that best suits the purpose of your site, how you want content structured, and how you want visitors to access that content.

Once you've identified at least one vocabulary, click the Manage link in the admin menu at the top of any page on your site and then click the Structure link. You'll see a list of options that includes a link to Taxonomy. Click that to reveal a page that lists all of the vocabularies that have already been defined for your site. By default, Drupal creates a vocabulary called Tags as a default generic "container" for terms. See Figure 4-1.

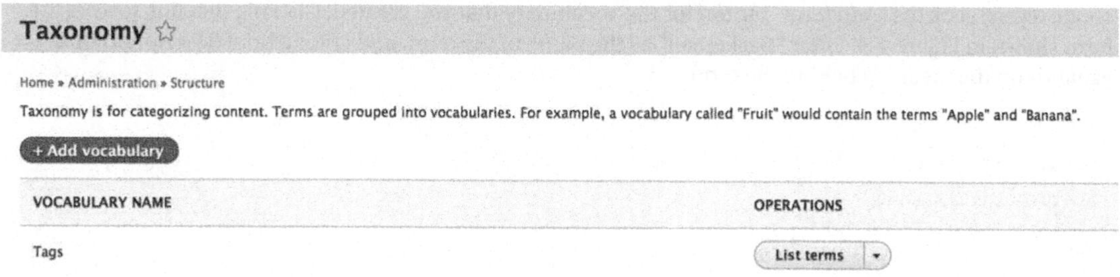

Taxonomy ☆

Home » Administration » Structure

Taxonomy is for categorizing content. Terms are grouped into vocabularies. For example, a vocabulary called "Fruit" would contain the terms "Apple" and "Banana".

+ Add vocabulary

VOCABULARY NAME	OPERATIONS
Tags	List terms ▾

Figure 4-1. *The Tags vocabulary*

To add a new vocabulary, click the "Add vocabulary" link at the top of the list, revealing the form shown in Figure 4-2. In the Name field, enter "Type of Sport," and enter a brief description in the Description field. The Description field is an optional field and by default is not displayed on the administrative interface for taxonomy. However, you may want to use this field when rendering lists of content as a description about the content that is contained in the list.

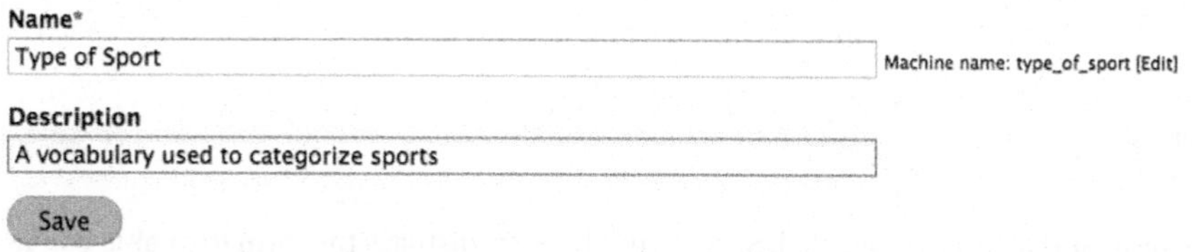

Name*

| Type of Sport | Machine name: type_of_sport [Edit] |

Description

| A vocabulary used to categorize sports |

Save

Figure 4-2. *Creating a new vocabulary*

Once you've entered values in both fields, click Save. Drupal then displays the list of terms associated with your vocabulary. Since this is a new vocabulary, the list is empty. See Figure 4-3.

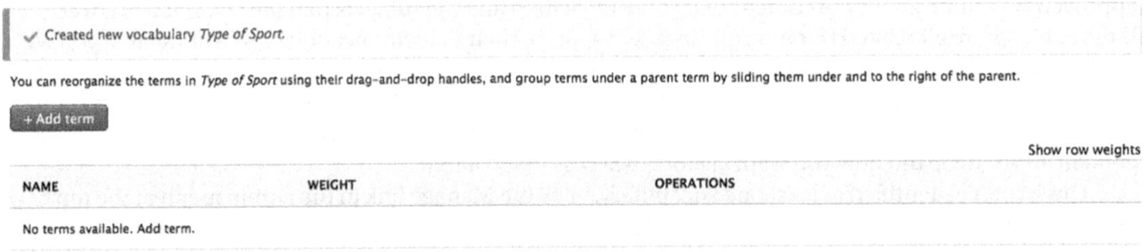

✓ Created new vocabulary *Type of Sport*.

You can reorganize the terms in *Type of Sport* using their drag-and-drop handles, and group terms under a parent term by sliding them under and to the right of the parent.

+ Add term

Show row weights

NAME	WEIGHT	OPERATIONS

No terms available. Add term.

Figure 4-3. *Your newly created vocabulary*

The next step is to create a list of terms that are associated with the "Type of Sport" vocabulary. To create terms, click the "Add term" button for the vocabulary that you created. Clicking that link reveals the form shown in Figure 4-4. Enter "Basketball" as the name of the term, and enter a brief description that expands on the meaning behind the term.

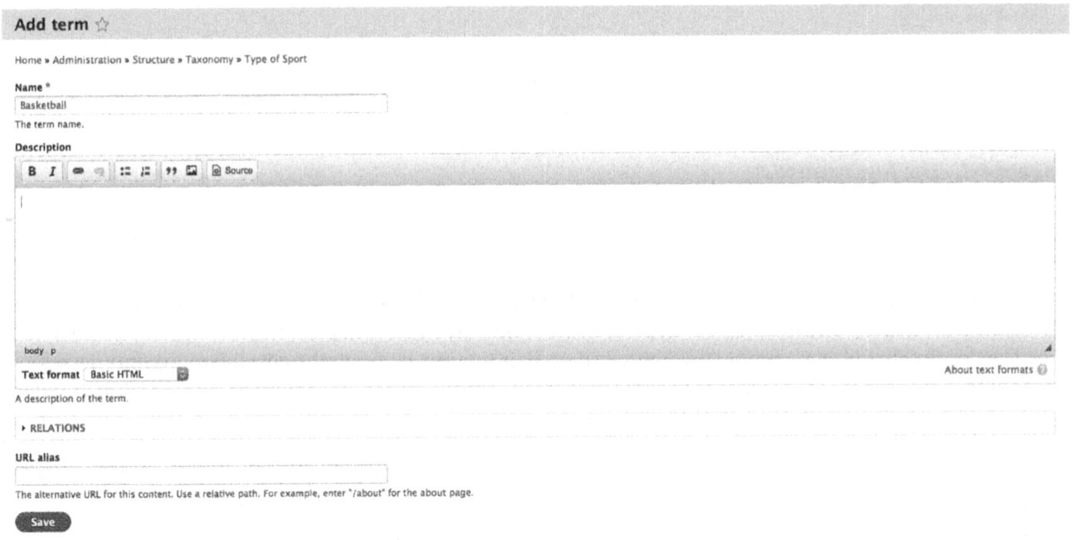

Add term ☆

Home » Administration » Structure » Taxonomy » Type of Sport

Name *

Basketball

The term name.

Description

B *I* ⚬ ⚬ ⁞⁞ ⁞⁞ " ▢ ▣ Source

body p

Text format Basic HTML ▢   About text formats ⓘ

A description of the term.

▸ RELATIONS

URL alias

The alternative URL for this content. Use a relative path. For example, enter "/about" for the about page.

Save

Figure 4-4. *Adding terms*

After entering the term and a description, click Save. Drupal then redisplays the form to enable you to enter another term. To practice, create terms for other sports, such as baseball, football, and soccer. Once you've completed the process of entering the terms associated with your vocabulary, click "Type of Sport" in the breadcrumb to return to the Edit Vocabulary page, and then click the List tab at the top of the page to see the complete list of terms for the vocabulary, shown in Figure 4-5.

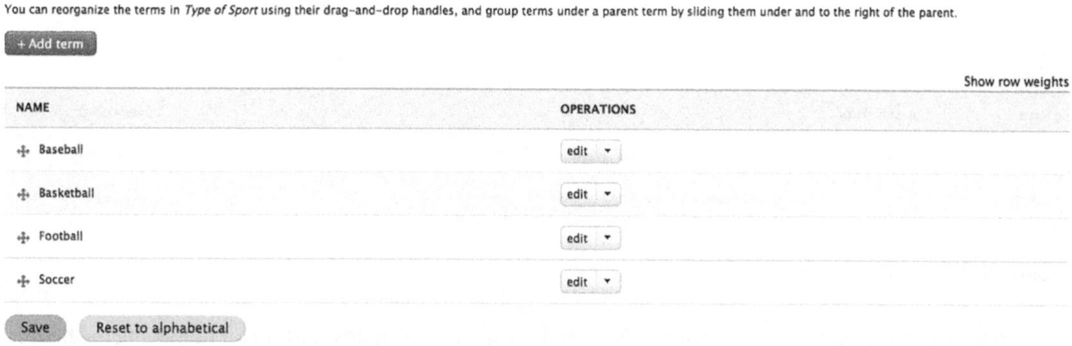

You can reorganize the terms in *Type of Sport* using their drag-and-drop handles, and group terms under a parent term by sliding them under and to the right of the parent.

+ Add term

Show row weights

NAME	OPERATIONS
✛ Baseball	edit ▾
✛ Basketball	edit ▾
✛ Football	edit ▾
✛ Soccer	edit ▾

Save   Reset to alphabetical

Figure 4-5. *The complete list of terms*

At this point we've created a vocabulary and the terms that we will use to categorize content. By default, taxonomy terms are sorted alphabetically, but in some cases you may need them to be sorted differently. For example, you may have a vocabulary for regions in the United States, with the terms East, Central, Mountain, and West. If the terms were sorted alphabetically, they would appear as Central, East, Mountain, and West. You may want the terms sorted in an east-to-west fashion, meaning the order should be East, Central, Mountain, and West, in which case you would want the order to differ from the default order. You may reorder the terms by simply clicking and holding the arrows icon to the left of a term and dragging that item to the position in the list where you want it to appear. Remember to click the Save button after reordering, as the order is not permanent until you save the list.

We now have to identify which content types will use this vocabulary as a method for categorizing content, and configure our vocabulary so that it will appear on the content creation screens for those content types.

Assigning a Taxonomy Vocabulary to a Content Type

Enabling content authors to assign one of the terms to a new piece of content requires that a site administrator make changes to the content types. The first step is to identify all the content types that you want to associate with the new vocabulary. You may decide that all content types will use the vocabulary to categorize the content created on your site, or you may decide the vocabulary is only appropriate for one or a few content types. For example, if you had a vocabulary that listed terms for event venues (e.g., cafeteria, gym, courtyard, soccer field, and so on), you might want to restrict which content types could be used. That vocabulary may only be appropriate for a Calendar event content type and not your Basic page content type.

As an example, let's update the "Article" content type on the test site to incorporate the ability to tag content with the type of sport vocabulary. The first step is to click the Manage link in the admin menu at the top of any page of your site, and then click Structure. Click the "Content types" link to get to the page that lists the available content types (shown in Figure 4-6).

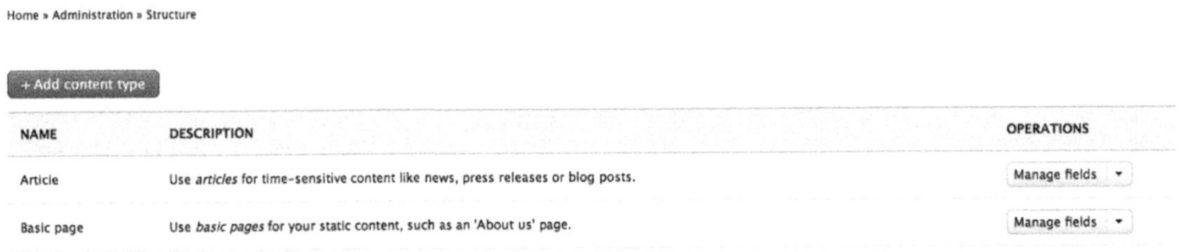

Home » Administration » Structure

+ Add content type

NAME	DESCRIPTION	OPERATIONS
Article	Use *articles* for time-sensitive content like news, press releases or blog posts.	Manage fields ▾
Basic page	Use *basic pages* for your static content, such as an 'About us' page.	Manage fields ▾

Figure 4-6. *Available content types*

To the right of each content type in the list, you'll see a "Manage fields" button for managing the fields associated with that content type. You'll learn in Chapter 5 how to add several types of fields to your content type (e.g., you may wish to add a file upload field, an additional text box to collect specific information, check boxes, radio buttons, or a select list to expand the content collected when someone uses that content type). For now we will concentrate on adding the taxonomy vocabulary to our content type so that an author can select one of the types of sports terms.

Click the "Manage fields" button to the right of the Article description to expose the form used to add your vocabulary (see Figure 4-7). On this form, you will find a button called "Add field." Click this button to begin the process of adding your taxonomy field.

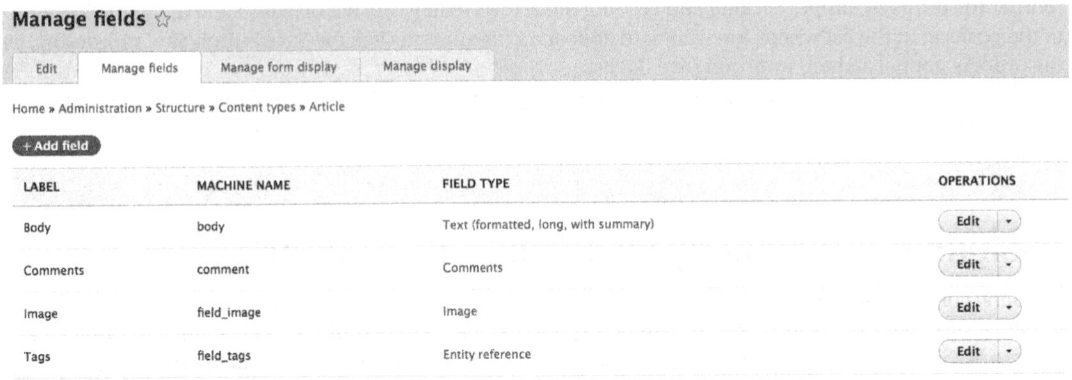

Manage fields ☆

Edit	Manage fields	Manage form display	Manage display

Home » Administration » Structure » Content types » Article

+ Add field

LABEL	MACHINE NAME	FIELD TYPE	OPERATIONS
Body	body	Text (formatted, long, with summary)	Edit ▾
Comments	comment	Comments	Edit ▾
Image	field_image	Image	Edit ▾
Tags	field_tags	Entity reference	Edit ▾

Figure 4-7. *Managing fields*

On the "Add field" screen, select "Taxonomy Term" from the drop-down list labeled "Add a new field." In the field titled Label, enter a descriptive title that will appear on the content editing form, informing the content author what the purpose of this field is. For our example, enter "Type of sport." Click the "Save and continue" button. On the next screen you have the option to specify how many values from the list the author may select when creating an article. The default value is Limited to one term from the list. For the example, we want the author to have the ability to select several of the terms in our "Type of sport" vocabulary, so we change the value in the select list from Limited to Unlimited. Next, click the "Save field settings" button to continue to the settings page.

On the settings page, we have options to change the label we previously created, enter help text that will be displayed on the content editing form beneath this field, set this field to Required (meaning the author must select a value from the list before saving the article), and set a default value should the author not select a value from the list. For the purposes of this demonstration, we'll leave the Label as previously set; enter a brief sentence instructing the author to select a value from the list if appropriate for this article; leave the check box for the Required field unchecked so that it's optional whether an author selects a type of sport for any given article; and leave the default value for "Type of sport" set to None. In the reference type leave the Reference method set to Default. The other option utilizes Views to customize the list of available values, I'll talk about Views in Chapter 10. In the list of Vocabularies select Type of Sport by clicking on the checkbox. This instructs Drupal to only display items from the Type of Sport vocabulary when presenting values to select from to the author. To complete the addition of the new field, click the "Save settings" button, which will return you to the main admin page for the "Article" content type. By default taxonomy terms are autocomplete fields, meaning that an author simply types a portion of the term they wish to add and Drupal looks to see if a term matching that pattern exists. Autocomplete works well when the taxonomy terms are known by the author, but in this case we want to present a list of terms for the author to select from. To change the Type of sport field widget from autocomplete to a select list click on the Manage form display tab at the to of the list of fields and change the value for List of sports from autocomplete to select list. After changing the value click the Save button. Authors can now select from the list of terms in the "Type of sport" vocabulary when authoring an article.

Selecting a Taxonomy Term when Creating Content

Based on our actions in the previous section, creating a new content item using the "Article" content type will now present the author with a list of values that they can select from to categorize the content they are authoring. To test this feature, click any of the "create content" links described previously. From the list of content types listed, click the "Article" content type. When the Create Article page is displayed, notice that there is a new "Type of sport" select list field where the author can select the type of sport to assign to this content item (see Figure 4-8). Create a new Article by entering a title, body text, and selecting a type of sport from the select list.

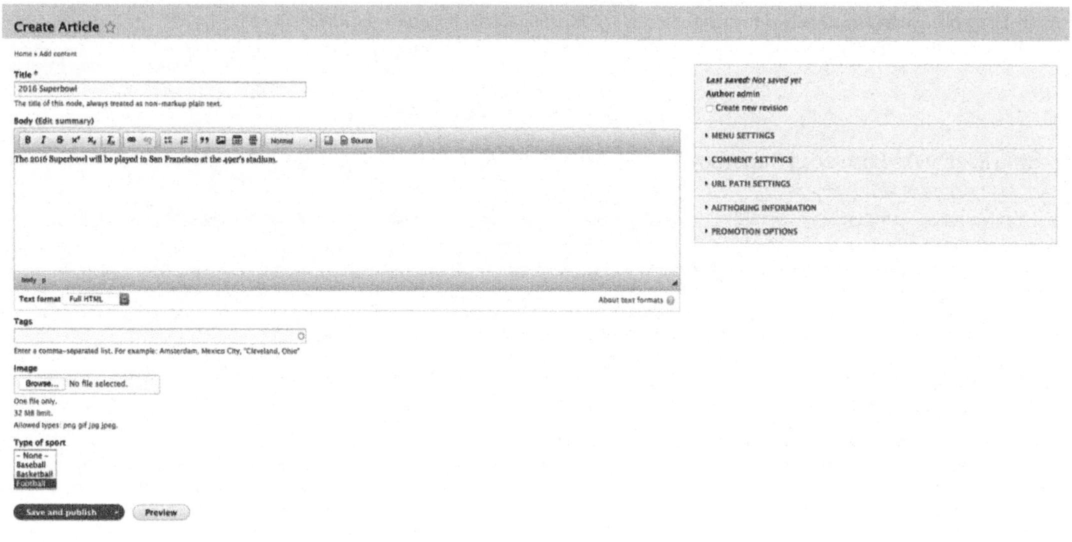

Figure 4-8. *Creating an article*

41

Clicking the "Save and publish" button results in Drupal displaying our new page with a new field, "Associated Sport," with the value you selected in the "Type of sport" field listed.

To demonstrate the power of taxonomy, create two additional pages using the same taxonomy term you selected in the first example. On the final content item that you create, once you have saved it, click the term that you used. In Figure 4-9 you would click Football.

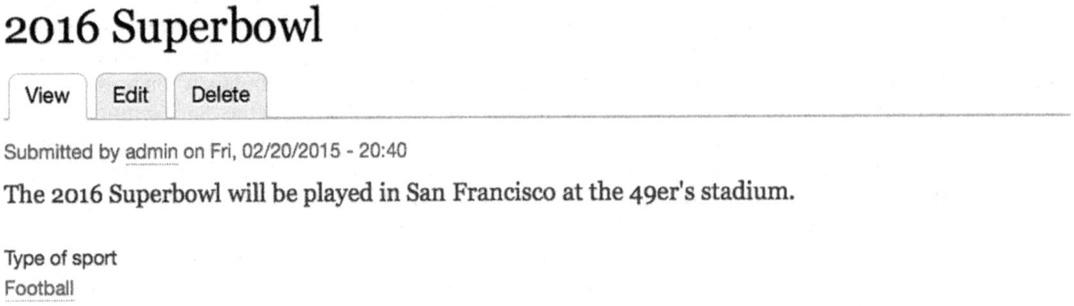

2016 Superbowl

View   Edit   Delete

Submitted by admin on Fri, 02/20/2015 - 20:40

The 2016 Superbowl will be played in San Francisco at the 49er's stadium.

Type of sport
Football

Figure 4-9. A new content item assigned to the Football taxonomy term

The result of clicking the term is a page that lists all other pages that were created and assigned to the Football taxonomy term (see Figure 4-10).

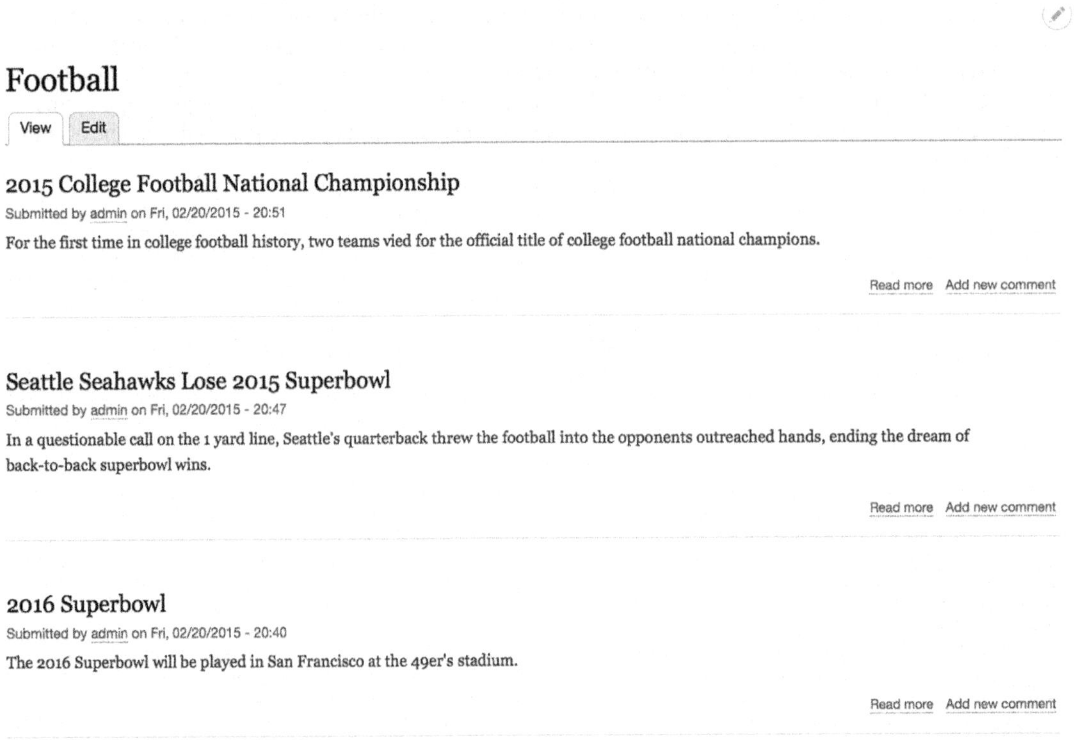

Football

View   Edit

2015 College Football National Championship

Submitted by admin on Fri, 02/20/2015 - 20:51

For the first time in college football history, two teams vied for the official title of college football national champions.

Read more   Add new comment

Seattle Seahawks Lose 2015 Superbowl

Submitted by admin on Fri, 02/20/2015 - 20:47

In a questionable call on the 1 yard line, Seattle's quarterback threw the football into the opponents outreached hands, ending the dream of back-to-back superbowl wins.

Read more   Add new comment

2016 Superbowl

Submitted by admin on Fri, 02/20/2015 - 20:40

The 2016 Superbowl will be played in San Francisco at the 49er's stadium.

Read more   Add new comment

Figure 4-10. All pages assigned to the term Football

Drupal automatically renders all of the articles that are associated with the selected term. The list is sorted by default in date/time order, with the most recently added article listed at the top of the list. You may change the order in which the articles appear by modifying the default view. We'll cover views in detail in Chapter 9. You will also notice an RSS feed icon at the bottom of the page. RSS feeds are an industry-standard approach for delivering lists of content to external sources, such as news reader applications. Drupal also created an RSS feed for all the pages that are associated with this taxonomy term. Clicking the RSS icon will render the list as a standard feed.

Creating Human- and Search Engine–Friendly Lists

By default, Drupal creates URLs for lists of content that are related to taxonomy terms, as shown in Figure 4-11.

Figure 4-11. *Drupal-created URL*

The structure of the URL is "taxonomy/term/*X*," where *X* is the "term ID" of the taxonomy term that you are referencing. While Drupal understands what this refers to, a human and, more important, a search engine wouldn't have a clue what this URL was related to other than looking at the title of the list and the content of the list. A simple remedy is to provide a *URL alias*. You can provide a URL alias by editing the taxonomy term and entering a value in the field that is shown on the form for adding a URL alias. To navigate back to your taxonomy term list, click the Manage link at the top of the page and select Structure. On the Structure page, click the Taxonomy link. On the Taxonomy page, click the "List terms" button that is associated with the vocabulary where the term you wish to supply a URL alias resides. Locate the term you wish to update and click the Edit tab. In the "URL alias" field (shown in Figure 4-12), enter a descriptive URL that is easily understood by humans and search engines. For consistency and simplicity, use all lowercase letters with hyphens between words. For our example, we're using a single word, "football." Click the Save button after entering your URL alias. In the address bar of your browser, enter the URL to your site followed by the URL alias that you just created for your taxonomy term. In the preceding example, the URL would be http://localhost/football.

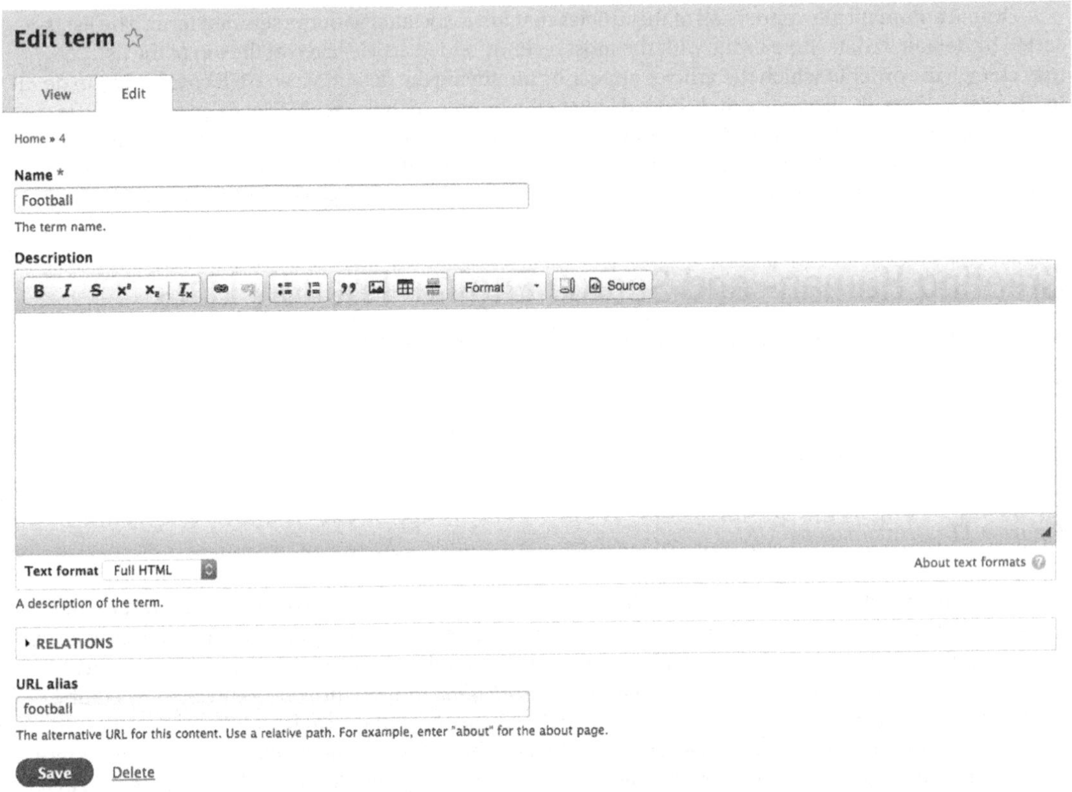

Edit term ☆

View	Edit

Home » 4

Name *

Football

The term name.

Description

B	I	S	x²	x₂	Iₓ		⚭	⚮		⦂	⦂		🗎	🖼	⊞	≡		Format	▾		🔲	🔳 Source

Text format Full HTML ⬍

About text formats 🕐

A description of the term.

▸ RELATIONS

URL alias

football

The alternative URL for this content. Use a relative path. For example, enter "about" for the about page.

Save   Delete

Figure 4-12. *Setting the URL alias for a taxonomy term*

Hierarchical Terms

What if you need to define a hierarchical structure of taxonomy terms, say, for example "basketball." You need the ability to further categorize basketball content by:

- Basketball
  - High School
  - College
    - Division 1
    - Division 2
    - Division 3
  - NBA
    - Eastern Conference
    - Western Conference

Fortunately, Drupal provides a simple mechanism for creating a hierarchical structure of taxonomy terms. To update our example click the Manage link at the top of the page, the Structure link in the submenu, and then the Taxonomy link. Click the "Add term" button, which reveals the term creation screen. Begin by adding the term for High School. Enter "High School" as the term name and then click the Relations link at the bottom of the form. In the list of "Parent term" select Basketball and then click Save. Continue the process by entering "College" and "NBA," also selecting Basketball as the parent term. To create the third level of the hierarchy, enter "Division 1" as the term name and, for the relationship selected, "College" as the parent. Continue the process until you've created all of the terms in the preceding list. The resulting structure should look something like the list shown in Figure 4-13.

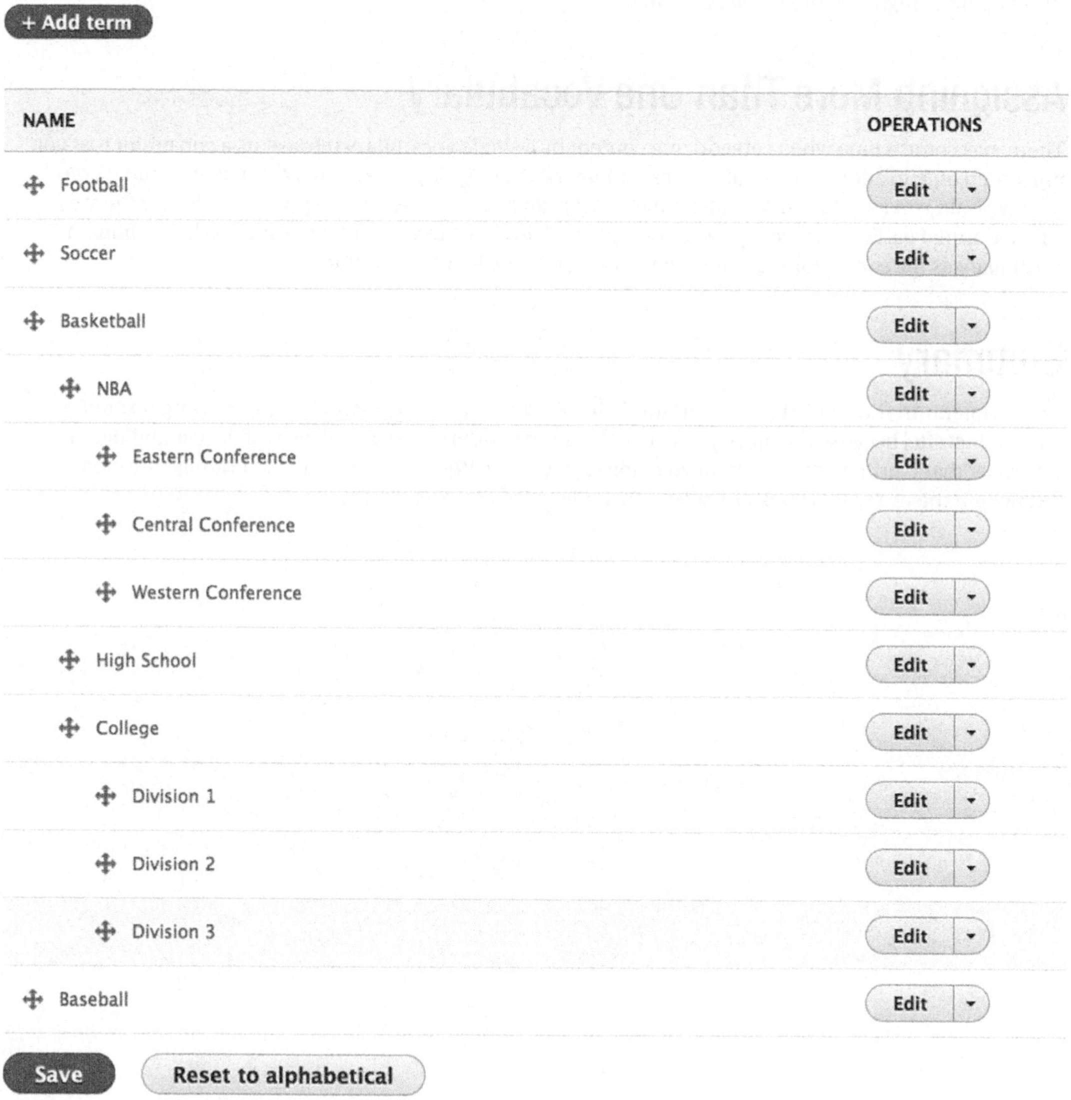

+ Add term

NAME	OPERATIONS
✛ Football	Edit ▾
✛ Soccer	Edit ▾
✛ Basketball	Edit ▾
✛ NBA	Edit ▾
✛ Eastern Conference	Edit ▾
✛ Central Conference	Edit ▾
✛ Western Conference	Edit ▾
✛ High School	Edit ▾
✛ College	Edit ▾
✛ Division 1	Edit ▾
✛ Division 2	Edit ▾
✛ Division 3	Edit ▾
✛ Baseball	Edit ▾

Save   **Reset to alphabetical**

Figure 4-13. The resulting list

If you happen to forget to select a parent term before saving, you can always position a term by clicking the arrows icon, holding the button down and dragging it to the position in the hierarchy where it should reside. You may also assign the term to the appropriate parent term by clicking the Edit button and modifying the value in the Relations section.

We now have the ability to assign taxonomy terms to content items at the child level as well as at the parent level.

The resulting web page that is created using this method now shows the associated sport as "High School." Clicking High School would render a list of all pages that are associated with the term "High School." Using views, which are described in detail in Chapter 5, provides you with the additional capability of listing all content within the hierarchy—for example, all articles categorized as Basketball, regardless of whether they pertain to high school, college, or NBA.

Assigning More Than One Vocabulary

There may come a time when categorizing content by a single vocabulary represents a constraint that you must overcome to address a complex requirement for content categorization. Fortunately, Drupal does not constrain you as to how many vocabularies you can assign to a content type. Simply follow the steps you performed earlier in this chapter to add a second field to the content type. Simply select a different vocabulary as the source for the values that you wish to present to the author.

Summary

This chapter introduced the power and simplicity of taxonomy. I suggest that you start using taxonomy on your first site, because the more you use it, the more comfortable you will be with its capabilities and the power that it brings to the content you deliver to your visitors. I will continue to leverage taxonomy throughout the rest of this book as I cover other advanced Drupal features.

CHAPTER 5

■ ■ ■

Content Types

If you ask Drupal developers what the most powerful feature of Drupal is, many will say it's Drupal's ability to create custom content types. What is a content type? Think of a content type as a template that you provide to users who author content on your site. You may decide that the standard content types that come with Drupal out of the box, "Basic page" and "Article," provide all the features you need for your site. But it's likely that you'll encounter situations where you want more control over how users enter information and how that information is displayed on your site, and that's where custom content types come into play. In this chapter I'll show you how simple it is to create a new content type from scratch. Hold on to your tickets, we're about to take off!

The Basic Page and Article Content Types

When you install Drupal 8 you automatically receive two content types that have been defined by the team who maintains Drupal core: the Basic page and Article. If you author a piece of content using the Basic page content type, you will see that it provides two basic fields: a title and a body.

An author using the Basic page content type simply enters a title (a required field as indicated by the red asterisk) and the text of their content in the Body field. The Body field is flexible and can contain whatever the author feels like writing about. The author could

- Write an entire book in the Body field, including HTML markup (headings, tables, CSS, and so on).

- Insert pictures.

- Write a single sentence.

The Article content type is similar to the Basic page, except it offers the ability to upload a picture as a stand-alone element, such as a banner image for the article (not embedded in the body text), and define a set of tags that can be used to categorize the content (see Chapter 4 for details on categorizing content).

Like a Basic page, an Article can be used to author content about any subject, and the body area allows for entering free-form text.

While the Basic page and Article content types are perfect for general content, there will likely be cases where you want to provide some form of structure around the information that is captured. You may want to

- Require that certain information is entered before the author submits the content item for publishing; for example, the start date and time for an event, the address of the venue where the event is being held, and a link to the event on a Google map.

- Have the ability to perform calculations based on the information that is captured in a content item.

- Have the ability to sort content items by specific "fields."

- Have the ability to "filter" or restrict which content items are displayed on a page based on a value in a field.

- Enforce the structure of how a piece of content is rendered on a page; for example, you may want to display information about a book and want the title to be followed by the author, followed by the ISBN, followed by the price, followed by the description of the book.

While you could publish all of this information in a Basic page or an Article, providing the features for sorting, filtering, making values required, calculating, and structuring how a content item is rendered on a page would be extremely difficult. Fortunately, Drupal's ability to define custom content types makes all of the above possible, and provides many more features that you will find invaluable over time.

Defining a Custom Content Type

A custom content type is defined by you, the Drupal administrator, over and above the Basic page and Article content types. The ability to create custom content types is included in Drupal 8 core.

To demonstrate the power and flexibility of custom content types, let's create a new custom content type for capturing information about upcoming events. An event could be a concert, a play, a class, a game, or any other activity that is scheduled in advance.

When authoring information about an event, you may want to include the following details:

- The name or title of the event

- The date and time when the event begins

- The date and time when the event ends

- The venue or address where the event will be held

- A description of the event

- The price for attending the event

As you will see in a few moments, Drupal provides a simple-to-use administrator's interface for creating and modifying custom content types. As soon as you define a custom content type, it is immediately available to those users who have the proper privileges to author, edit, publish, and delete that specific content type (Drupal provides the ability to restrict access to custom content types by user role).

Creating a Custom Content Type

Creating a custom content type takes two basic steps: sitting down and listing the types of information you want to collect, and building the custom content type using Drupal's custom content type administration screens.

For this example, let's create a custom content type for an event that includes the types of information listed in the previous section.

To get started, click the Manage link at the top of the page and the Structure link in the submenu. On the Structure page (shown in Figure 5-1), click "Content types."

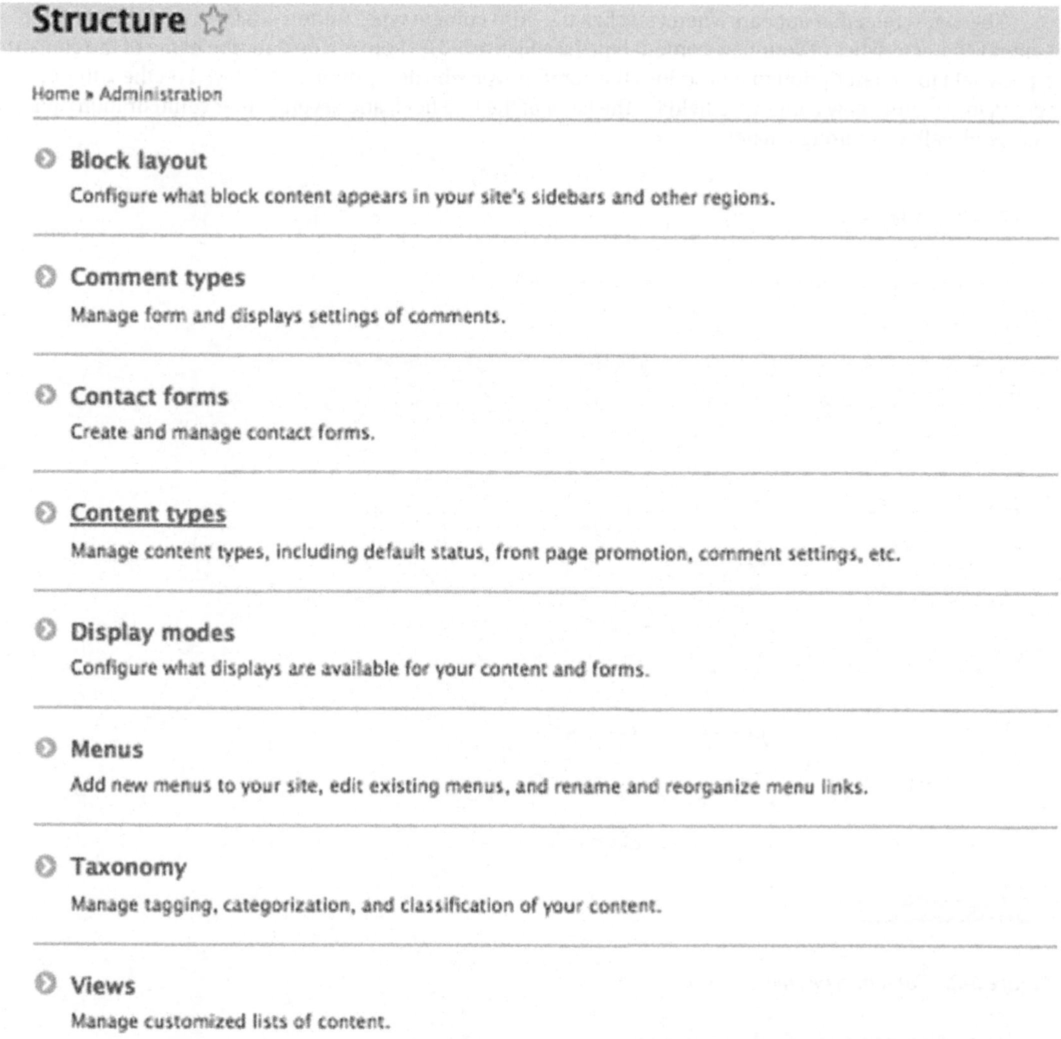

Structure ☆

Home » Administration

⊙ **Block layout**

Configure what block content appears in your site's sidebars and other regions.

⊙ **Comment types**

Manage form and displays settings of comments.

⊙ **Contact forms**

Create and manage contact forms.

⊙ **Content types**

Manage content types, including default status, front page promotion, comment settings, etc.

⊙ **Display modes**

Configure what displays are available for your content and forms.

⊙ **Menus**

Add new menus to your site, edit existing menus, and rename and reorganize menu links.

⊙ **Taxonomy**

Manage tagging, categorization, and classification of your content.

⊙ **Views**

Manage customized lists of content.

Figure 5-1. *Structure page with "Content types" link*

The "Content types" screen (shown in Figure 5-2) lists all of the existing content types, which in our case are the Article and Basic page content types that are included with Drupal 8 core. The "Content types" screen also provides a link to create a new content type. Click the "Add content type" button to start the process of creating our Event content type.

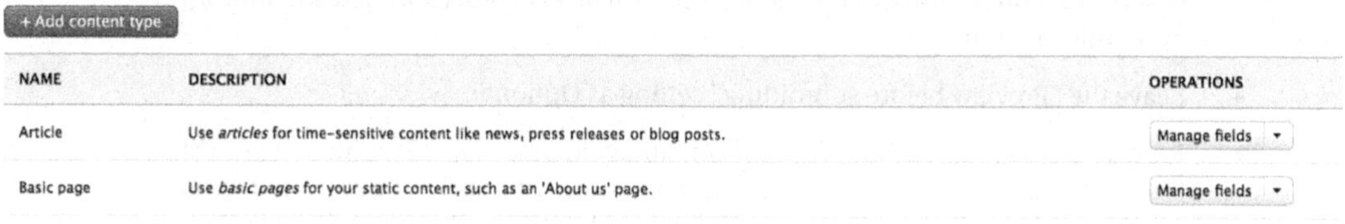

+ Add content type

NAME	DESCRIPTION	OPERATIONS
Article	Use *articles* for time-sensitive content like news, press releases or blog posts.	Manage fields ▾
Basic page	Use *basic pages* for your static content, such as an 'About us' page.	Manage fields ▾

Figure 5-2. *A listing of content types*

The first screen that appears when you click the "Add content type" button is a form that defines the general characteristics of your new content type (see Figure 5-3). There is a field for the name of the content type, a field for a description that describes the content type (the description is displayed on the author's screen for creating new content), a field for the label of the title field, and several other configuration options that I will walk you through in detail.

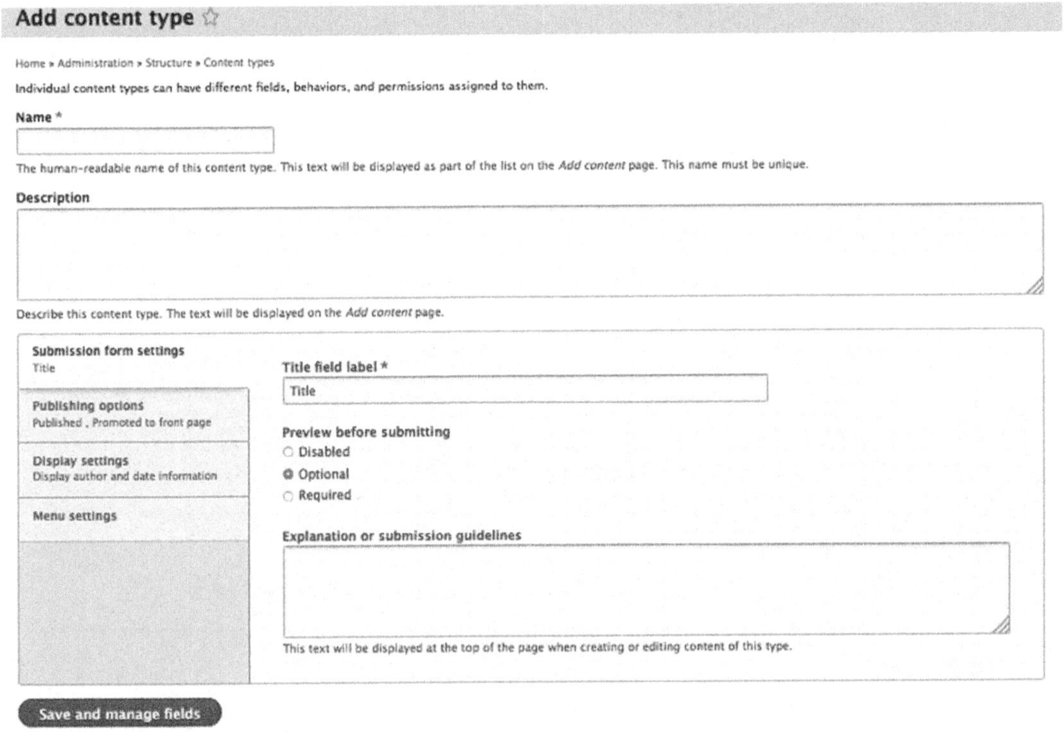

Add content type ☆

Home » Administration » Structure » Content types

Individual content types can have different fields, behaviors, and permissions assigned to them.

Name *

[   ]

The human-readable name of this content type. This text will be displayed as part of the list on the *Add content* page. This name must be unique.

Description

[   ]

Describe this content type. The text will be displayed on the *Add content* page.

Submission form settings Title	**Title field label *** [Title]
Publishing options Published , Promoted to front page	**Preview before submitting** ○ Disabled ◉ Optional ○ Required
Display settings Display author and date information	
Menu settings	**Explanation or submission guidelines** [ ] This text will be displayed at the top of the page when creating or editing content of this type.

(Save and manage fields)

Figure 5-3. Content type creation form

To begin the process, do the following:

- Fill in the name of the content type, which in our case is "Event." The text below the Name field provides a set of guidelines that you should follow when creating a name for a new content type.

- Provide a description of how this content type should be used, such as "A content type used to capture the details about upcoming events."

- Change the "Title field label" from just Title to "Event Title," making it more descriptive and intuitive to the author who will be using this template for authoring event information.

- Leave the "Preview before submitting" setting as Optional.

- Provide a brief explanation of the submission guidelines for this content type. This is an optional value, and may not apply to your content type. For our Event content type, we will use "Please fill out all required fields before submitting the event" as the submission guidelines. You can choose to use or ignore this field when creating new content types.

There are other optional settings that you should consider carefully when creating a new content type. First are the publishing options. In the left vertical menu, click the "Publishing options" tab (see Figure 5-4).

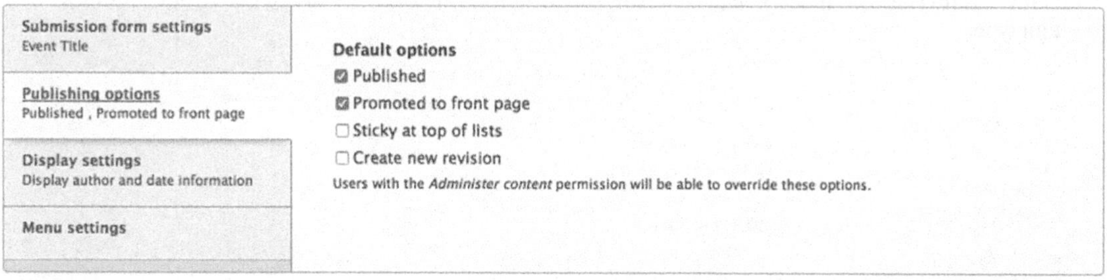

Figure 5-4. Publishing options

Depending on whether you want content to be automatically published (made viewable on your site immediately upon saving) and whether you want the content to automatically appear on the homepage of your website, you may wish to adjust these options. For our Event content type, we want an Event to be automatically published when they are saved, but we don't want them to automatically show up on the homepage. So we will uncheck the "Promoted to front page" check box. We can also set whether an Event is sticky at the top of lists (meaning that, in a list of various content types on a page, the Event content would always be at the top of the list), and whether we want to automatically create a new version of a content item created as an Event when the author makes an update (typically a good idea, but it depends on whether you want the ability to see the changes made to an individual piece of content over time, and the ability to republish a previous version in the case where the current version is incorrect). For our Event content type, we'll check the "Create new revision" check box.

The next set of options is for display settings. Click the "Display settings" tab in the left column to reveal the option that is available with this configuration parameter (see Figure 5-5). You can set whether Drupal should display the name of the author who created the Event content item and the date that the item was authored. Let's say in our case we don't feel that having the author and date published is relevant, so we'll uncheck that box. You may, depending on the type of content being authored, decide that it is important to display the author's name and the date that the content was published. If so, leave the box checked.

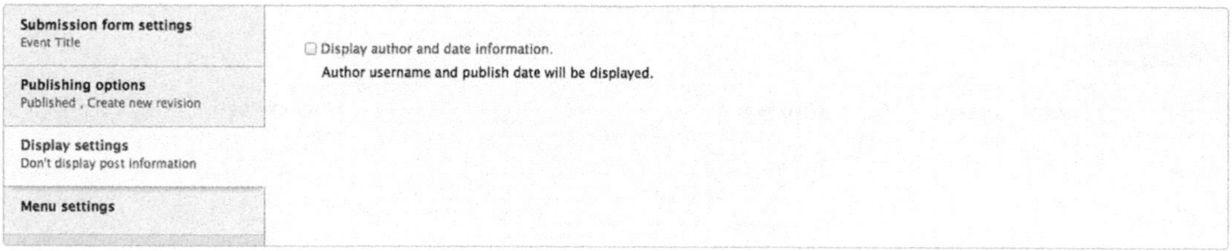

Figure 5-5. Display settings

The final set of parameters defines the menu options that are presented to the author. Click the "Menu settings" tab to reveal the menu parameters (see Figure 5-6). The "Available menus" section lists the menus on which this content item may optionally appear. During content creation using this content type, the author will have the ability to specify whether the content item being created will appear as an item in the selected menu. In the example shown in Figure 5-6, the only menu that will appear as available to the

51

content author is the "Main navigation" menu. You can uncheck Main navigation to hide all menus from the list that may be selected from, or you can check more than one menu to allow the author to choose from multiple menus. The "Default parent item" option allows you to set which menu is automatically selected when the "Menu settings" page is displayed when an author creates a new content item from your new content type.

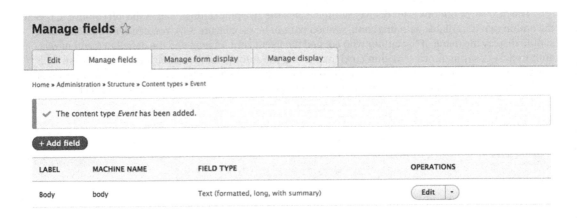

Figure 5-6. *Menu settings*

For our example, leave the default values and click the "Save and manage fields" button. Drupal now displays the "Manage fields" page (see Figure 5-7).

Manage fields ☆

| Edit | Manage fields | Manage form display | Manage display |

Home » Administration » Structure » Content types » Event

✓ The content type *Event* has been added.

+ Add field

LABEL	MACHINE NAME	FIELD TYPE	OPERATIONS
Body	body	Text (formatted, long, with summary)	Edit ▾

Figure 5-7. *The "Manage fields" page for the Event content type*

Customizing Your Content Type

At this point we could create a new content item using our Event content type. However, the Event content type only has two fields, an Event Title and a Body. Our requirements call for an event description, start date, end date, venue/address, type of seating, assistance available at the venue, type of event and the ability to provide a file that can be downloaded by the site visitor (e.g., a program). As you can see in Figure 5-8, Drupal automatically creates a Body field, which we will use for the event description.

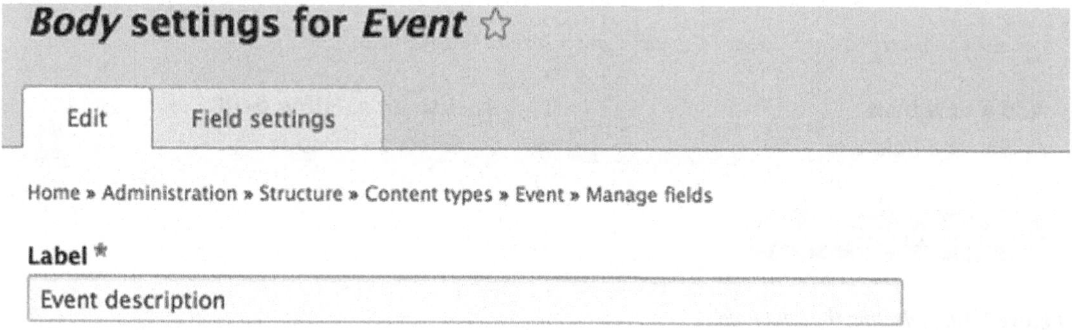

Figure 5-8. *Changing the Label field*

We'll start with changing the Body field by modifying the label that appears on the screen from "Body" to "Event description," a better indicator of the type of text to be entered for the person creating the event. Click the Edit button for the Body field. In the Label field, change "Body" to "Event description" (see Figure 5-8), and then click the "Save settings" button at the bottom of the form.

After saving the update to the body label, Drupal returns you to the "Manage fields" page with the updated Label, as shown in Figure 5-9.

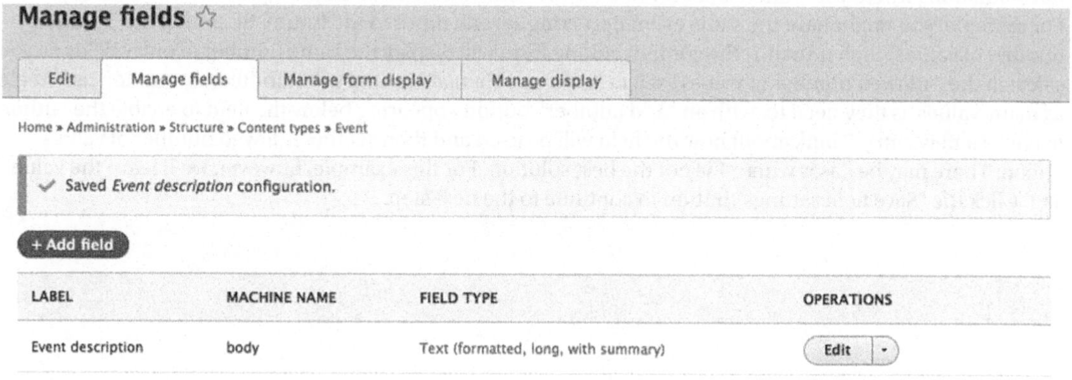

Figure 5-9. *Revised field label*

The next step is to add the Start Date field. Click the "Add field" button. The next step is to select what type of field to add or alternatively what existing field to add to this content type. A previously created field may reside in another content type and instead of recreating that field, we can reuse the definition by selecting that field from the list of existing fields (see Figure 5-10).

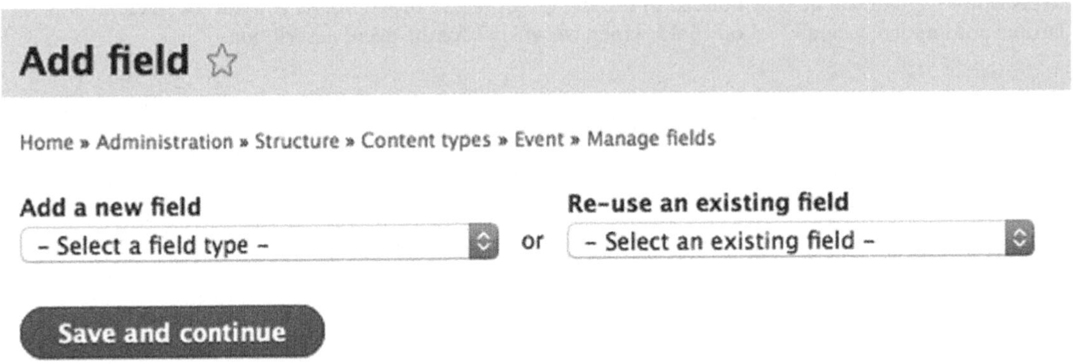

Add field ☆

Home » Administration » Structure » Content types » Event » Manage fields

Add a new field

– Select a field type – ◇   or   **Re-use an existing field**

– Select an existing field – ◇

Save and continue

Figure 5-10. *Selecting the field type*

After clicking Date, you will see a new field on the screen where you will enter the label for the new field. This label is displayed on the content editing form so the author knows which field they are entering a value for, and is displayed to the end user when the content item is rendered on the site. Since we're creating the start date for the event, enter "Start Date" into the Label field and click the "Save and continue" button.

The next step in the field creation process is to set the format for our date field, either date and time or just the date, and the number of allowed values (see Figure 5-11). Since events typically have a time associated with them, we'll leave the value set to "Date and time" for the "Date type" select list. We'll also leave the "Allowed number of values" option set to "Limited" and "1" because our events only occur once. You will see the "Allowed number of values" configuration option on every field that you create. You may have situations where you want the author to have the ability to create multiple values for this field. For example, you might have the same event occurring several times in the future. By setting the "Allowed number of values" higher than 1, the content editing form will display the same number of entry fields as you select in the "Allowed number of values" select list. If you change Limited to Unlimited, the author can create as many values as they need to, with an "Add another" button appearing below the field to enable the author to create a new entry. Think about how the field will be used and then set the "Allowed number of values" option. There may be cases where 1 is not the best solution. For this example, however, we'll leave the value as 1. Click the "Save field settings" button to continue to the next step.

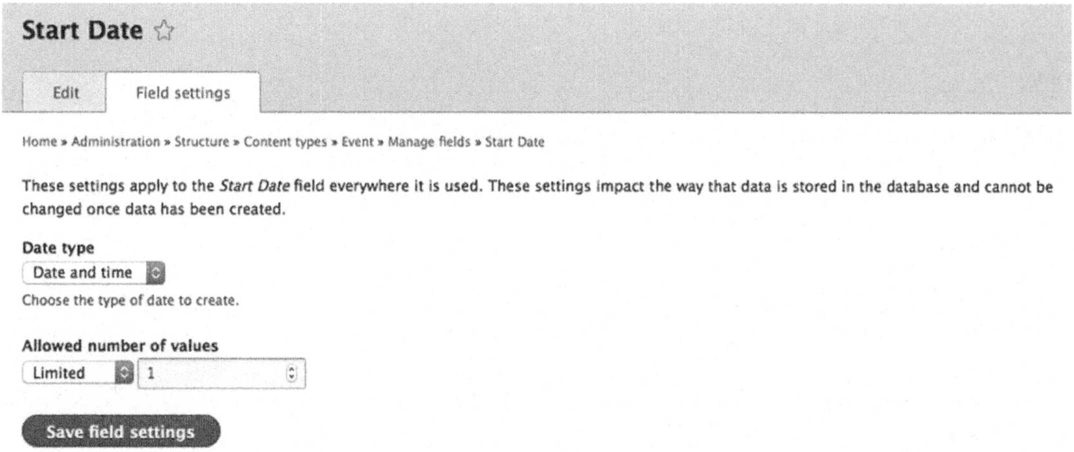

Start Date ☆

Edit	Field settings

These settings apply to the *Start Date* field everywhere it is used. These settings impact the way that data is stored in the database and cannot be changed once data has been created.

Date type

Date and time ⌄

Choose the type of date to create.

Allowed number of values

Limited ⌄   1 ⌄

Save field settings

Figure 5-11. *Setting the date type and number of allowed values*

The next form that Drupal displays (shown in Figure 5-12) enables you to set additional detailed parameters for the event Start Date field. On this form you have the ability to

- Change the label that we previously defined for this field. Unless you made a mistake or changed your mind, you can leave the value as it is shown.

- Enter content in the "Help text" field to be displayed beneath the text field on the screen. This is a great place to describe requirements for data that will be entered in this field, such as requesting that authors enter dates as mm/dd/yyyy. This is an optional field.

- Define whether this field is required. A required field is displayed with a red asterisk, and Drupal forces the user to enter a value in this field before the content item can be saved. Because our content type is about an Event and dates are important attributes of an Event, you want a date to be required, so check the "Required field" check box.

- Define whether a default value is assigned to the field before the content creation screen is displayed to the author. Because our field deals with dates in the future, providing a default value doesn't make sense. There may be cases for other fields where a default value does make sense, such as selecting a seating preference for the event: you may wish to set a default value to "best available." In those cases, this is the place where you would enter the default value.

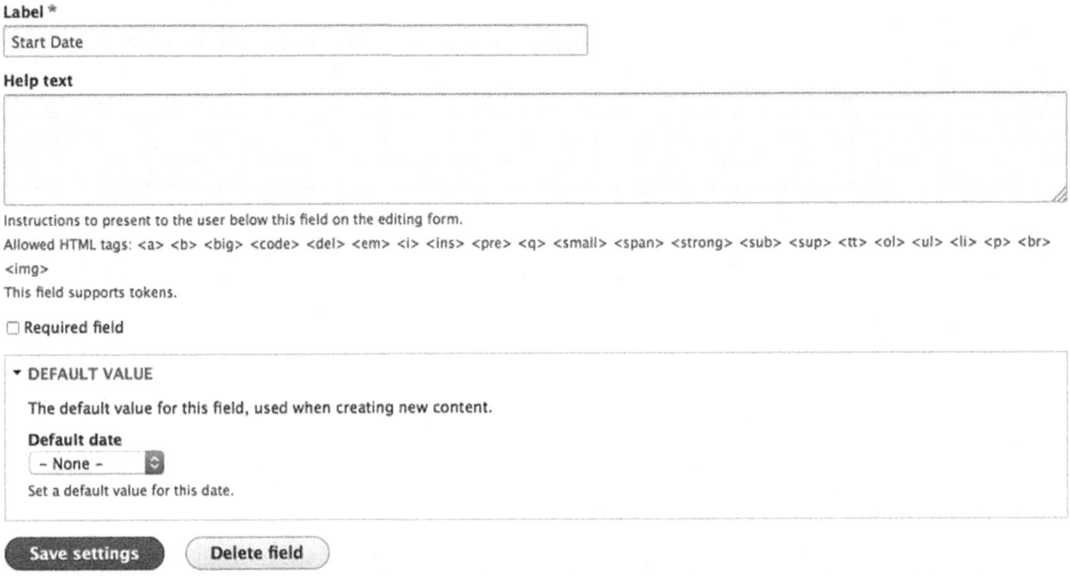

Label *

Start Date

Help text

Instructions to present to the user below this field on the editing form.

Allowed HTML tags: `<a>` `<b>` `<big>` `<code>` `<del>` `<em>` `<i>` `<ins>` `<pre>` `<q>` `<small>` `<span>` `<strong>` `<sub>` `<sup>` `<tt>` `<ol>` `<ul>` `<li>` `<p>` `<br>` `<img>`

This field supports tokens.

☐ Required field

▾ DEFAULT VALUE

The default value for this field, used when creating new content.

Default date

– None –

Set a default value for this date.

Save settings   **Delete field**

Figure 5-12. *Setting the detailed parameters for the event Start Date field*

Click the "Save settings" button to complete the configuration of the Start Date field. Drupal then redisplays the general "Manage fields" page with the new Start Date field added to the Event content type (see Figure 5-13).

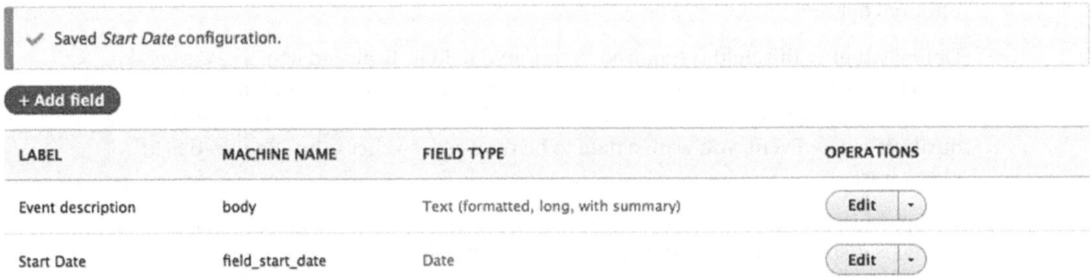

✓ Saved *Start Date* configuration.

+ Add field

LABEL	MACHINE NAME	FIELD TYPE	OPERATIONS
Event description	body	Text (formatted, long, with summary)	Edit ▾
Start Date	field_start_date	Date	Edit ▾

Figure 5-13. *A list of fields for the Event content type including the Start Date field*

We are now ready to add the other fields that we defined earlier: End Date, Event description, and Event Venue/Address. Follow the same steps as previously described to create the End Date field. When creating the Event Venue/Address field, select "Text (formatted, long)" for the field type instead of "Date," since the values entered for the venue will be a paragraph or two of text. When you're finished, your list of fields should look similar to Figure 5-14.

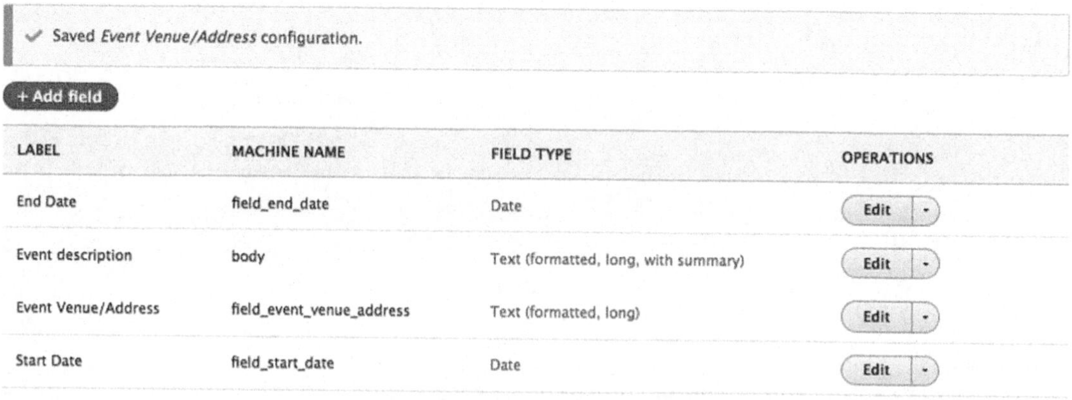

✔ Saved *Event Venue/Address* configuration.

+ Add field

LABEL	MACHINE NAME	FIELD TYPE	OPERATIONS
End Date	field_end_date	Date	Edit ⏷
Event description	body	Text (formatted, long, with summary)	Edit ⏷
Event Venue/Address	field_event_venue_address	Text (formatted, long)	Edit ⏷
Start Date	field_start_date	Date	Edit ⏷

Figure 5-14. *All of the Event fields are now listed*

Our Event content type is now ready for authors to use. To try our new content type, click the "Back to site" link in the top left corner of the screen and then click one of the "Add content" links, revealing the list of content types that we have available on our site.

Our Event content type appears in the list of available content types. Click Event to reveal the content creation page for our Event content type (see Figure 5-15). The page shows the Event Title, Event description, Start Date, End Date, and Event Venue/Address fields.

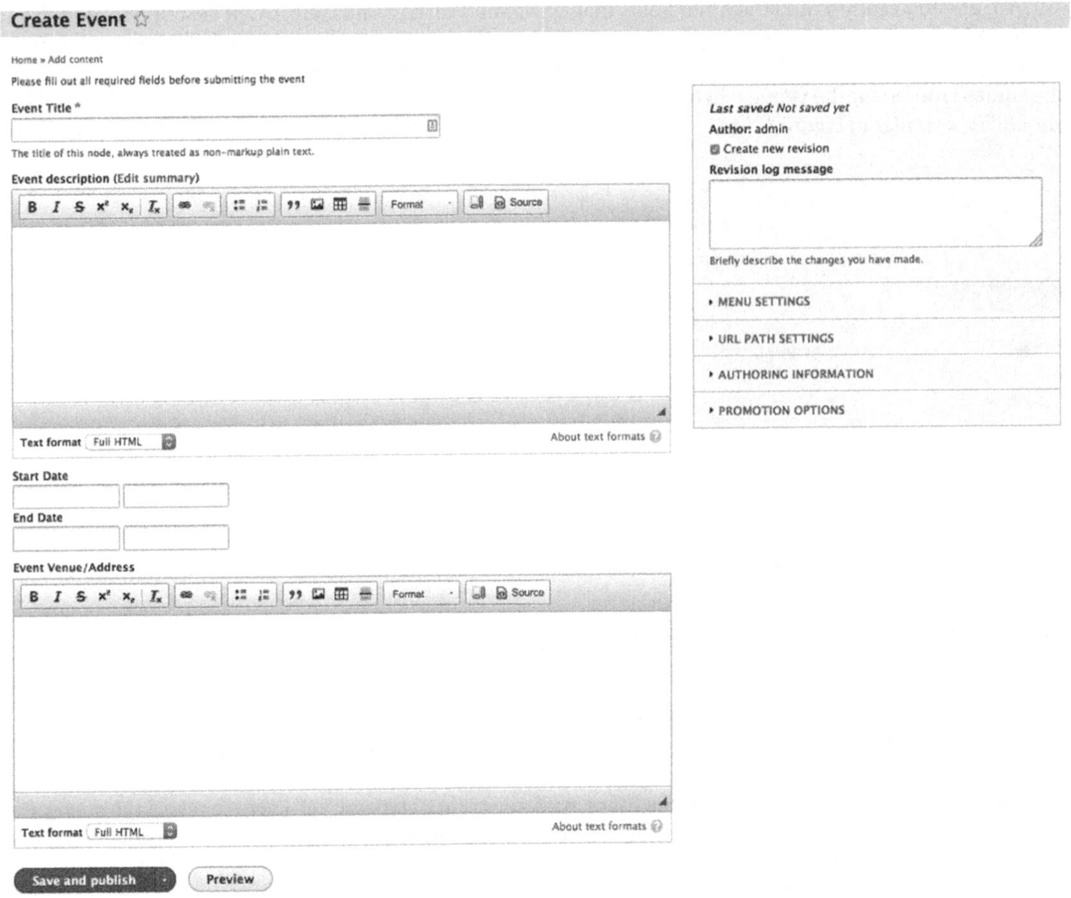

Figure 5-15. *Creating a new event form*

Create a sample event using the event creation form. When you've finished entering values, click "Save and publish." Drupal will render your new Event content item using the values you specified. The example Event entered on the form in Figure 5-15 appears as a new Event in Figure 5-16.

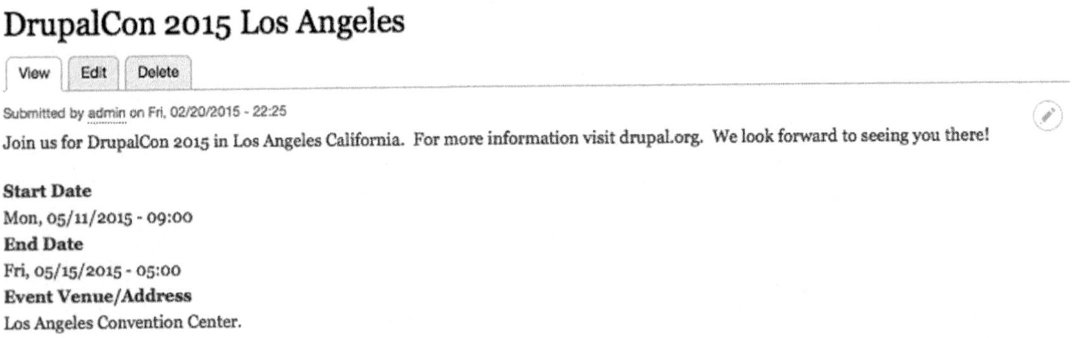

DrupalCon 2015 Los Angeles

View	Edit	Delete

Submitted by admin on Fri, 02/20/2015 - 22:25

Join us for DrupalCon 2015 in Los Angeles California. For more information visit drupal.org. We look forward to seeing you there!

Start Date
Mon, 05/11/2015 - 09:00
End Date
Fri, 05/15/2015 - 05:00
Event Venue/Address
Los Angeles Convention Center.

Figure 5-16. *The completed example event*

Other Field Types

In our Event content type, we created a set of fields for authors to enter values for date and venue. There may be instances where a text field is less effective than using one of the following field types:

- *Radio buttons*: Great for providing a list of options to the author and only allowing the selection of a single item from the list.

- *Check boxes*: Perfect for providing a list of options to the author, allowing selection of one or more items in the list.

- *Select list*: Great for long a list of items to select from; for example, all of the countries in the world.

- *File upload*: The right field to use when you want to provide the ability to upload and attach a file to a piece of content.

- *Image upload*: The field type to use when you want to upload and display an image.

- *Text area:* The field to use when the author is expected to enter paragraphs of content. It provides a box with multiple lines, whereas a text field has only a single line of text.

- *Numeric field*: Perfect when you want the author to enter numbers only.

- *Entity reference fields:* It's the field to use when you want to associate and display another content item with the item that you are creating. An example could be that your site has a content type called Biography that contains a headshot and biographical information about performing artists. If you wanted to include an artist's headshot and biography on an Event content item you could use the entity reference field to link the event to the artist's Biography, displaying the headshot and biography from the existing content item instead of having to manually re-enter the biographical information the Event.

- *Term reference field*: When you want to include taxonomy terms as part of your content item, this is the field to use.

The field types listed here are part of Drupal 8 core. There are other custom field types that are available as contributed modules. For a list of those modules, please visit `www.drupal.org/project/modules`, choose the Fields item in the "Module categories" filter, and click Search. You'll find a list of add-on modules that provide value-added capabilities, like other field types. You can install additional modules by following the process described in Chapter 12.

It is likely that you will come across the need to use one of the other field types as you create new content types. We will expand on our Event content type by adding several additional fields using other types of fields.

Radio Buttons

Radio buttons are useful when you want to present the author with a list of values from which they can select only a single item (check boxes are used when you want the author to have the ability to select one or more values). We will expand our Event content type to include the ability to select the type of seating that will be available at the event: either reserved seating or general admission. To start the process, click the Manage link at the top of the page, click Structure in the submenu, followed by the "Content types" link on the Structure page and the "Manage fields" tab for the Event content type. Click the "Add field" button to start the process. Figure 5-17 shows the list of field types. Since we are creating a radio button–based list, select the "List (text)" option. A field for the Label will appear after selecting the List option. Enter "Type of Seating" in the Label field, and then click the "Save and continue" button.

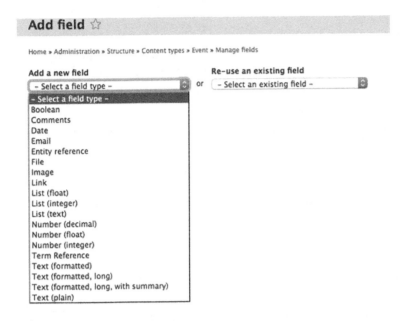

Figure 5-17. *Adding a list field*

The next step in the process is to provide the values that will appear in the list (see Figure 5-18). On this screen we have to specify the "Allowed values list," which is the list of options that will be presented to the author. Drupal requires that options be listed as a "*key|label*" pair, where *key* is a value representing which option that was selected (the key value will be stored in the database), followed by the "pipe" character (press the Shift key and \ to enter a pipe character), and *label* is the value that will be displayed on the screen. In the example in Figure 5-18, I used reserved|Reserved and general|General Admission, resulting in the values of reserved or general being stored in the database. By setting the "Allowed number of values" field to "Limited" and "1," Drupal will render this list as radio buttons, as the user is restricted to selecting a single value. If the number is greater than 1, Drupal will render this list as check boxes. After entering the values, click the "Save field settings" button to continue the process.

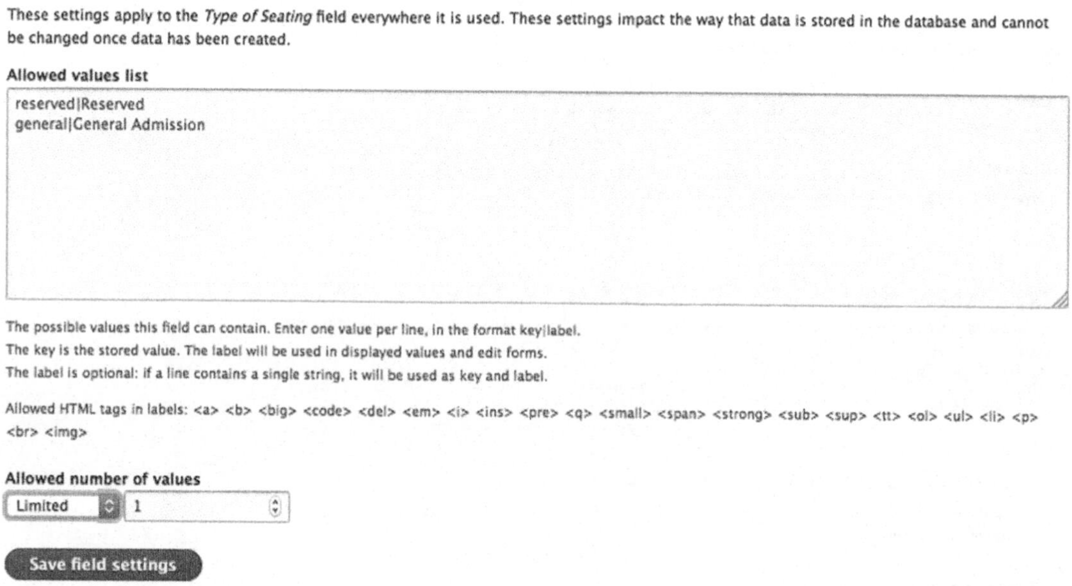

These settings apply to the *Type of Seating* field everywhere it is used. These settings impact the way that data is stored in the database and cannot be changed once data has been created.

Allowed values list

```
reserved|Reserved
general|General Admission
```

The possible values this field can contain. Enter one value per line, in the format key|label.
The key is the stored value. The label will be used in displayed values and edit forms.
The label is optional: if a line contains a single string, it will be used as key and label.

Allowed HTML tags in labels: <a> <b> <big> <code> <del> <em> <i> <ins> <pre> <q> <small> <span> <strong> <sub> <sup> <tt> <ol> <ul> <li> <p>
 <img>

Allowed number of values

Limited	⬍	1	⬍

Save field settings

Figure 5-18. Creating radio button options

The next step in the configuration process for this field is shown in Figure 5-19. On this form we can

- Change the label.
- Create help text.
- Mark the field as required.
- Set the default option that will be selected by default when the page is rendered.

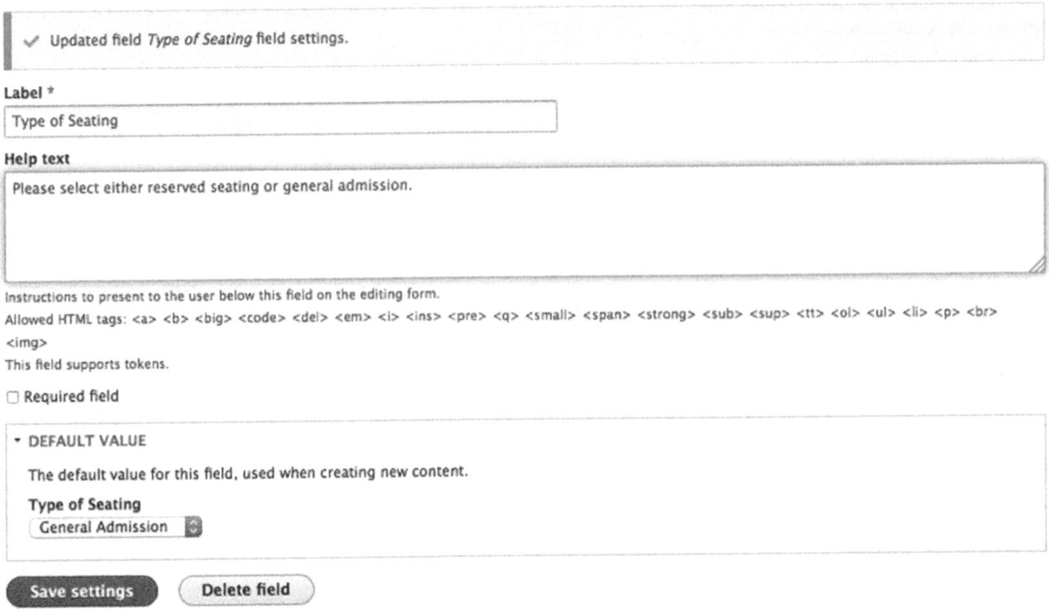

Figure 5-19. *Configuring a radio button field*

Enter help text that will help the visitor understand what this field is about, and set the General Admission option as the default value that will be selected automatically when the Create Event page is displayed. After setting the values, click the "Save settings" button.

The last step in the process is to define how we want Drupal to render the list of values, either as a select list or as check boxes/radio buttons. If you set the "Allowed number of values" to 1, a select list will render as a drop-down list, enabling the user to select a single item. If the "Allowed number of values" is set to more than one, the full list of values will be displayed instead of a drop-down select list. A list will render as radio buttons if you set the "Allowed number of values" to 1, and as check boxes if the "Allowed number of values" is greater than one. To set which type of widget will be used to display the Type of Seating list, click the "Manage form display" tab at the top of the "Manage fields" page (see Figure 5-20). Locate the Type of Seating field in the list of fields for this content type and change the Widget column from "Select list" to "Check boxes/radio buttons." Click the Save button to record your change.

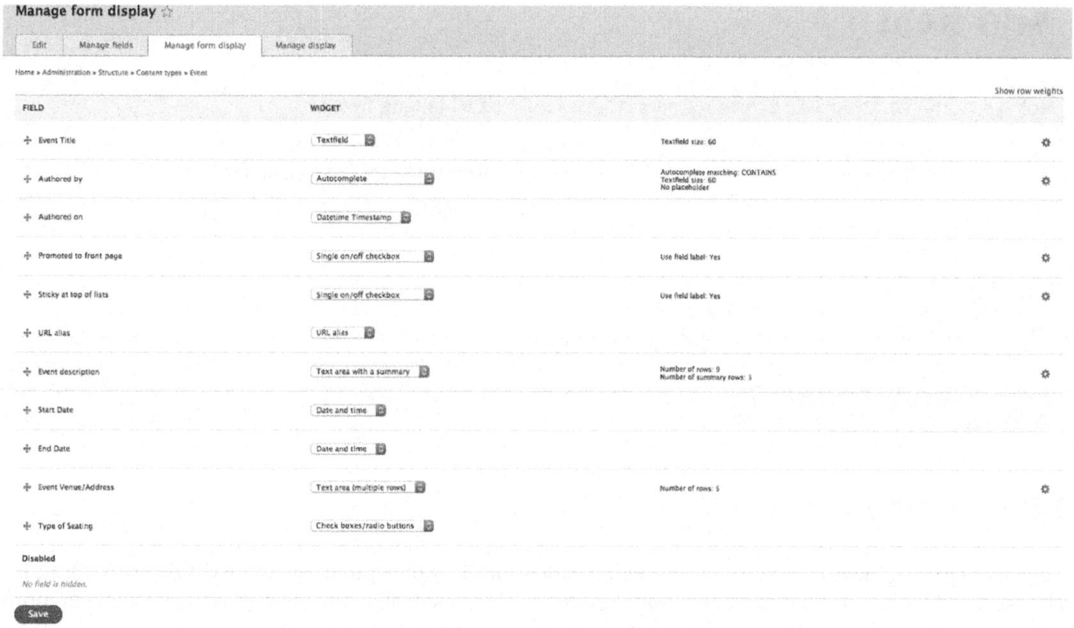

Figure 5-20. *Setting the widget type to "Check boxes/radio buttons"*

After clicking the Save button, the new field is ready for use, as shown in Figure 5-21. You'll note that Drupal added a third option to our list, the N/A option. Since we did not check the "Required field" check box for this field (see Figure 5-19), Drupal automatically inserts the N/A option because a visitor may wish to not select an option. If you want to remove the N/A option, check the "Required field" check box and Drupal will remove that option from the list.

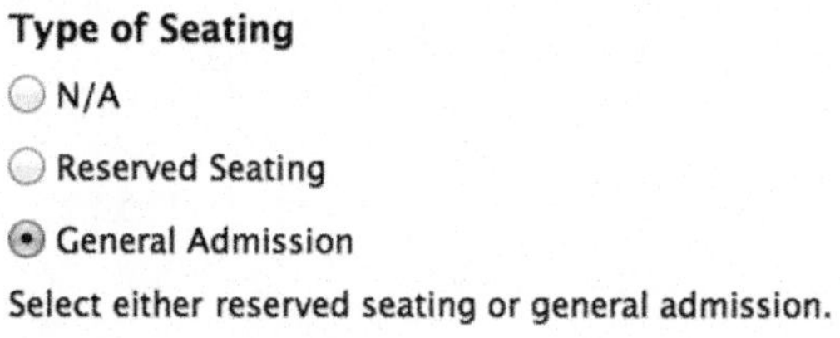

Type of Seating

○ N/A

○ Reserved Seating

◉ General Admission

Select either reserved seating or general admission.

Figure 5-21. *The "Type of Seating" radio buttons field*

Check Boxes

Check boxes are similar to radio buttons but allow the user to select more than one value from the list. We will now expand on our Event content type by adding a list of check boxes that addresses special accommodations available at this event for attendees with disabilities. We will create check boxes that specify whether audio-assisted devices, visual-assisted devices, and wheelchair seating are available for this event. To define the list of check boxes, return to the Event content type's "Manage fields" page and click the "Add field" button. Select "List (text)" from the "Add a new field" select list (refer to Figure 5-17) and enter a title of "Assistance" in the Label field (see Figure 5-22).

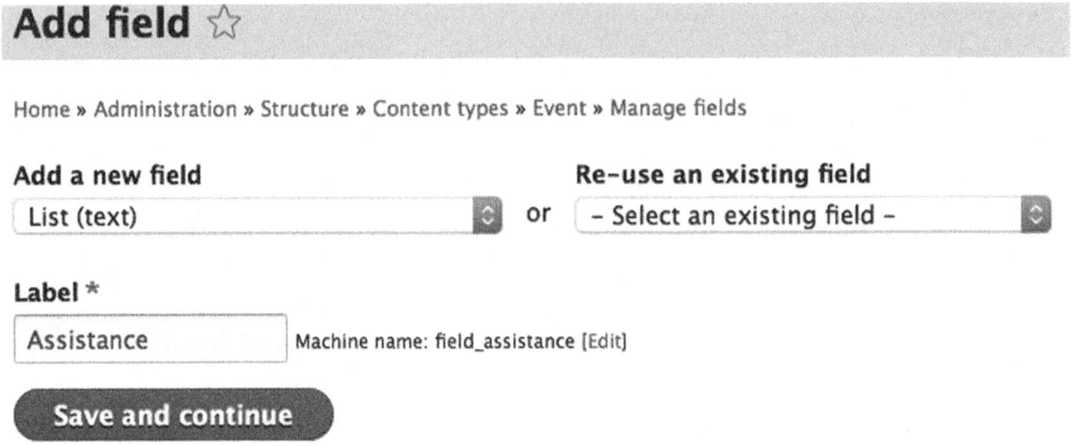

Add field ☆

Home » Administration » Structure » Content types » Event » Manage fields

Add a new field   **Re-use an existing field**

List (text) ◊   or   – Select an existing field – ◊

Label *

Assistance   Machine name: field_assistance [Edit]

Save and continue

Figure 5-22. Adding a check box field

After clicking "Save and continue," enter the values for the three options, as shown in Figure 5-23, and change the "Allowed number of values" from Limited to Unlimited, allowing the visitor to select one or more values from the list. Click the "Save field settings" button to continue the process.

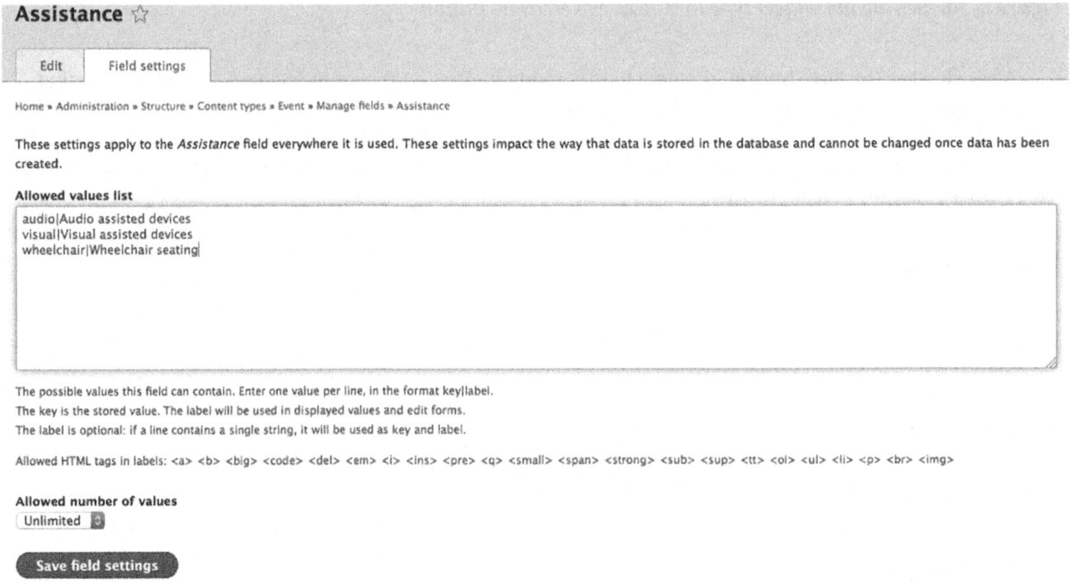

Assistance ☆

Edit   Field settings

Home » Administration » Structure » Content types » Event » Manage fields » Assistance

These settings apply to the *Assistance* field everywhere it is used. These settings impact the way that data is stored in the database and cannot be changed once data has been created.

Allowed values list

audio|Audio assisted devices
visual|Visual assisted devices
wheelchair|Wheelchair seating|

The possible values this field can contain. Enter one value per line, in the format key|label.
The key is the stored value. The label will be used in displayed values and edit forms.
The label is optional: if a line contains a single string, it will be used as key and label.

Allowed HTML tags in labels: <a> <b> <big> <code> <del> <em> <i> <ins> <pre> <q> <small> <span> <strong> <sub> <sup> <tt> <ol> <ul> <li> <p>
 <img>

Allowed number of values
Unlimited ◊

Save field settings

Figure 5-23. Creating a check box field

The next step in the process is to enter help text to guide the author in what to do with the Assistance field, set the field to required if necessary, set the default value if a default is desired (see Figure 5-24), and then click the "Save settings" button. For our example, we will not make the Assistance field required, nor will we set a default value, as a majority of the visitors to our events are likely to not require assistance.

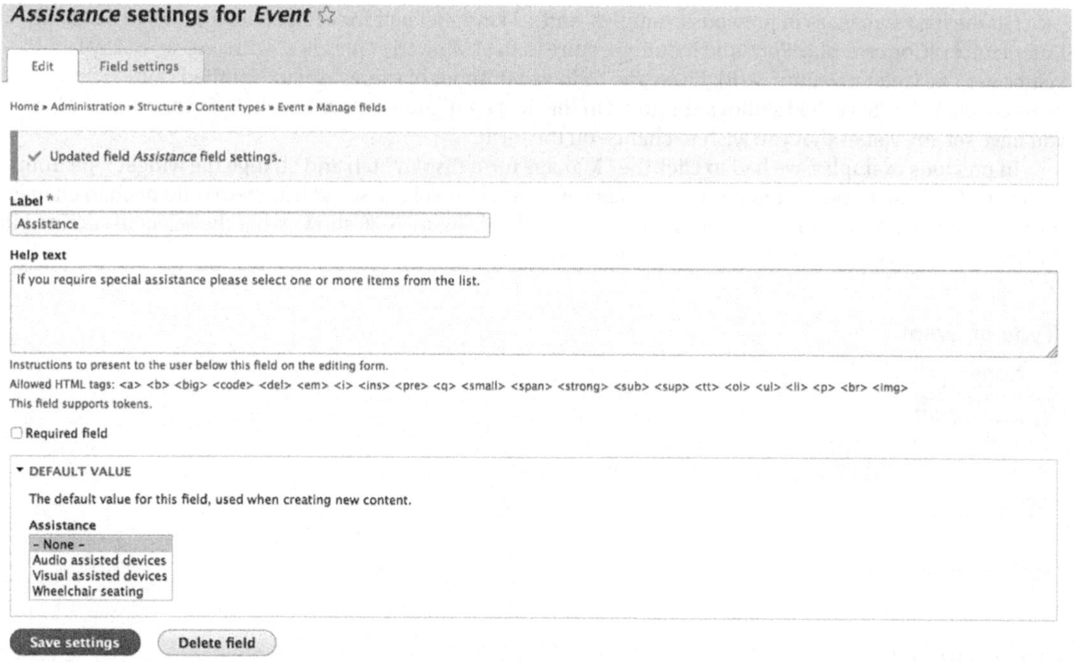

Assistance settings for *Event* ☆

Edit	Field settings

Home » Administration » Structure » Content types » Event » Manage fields

✓ Updated field *Assistance* field settings.

Label *

Assistance

Help text

If you require special assistance please select one or more items from the list.

Instructions to present to the user below this field on the editing form.
Allowed HTML tags: `<a> <b> <big> <code> <del> <em> <i> <ins> <pre> <q> <small> <span> <strong> <sub> <sup> <tt> <ol> <ul> <li> <p> <br> <img>`
This field supports tokens.

☐ Required field

▼ DEFAULT VALUE

The default value for this field, used when creating new content.

Assistance

```
- None -
Audio assisted devices
Visual assisted devices
Wheelchair seating
```

[Save settings]   [Delete field]

Figure 5-24. *Completing the settings for the check box field*

After completing the field settings for the Assistance field, you must then instruct Drupal to render this field as "Check boxes/radio buttons." Click the "Manage form display" tab at the top of the content edit form and change the widget type value from "Select list" to "Check boxes/radio buttons," and click the Save button. To see the result of adding this field, click one of the "Add content" links and add a new event. The new check box field will appear as shown in Figure 5-25.

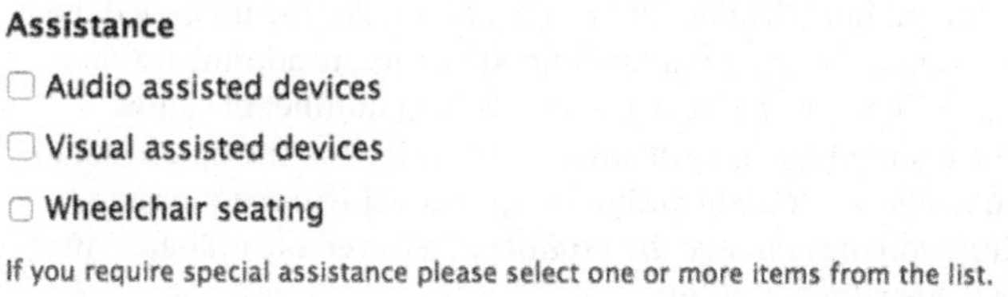

Assistance

☐ Audio assisted devices

☐ Visual assisted devices

☐ Wheelchair seating

If you require special assistance please select one or more items from the list.

Figure 5-25. *The list of check boxes for the Event content type's Assistance field*

Select Lists

Select lists are often called drop-down lists. To demonstrate select lists, let's create a new field for the Event content type that lists whether the event is a concert, a play, or a lecture. Creating a select list is similar to creating the previous field types covered. On the "Manage fields" page for the Event content type, click the "Add field" button. Select "List (text)" for the field type (refer to Figure 5-17) and enter "Type of Event" in the Label field. After setting these values, click the "Save and continue" button to proceed with the definition of your new select list field.

On the next screen, as in previous examples, enter a key|label pair for each of the options to be listed. Enter concert|Concert, play|Play, and lecture|Lecture in the "Allowed values list," with one set of key|label values per line (refer to Figure 5-18). Leave the "Allowed number of values" set to "Limited" and "1." To proceed, click the "Save field settings" button. On the next configuration screen, click "Save settings" after you have set any values that you wish to change on the form.

In previous examples, we had to click the "Manage form display" tab and change the widget type from "Select list" to "Check boxes/radio buttons." Since we want to display a select list, there is no need to change the value. You are now ready to use your new select list field. Figure 5-26 shows what the select list defined in the previous steps looks like when creating a new event.

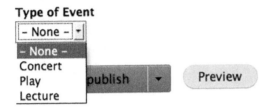

Figure 5-26. *Select list*

File Uploads

The file upload field type presents a file browser button that allows an author to browse their local computer for a file to upload to Drupal and attach to the content item that they are creating. Creating a file upload field is nearly identical to the procedure for creating other field types. We will expand our Event content type to include the ability to attach the program for the event. As with previous fields, navigate to the Event content type's "Manage fields" page and click the "Add field" button. On the "Add field" screen (refer to Figure 5-17), select "File" as the field type and enter "Event Program" in the Label field. Click "Save and continue" to proceed to the next step.

On the "Field settings" page (see Figure 5-27), check the "Enable *Display* field" check box and the "Files displayed by default" check box. Checking these boxes provides the author with the option of displaying a link to the file when visitors are viewing that content item. By default, the destination for the uploaded file will be the "Public files" directory, which is a configurable destination defined by the site administrator. (I'll cover configuration options in more detail in Chapter 14.) Next, in the "Allowed number of values" field, set the number of file uploads that will be enabled for content authors. We will leave the option set to "Limited" and "1" as we only foresee the need to allow a content author to upload a single event program file per event. Depending on your requirements, you may change the number of allowed file uploads. After setting the values on the form, click the "Save field settings" button.

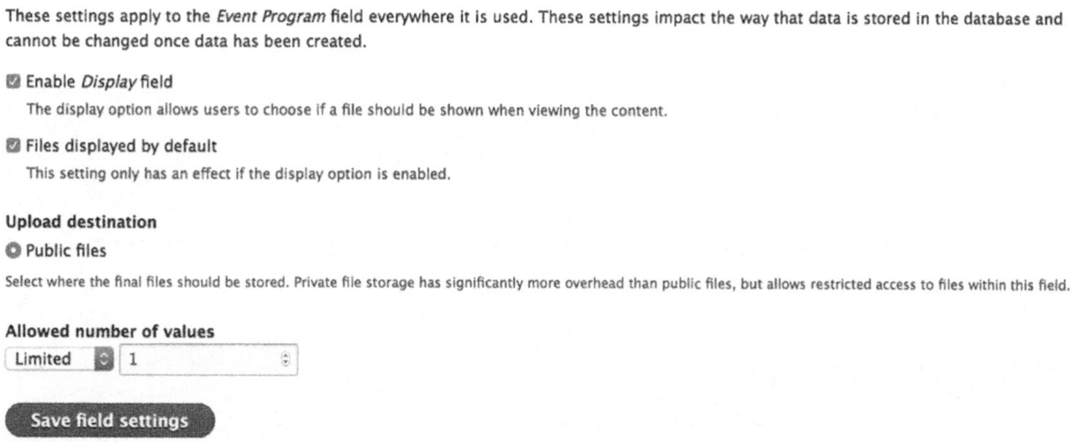

These settings apply to the *Event Program* field everywhere it is used. These settings impact the way that data is stored in the database and cannot be changed once data has been created.

☑ Enable *Display* field
The display option allows users to choose if a file should be shown when viewing the content.

☑ Files displayed by default
This setting only has an effect if the display option is enabled.

Upload destination
◉ Public files

Select where the final files should be stored. Private file storage has significantly more overhead than public files, but allows restricted access to files within this field.

Allowed number of values

Limited ⬍	1 ⬍

Figure 5-27. Setting the file upload parameters

On the final configuration screen (see Figure 5-28), you will find fields and options for entering help text that explains what this field is used for ("Upload the events program" in our example), indicating whether a file upload is required when creating an event (unchecked in our example), specifying the allowed file extensions (in our case we'll allow an author to upload a file with either a txt, doc, docx, ppt, pptx, or pdf file extension), optionally identifying the directory within the public files directory where these files will be uploaded (leave blank), setting the "Maximum upload size" (for our example we'll allow files up to 1MB to be attached to the event), and enabling a Description field that may be used by the content author to describe the file. Once you've updated the values, click the "Save settings" button at the bottom of the form.

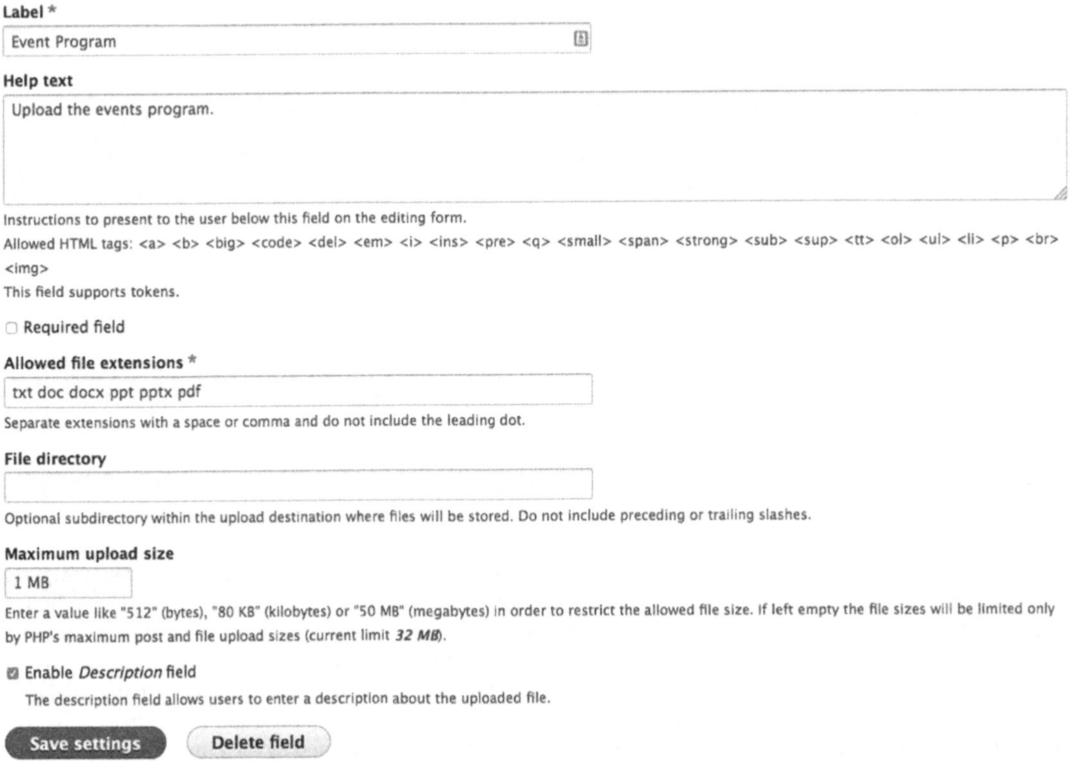

Label *

| Event Program | 🔡 |

Help text

Upload the events program.

Instructions to present to the user below this field on the editing form.
Allowed HTML tags: <a> <b> <big> <code> <del> <em> <i> <ins> <pre> <q> <small> <span> <strong> <sub> <sup> <tt> <ol> <ul> <li> <p>
<img>
This field supports tokens.

☐ Required field

Allowed file extensions *

| txt doc docx ppt pptx pdf |

Separate extensions with a space or comma and do not include the leading dot.

File directory

Optional subdirectory within the upload destination where files will be stored. Do not include preceding or trailing slashes.

Maximum upload size

| 1 MB |

Enter a value like "512" (bytes), "80 KB" (kilobytes) or "50 MB" (megabytes) in order to restrict the allowed file size. If left empty the file sizes will be limited only by PHP's maximum post and file upload sizes (current limit *32 MB*).

☑ Enable *Description* field

The description field allows users to enter a description about the uploaded file.

Save settings   **Delete field**

Figure 5-28. *File upload configuration parameters*

Figure 5-29 shows the new file upload field on the event creation form.

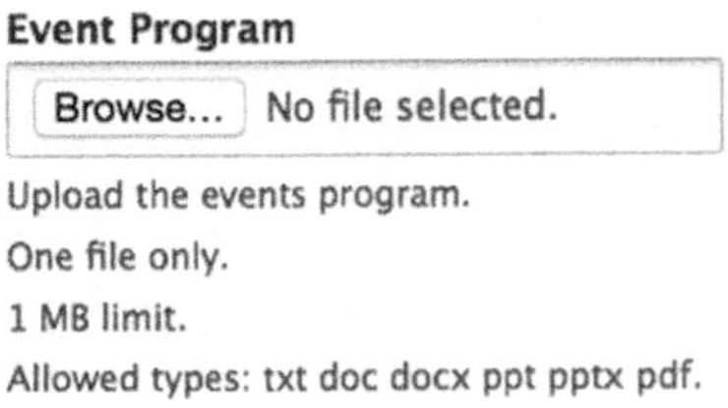

Event Program

| Browse... | No file selected. |

Upload the events program.
One file only.
1 MB limit.
Allowed types: txt doc docx ppt pptx pdf.

Figure 5-29. *File upload field*

Text Area

There will likely be scenarios where you want to provide a field on a content creation form that enables an author to enter a paragraph or more of text. While you could provide this capability through a text field (a single-line text-entry box), the more acceptable and standard way is to provide a text area. Extending our event example, let's add a new field that will be used to capture driving directions to the venue. To create a text area, follow the same steps as we used to create other fields in the previous sections. Click the "Add field" button on the "Manage fields" page for our Event content type and select "Text (formatted, long)" from the "Add a new field" list of options (refer to Figure 5-17). Enter "Driving directions" in the Label field and then click the "Save and continue" button.

The next form allows you to set how many text boxes will be created for this field. Leave the value set to 1 and click the "Save field settings" button. The next form provides you with the option to enter help text, set the field as required, specify a default value, and define what type of text processing will be enabled for the author. Choosing Full HTML allows authors to use the full capabilities of the WYSIWYG editor, whereas Basic HTML restricts the number of available formatting options to just the basics (see Figure 5-30 for the Limited HTML options). Choose Basic HTML and click the "Save settings" button. The new field is now available for use. Try creating a new event, and you'll see the new text area where you can enter driving directions (see Figure 5-30).

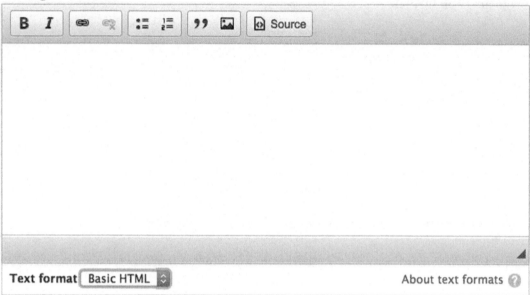

Figure 5-30. *The new text area for driving directions*

Numeric Fields and Other Field Types

By walking through the various field types listed previously, you can see that there is a pattern and a common set of parameters for nearly every field type we created. A numeric field is essentially a text field, but restricted automatically by Drupal so that it will only accept numeric characters (0–9). As you expand on the types of fields that you can create by downloading and enabling contributed Fields modules, you will find slight variations in the process due to the structure of the fields you are creating. However, the overall process will be the same. If you haven't done so, now is the perfect time to browse the list of Fields modules that are available to extend the capabilities of what is available in Drupal 8 core. Visit http://drupal.org/project/modules, click the Fields item in the "Module categories" filter, and click Search. When you browse, make sure that you're focusing on Fields modules that are built for Drupal 8, as many of the capabilities inherent in Fields are now part of Drupal core, whereas in previous versions of Drupal you had to download and install CCK to do what we just accomplished using Drupal out of the box. To narrow the list to only Drupal 8, select 8.x from the Core compatibility drop down and click the Search button.

Formatting the Input Form for a Custom Content Type

Sometimes you may find that the visual representation of your new content creation form doesn't fit with how you would like it to appear. You may want to change the order of fields on the form, the type of widget used to create content in a field, or the format of the widget itself. To change how the form is displayed, edit a content type following the steps you've performed previously. Click the "Manage form display" tab at the top of the page, resulting in the list of fields with their widget types and widget configurations displayed (see Figure 5-31).

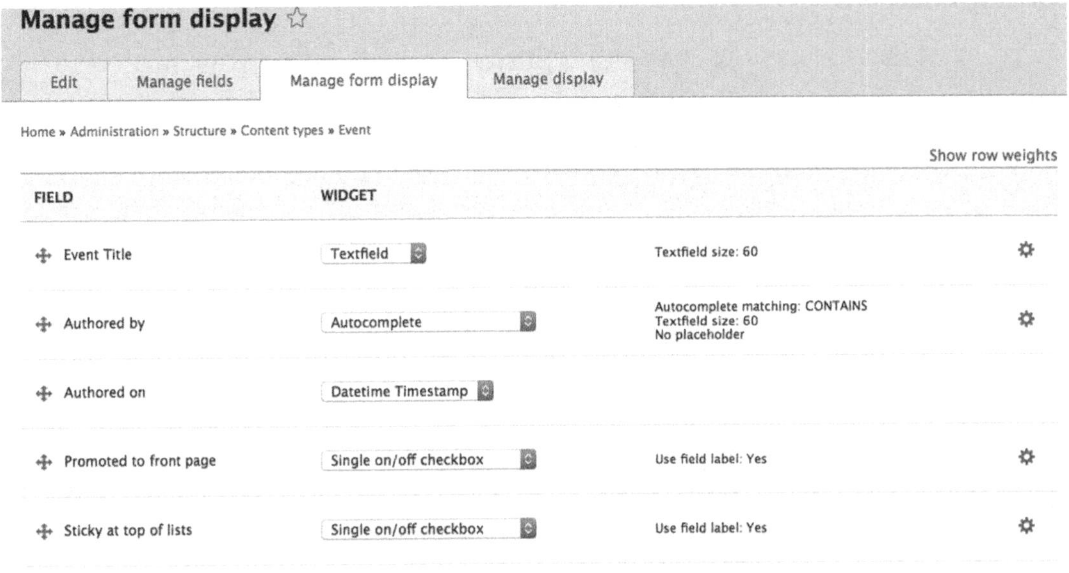

Figure 5-31. *The "Manage form display" tab*

To rearrange the order of the fields on the form, click and hold the arrows icon next to the field you wish to move, drag the field to the position where you want it to appear, and release your mouse button. To change the widget type, simply select a new value from the widget select list, and to change the appearance of a widget (for example, changing a text area so that it displays more than the default five lines), click the gear icon in the right column (see Figure 5-31).

As an example, let's change the text area field for driving directions from the default five lines of text to ten lines of text. To do so, click the gear icon in the right column of the "Driving directions" field. The form will expand to display a field where you can change the number of rows as well as enter placeholder text that will appear in the field until the author begins entering text in that field. Change the number of rows from 5 to 10 and then click the Update button, followed by the Save button. The number of rows displayed when creating a new event is ten, providing the author more room to enter directions.

Formatting the Output of a Custom Content Type

There will be times when the visual representation of your new content type as displayed to the end user of a site doesn't fit with how you would like the content created with your new content type to be rendered on the screen. In the previous section we looked at rearranging the fields on the form used by content authors to create an event; in this case we are rearranging the content as it appears when an event is rendered to an end user.

Adjusting the order and positioning of the labels in relation to the field can be accomplished by clicking the "Manage display" tab on the custom content type edit form.

We will use our Event content type to demonstrate the capabilities. Clicking the "Manage display" tab reveals the page shown in Figure 5-32.

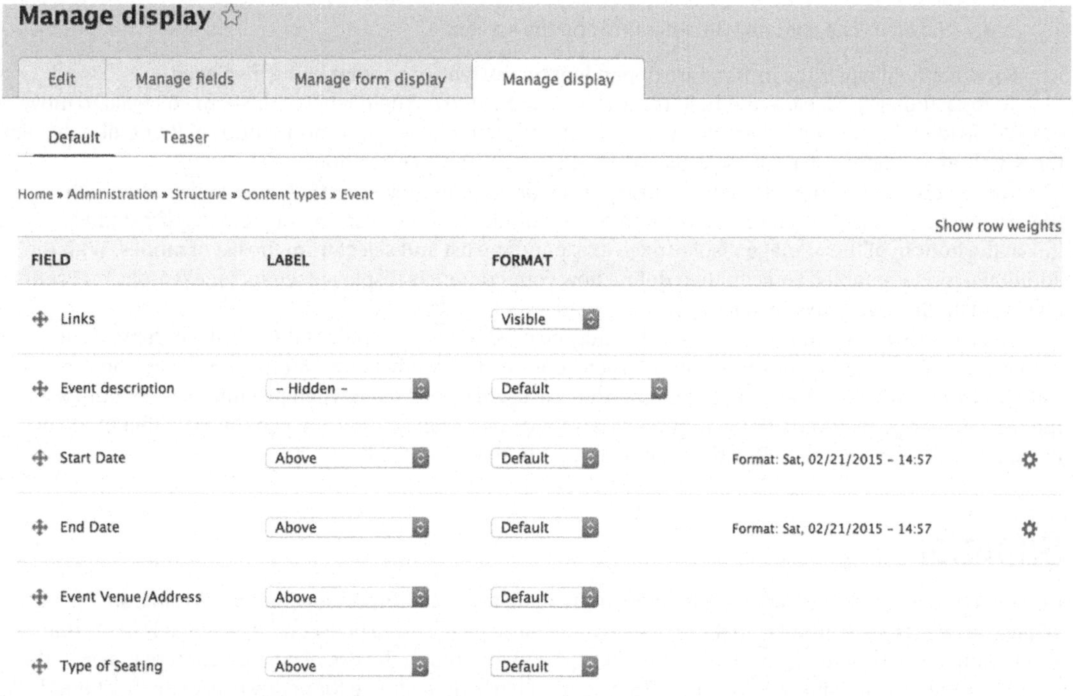

Manage display ☆

| Edit | Manage fields | Manage form display | Manage display |

Default   Teaser

Home » Administration » Structure » Content types » Event

Show row weights

FIELD	LABEL	FORMAT		
⊹ Links		Visible ◌		
⊹ Event description	– Hidden – ◌	Default ◌		
⊹ Start Date	Above ◌	Default ◌	Format: Sat, 02/21/2015 – 14:57	⚙
⊹ End Date	Above ◌	Default ◌	Format: Sat, 02/21/2015 – 14:57	⚙
⊹ Event Venue/Address	Above ◌	Default ◌		
⊹ Type of Seating	Above ◌	Default ◌		

Figure 5-32. *"Manage display" page*

This page lists all of the fields that are associated with our content type, and provides the ability to define basic display attributes for the label and content for each of the fields. By default there are two sets of values that we can set: one for the Default (full node) and one for the Teaser view. The Default option displays the complete content item and Teaser displays just the content item's title and a trimmed version of the body field. You can switch between these using the two links at the top left of the page. If you click the select list for the Label of each field , you will find that there are three options:

- *Above*: The label will be displayed on a line immediately above the widget that you selected for your field.

- *Inline*: The label will be displayed to the left of your widget, on the same line as the widget.

- *Hidden*: The label will not be displayed on the screen.

71

If you click the select list for the Format of each field, you will find a selection of options depending on the field type. For text-related fields, the options are

- *Default*: The content will be rendered on the screen as you specified when you created the field.

- *Summary or Trimmed*: If the field type has a summary value and a body value, the summary value will be displayed. If there isn't a summary, the body value will be trimmed to a specified length.

- *Trimmed*: The content will be "trimmed" to a specified number of characters. If the content is longer than the specified number of characters, a "Read more" link will be displayed.

- *Hidden*: The content will not appear on the screen.

For other field types, the options are dependent on the type of content being displayed.

To reposition a field, click and hold the arrows icon next to the field label of the item you wish to move, drag the field to the position where you want it to appear, and release your mouse button. Remember to click the Save button after you have moved all of the fields to their proper position.

We can also define how the content is displayed for other modes beyond default and Teaser, such as RSS, Search index, and Search result. To enable those modes simply click the "Custom display settings" link at the bottom of the Manage display page to expand the list and select from the list of modes. With the additional modes enabled you can then define how your content is displayed when, for example, an Event is displayed on the search results page.

You can also define your own modes that may be used to display content differently under various scenarios. To create a new view mode visit Structure ➤ Display Modes ➤ View modes and click on the "Add new view mode" button. Select Content from the list of options and when prompted, give your view mode a name (e.g., featured). Once your new view mode has been created you can then use that mode on the Manage display page to define the unique output for that view mode.

Summary

Content types is one of the "killer app" aspects of Drupal, and is an important concept to understand. While you could construct a Drupal site with just the Basic page and Article content types, it is likely that you'll want to leverage the features and functions provided through the use of custom content types. In this chapter I demonstrated just one of the custom content types that I create for nearly every site that I build for my clients. Other custom content types that I frequently use include Customers, Products, Departments, FAQs, Locations, and Employees. As you design and develop your new site, I'm sure you'll identify one or more custom content types that you could use.

Another powerful feature of custom content types is the ability to develop custom reports or "views" of custom content type data that is stored in the Drupal database. If you think about the Event content type we created in this chapter, it might be valuable to generate a list of events sorted by the start date, or a list sorted by venue.

The next chapter provides an overview of Drupal themes. Now that we have content, let's make it look good!

CHAPTER 6

■ ■ ■

Using Drupal Themes

In this chapter I will explain the process of changing the overall look and feel of your site by installing a new theme. I will walk you through the process of selecting, downloading, and enabling your selected theme. You've added some neat things to your site in previous chapters, and we've seen some exciting features of Drupal; but this chapter will have you exclaiming "wow!"

The visual layout and presentation of your new Drupal site is defined through a Drupal component called a *theme*. A theme defines

- The colors used on the page.

- The fonts used for text, headings, links, and other elements.

- The placement of images and graphics that are present on every page of the site (images and graphics that are associated with the page itself rather than a content item).

- The layout of the page (such as a menu at the top, a banner area, a secondary menu below the banner, a column on the left, or a footer).

Themes can be as simple as a plain white canvas or as complex and visually energizing as your imagination can conjure up. Drupal themes are designed and developed using HTML, cascading style sheets (CSS), and elements such as variables, expressions, and tags from the Twig templating engine. Twig makes it easier for nondevelopers to create Drupal themes because they don't have to know PHP, the programming language that Drupal is built upon.

We have already worked with a Drupal theme; the basic Drupal 8 site that we installed as part of the earlier chapters in this book uses the default Bartik theme. Bartik is a predominantly "black and blue" theme, with a relatively simple structure (see Figure 6-1). The theme provides 17 different regions where you can place content, widgets, images, videos, forms, or other elements. In Chapter 9 we will look at the administrative tools for placing elements within regions.

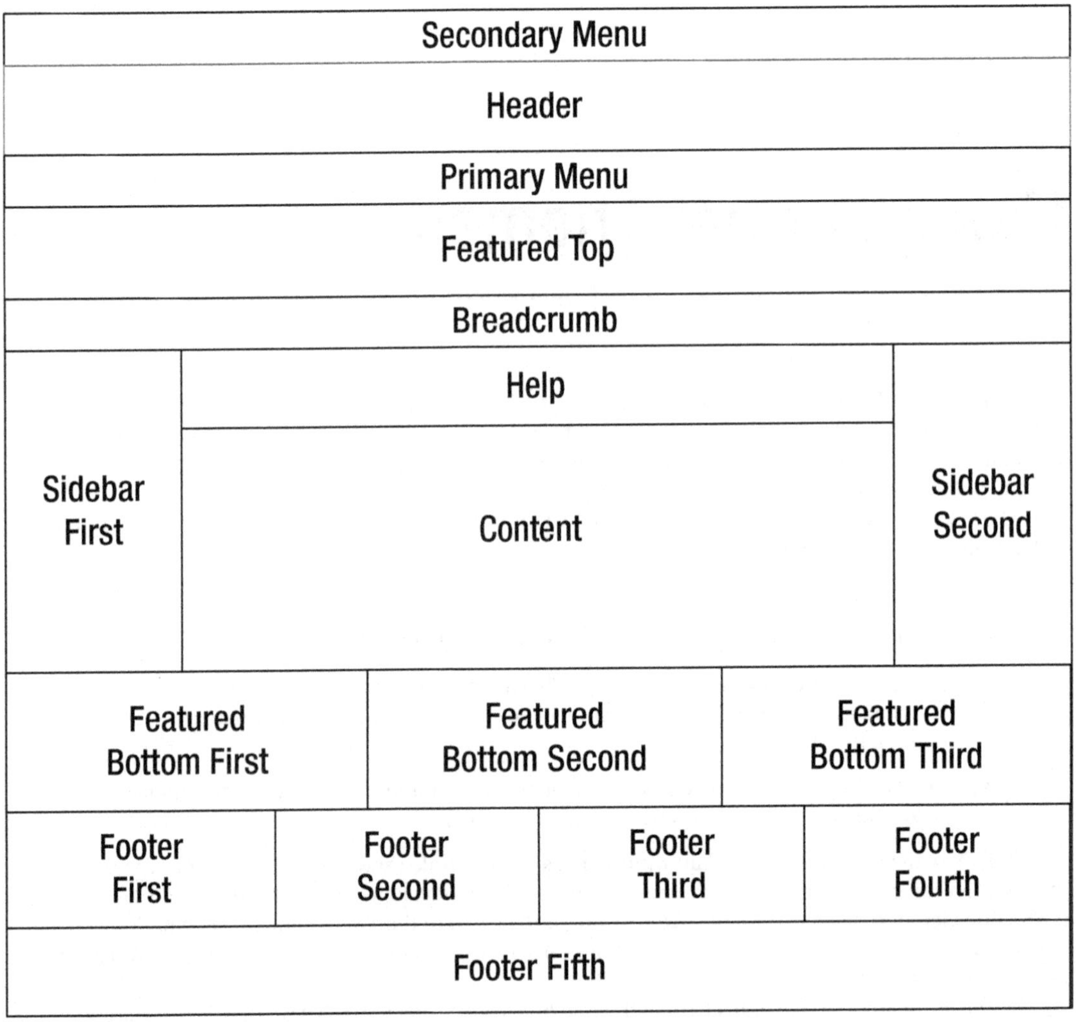

Secondary Menu			
Header			
Primary Menu			
Featured Top			
Breadcrumb			

Sidebar First	Help	Sidebar Second
	Content	

Featured Bottom First	Featured Bottom Second	Featured Bottom Third

Footer First	Footer Second	Footer Third	Footer Fourth

Footer Fifth			

Figure 6-1. *The Bartik theme*

You'll find as you browse through various Drupal themes that many of them follow this same generic layout, which for many people is a negative because it makes them believe that every Drupal site looks nearly identical. The truth of the matter is that, yes, many off-the-shelf themes follow this same layout pattern. However, you have the ability to create a layout that significantly deviates from the standard. Figure 6-2 demonstrates how I used the capabilities of Drupal's theme engine to create a Drupal site for the University of Oregon that is used by high school students to manage their electronic portfolio of learning assets and track their progress toward graduation. The area at the top of the page with the brown background is the header, the area in the middle of the page with the green background is the content area, and the brown area at the bottom is the footer.

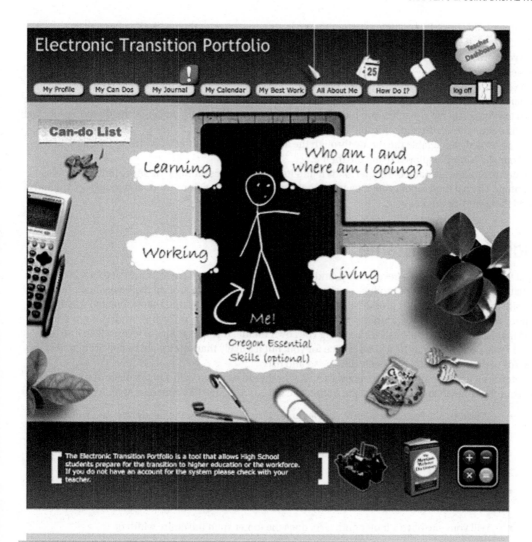

Figure 6-2. A creative, nontraditional Drupal theme

How a Drupal Theme Works

Understanding some of the basics behind how a Drupal theme works will help lay the foundation for some topics that I will cover in later chapters. The fundamentals of how a theme works can be distilled into a few basic concepts, which I explain here.

As the administrator, you have the ability to pick which theme your site will use. You can download a stock theme from www.drupal.org/project/project_theme, you can purchase a commercial theme from various providers that sell Drupal themes, you can create your own theme using one of the starter themes available on Drupal.org, or you can start from scratch and create a custom theme. It is likely that you will find something that matches or closely matches what you want from a visual design perspective on the Drupal theme download site or by creating a custom theme leveraging a starter theme like Zen (`www.drupal.org/project/zen`). If you scan through the hundreds of themes and can't find one you like, you can always create your own. *Pro Drupal Development*, also published by Apress, covers many of the aspects of creating a theme from scratch.

If you find a theme that you like, download it, and save it in the `/themes` directory of your site. The file that you download will be a Zip file, which needs to be unzipped using the tools provided by your operating system to expand zip files (just like you did when you downloaded Drupal), and copy the theme to your web server into the `/themes` directory located in the root directory of your site.

Once copied, you enable the theme through the administration features provided in Drupal 8, and voila! Your site is now displayed using the theme.

Once the theme is enabled, Drupal loads it and its associated cascading style sheets and assembles the content. Drupal then renders each page using the structure, style, colors, fonts, and images as you have defined them in your theme.

Finding a New Theme

Drupal 8 ships with the Bartik, Seven, Stark, and Classy themes. Although Bartik is a great theme, it's likely one that you won't use on your production site (although when browsing around the Web you'll often run into a site that uses Bartik as its production theme). Seven is the default admin theme, created specifically to render administrative pages. Stark is a very simple theme with virtually no styling, and Classy is a base theme that is meant to be the basis for building your own theme. If you're going for a very clean and text-heavy theme, then Stark may be a good choice for you, but it's likely that you'll want to pick from one of the hundreds of themes that you can freely download and use.

Before you begin your search for a new theme, you should sit down with a blank piece of paper and sketch out the general layout of at least the homepage of your new site. Key concepts to focus on include:

- Will your site have a header or banner area? If so, how tall will the header be, and will it span the entire width of your page?

- Will your site use horizontal menus and, if so, how many will you have and where will they be placed?

- Does your design call for a left or right side bar? Or does your design call for two sidebars on the right or two on the left?

- Will your site have a footer and, if so, does the footer span the entire width of the page?

- Will you have a fixed width (say, 960px wide), or will the site need to adjust for different screen widths across a variety of desktops, laptops, tablets, and smartphones?

Answering these questions will help you narrow the choice of themes to only those that support your general layout and design goals.

The best place to begin your search for a theme is the Drupal.org website. To view a list of the available Drupal themes, visit `www.drupal.org/project/project_theme` (see Figure 6-3).

For demonstration purposes, let's search the Drupal.org site for a Drupal 8 theme that matches our intended layout and color scheme. On `www.drupal.org/project/project_theme`, select 8.x from the "Core compatibility" select list to limit the list to only themes that are Drupal 8 compatible, and then click the Search button. Drupal will display the list of themes, only listing those that are compatible with Drupal 8.

You can narrow the list of themes by filtering the results by theme name, maintenance and/or development status, and theme status (full projects or only sandbox projects, the latter of which are themes that are under development and have not yet been released). You can also use the "Sort by" filter to sort the results by creation date, last release, last build, title, author, or most installed. Choosing "Last release" shows all of the newly added themes (or updates to existing themes), which is a nice feature when you visit this page often and want to see what the community has contributed recently. For this demonstration, let's sort by Title to list the Drupal 8 themes in alphabetical order.

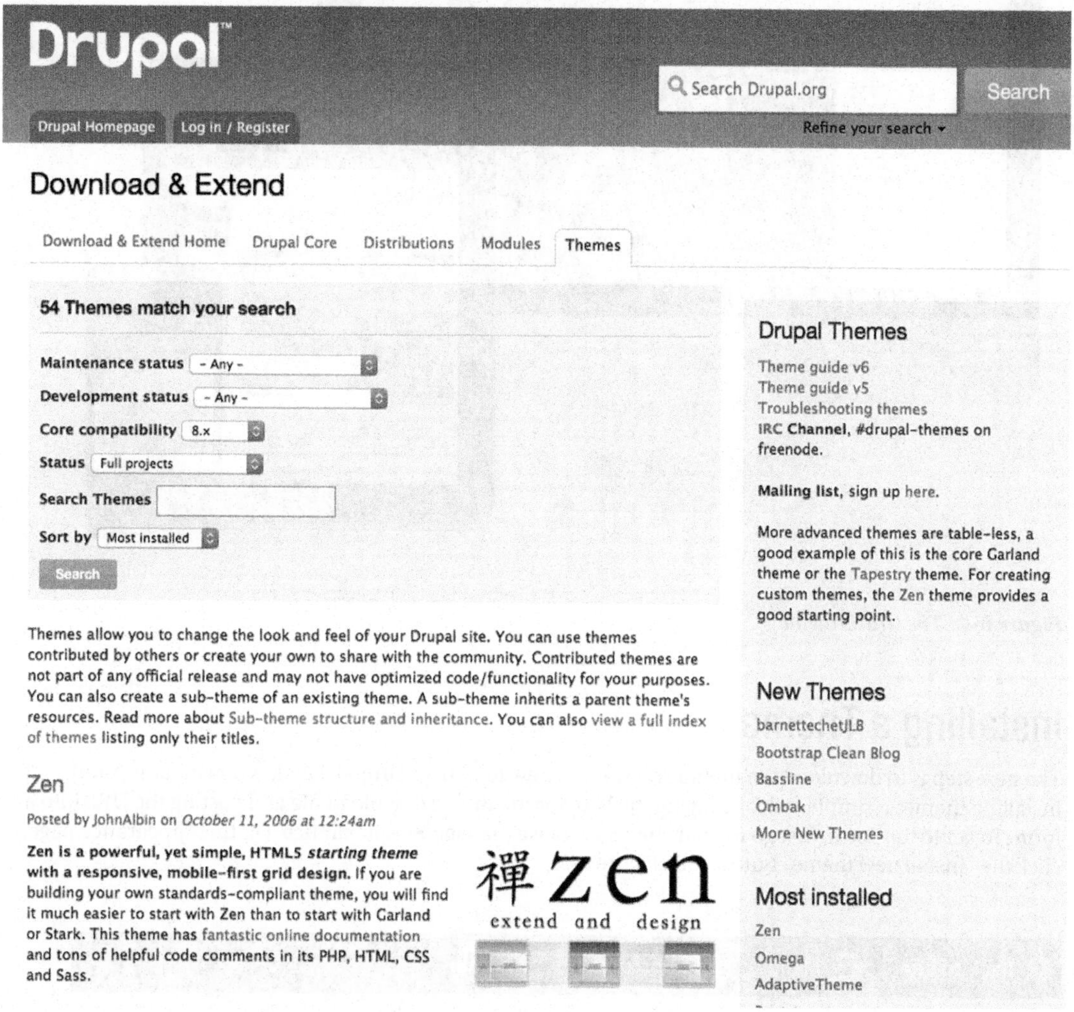

Figure 6-3. *Sort options for Drupal themes*

Browse through the pages of themes to see the variety that is available. Most theme developers provide a sample screenshot of their design so you can see the general layout and design of their theme. As an example, select the Gratis theme (`www.drupal.org/project/gratis`). This theme provides a clean and simple layout that is responsive, meaning it will display well on desktops, laptops, tablets, and smartphones. See Figure 6-4.

Figure 6-4. *The Gratis theme*

Installing a Theme

The next step is to download the theme you want. A new feature in Drupal 8 makes downloading and installing themes a simple task of copying the URL for the theme download file and pasting the URL into a form. To get to this form, first go to your site and choose Manage ➤ Appearance. On the Appearance page, click the "Install new theme" button. See Figure 6-5.

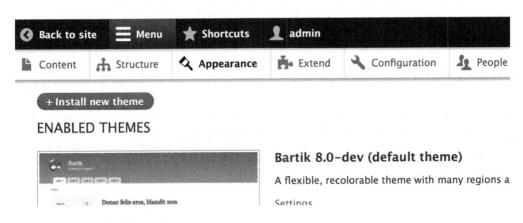

Figure 6-5. *Installing a new theme*

There are two methods for installing a new theme: using the Drupal admin interface to upload the file to your server, or manually copying the theme file to your web server and unarchiving that file in the / themes directory. The first option is the easiest if your web server is set up with FTP access, you have a valid FTP account (user ID and password), and your directories have the correct permissions to allow this user to create directories and copy files. If you're not sure about all of this, the simple method is to manually copy the theme file.

Let's take the easier approach for this example and manually copy the theme to our site. Open a new browser window (or a tab in an open window) and navigate to the theme that you wish to install (www.drupal.org/project/project_theme). We'll use the Gratis theme for Drupal 8 (www.drupal.org/ project/gratis) in this example. Scroll down the Gratis homepage to the Downloads section and click the tar.gz link for the 8.x version in the recommended releases section. If there isn't an 8.x version in the recommended releases section you can try the 8.x version in the Other releases or Development releases. Other and development releases may have issues as they are not quite ready for production.

Save the theme file to your computer. The next step is getting the tar.gz file to your server. If you are running Drupal locally, then simply copy the tar.gz file to the /themes directory for your site. If you are installing Drupal on a remote server, you will need some means for getting that file to your server, such as the file manager tools available through your hosting provider's administrative interface, to upload and expand the tar.gz file. Since I'm working on a local copy of Drupal on my laptop, I'll copy the tar.gz file to the /themes directory and, using my operating system's tools, expand the archive file. If you are using OS X, simply double-click the tar.gz file to expand the archive. Other operating systems may require third-party tools to expand a tar.gz file; check your operating system vendor's documentation for details.

If your web server is set up with FTP access and you have an FTP account with access to your site's directory, you may follow the first approach, the admin interface, to install the theme. To leverage this capability, click the Manage link in the admin menu followed by the Appearance link. At the top of the page, you'll see a button labeled "Install new theme." Click that button, and the interface for installing themes will be displayed as shown in Figure 6-6.

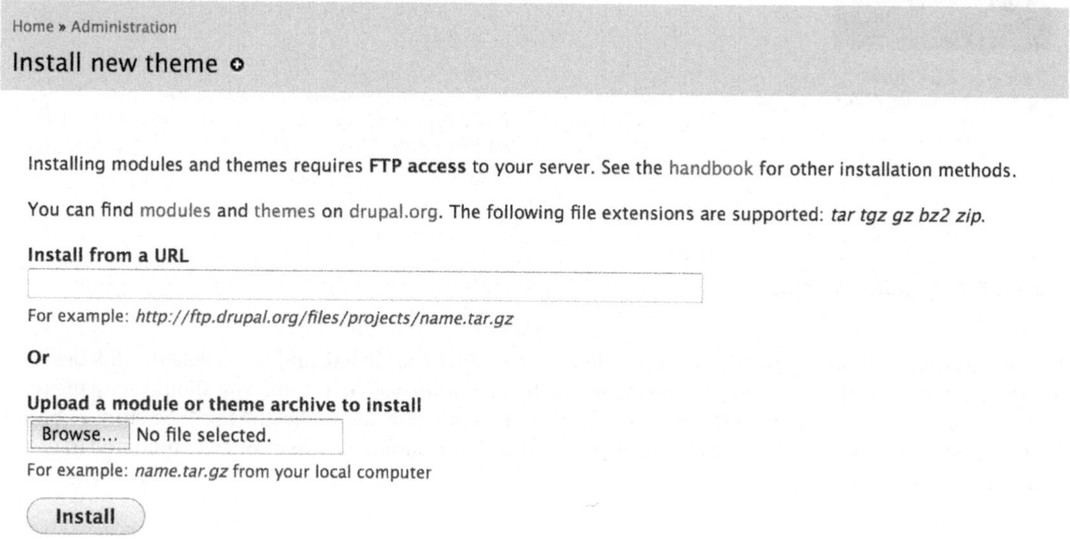

Home » Administration

Install new theme ○

Installing modules and themes requires **FTP access** to your server. See the handbook for other installation methods.

You can find modules and themes on drupal.org. The following file extensions are supported: *tar tgz gz bz2 zip*.

Install from a URL

_____

For example: *http://ftp.drupal.org/files/projects/name.tar.gz*

Or

Upload a module or theme archive to install

[Browse...] No file selected.

For example: *name.tar.gz* from your local computer

(Install)

Figure 6-6. The theme upload/download form

On this form you will see two fields, providing two ways to install the new theme:

- *Install from a URL*: This option enables you to paste (or type) the URL of the theme's distribution file that you wish to install. You'll need to visit the theme's homepage, scroll to the Downloads section of that page, right-click the tar.gz file name for the Drupal 8 version of the theme, copy the link location for that file, and paste that link in the first text box shown in Figure 6-6.

- *Upload a module or theme archive to install*: This method requires that you first download the tar.gz file to your local computer. Scroll to the Downloads section of the theme's homepage, click the tar.gz link for the Drupal 8 version of the theme, and save the file locally. Then, using the Browse button, locate that file and select it in preparation for the installation process.

Once you have either pasted the URL or located the tar.gz file locally, click the Install button. The next page in the process asks you for the FTP information for your site (Username and Password). Enter valid credentials and click the Continue button. Drupal will copy the tar.gz file to your server and expand the file ready for you to enable and set default as outlined in the steps below.

With the theme file expanded in the /themes directory, return to your site and click the Manage link in the admin menu and then Appearance link. Scroll down the page and you should see a section titled Uninstalled Themes (see Figure 6-7).

UNINSTALLED THEMES

Gratis 8.x–2.0–beta6
Drupal 8.x-2.x version of the Gratis Theme by Danny Englander

Install │ Install and set as default

Stark 8.0.0–beta6
An intentionally plain theme with almost no styling to demonstrate default Drupal's HTML and CSS. Learn how to build a custom theme from Stark in the Theming Guide.

Install │ Install and set as default

Figure 6-7. *Uninstalled themes*

Gratis should appear in the list of uninstalled themes. Click the "Install and set as default" link below the description of Gratis to enable the new theme. If the operation was successful, you should see a message that says Gratis is now the default theme. Visit the homepage of your site by clicking the "Back to site" button at the top left of the page and prepare yourself to be wowed. You should now see your site rendered in the new theme. See Figure 6-8.

Figure 6-8. *The site rendered in the new theme*

The Administration Theme

Administration forms tend to be wide and long, sometimes not fitting too well within the confines of the content area defined for a given theme. To address this problem, Drupal 8 lets you specify a theme that should be used for administrative functions. You can try your new theme to see if it works for administration screens, or you can pick a different theme to use whenever a site administrator is performing site administration tasks. Typically, a simple clean theme that is at least 960px wide works best as the admin theme. To change the administration theme, simply click the Appearance menu item at the top of the page and scroll to the bottom. You'll see a section titled Administration Theme. From the list of themes in the drop-down list, select a theme that you know will work with administration forms. By default Drupal 8 enables Seven as the administration theme, because it accommodates administration screens. You may also change the administration theme to any other theme listed in the drop-down list. If you change the value, make sure you click the "Save configuration" button.

Configuration Options

Drupal 8 provides a set of configuration options that, when changed, updates certain aspects of what is displayed within your theme. Depending on whether the theme author adhered to Drupal standards, you can use this form to determine which elements are displayed on the page (Logo, Site Name, Site Slogan, and so on), whether the theme should use its default logo, and whether the shortcut icon should be used (the shortcut icon is also known as the *favicon*; it's the little logo that appears to the left of your browsers address bar). To get to this screen, simply click the Appearance menu item in the top menu and click the Settings tab at the top of the Appearance page. See Figure 6-9.

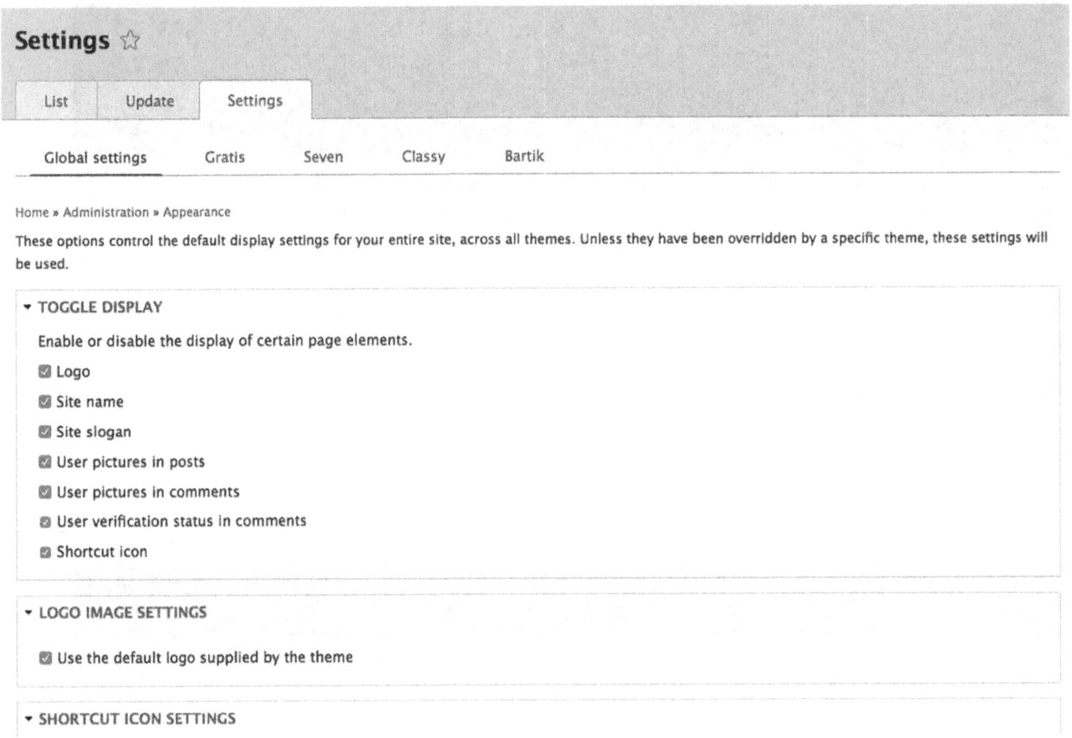

Settings ☆

| List | Update | Settings |

Global settings   Gratis   Seven   Classy   Bartik

Home » Administration » Appearance

These options control the default display settings for your entire site, across all themes. Unless they have been overridden by a specific theme, these settings will be used.

▾ TOGGLE DISPLAY

Enable or disable the display of certain page elements.

☑ Logo
☑ Site name
☑ Site slogan
☑ User pictures in posts
☑ User pictures in comments
☑ User verification status in comments
☑ Shortcut icon

▾ LOGO IMAGE SETTINGS

☑ Use the default logo supplied by the theme

▾ SHORTCUT ICON SETTINGS

Figure 6-9. Appearance configuration options

Try changing some of the display options such as the logo. Uncheck the "Use the default logo supplied by theme" check box and use the Browse button that appears after unchecking the box to upload a new logo for your site. Click the "Save configuration" button at the bottom of the Settings page and return to your site's homepage to see the change in appearance.

■ **Note**   A great site to visit to see what others have done with Drupal is Dries Buytaert's personal page. On his site, he lists many of the highest-profile sites on the Web that are deployed on Drupal. You can find the list at `http://buytaert.net/tag/drupal-sites`.

Summary

In this chapter we stepped into the "wow!" part of building a Drupal-based site: themes. In a matter of minutes, we changed the entire look and feel of our site through a few simple steps. Spend some time browsing through the themes on Drupal.org. You'll be amazed at the breadth of options that are literally a few clicks away from changing the entire look of your site.

CHAPTER 7

■ ■ ■

Creating Menus

A key factor in defining the success or failure of your new website is whether visitors can find information on your website, particularly the information that you want them to find. There are three basic mechanisms in Drupal to provide navigational capabilities to your site:

- Text links embedded in content that direct the user to a new page

- Images and buttons that direct the user to a new page when clicked

- Menus, which are horizontal or vertical lists of text or image links

In this chapter, you will learn how to use Drupal's administrator's interface for creating and managing menus.

Ordering from the Menu

A menu, in its simplest form, is a horizontal or vertical list of links that directs a user to a new page or pages. If you examine the homepage of your new website, you'll see that there are at least six menus on that page alone. See Figure 7-1.

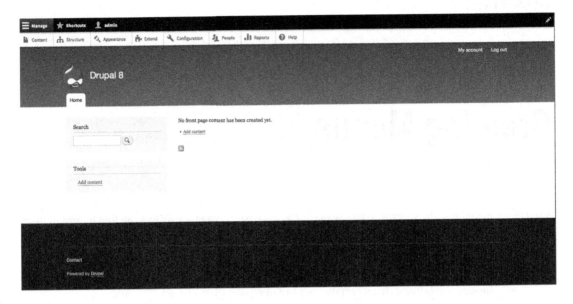

Figure 7-1. *Menus on a site*

From top to bottom, the menus are

- the Administrative menu, starting with Manage;
- the Administrative submenu bar at the top of the page, starting with Content;
- the User account menu (top of the header), with My account and Log out;
- the Main navigation menu, starting with the Home tab;
- the Tools menu in the left column, starting with Add content; and
- the Footer menu, starting with Contact.

Menus help a visitor to a site understand (and access) the content, features, and functions that the site provides.

On our example site that we're creating in this book, the menus shown on the page are all text links. Drupal also provides mechanisms for creating menus that are button and/or image based.

Creating menus is facilitated through a set of screens that are part of Drupal 8 core. There are three basic activities for creating menus and items that appear on menus:

- Adding an item to an existing menu. Drupal 8 comes with several menus already created. All you need to do is to add items to those menus.
- Creating a new menu. If you need more than the five menus that come with Drupal 8, you can create a new one.
- Assigning the menu to a region of on a page. If you created a new menu, you'll need to assign it to a region on the page.

Adding an Item to a Menu

There are two general items that we can add to our page as menu items: a link to an existing element on our site (a page, a content item, a list of content associated with a taxonomy term, and so on), or a link to a page that is external to our site (e.g., www.drupal.org).

Adding a Content Item to a Menu

There are two approaches for adding items to menus:

- The best practice is to use the content creation form (see Figure 7-2) or, as we will see later in the book, other element creation forms such as a panel page or a view. The reason for using this approach is that when you delete that content item, Drupal automatically removes the item from the menu to which it was assigned. If you use the manual approach of creating a menu item using the menu administration form, you as the site owner must remember to remove that item manually from the menu

- You can also use the menu administration form (see Figure 7-3) to create a new menu item, or you can create a menu link from the content item that you wish to reference from within the form used to create or edit that content item...

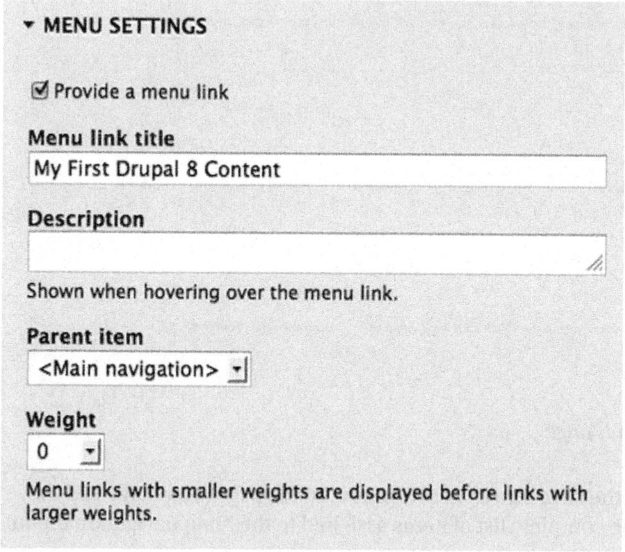

▼ MENU SETTINGS

☑ Provide a menu link

Menu link title

My First Drupal 8 Content

Description

Shown when hovering over the menu link.

Parent item

\<Main navigation\> ▾

Weight

0 ▾

Menu links with smaller weights are displayed before links with larger weights.

Figure 7-2. *Adding a content item to a menu*

To create a new content item, click any of the "Add content" links that are available on the homepage of your website (assuming you are still logged in as the administrator), and select the "Basic page" content type. As an example, enter a title and body for the new content type and then click the Menu Settings link in the right column. Check the "Provide a menu link" box, which reveals the fields for defining your menu (see Figure 7-2). Enter the title for the item as you wish it to appear on the menu, and in the "Parent item" drop-down list select the "Main navigation" menu as the one where you want the item to appear. After entering the values for your menu item, click the "Save and publish" button at the bottom of the page. Drupal then displays the page that you just created, with the menu item associated with this page now appearing in the Main navigation menu at the top left of the header area of the page.

Clicking that link will take you directly to the page we just created, regardless of where you are on the website.

Adding a Menu Item for an External Page

You can add links to external sites by adding a menu item. To do so, click the Manage link at the top of the page and the Structure link in the submenu. On the Structure page, click the Menus link. On the Menus page, click the triangle icon next to the "Edit menu" button for the Main navigation menu and select the "Add link" option. You should now see the "Add menu link" form (see Figure 7-3). Enter a title (in this example, I used Apress as the menu title), the link, which is the full URL to the external page to which we want to link (in the example I used `http://apress.com`), ensure that the Enabled check box is checked, and for demonstration purposes, select "Main navigation" from the "Parent link" drop-down list.

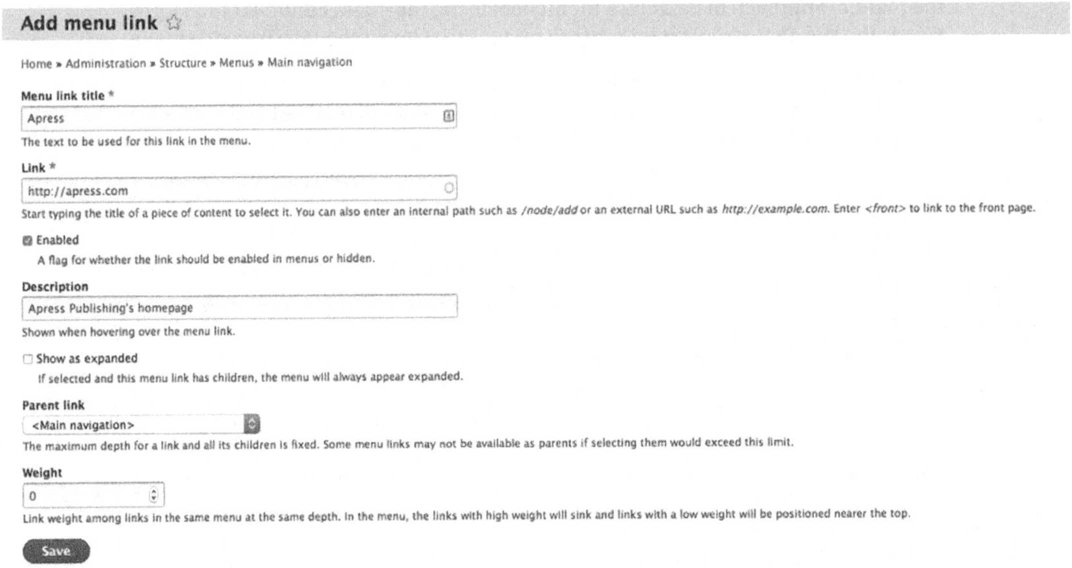

Add menu link ☆

Home » Administration » Structure » Menus » Main navigation

Menu link title *

| Apress | ⊡ |

The text to be used for this link in the menu.

Link *

| http://apress.com | ○ |

Start typing the title of a piece of content to select it. You can also enter an internal path such as /node/add or an external URL such as *http://example.com*. Enter *<front>* to link to the front page.

☑ **Enabled**
   A flag for whether the link should be enabled in menus or hidden.

Description

| Apress Publishing's homepage |

Shown when hovering over the menu link.

☐ **Show as expanded**
   If selected and this menu link has children, the menu will always appear expanded.

Parent link

| <Main navigation> | ◇ |

The maximum depth for a link and all its children is fixed. Some menu links may not be available as parents if selecting them would exceed this limit.

Weight

| 0 | ◇ |

Link weight among links in the same menu at the same depth. In the menu, the links with high weight will sink and links with a low weight will be positioned nearer the top.

[Save]

Figure 7-3. *Adding a menu item for an external page*

Once you've entered all the values, click the Save button at the bottom of the page (you may need to scroll down to see it). Drupal then displays the complete list of items assigned to the Main navigation menu, including the new item that we just created.

Navigate back to the homepage of your site by clicking the "Back to site" link in the admin menu. You should now see the new menu item that you just added. Clicking that menu item will take you to the external link that you entered when you created the menu item.

Creating a New Menu

There may be situations where you need to create additional menus beyond the standard menus created and enabled with Drupal 8. As an example, when creating Drupal-based websites for public libraries, I am often asked to build unique menus for each department in the library (a menu each for Adult Services, Youth

Services, Teen Services, Circulation, and so on). In such a case, the basic menus shipped with Drupal 8 are not enough to fulfill the library's requirements. To create a new menu, click the Manage link at the top of any page on your site and select the Structure link in the submenu. On the Structure page, click Menus, and on the Menus page click the Add Menu link. The form for creating a new menu is displayed (see Figure 7-4). Enter the title of the menu and a description (which is optional). Click the Save button, and you now have a new menu ready to assign items to using the same methods as described earlier in this chapter.

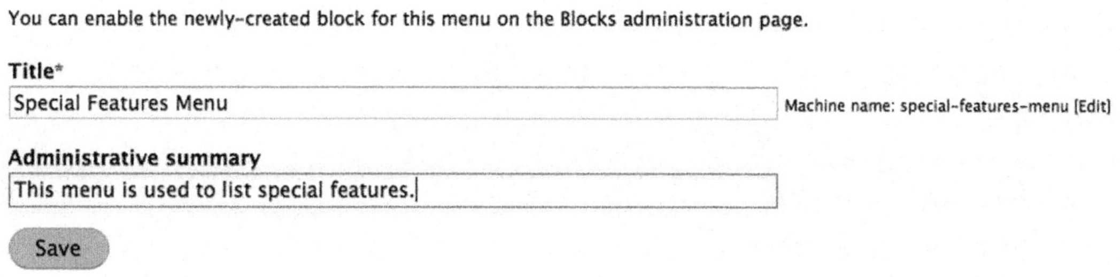

You can enable the newly-created block for this menu on the Blocks administration page.

Title*

Special Features Menu   Machine name: special-features-menu [Edit]

Administrative summary

This menu is used to list special features.|

Save

Figure 7-4. *Creating a new menu*

After saving the menu, you can now add items to it. As practice, create menu items for the following external links, using the process described in the section "Adding a Menu Item for an External Page": apress.com, yahoo.com, google.com, and bing.com. When completed, your menu should look something like that shown in Figure 7-5.

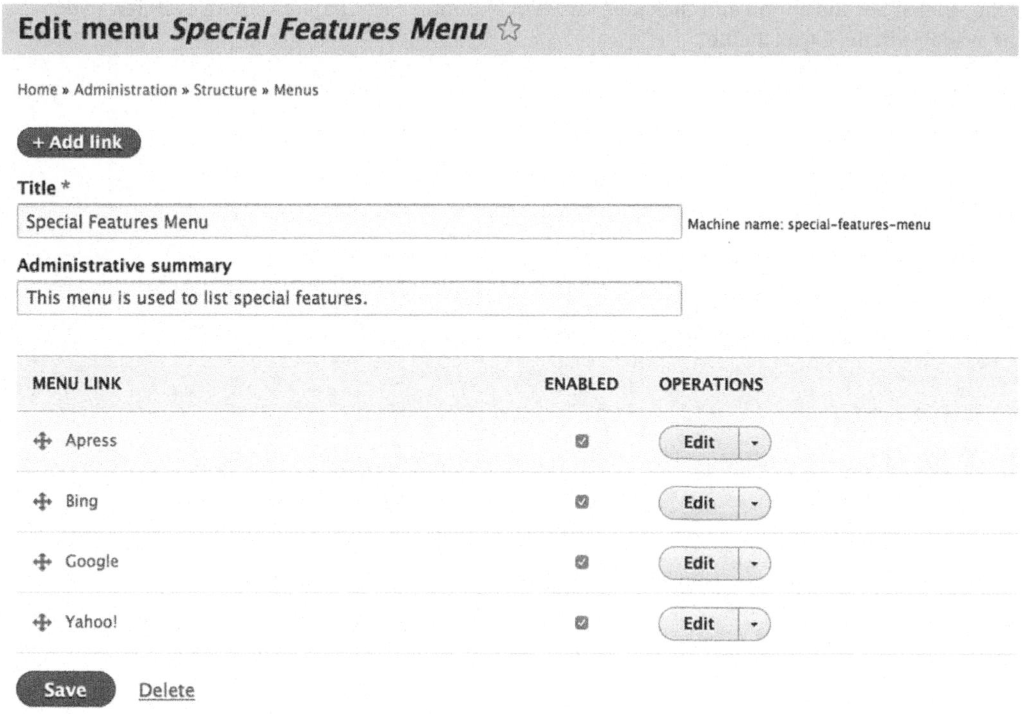

Edit menu *Special Features Menu* ☆

Home » Administration » Structure » Menus

+ Add link

Title *

Special Features Menu   Machine name: special-features-menu

Administrative summary

This menu is used to list special features.

MENU LINK	ENABLED	OPERATIONS
✛ Apress	☑	Edit ▾
✛ Bing	☑	Edit ▾
✛ Google	☑	Edit ▾
✛ Yahoo!	☑	Edit ▾

Save   Delete

Figure 7-5. *Your menu with items*

At this point the menu exists in Drupal, but it isn't assigned to a region on a page and, therefore, isn't visible to site visitors. To make your new menu visible, click the Manage link at the top of any page and then the Structure link in the submenu. On the Structure page click the "Block layout" link. On the "Block layout" page, scroll down until you find Special Features Menu (see Figure 7-6) in the "Place blocks" column on the right side of the page.

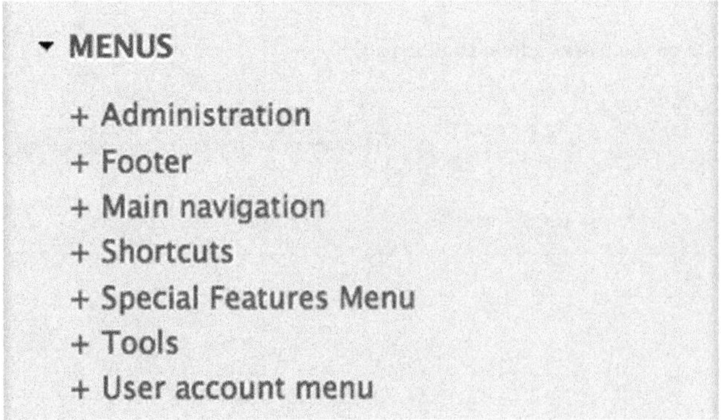

Figure 7-6. The "Block layout" page

Click the Special Features Menu link, which opens the "Configure block" form (see Figure 7-7). On this form select the region where you would like the menu to appear. Assuming you are using the Bartik theme, select the Sidebar Second option and click the "Save block" button. See Chapter 6 for an overview of the regions available in the Bartik theme.

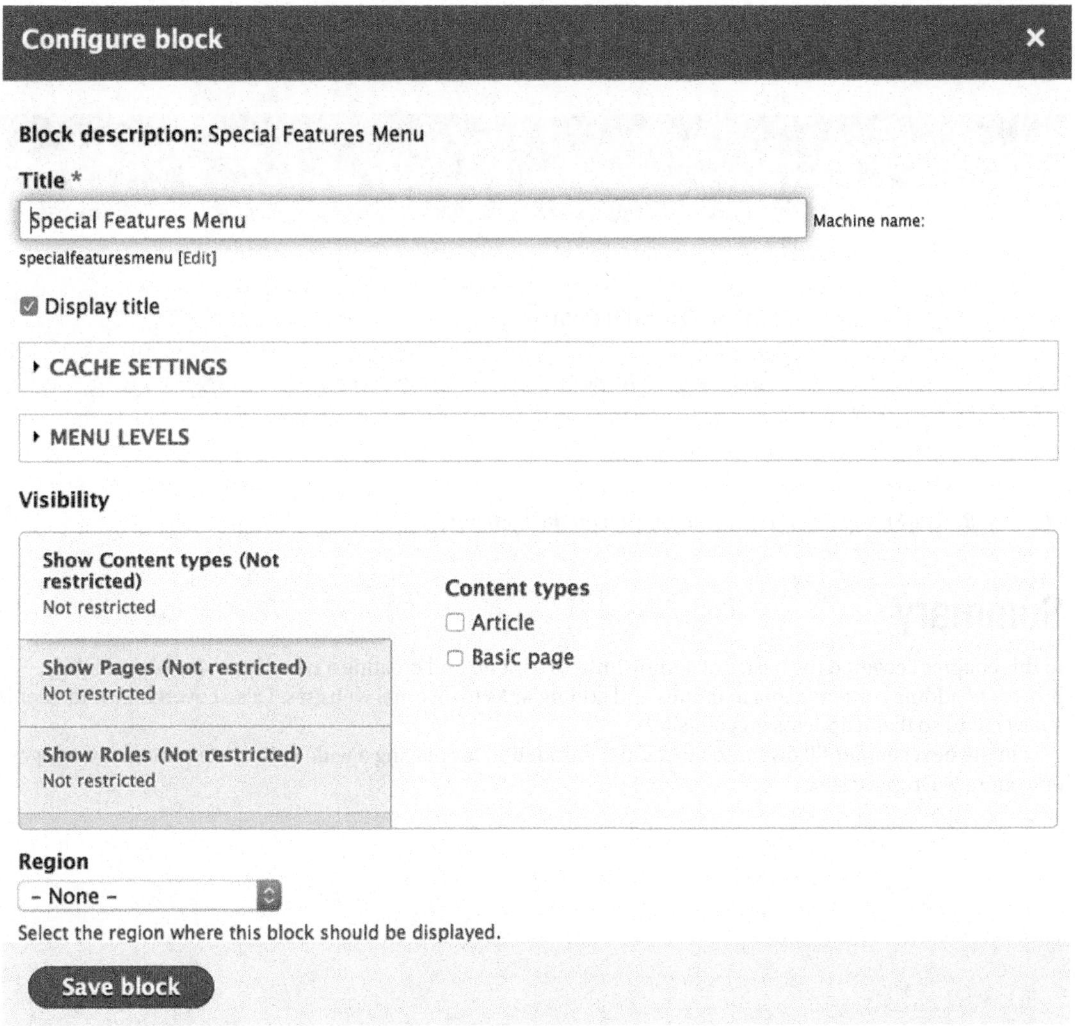

Configure block   ✕

Block description: Special Features Menu

Title *

Special Features Menu   Machine name:
specialfeaturesmenu [Edit]

☑ Display title

▸ CACHE SETTINGS

▸ MENU LEVELS

Visibility

Show Content types (Not restricted) Not restricted	**Content types** ☐ Article ☐ Basic page
Show Pages (Not restricted) Not restricted	
Show Roles (Not restricted) Not restricted	

Region

- None - ⬍

Select the region where this block should be displayed.

Save block

Figure 7-7. *Assigning the Special Features Menu to a region*

Click the "Back to site" button at the top left of the screen to return to the homepage and voila! There's your new menu (see Figure 7-8). You may now place your order.

Figure 7-8. *The Special Features Menu appears on the homepage*

Summary

In this chapter I covered the basics of adding links to a menu and creating a new menu. I explained the process of adding content items to menus and adding links to external websites. I also covered how to enable a new menu so that it appears on your site.

In the next chapter I'll dive into blocks, the foundation for placing a wide variety of content and images on your new Drupal 8 site.

■ ■ ■

## CHAPTER 8

Drupal Blocks

In this chapter I focus on using blocks to assign content and what are commonly called "widgets" (which include the user login form, latest blog posts, a list of who is currently logged into your site, the current weather conditions, and the like) to specific positions on a page. I will cover standard blocks that ship with Drupal 8, blocks that come with contributed modules, and information on how to build a custom block from scratch. At the end of the chapter you will have the ability to construct a page with some pretty exciting features.

Blocks, Blocks, and More Blocks

A *block* is a generic term that is applied to any self-contained piece of content, menu, or code. There are standard prebuilt blocks that come with Drupal 8: the "User login" block, the Search block, the "Who's online" block, the "Who's new" block, the "Recent content" block, and more. There are also blocks that come with contributed modules, such as blocks that share the latest weather report, your recent Twitter posts, or your current Facebook status. As a site administrator you can construct your own custom blocks, such as a list of upcoming events.

Making Blocks Appear on Pages

In Chapter 6 I covered the structure of themes and how themes define "regions" on a page. Figure 6-1 showed how the theme was divided into Sidebar First, Sidebar Second, Featured Top, Content, and several other regions. I'll now show you how to assign anywhere from one to dozens of blocks to the various regions on your theme, and explain how doing so increases visitor interest in your site by providing interesting and high-value features.

Figure 8-1 is an example of blocks that are assigned to various regions on a page. Seven blocks appear on this page.

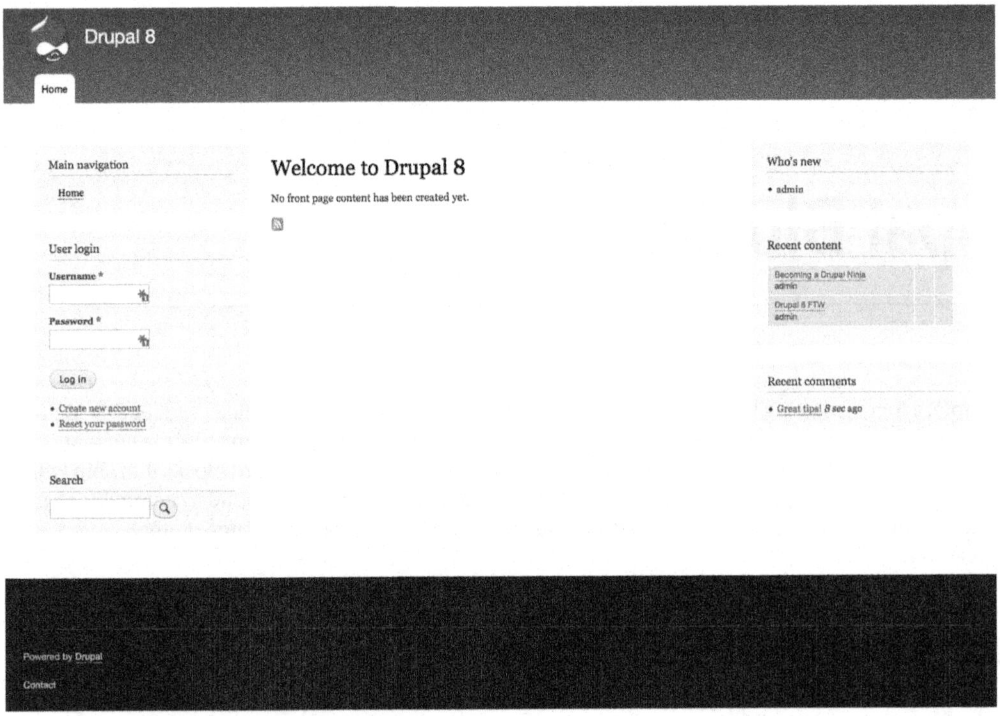

Figure 8-1. *See if you can spot the blocks*

This example includes a menu block (Main navigation), interactive blocks (Search and User login), and informational blocks (Who's new, Recent content, Recent comments, and Powered by Drupal).

Let's take a look at the blocks that come with Drupal 8 and assign a few of those blocks to regions on your site. We'll then install a module or two that provide cool blocks that you can add to your site, and then we'll create a custom block from scratch.

Finding the List of Available Blocks

To find the list of blocks that are available for you to use on your new website, click the Manage link at the top of the page, then click the Structure link in the secondary menu. This takes you to the Structure page. On the Structure page, click the "Block layout" link to reveal the "Block layout" page, which lists all the defined blocks on your system, including those that are already assigned to regions and those that are not assigned to a region. See Figure 8-2.

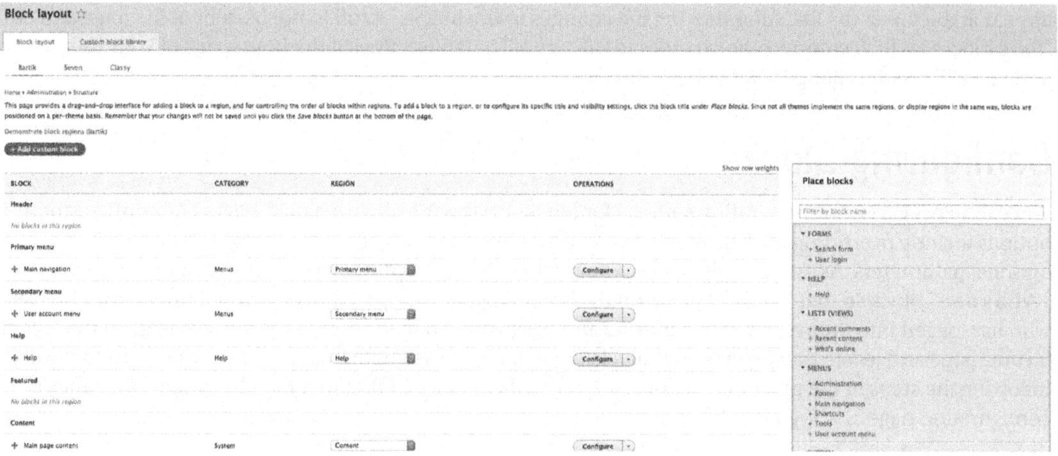

Figure 8-2. *The "Block layout" page*

On the "Block layout" page you will see that Drupal 8 provides a number of prebuilt blocks that can be placed on pages on your site. Pick a few by selecting from the list of blocks in the "Place blocks" box in the right column of the page. Click the title of a block and, on the "Configure block" form, pick a region from the select list (e.g., Sidebar First if you are using the Bartik theme). After assigning the blocks to regions, click the "Save blocks" button. If you return to your site's homepage, you'll now see the blocks that you enabled in the regions where you assigned them.

Rearranging Blocks

It is likely that, at some point in time, you're going to want to reorder how blocks appear on a page. In the previous example shown in Figure 8-1, we may want to have the "Recent content" and "Recent comments" blocks appear above the "Who's new" block. To reorder the blocks, navigate to the "Block layout" page as described in the previous section. On the "Block layout" page, shown in Figure 8-2, simply click and hold the plus sign (+) next to the block that you want to move, and drag that block to the position where you want it in the list of blocks for that region. When you release the mouse button, you'll see that Drupal reordered the items (temporarily). You'll see a message at the top of the list of blocks stating "You have unsaved changes." Scroll to the bottom of the page and click "Save blocks." Drupal will save the changes and display a message stating that the changes were made. Return to the homepage by clicking the "Back to site" link at the top left of the page and you will see the blocks in their new order.

Reassigning and Deactivating Blocks

Drupal also provides the mechanisms for moving a block to a different region and deactivating a block that is already visible on a page. To make the changes, navigate to the "Block layout" page (Structure ➤ Block layout).

On the "Block layout" page (refer to Figure 8-2), click the Region drop-down list for one of the blocks you enabled and assigned to a region and select the <none> option. Immediately upon selecting <none>, that item will disappear from the region section of the "Block layout" page and will reappear at the bottom of the page in the Disabled section. Next, click the Region drop-down list for another one of the blocks that you assigned to a region and select a different region from the select list. Immediately after selecting the new location, the block you selected will move to the newly assigned region within the block listing, and it will appear at the top of the list. After making the changes to the blocks, scroll to the bottom of the page and click "Save blocks," which commits the changes to the Drupal database. Revisit the homepage of your website, and you will see the changes that you just made.

Configuring Blocks

You can select various configuration settings for blocks on the "Configure block" page. The configuration options include overriding the title of the block and setting the visibility of the block based on several optional parameters. As an example of how you might use these features in the future, let's change the "Who's new" block so that it only appears on the homepage of your site, and only when the visitor is a user who has logged into the system with a user ID and password. To make these changes, navigate to the "Block layout" page and locate the "Who's new" block. If you haven't assigned that block to a region, do so now by following the steps in the previous section. Next, click the block's Configure link. This reveals the block's configuration page. See Figure 8-3.

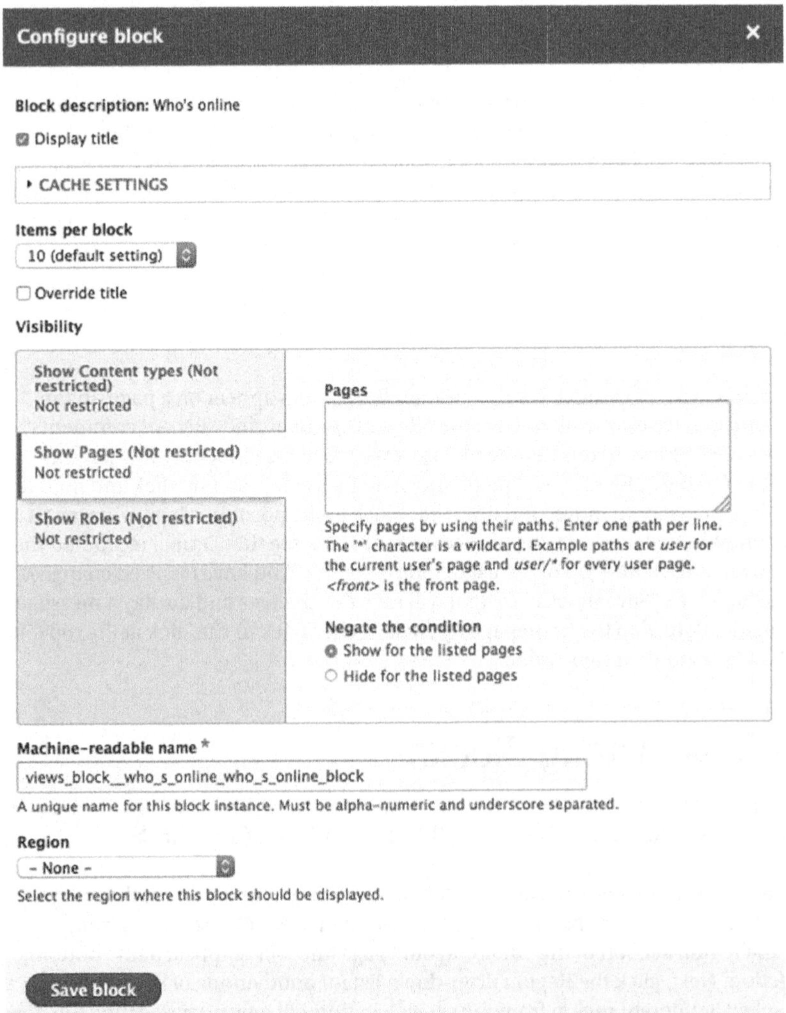

Figure 8-3. *The configuration page for the "Who's online" block*

On this form, you can override whether the title of the block "Who's new" appears on the page when the block is displayed (uncheck the "Display title" check box), specify how many users will appear in the list of who's new ("Items per block"), override the title by checking the Override title box and entering a new title in the text field that appears when you check the box, and assign the block to a new region.

You may wish to only have this block appear on certain pages on your site. By default it appears on every page. For example, you may want the "Who's new" block to only appear on the homepage of your site. At the bottom of the "Configure block" page (see Figure 8-4), you will see the Pages tab in the Visibility section. To set the block to only appear on the homepage, click the "Show for the listed pages" radio button and enter <front> in the text box (<front> is the special term used to represent the homepage of your site). You could also specify other pages by entering the URL of that page in the text box (for example, /content).

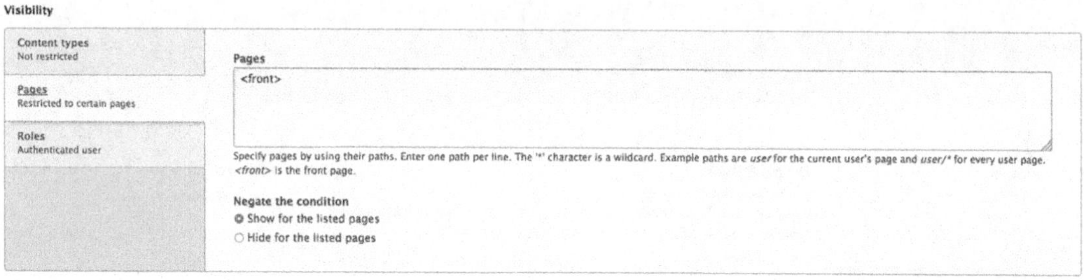

Figure 8-4. Choosing Visibility settings

It is also possible to set a block so that it only appears for specific types of users based on their assigned roles. Click the Roles tab to examine and set the visibility by user role options. As an example, let's set the block to only appear when the person visiting the site is logged in. (See Figure 8-5).

Figure 8-5. Choosing roles-based settings

Once you have clicked the "Authenticated user" check box, you can click the "Save block" button at the bottom of the page and return to the homepage of your site.

To test your changes, navigate to a page other than the homepage and you'll see that the "Who's online" block is no longer displayed. Log out and return to the homepage and you'll see that the "Who's new" block no longer appears because you are no longer logged in.

Using Blocks from Contributed Modules

There are literally thousands of contributed modules available for Drupal. Many of those modules generate blocks as their primary means of displaying information to visitors, such as the local weather. If the module is already installed and enabled on your site, the blocks that are generated by that module will appear on the "Block layout" page. Simply place the desired block(s) in a region as previously described in this chapter. If you have not yet installed the module, follow the steps outlined in Chapter 11.

An example of a using a contributed module's block is the Wunderground weather block that displays the current forecast (see Figure 8-6).

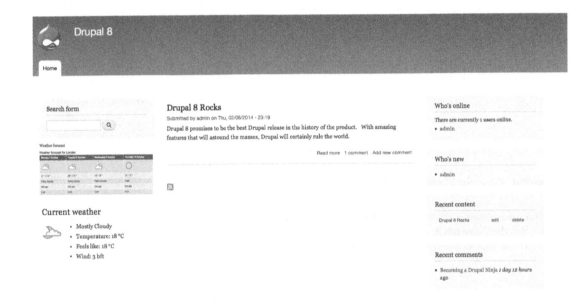

Figure 8-6. *London's weather (or any other city!), now available on your site*

There are hundreds of modules that generate blocks. Visit `www.drupal.org/project/project_module` and browse through the list.

Creating Custom Blocks

There may be cases where you need a block and, even after looking through the list of contributed modules, you can't find anything that meets your specific requirements. In that case, you have the opportunity to create a custom block yourself. Custom blocks can contain any combination of static HTML and JavaScript and can be as simple as the example that follows or as complex as you would like to make it.

To demonstrate creating a custom block, we'll create one that displays static HTML text in the form of "Hello World!" Although it may not be exciting, it does demonstrate the process for creating a new block. The first step is to navigate back to the "Block layout" page. Once there (refer to Figure 8-2), click the "Custom block library" tab in the upper-left corner of the page. On the "Custom block library" page, click the "Add custom block" button.

On the "Add custom block" form, enter a description of the block in the "Block description" field; for this example, we'll use "My First Custom Block." Next enter "Hello World!" in the Body text area and then click the Save button. See Figure 8-7.

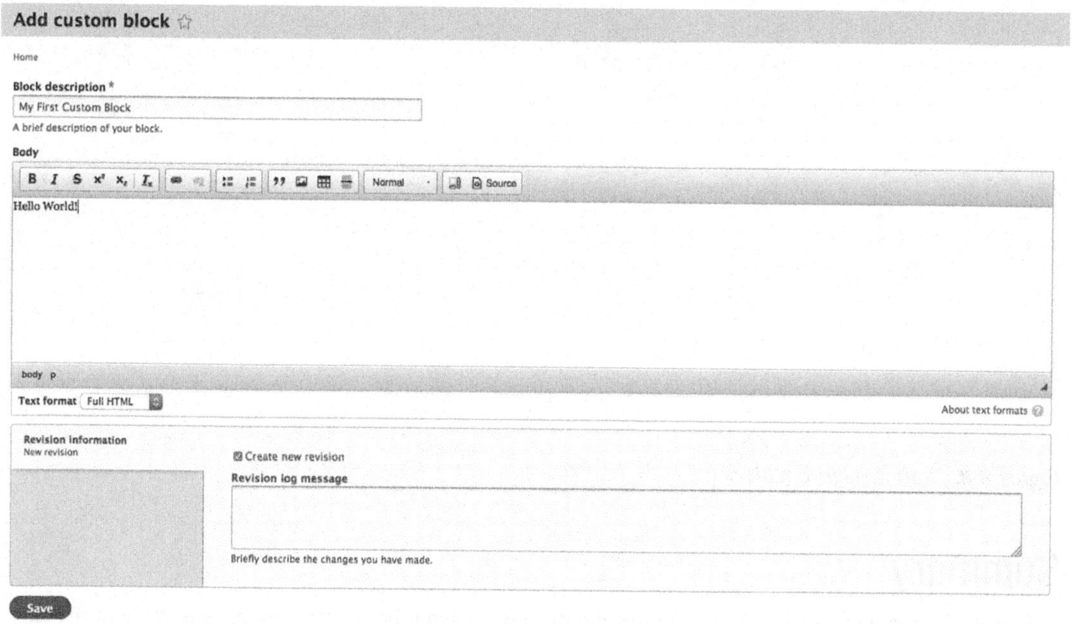

Add custom block ☆

Home

Block description *

My First Custom Block

A brief description of your block.

Body

| B | I | S | x² | x₂ | I_x | ⚓ | | ≔ | ⁝≔ | 99 | 🖾 | ⊞ | ≡ | Normal | ⋅ | | 🗐 | 🗋 Source |

Hello World!

body p

Text format Full HTML

About text formats ⑦

Revision information
New revision

☑ Create new revision

Revision log message

Briefly describe the changes you have made.

Save

Figure 8-7. Block settings for a custom block

After saving the block, click the "Block layout" tab at the top of the page and look for your new block in the "Place blocks" box under the Custom category. Click the name of the block you created and assign the block to a region on the page. Click the "Save block button" and return to the homepage of your site where you'll see the block you created in the region you specified (see Figure 8-8).

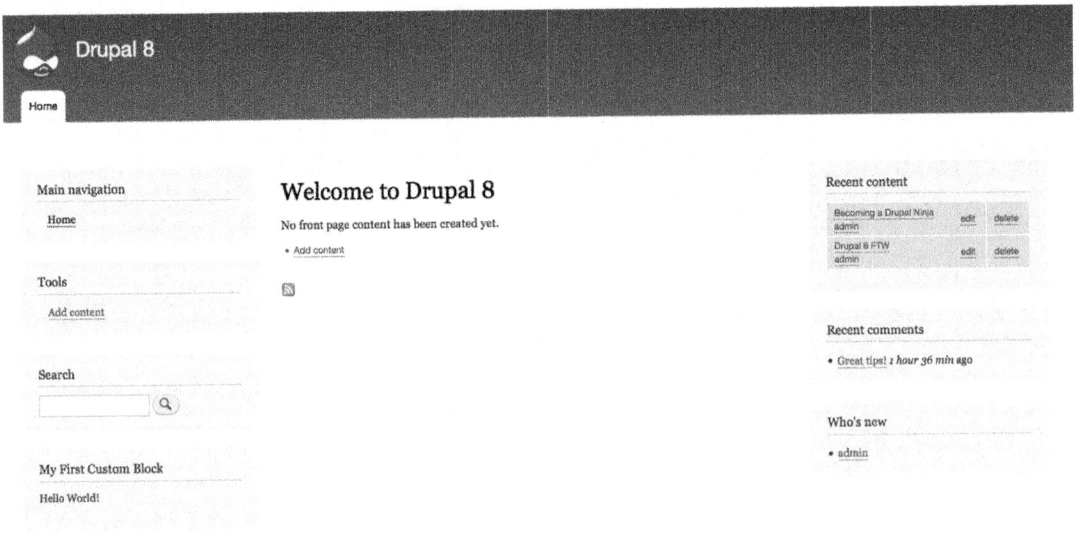

Figure 8-8. *Your first custom block*

Summary

Blocks are powerful mechanisms for creating and displaying dynamic content and interactive features on your site. In this chapter we explored blocks that ship with Drupal 8, using blocks from contributed modules, and how to create a custom block from scratch. We will continue to expand on the use of blocks as I cover additional topics in upcoming chapters.

CHAPTER 9

■ ■ ■

Views

If you ask anyone who has used Drupal for a while what the "killer module" is, the answer will likely be Views, Panels, or custom content types. In that list, Views is usually mentioned first, and it's the module that many users say they can't live without. What does the Views module do that is so special? Simply stated, Views provides an easy-to-use interface for selecting and displaying lists of content on your website. Examples of how you might use Views include

- Displaying the most recent news articles posted to your website, sorted in descending order by the date of posting.

- Displaying a list of company locations as a table that is sortable by clicking the titles for the location name, city, state, and country.

- Displaying a photo gallery.

- Displaying a slideshow.

- Displaying a calendar.

- Displaying a list of blog postings that is filterable by subject.

- Creating an RSS feed that lists the most recent content posted on your website.

- Displaying just about any kind of list that you can think of, created from the content that is stored on your website, as a list, table, or RSS feed.

In Chapter 5, we created the Event content type. Let's put it to work by creating lists of events that will be useful to site visitors using the Views module. If you haven't completed Chapter 5, now would be an excellent time to return to that chapter and work through the example so that you have the content required to support the upcoming activities.

The Views Module

Views is a Drupal 8 core module and is enabled by default during installation. To verify that Views is installed and enabled, click the Manage link at the top of the page and the Extend option in the submenu. Using the Search feature of the Extend page, enter Views in the search box. If the Views module exists you should see two modules listed as shown in Figure 9-1. If either of the check boxes is unchecked, please check it and click the "Save configuration" button.

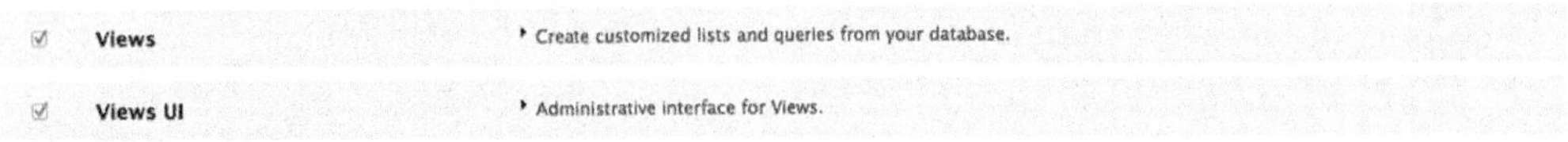

| ☑ | **Views** | ▸ Create customized lists and queries from your database. |
| ☑ | **Views UI** | ▸ Administrative interface for Views. |

Figure 9-1. *Verifying that Views is installed and enabled*

The Views module is the behind-the-scenes component that handles the extraction and display of content from the database. The Views UI module, where UI stands for User Interface, is the administrator's interface for creating and configuring views. We'll spend the majority of the rest of this chapter in Views UI.

Creating Your First View

With Views installed and enabled, we're ready to proceed. But a view without content is, well, just a blank page, so the first step is to create some content. We've created several articles prior to this chapter, so let's use those as the basis for our first foray into views. If you skipped the previous exercises or have deleted the articles that you created, then take a moment to create several.

We are now ready to create a view that will display a list of articles. Click the Manage link at the top of the page, the Structure link in the secondary menu, and then the Views link, which brings you to the Views administration page. You'll notice that there are already several views listed on this page. These are views that are part of Drupal core and provide lists of items such as recent content, recent comments, who's new, who's online, and others. You'll recognize the output of some of these views if you stepped through Chapter 8, as these are the views that generate the output that is displayed in several of the blocks that we used in that chapter.

To add a View, click the "Add new view" button at the top of the page, which reveals the page for creating a new view (see Figure 9-2). On this page, define the following:

- *View name*: The name must be unique (a name that has not been used for another view on your site). It's a good idea to pick a descriptive name that conveys the purpose of the view so that others looking at the list can easily identify the right one to use. For the first view, use Recent Articles as the name.

- *Description*: This is another field that you can use to provide additional information about the view. Check the box next to Description and enter "A list of recent articles published on the site."

- *View Settings*: This group of fields defines what type of content is going to be rendered by the view. If you click the Show list, you'll see various options such as Content, Log Entries, Files, Comments, Content Revisions, Taxonomy Terms, and Users. The focus of our view is on Article content, so select Content. In the "of type" field, select Article, the name of our content type. The "tagged with" field provides the ability to limit the results of our view to only articles that contain those terms. We'll skip the "tagged with" field and move to the "sorted by" option. Choose Unsorted (I'll cover sorting later in this example).

- *Page Settings*: Views provides the ability to create a list of content and have that list available as a stand-alone page on your site accessible through a URL. For demonstration purposes, check the "Create a page" box. You must then enter a page title (or keep the default value) and enter a URL path to reach the list (or keep the default value). In the Display format, leave it as an unformatted list of teasers, and set the Items to display at 10 with "Use a pager" checked. This will render a list of articles; if there are more than 10 articles in the list, a pager will appear at the bottom of the list to enable the visitor to view all of the articles, 10 articles at a time.

- *Block Settings*: We covered blocks in Chapter 8, but for demonstration purposes, we will allow our view to create a block (a page-level element that can be placed anywhere on a page) that lists the latest three events. Check the "Create a block" box and enter a block title (or keep the default), leave the display format as an unformatted list of titles (linked), and set the items per block to 3. Leave the "Use a pager" check box unchecked.

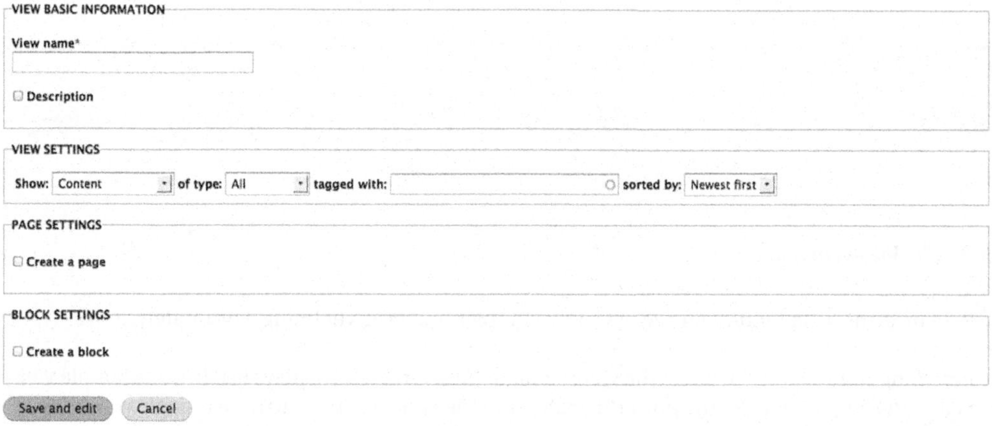

Figure 9-2. *Creating a new View*

Click the "Save and edit" button to proceed. The next step in the process is to configure your view, as shown in Figure 9-3.

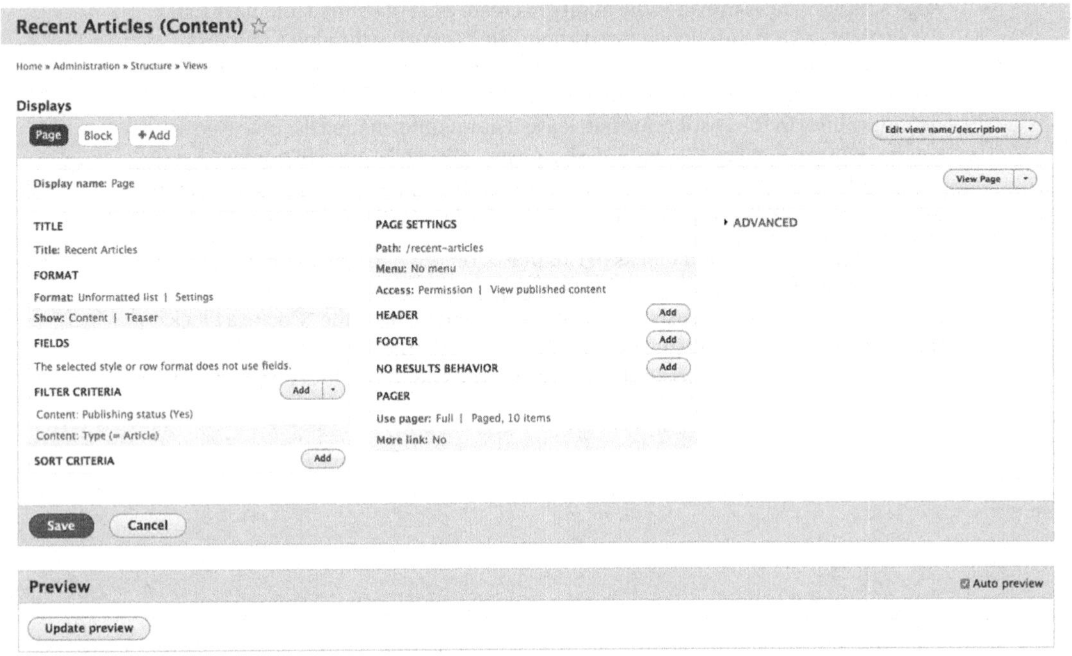

Recent Articles (Content) ☆

Home » Administration » Structure » Views

Displays

| Page | Block | + Add |

Edit view name/description | ▾

Display name: Page

View Page | ▾

TITLE

Title: Recent Articles

FORMAT

Format: Unformatted list | Settings

Show: Content | Teaser

FIELDS

The selected style or row format does not use fields.

FILTER CRITERIA   Add | ▾

Content: Publishing status (Yes)

Content: Type (= Article)

SORT CRITERIA   Add

PAGE SETTINGS

Path: /recent-articles

Menu: No menu

Access: Permission | View published content

HEADER   Add

FOOTER   Add

NO RESULTS BEHAVIOR   Add

PAGER

Use pager: Full | Paged, 10 items

More link: No

▸ ADVANCED

| Save | Cancel |

Preview   ☑ Auto preview

| Update preview |

Figure 9-3. *The Views edit page*

At first glance, the form for defining a view looks complex and overwhelming. Fortunately, looks are deceiving.

The first thing you'll see at the top of the view configuration form is a Displays list. In our example view, we have a Page and a Block. One of the powerful features of Views is the ability to have a single view render multiple displays. Examples of the types of displays that we might use for recent articles include

- A full page display that displays all the details of every Article published on the site.

- A block that lists the five most recent Articles, displaying only the title for each article.

- Another block that lists the five most recent Articles, displaying the title and a shortened version of the article body.

- Yet another block that lists the ten most recent Articles, displaying the title, the date the article was published, the author who wrote the article, and a shortened version of the article body.

This single view can be used to create several different types of displays that each display Articles in slightly different formats.

We will start by defining the two displays, Page and Block, that were automatically created by Views when we selected the options on the first configuration screen (refer to Figure 9-2). We'll add to that list of displays after we have the first two working.

Page Display

Let's define the Page display first. Click the Page button that appears directly under Displays to configure the Page display. On this page we will display the complete Article, which includes the title, body, author of the article, and the date and time that it was published. Let's work top to bottom, left to right through the configuration parameters that we need to set to make this page display what we want it to:

1. Change the "Display name" from "Page" to something a little more descriptive, something like "All Articles Page." To change the value, click "Page" to the right of "Display name" and in the pop-up form enter the new value in the "Administrative name" field, followed by clicking the Apply button. You'll see that the new value is displayed both in the Displays area of the view edit form and in the "Display name" field in the left column.

2. In the Title section, change the Title of the view. This value is displayed at the top of the output generated by views for this display. Let's change it to "All Articles." Click "Recent Articles" and select "This page (override)" from the For select list. This means that the changes we are making to this value will only be applied to this specific view display. If you leave the value set to "All displays," every display will show this new title. Since we're going to have different displays for different purposes, "All Articles" is likely a poor choice of titles for other displays.

3. In the Format section, we have the option to generate a list using different output formats. Click the "Unformatted list" value for Format to see a list of output options:

    - *Grid*: The output is displayed in rows and columns; in our example, each article would fill one column on a row in the grid. This is a great option for displaying photos in a photo gallery.

    - *HTML list*: The output is displayed as either an ordered list or an unordered list. In our example, each article would be listed as a <li> within a <ol></ol> or <ul></ul> tag. If you're not familiar with HTML tags, check out the great tutorial at www.w3schools.com/html or pick up one of the great introductory books on HTML development at www.apress.com.

    - *Table*: The output is displayed as an HTML table, where each field is displayed in a column. A table is great when you want to provide visitors with the ability to sort the output of a view by the values within a column.

    - *Unformatted list*: The output is displayed as a list, but unlike the HTML list, there are no enclosing <ul>, <ol>, or <li> tags.

    For our example Page, we'll leave the value set to "Unformatted list." Remember to select "This page (override)" from the For select list when changing the value to something other than "Unformatted list." If you click Settings to the right of "Unformatted list," you'll see the configuration options available for that type of list. Each of the options has its own set of parameters that you can set.

4. The Show parameter in the Format section defines how we want to handle the content that we are going to display. The two most common options are Content and Fields:

   - *Content*: Displays the complete entity that is being selected and displayed. In the case of Articles, the complete Article would be displayed.

   - *Fields*: Enables you to display specific fields from the entity that you are rendering. In our example, we are selecting and displaying Articles. We may have a View Display where we only want to show the Article title and the published date. Using the Fields option, we can specify which fields are to be displayed and the order in which those fields will be displayed on the page.

   For our example Page, we'll select Content and display the content as teasers, a shortened version of the article, displaying the first 600 characters. When we defined the view we set the page to display content in teaser mode, so the values for Show are already set for us. If we wanted the entire article to be rendered by the view, we would click the word Teaser and select "default" from the list of View modes. For the purposes of our demonstration, leave the display mode set to Teaser.

5. In our example, the Fields configuration parameters are not displayed because we are going to display the whole Article. We'll cover fields later in this chapter when we create block displays.

6. Filter Criteria is the next section to configure. You may restrict what content is rendered in the view by adding filter criteria to the view display. On the very first configuration screen when we created the view (refer to Figure 9-2), we selected the View Settings option to only display Articles. By selecting Articles we set a filter to only display Article content types. Additionally Views also creates an additional filter for content that is published (vs. unpublished). We can add other filter criteria to our views; for example, in the case of Articles, we might want a View display that only shows Articles that have been published in the past 30 days. We can restrict the output of the view by adding filter criteria on any of the values stored on a content item. For demonstration purposes, we'll leave the filter criteria alone. We'll cover adding filter criteria later in this chapter when we create block displays.

7. The Sort Criteria section provides the ability to specify the order of the content in the list. By default, the values rendered will be sorted in ascending order by Node ID (the unique identifier assigned to each content item by Drupal). Typically, you will want to set the sort criteria to Title, for lists you want alphabetically ordered, or by the date that the content was published with newest articles at the top of the list. Let's add a sort criteria on title by clicking the Add button to the right of the Sort Criteria label. After clicking the Add button, you will see a complete list of all fields that are defined for your site. We'll want to filter the list to only fields with "title" in their name. To do so, enter "title" in the Search field and select "Content: title" from the list of fields. In the revised list of fields, scroll down until you find Content: Title. Check the checkbox for that field and change the value of the For select list at the top of the form to "This page (override)," then click the "Apply (this display)" button. The next screen allows you to set the sort order, ascending or descending, as well as expose this option to site visitors. We will leave the check box for Expose unchecked for our example Page, and we want titles to appear in ascending alphabetical order. Click the "Apply (this display)" button to continue. Scroll to the bottom of the screen and you should now see how the output will be rendered on the page.

In the second column of configuration options (refer to Figure 9-3), we'll begin by defining the Page Settings for our example.

8. Every View display that is defined as Page must have a unique URL, specified in the Path field. For our example, let's use "/all-articles" as the URL. Click "No path is set" and on the "The menu path or URL of this view" form enter all-articles in the Path text field. Click the Apply button to continue.

9. The Menu field gives us the option to add our View display page to a menu. For demonstration purposes, we'll add it to the "Main navigation" menu. Click the "No menu" parameter and click the "Normal menu entry" option. On the configuration page for adding the menu entry, enter a title, a description, and select "Main navigation" as the menu on which this item will be displayed. For sites that you are building, you may want to add a View page to a menu other than the "Main navigation" menu. Click the Apply button after entering the values on the form.

10. Views provides the ability to restrict who can see the output generated by this View display. You can set the Access restrictions to

   • *None*: Anyone can see the output.

   • *Permission*: The visitor must be assigned to a role that has permissions to view the output.

   • *Role*: The visitor must be assigned to a specific role to see the output.

   By default the value is set to Permission, where the default permission is that the visitor must have the ability to view content on the site (see figure 9-3). In most cases the default values are appropriate. For our example page, we will leave them set to the defaults, which is that only visitors who have the ability to view content will be able to see the output of the view.

11. The Header setting enables you to add several things to the top of your view. For example, you could provide an introductory paragraph that describes the content rendered by the view, or a block that you have defined on your site, the output of another view, or several other elements. Click the Add button and select from the list of options. The most common option is to add an introductory paragraph; to do so, click the "Global: text area" option, select the "This page (override)" option in the For select list at the top of the options, and click the "Apply (this display)" button. On the next form, enter the text that you want to display at the top of the view. If you want the header text to display even when there are no results for your view, check the "Display even if view has no results" box, followed by clicking the "Apply (this display)" button.

12. The Footer setting, similar to Header, enables you to add a footer to the output of a view. Follow the same steps as listed in step 11 to insert a footer at the bottom of the view.

13. If your view returns no content—for example, there are no published Articles on your site—you can alert the visitor that no content exists by displaying a message via the No Results Behavior setting. The process for creating the message is the same as for creating the header and footer. Follow the directions in step 11 to add a message when no results are found.

14. If your view returns a long list of items, consider using a pager at the bottom of the view and restricting the number of results displayed at any given time. For example, a view may return 100 content items. Instead of showing all 100 in a long list, you may use a page to show 10 items at a time, with a pager at the bottom of the view to navigate through the list of content. The Pager configuration option also provides the ability to list a specific number of items (e.g., three most recent articles), or list all items that fit the filter criteria set in the previous column.

    In the third column (refer to Figure 9-3), there are several advanced configuration options, two of which we'll focus on. To reveal the options, click Advanced.

15. Contextual Filters is a powerful configuration option that allows you to utilize values passed in the URL to filter content that is returned by the view. For example, we may wish to limit the Articles returned by our view to only those Articles tagged for a specific category. If our Article content type has the "Event" taxonomy vocabulary as a field that editors can use to specify which category an Article is associated with, we can then use values passed in the URL to filter which Articles are displayed. By selecting a contextual filter of "Has taxonomy term ID" and setting the content type to Article, the vocabulary to Category, and Filter value type to Term name converted to Term ID, you can now update the Path value to `all-articles/%`, where % represents a value that will be passed to the view through the URL. The benefit is that we can have one view that can display any Article tagged by any category in our taxonomy vocabulary. This single view can render a list of Articles about Drupal by using a URL of `/all-articles/drupal`, or all Articles about dinosaurs by using `/all-articles/dinosaurs`, or any other term in our type of category vocabulary. Amazing! But for simplicity's sake, let's not use contextual filters in out example.

16. Relationships is use in cases where you need to pull content from two different content types in order to meet the requirements of a specific view. For example, you may have a content type for Venue that lists the address, hours of operation, and accessibility options. Instead of typing that information on every event that happens at that venue, you can create a relationship between the Event content type and the Venue content type to combine the information stored in both content types. Once you have created the relationship, fields on both content types are then available to display in your view. Since we are keeping it simple, we'll leave off relationships for now.

At this point we're ready to test our view. Make sure you click the Save button before proceeding. After saving, return to the homepage of your site and you should see the All Articles link in the Main navigation menu (if you are using the Bartik theme, it should appear as a tab on the screen). Click the All Articles link (or tab) and you will see the fruits of your labor (see Figure 9-4).

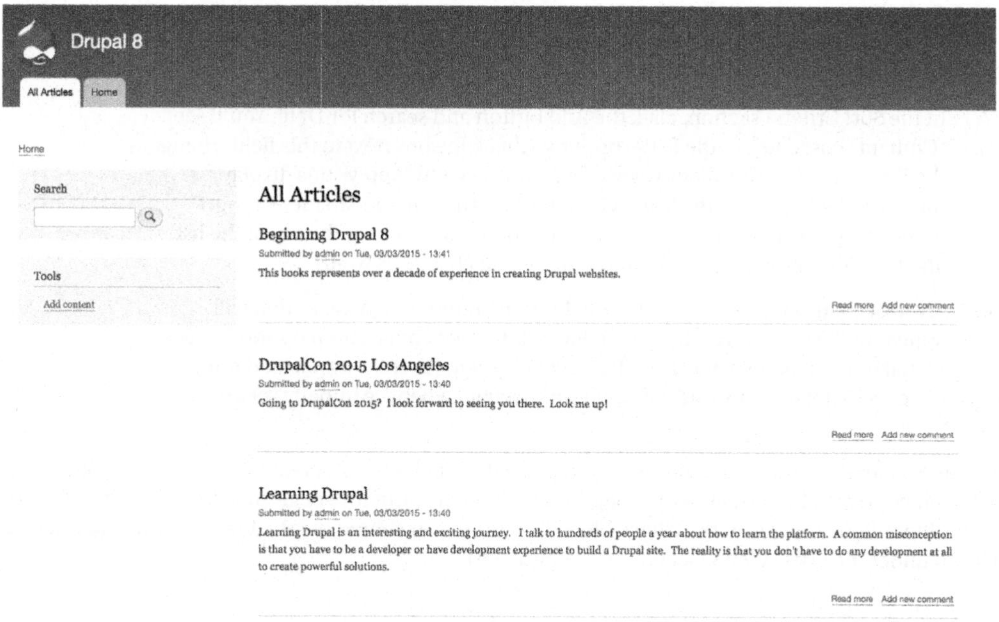

Figure 9-4. The All Articles view page

Block Display

With the full listing of Articles page under our belt, let's now revise the Block display. Return to the Views administration page by navigating to Manage ➤ Structure ➤ Views. Locate the Recent Articles view and click the Edit link in the Operations column. You should now see the Recent Articles view configuration page (see Figure 9-3).

The first step in the process is to click the Block button in the View display list. You should be able to find it directly to the right of the All Articles Page button. Clicking the Block button displays all of the configuration parameters for the block. Let's update the display to only show the three most recent Article titles, sorted in date-published order, descending so that the most recent Article appears at the top of the page. Let's start the process by updating the name of our display from Block to something more descriptive, followed by making the changes we need to make to the display itself:

1. In the first column, next to "Display name," click Block and change the value of the "Administrative name" field to "Recent Articles Block."

2. Leave the Title as Recent Articles, as it still applies to what we are going to display.

3. Leave the Format as "Unformatted list," as we still want the articles to appear as a list.

4. Change the value of the Show option to Fields, as we only want to display the title of the Articles in our list.

5. In the Fields section, leave the item to be displayed as the title. If it doesn't say Title, click the Add button for that section and search for Title, adding it to the display.

6. In the Filter Criteria section, leave the Content Publishing status and Content Type criteria set as only showing published content (Yes) and only content that is of type Article.

7. In the Sort Criteria section, click the Add button and search for Date. You'll see "Content: Post date" in the list of options. Check the box next to this field, change the For option to "This block (override)," and click the "Apply (this display)" button at the bottom of the form. On the next form that appears, select "Sort descending," as we want the most recent Articles to appear at the top of the list, and the oldest articles at the bottom. Apply that change as well.

8. The last change we need to make is to limit the number of Articles that will appear in the list to three. In the second column of configuration options, check to make sure that the value for "Use pager" is set to "Display a specified number of items | 3 items." This was the value we specified when we initially set up the view.

Click the Save button, and you're now ready to place the block you just created on a page on your site. To place the block created by your view on a page, navigate to the Structure page and click the "Block layout" link. On the "Block layout" page, in the "Place blocks" column, you should see the View display that you just created listed under the Lists (Views) section (see Figure 9-5).

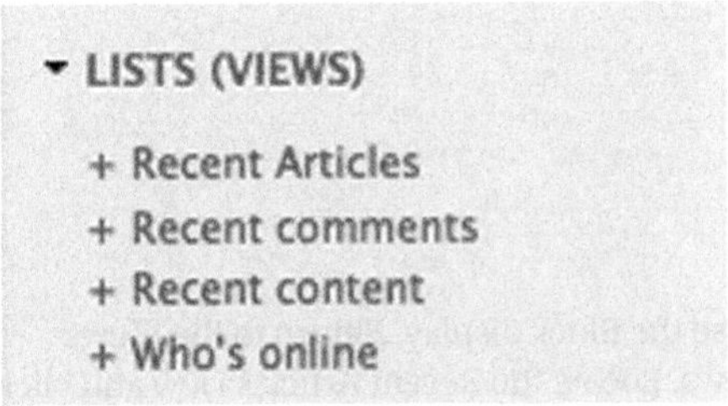

Figure 9-5. *The List (Views) blocks*

Click the Recent Articles: Recent Articles Block link and assign the block to a region. After selecting a region from the list, save the block and return to the homepage of your site. You should be happy to see the list of articles that you created displayed through the block that you created using views (see Figure 9-6).

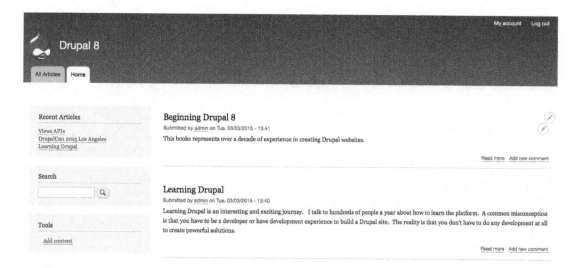

Figure 9-6. *The homepage displaying the list of Recent Articles block*

Filtering

In the previous example, we filtered the output of our view based on content type and publishing status. Those are pretty typical filters on most views, but what if you wanted to restrict the output of the view beyond just content type and status? Let's use tagging as an example of demonstrating the power of views filtering. In this section we are going to add a few tags to the example articles on the demonstration website. Edit several of your articles, and in the Tags field, enter several keywords, separated by commas, that describe the content of each article. Use similar words in at least two of your articles so that we can use those articles in upcoming examples. To find articles to update, click the Content link in the admin menu, and from the list, click the Edit button to add tags to existing articles. After adding the tags, return to the Recent Articles page that we built in the previous sections and note that the tags that you added are now displayed beneath the teaser of each article (see Figure 9-7).

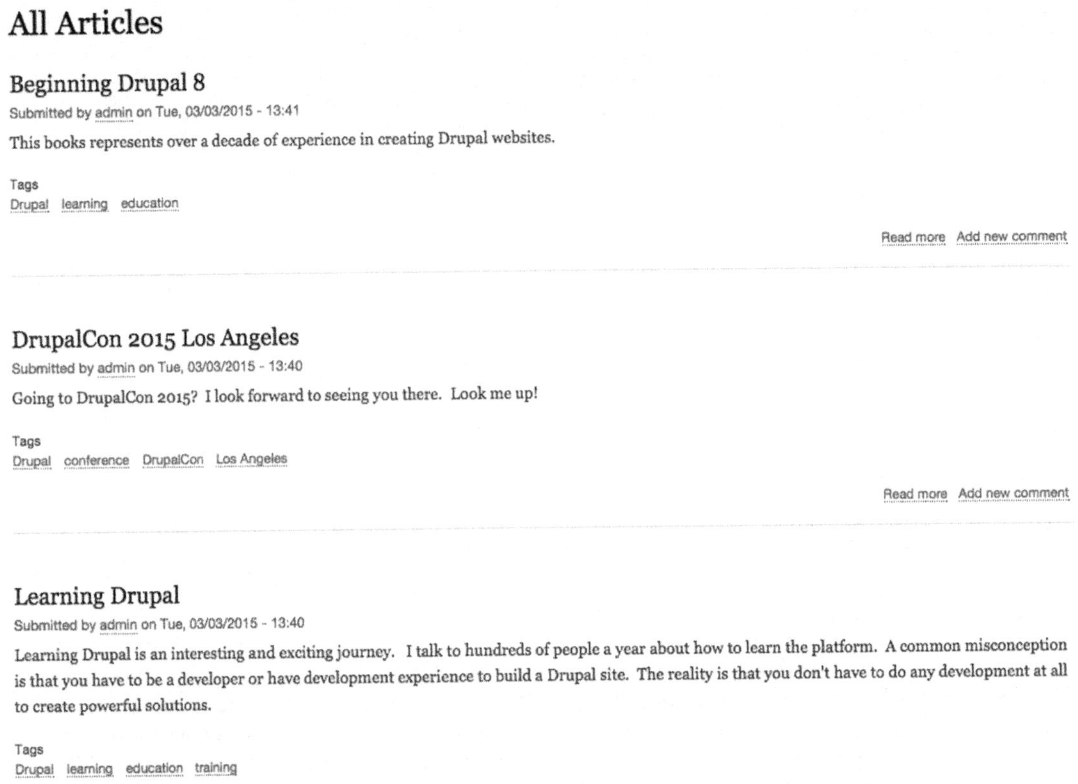

All Articles

Beginning Drupal 8

Submitted by admin on Tue, 03/03/2015 - 13:41

This books represents over a decade of experience in creating Drupal websites.

Tags
Drupal   learning   education

Read more   Add new comment

DrupalCon 2015 Los Angeles

Submitted by admin on Tue, 03/03/2015 - 13:40

Going to DrupalCon 2015? I look forward to seeing you there. Look me up!

Tags
Drupal   conference   DrupalCon   Los Angeles

Read more   Add new comment

Learning Drupal

Submitted by admin on Tue, 03/03/2015 - 13:40

Learning Drupal is an interesting and exciting journey. I talk to hundreds of people a year about how to learn the platform. A common misconception is that you have to be a developer or have development experience to build a Drupal site. The reality is that you don't have to do any development at all to create powerful solutions.

Tags
Drupal   learning   education   training

Figure 9-7. *Rendering tags through views*

As a quick demonstration of the power of taxonomy, tags, and views, click one of the tags that you entered and Drupal will render a list of all content tagged on your site with that term. Behind the scenes, Drupal is using Views to generate this list. But let's take it one step further and allow users to filter content that is rendered from our All Articles view by entering a tag.

Return to the Views administration page by clicking the Views link on the Structure page. Locate the Recent Articles view that we have been working on and click the Edit button. Click the All Articles Page display button in the Displays area of the view configuration page. Add a new filter for tags by clicking the Add button in the Filter Criteria section. Search for the Tags field by entering "tags" in the Search box at the top of the "Add filter criteria" form, and check the box for the "Content: Tags (field_tags)" field. Change the For option to "This page (override)" so that the filter is only applied to the All Articles Page display, and click the "Apply (this display)" button.

The next step in the process is to select the type of interface we wish to provide, either a Dropdown list of terms to select from, or an Autocomplete field where the user types in the keyword to search for. The Dropdown field will show the user what terms are available, whereas the Autocomplete approach requires that the user know what terms they wish to search for. The option is dependent on your desired user experience. For demonstration purposes, select Dropdown, and click the "Apply and continue button."

The next step in the process is to configure the filter and how it will work. We want to allow users to select which terms to filter on, so we'll expose the filter to the user so they can control what content is displayed by the view. To do so, check the "Expose this filter to visitors, to allow them to change it" check box, leave the "Filter type to expose" setting to "Single filter," and change the Label to "Select one or more tags". Leave the Operator set to "Is one of," meaning the values that we want the user to select from are only the tags that exist within the Articles on the site. Also check the "Allow multiple selections" check box to allow the visitor to select more than one tag to search for. Click the Apply button to continue the process (see Figure 9-8), and the Save button to save the changes made to the view.

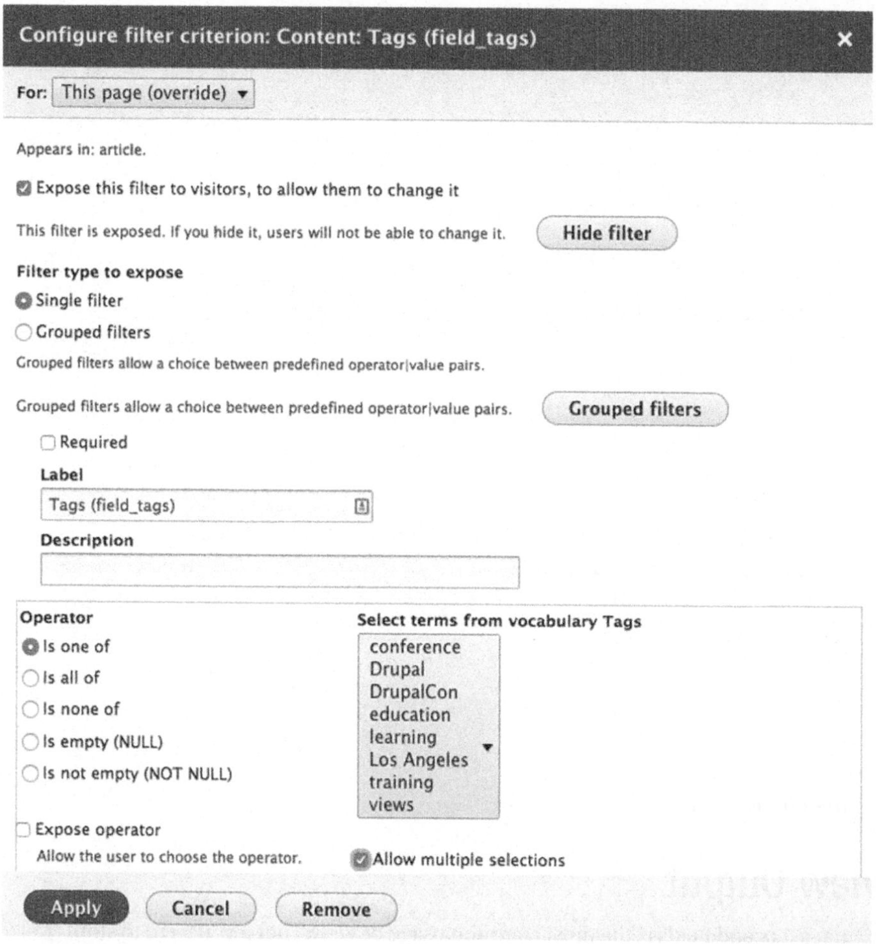

Figure 9-8. *Configuring filters*

Return to the All Articles page by clicking the All Articles link on the main menu, or visit the /recent-articles URL on your site. You'll see your exposed filter at the top of the list of articles. Select one or more tags and click the Apply button to see the new filter in action (see Figure 9-9). Amazing! And you've just scratched the surface of what Views can do for you.

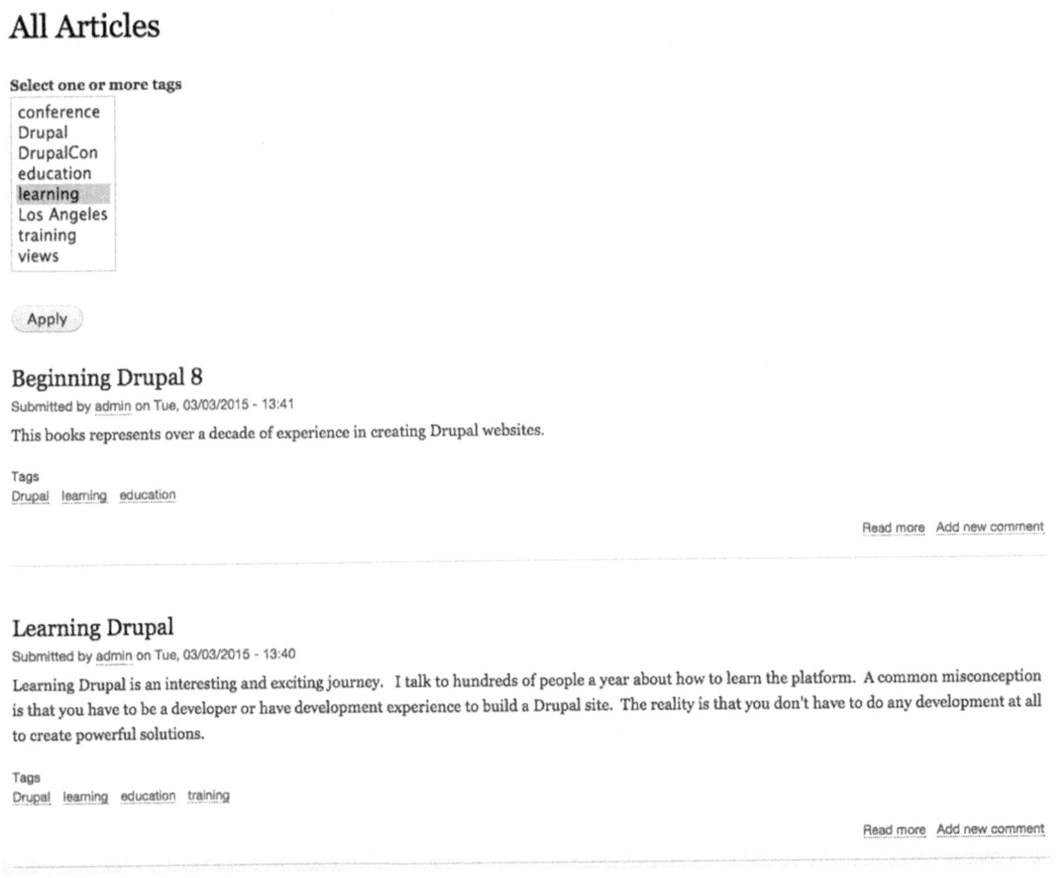

All Articles

Select one or more tags

```
conference
Drupal
DrupalCon
education
learning
Los Angeles
training
views
```

(Apply)

Beginning Drupal 8

Submitted by admin on Tue, 03/03/2015 - 13:41

This books represents over a decade of experience in creating Drupal websites.

Tags
Drupal   learning   education

Read more   Add new comment

Learning Drupal

Submitted by admin on Tue, 03/03/2015 - 13:40

Learning Drupal is an interesting and exciting journey. I talk to hundreds of people a year about how to learn the platform. A common misconception is that you have to be a developer or have development experience to build a Drupal site. The reality is that you don't have to do any development at all to create powerful solutions.

Tags
Drupal   learning   education   training

Read more   Add new comment

Figure 9-9. *Filtered output based on user input*

Advanced View Output

Creating lists of content teasers and fields is the most common usage of Views, but if you were to stop there you would miss many of the powerful capabilities available to you through Views. In this section I'll demonstrate common scenarios that I encounter while building Drupal sites.

Creating RSS Feeds

One of the common uses of Views is to create RSS feeds. An RSS feed is an industry-standard format for publishing content that can then be consumed by applications such as newsreaders, or by other systems such as another Drupal site. While RSS feeds are not as popular as they once were during the heyday of online newsreaders, there are still cases where using RSS feeds make sense, such as providing feeds of content to other sites.

Let's take the Recent Articles view and create an RSS feed for all articles. To begin, return to the Views page by clicking the Manage link in the admin menu, followed by the Structure link, and finally the Views link on the Structure page. Find the Recent Articles view and click the Edit button for that view. We will create a new Display for the RSS feed by clicking the Add button in the Displays section of the page. From the list of options, choose Feed. The next step is to enter a URL where the feed will be accessed. In the second column in the "Feed settings" section, click the "No path is set" link to enter a URL. For demonstration purposes, I'll enter a URL of rss/all-articles. I could have used any URL, but I find it easier to prefix all of my RSS feed URLs with rss so that it is apparent what that URL renders. Complete the process by clicking the Apply button to save the changes to the URL, and then clicking the Save button at the bottom of the form to save the updates to the view. You now have an RSS feed that other sites can use to consume articles from your site. Visiting that URL shows the output of the feed (see Figure 9-10).

Figure 9-10. *A Views-generated RSS feed*

Creating Tables

Rendering content as lists works well in most cases, but you'll likely encounter scenarios where listing content in a table format is more representative of how users prefer to view the content. For demonstration purposes, return to the Recent Articles view edit form to create a new display that will render fields from articles in a spreadsheet-like format. Click the Add button in the Displays area, and select Block as the display type. Change the "Display name" as you did previously, this time to "Table of articles." Click "Unformatted list" in the Format section, changing the type of output to be rendered to Table, and remember to change the For option at the top of the page to "This block (override)" before clicking the "Apply (this display)" button. The next screen that appears presents the style options that you can set for your new table(see Figure 9-11).

Table of articles: Style options   ✕

Place fields into columns; you may combine multiple fields into the same column. If you do, the separator in the column specified will be used to separate the fields. Check the sortable box to make that column click sortable, and check the default sort radio to determine which column will be sorted by default, if any. You may control column order and field labels in the fields section.

FIELD	COLUMN	ALIGN	SEPARATOR	SORTABLE	DEFAULT ORDER	DEFAULT SORT	HIDE EMPTY COLUMN	RESPONSIVE
Content: Title	Content: Title	None		☐	○	☐		High
None					◉			

Grouping field Nr.1

- None -

You may optionally specify a field by which to group the records. Leave blank to not group.

Row class

The class to provide on each row. You may use field tokens from as per the "Replacement patterns" used in "Rewrite the output of this field" for all fields.

☑ Add views row classes

Add the default row classes like views-row-1 to the output. You can use this to quickly reduce the amount of markup the view provides by default, at the cost of making it more difficult to apply CSS.

☑ Override normal sorting if click sorting is used

☐ Enable Drupal style "sticky" table headers (Javascript)

(Sticky header effects will not be active for preview below, only on live output.)

Caption for the table

A title which is semantically associated to your table for increased accessibility.

▸ TABLE DETAILS

☐ Show the empty text in the table

Per default the table is hidden for an empty view. With this option it is posible to show an empty table with the text in it.

Place fields into columns; you may combine multiple fields into the same column. If you do, the separator in the column specified will be used to separate the

Apply   **Cancel**

Figure 9-11. *Table style options*

The option on this form that you'll want to use most commonly is the Sortable option. Right now our table only has a single column, the article's Title field, but we have the ability to add other fields after completing this step, and we may want one or more of those columns to be sortable by the end user. To sort the column, the user clicks the title of that column, and Views automatically orders the table based on sorting that column in ascending order (or, if the user clicks the title again, descending order). Click the Sortable check box for the Title column; we will return to this form after adding other columns in the next few steps.

Below the list of fields you'll find a select list titled "Grouping field Nr.1." You can group the output rendered in the table, grouping like items in your table into different sections by simply selecting the field that you want to sort and group results by. For example, if you had a list of properties for sale, you could group the output of that table by ZIP code or by city. All properties that share a ZIP code would appear as a separate section of the table. For demonstration purposes, leave the option set to None.

There are additional styling options, but in most instances leaving the default values for those options is sufficient. Click the Apply button to complete this step in the process.

A table with a single column is pretty boring, really nothing more than just a list. So to spice up the table let's add two additional fields, one for the date that the article was created, and another for the tags associated with the article. We'll add each field as a separate column. To add the fields, click the Add button in the Fields section of the page (see Figure 9-3), which reveals the list of every field available to display on our view. To simplify finding the fields that we want, enter "created" in the Search box at the top of the list of fields, and from the list of results that is displayed, check the box next to the "Content: Authored on" field. Select the For option of "This block (override)" to prevent this field from being added to all of the other view displays that we've created, and then click the "Apply (this display)" button. The next screen provides options to configure how the "Authored on" field will be rendered, including the label displayed for that field, CSS styling options, what to do when there isn't a value present for a given article, and other options. Leave all the values set to their defaults for the remaining options and click Apply.

Views Add-on Modules

The Views module itself is a powerful tool for rendering content on your site. When you combine Views with other specialized modules, you get a whole new level of powerful capabilities. There are several "must have" Views add-on modules that you may wish to consider as you build out your site. Here are a few of my favorites:

- *Views Slideshow* (`www.drupal.org/project/views_slideshow`): This module provides a simple-to-use interface for creating views that display content as a slideshow. There are a number of slideshow modules for Views, but this happens to be one of the easiest to use.

- *Calendar* (`www.drupal.org/project/calendar`): Need to display events on a calendar? This is the module for you. It provides you with a rich set of tools for creating and displaying any content that contains a date field and date values on a calendar (day, week, month, year). It's one of the must-have modules on all my sites.

- *JCarousel* (`www.drupal.org/project/jcarousel`): Most of my projects involve some form of displaying content in a carousel. This module makes it simple to create a list of content items and render them as a carousel.

- *Draggable Views* (`www.drupal.org/project/draggableviews`): Want to provide an administrative interface that allows content editors to rearrange the items that appear in a view? This module provides a simple drag-and-drop interface to rearrange items in your view.

- *GMap* (`www.drupal.org/project/gmap`): Want to render content that has geographic (address) information on a map? This module integrates Google Maps with Views to provide an easy-to-use solution for rendering content items on a map.

- *Views data export* (`www.drupal.org/project/views_data_export`): Want to export content from your site into a CSV file, spreadsheet, Word document, text file, or XML? This module provides the ability to do just that.

There are also add-on modules for Views that we did not cover in this section. Please visit `www.drupal.org/project/project_module` and click the Views link in the categories listed in the right column. At the time of writing, there are 756 contributed modules just for Views! Browse through the list (remembering to look to see if there is a Drupal 8 version of the modules you may be interested in). People have created many amazing capabilities for Views.

Summary

I've only scratched the surface of how you can use Views on your new site. Views is extremely powerful, and one of the "killer" modules for Drupal.

Up to this point we have focused on the basic building blocks of creating content, menus, and blocks. In the next chapter we'll look at using those elements to create pages.

■ ■ ■

## CHAPTER 10

Creating Pages

Now that you have a general understanding of content types, blocks, views, and themes, you're ready to start assembling pages on your website using a combination of each of those elements. A page may represent a single piece of content (for example, a news story about the first day at DrupalCon), or it may represent a landing page similar to the front page of Drupal.org. Each page on your site may vary in structure, thanks to the flexibility of the theme that you select for your site as well as the blocks mechanism and the ability to specify on which page (URL) a block is to be displayed. Using Views to create blocks provides a dynamic mechanism for extracting content along with static blocks created through the blocks interface. The combination of Drupal 8 tools provides a powerful mechanism for creating an awesome site.

Foundation for Creating Pages

Drupal 8 core in conjunction with your theme provides all the capabilities required to create a typical page found on a website. The theme provides the regions that can contain content, while Drupal 8 core's content types, blocks, and views provide the mechanism for creating content that will appear within those regions.

In Chapter 6 you discovered the regions that the Bartik theme provides as containers for content on your website. As a review, Figure 10-1 depicts the regions that may be used to place content and blocks.

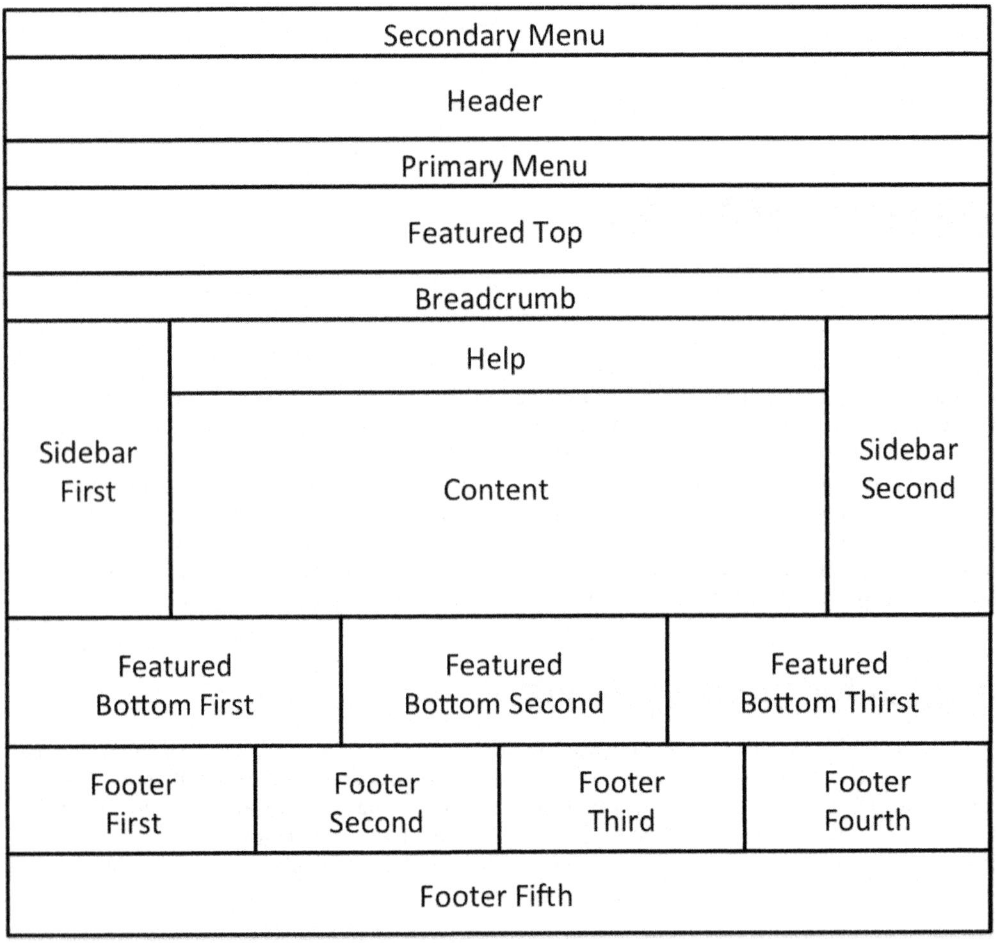

Secondary Menu			
Header			
Primary Menu			
Featured Top			
Breadcrumb			

| Sidebar First | Help | | Sidebar Second |
| | Content | | |

Featured Bottom First	Featured Bottom Second	Featured Bottom Thirst

Footer First	Footer Second	Footer Third	Footer Fourth
Footer Fifth			

Figure 10-1. *Regions provided by the Bartik theme*

Bartik provides 17 regions where we can place content and blocks, including the Header region that is typically used to display a site's logo, a search box, and navigational elements such as the main menu. Bartik is only one of several hundred themes that are available on Drupal.org, each with its own arrangement and number of regions. Alternatively, you can use one of the starter themes, such as Zen, and design the exact layout of regions that you need to achieve the look that you desire for your site. For the purposes of demonstrating page building in Drupal 8, we'll stick with the flexibility offered in the Bartik theme's regions and layout.

The first page that we will create is an example of a content detail page, meaning a single piece of content is displayed on a page with various associated blocks that augment the page beyond just the single piece of content. To demonstrate creating a content detail page, we'll use the Article content type and create an article that describes the upcoming DrupalCon. After logging on, navigate to Manage ➤ Content. On the Content page, click the "Add content" button and select Article. Enter the title of the article and body text, and click the "Save and publish" button. Take note of the URL associated with your article, because you are going to use it to place blocks that appear only on this article's page.

At this point all of the blocks that are defined to be site-wide blocks will appear on the page, along with the article for DrupalCon. But what if you wanted more things to display on this page other than the standard blocks and the article? The answer is to use Views to generate blocks from content, or use the block interface to create or assign a block to appear on this page. Let's begin by creating a custom block through the "Block layout" page and assigning that block to appear only on the DrupalCon page (see Chapter 8 for a refresher on blocks):

1. Click the Manage link in the top menu followed by the Structure link in the secondary menu. Click the "Block layout" link to display the "Block layout" page.

2. Click the "Add custom block" button to create a new custom block.

3. In the "Block description" field, enter "DrupalCon 2015 Los Angeles."

4. In the Body field, enter "May 11-15, 2015 in the Los Angeles Convention Center."

5. Click the Save button.

6. On the "Configure block" page that appears, locate the Region select list and set the region to "Featured top" (if you are not using Bartik, select another prominent region).

7. To restrict which pages this block will appear on, click the Pages tab in the vertical navigation bar and, in the Pages text area, enter the URL associated with the article you created, starting with /node. For my example, it's the first article that I've written on the site, so the value that I will enter in the box is /node/1. Next, click the "Show for the listed pages" radio button, as we only want this block to appear on our article's page.

8. Click the "Save block" button to save the new block, and then navigate back to the article page that you are working on by clicking the Content link in the secondary menu and clicking the title for the article in the list of content.

After adding the block you should see something similar to Figure 10-2.

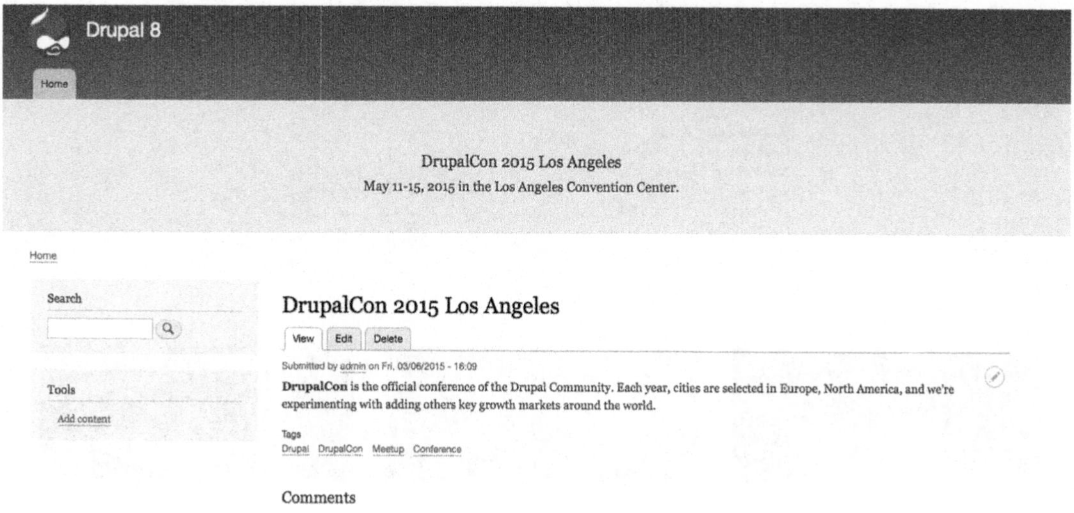

Figure 10-2. *Adding a block to an article detail page*

We can continue the process of adding other blocks to the other regions on this page until we have the content and elements that we want to display to our targeted users when they land on the DrupalCon 2015 Los Angeles page.

Creating Landing Pages

A landing page is typically a page that is not associated with a single piece of content and may display several different pieces of content and several blocks on the page. Drupal.org's homepage is an example of a landing page. Let's continue the process of creating pages by creating a new page for attractions in and around Los Angeles for those who are going to attend DrupalCon. This page will utilize many of the regions provided by the Bartik theme in order to generate a page that looks like the one depicted in Figure 10-3.

Figure 10-3. The "What to do Around Los Angeles" page

The first step in generating this page is to use the Basic page content type to create the base information that will be used (see Chapter 1 for a refresher on creating a Basic page). To keep things interesting, we'll only enter a title for this page, leaving the Body field empty. In the Title field, enter "What to do Around Los Angeles," and then click the "Save and publish" button. We now have a blank page with the title "What to do Around Los Angeles," without anything else other than the standard blocks that appear on every page. Let's create a few blocks and views and assign them to this page to make it look like a landing page.

First let's create a new taxonomy vocabulary named Event, and in that vocabulary let's create a single term for DrupalCon Los Angeles. Click the Manage link in the admin menu, click the Structure link in the secondary menu, and on the Structure page select Taxonomy. On the Taxonomy page, click the "Add vocabulary" button and enter "Event" in the Name field. Click the Save button to reveal the Events taxonomy page. Click the "Add term" button and create a term by entering "DrupalCon Los Angeles" in the Name field. Click Save to save the taxonomy term. We also need another taxonomy vocabulary for Subject. Follow the same steps for creating the Events taxonomy, only this time name the vocabulary "Subject" and add a term named "Things to do."

We now need a means for authors to specify that an article they are writing is about things to do around Los Angeles. We can enable that ability by adding two term reference fields to our Article content type, allowing authors to select from a subject and an event. On the Structure page, click the "Content types" link and click the "Manage fields" link for the Article content type. Following the general steps in the "Customizing Your Content Type" section of Chapter 5, create two new term reference fields, one for Event and one for Subject. As a refresher, select Term Reference as the field type, and on the Field settings page, select the appropriate vocabulary for each field. After adding the two fields, your list of fields should appear similar to that shown in Figure 10-4.

LABEL	MACHINE NAME	FIELD TYPE	OPERATIONS
Body	body	Text (formatted, long, with summary)	Edit ▾
Comments	comment	Comments	Edit ▾
Event	field_event	Term Reference	Edit ▾
Image	field_image	Image	Edit ▾
Subject	field_subject	Term Reference	Edit ▾
Tags	field_tags	Term Reference	Edit ▾

Figure 10-4. *Event and Subject fields added to Article content type*

The next step is to create several articles, selecting DrupalCon Los Angeles as the event and Things to do as the subject. Let's start with creating five articles and using those articles as the basis for creating a landing page.

Creating Views

In the main Content area of the page, we'll create a listing of the five most recently published articles that are focused on what to do in Los Angeles. We'll use the Views module to create the listing of articles, using the Teaser display to give our site visitors an introduction to each of the articles and the ability to click a "Read more" link to see the full article. Using the techniques described in Chapter 9, create a new view for articles by clicking the Structure menu item and selecting Views. Click the "Add new view" button and name the view "Articles." We will use this single view with multiple displays to create the types of output we wish to display on our landing page. In the View Settings area of the "Add new view" page, select Article as the type of entity that we wish to render, leaving the remainder of the options in their default state. Click the "Save and edit" button to continue.

The first view display that we will create is the teaser list of the latest five articles. Click the Add button to create a new display, and select Block from the list of options. Click the Block link in the "Display name" field and change the "Display name" to "Latest Articles." Click the None link next to the Title field and enter "Latest Articles" as the title to display at the top of the view's output. Next, for the Show settings, change what to show from Fields to Content and select Teaser from the list of formats to display. Click the "Use pager" link and change it to "Display a specified number of items" and set the number of items to display to 5. Finally, click the Save button.

The second view display that we will create is a Featured Article block. We'll randomly select an article and display the full article on the page. To create this view display, click the Add button and select Block. Change the "Display name" to "Featured article" and the Title to "Featured Article." Make sure you select "This block (override)" in the For select list at the top of each element you change; otherwise your changes will apply to all the view displays. Change the Show settings to Teaser to display the shortened version of the article. Next, click the Add button in the Sort Criteria section and add a new sort order. Select Global from the Type drop down list and from the list of values available for Global, select Random and click Add and configure sort criteria. Leave the Export this sort to visitors checkbox unchecked and complete the addition of the new sort criteria by clicking the Apply button. Next, delete the "Post date (desc)" sort criteria by clicking the drop-down arrow next to the Add link (displayed to the right of Sort Criteria) and selecting Rearrange. On the "Rearrange sort" page, click the Remove link associated with "Content: Post date (desc)" and click the Apply button. Next, change the number of items to display in the Pager section from 5 items to 1. Finally, click the Save button.

We'll assign the two blocks that we've just created to the "What to do Around Los Angeles" page to demonstrate the fruits of our labor. Click the Structure link and select the "Block layout" link. In the right column you will see the list of available blocks to place. In the section titled Lists (Views), you will see the two blocks that we just created. Click the Article: Featured Article link and assign it to the "Sidebar second" region. Click the Show Pages vertical tab and click the "Show for the listed pages" radio button. In the text area enter the URL to the page. In my case the URL to my article about what to do around Los Angeles can be found at /node/7, so that is the value that I will use to restrict this block to only that page. Click the Save button. Do the same steps for Article: Latest Articles, but in this case select the Content region. Finally, click the "Save blocks" button at the bottom of the "Block layout" page. Next visit the "What to do Around Los Angeles" page to see the progress of our page-building efforts (see Figure 10-5).

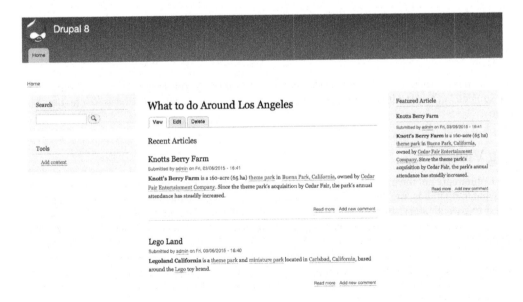

Figure 10-5. *Page build progress*

We will wrap up the landing page by adding three additional Featured Article blocks by creating three additional articles for restaurants around Los Angeles. We'll display the image uploaded for each restaurant article in the Featured Bottom regions near the bottom of the page (refer to Figure 10-1 for the region locations).

We'll first need to add a new term to the Subject vocabulary for Restaurants so that we can filter articles using DrupalCon 2015 Los Angeles as the event and Restaurants as the Subject. Follow the steps you performed earlier in the chapter (and in Chapter 4) to add the new term by navigating to Structure ➤ Taxonomy. Click the "Add term" link in the Operations column for the Subject vocabulary by clicking the drop-down arrow next to list terms and then select add terms. In the Name field enter Restaurant and click the Save button.

The next step is to create content. Click the Content link in the secondary menu and click the "Add content" button. Select the Article content type and create three new Articles selecting Restaurants from the list of subject taxonomy terms and upload images for each of the three restaurant articles. To upload an image click on the Browse button for the Image field, locate the image to upload, select it from the list of files presented, and click the Open button.

With the content in place, we're ready to create the view displays that will render the name and image of each restaurant as a block. Return to the Article view and:

1. Click the Add button to create a new block.

2. Give the first block a "Display name" of "Featured Restaurant 1."

3. We will want to display the name of the restaurant at the top of the block instead of using the Title field, so click the existing title, select "This block (override)" from the For select list at the top of the configuration panel for Title, blank out the existing title that appears in the text field, and click the "Apply (this display)" button.

4. We also want to show fields instead of teasers or full content in our blocks, so click the Content link to the right of Show and select Fields. Leaving the other configuration options at their default values. When we select Fields as the option for what to show, the Views module automatically adds the Title field to the list of fields to display. Click the Apply button to return to the Views configuration page.

5. We also want to display the image we uploaded for each restaurant, so click the Add link in the Fields section and scroll down through the list of fields until you find "Content: Image Appears in: article." Alternatively, enter "Image" in the Search box at the top of the list of fields to quickly take you to the appropriate field. Check the box next to the Image field and change the selected option of "All displays" at the top of the "Add fields" form to "This block (override)." Next, click the "Apply (this display)" button at the bottom of the "Add fields" form. The "Configure field: Content: Image" form will be displayed next, allowing you to set how the image will appear in the block. Uncheck the "Create a label" box, as we don't need a label to appear above the image. In the "Link image to select list," pick the Content item to automatically make the image a hyperlink to the article about that restaurant, and then click "Apply (this display)" button at the bottom of the form.

6. The next step in creating the first block is to set filter criteria so that only restaurants are displayed. Click the Add button for Filter Criteria, change the For option to "This block (override)," enter "term" in the Search box, check the "Content: Has taxonomy term" box from the list of fields returned, and click the "Apply (this display)" button. Views displays the "Configure extra settings for filter criterion" form, allowing you to pick which Vocabulary (choose Subject) and Selection type (choose Dropdown, and check the "Show hierarchy in dropdown" box). Click the Apply and continue button to proceed to the next page, select Restaurants from the list of terms in that vocabulary and click the "Apply (this display)" button.

7. The last step in creating the first restaurant block is to limit the number of items displayed to one article. Click the "Use pager" option to set the option to "Display a specified number of items" and set the number to display to 1.

8. Click the Save button to create the new block.

We need to create two more blocks to display additional restaurants. We'll make it a little easier by using the Duplicate feature in Views. With the Featured Restaurant 1 view display selected, click the Duplicate Featured Restaurant 1 link on the right side of the view configuration form. You will now see a new view display with the same name, ready to modify (see Figure 10-6).

Figure 10-6. *A duplicated view display*

There are two changes that we need to make to this duplicated display.

1. Change the "Display name" to "Featured Restaurant 2," and

2. Specify which restaurant to display.

Click the "Display name" link to change the name of the view, setting the value to "Featured Restaurant 2." Next, click the "Use pager" link to change the value to "Display a specific number of items" (making sure that you select "This block (override)" in the For select list at the top of the "Select which pager" configuration form). Click the number of items link and update the value of the "Items to display" field to 1 and enter 1 in the "Offset (number of items to skip)" field. Think of offset as the number of items to skip in a list before selecting the item we want to display. Since this specific block is supposed to display the second restaurant in the list we'll change the offset value to 1, meaning, skip the first one and show the second one. After completing the Featured Restaurant 2 block, click the duplicate Featured Restaurant 2 button and follow the same steps to update this duplicate of the Featured Restaurant 2 block using "Featured Restaurant 3" as the "Display name" and 2 as the value in the Offset field.

The next step in building our page is to place the Featured Restaurant blocks in the Featured Bottom regions (refer to Figure 10-1). Visit the "Block layout" page (click the "Block layout" link on the Structure page) and select the "Article: Featured Restaurant 1" block in the "Place blocks" section of the page. Select "Featured bottom first" as the region to assign the block to, click the "Show for the listed pages" radio button, and enter the URL to your "What to do around Los Angeles" page in the text area for "Show block on specific pages."

Repeat these steps for the Featured Restaurant 2 and 3 blocks, placing them in the Featured Bottom Second and Featured Bottom Third regions. The result of adding the Featured Restaurant blocks in the Featured Bottom regions is as shown in Figure 10-7.

Knotts Berry Farm
Submitted by admin on Fri, 03/06/2015 - 18:29

Knott's Berry Farm is a 160-acre (65 ha) theme park in Buena Park, California, owned by Cedar Fair Entertainment Company. Since the theme park's acquisition by Cedar Fair, the park's annual attendance has steadily increased.

Read more   Add new comment

Figure 10-7. *Featured restaurants*

You could continue to create additional views to display other lists of content, add other custom blocks, or look for modules that generate blocks that would augment the content on this page (e.g., Google Maps or Yelp), but for now we'll mark as complete our task of building a "What to do Around Los Angeles" page.

Summary

In this chapter we merged themes, content types, content, blocks, and views into a solution for creating complex pages on our site. We will use these techniques in Chapters 19 through 22 as we build a variety of Drupal 8 sites.

Next up we'll explore expanding the functionality of our site by adding contributed modules.

CHAPTER 11

■ ■ ■

Drupal Modules

Drupal is an amazing product in its off-the-shelf state. The features and functionality provided in Drupal 8 core are often more than adequate to meet the needs of many who build their websites with Drupal. But there are times when you need a feature that isn't possible with Drupal core alone, and in those cases you need look no further than the thousands of contributed modules that have been written to address just about anything you could think of doing on a Drupal based website.

In this chapter you will learn how to find, install, enable, and configure contributed modules.

Finding Contributed Modules

A Drupal-contributed module is essentially a program or set of programs that expands Drupal's capabilities beyond what is available in Drupal core. Contributed modules are designed, developed, and provided to the Drupal community free of charge by one or more of the thousands of developers who actively participate in the Drupal community. Modules can be downloaded from Drupal.org and enabled through the module administration pages. I will cover the process for adding modules in detail in a few moments.

A contributed module can be as simple as providing a mechanism to automatically create the title of an article or as complex as a fully featured e-commerce storefront with product management, inventory management, order management, shipment management, credit card processing, customer management, and returns management. There are thousands of modules of every shape and size, covering a wide variety of topics. To find a contributed module, visit `www.drupal.org/project/project_module` and browse through the categories of modules in the "Module categories" drop-down list. Example categories include the following (the parenthetical number after the category represents the number of modules available for that category at the time of writing):

- Administration (1,410)
- Commerce/Advertising (653)
- Community (687)
- Content (2,370)
- E-commerce (1,109)
- Import/Export (496)
- Mobile (176)Multilingual (244)
- Performance and Scalability (379)
- User Management (540)
- Third-party Integration (2,302)
- Utility (2,393)

As you can see from these examples, there are thousands of modules that span a wide variety of categories. The general titles of the categories listed here often do not do justice to the rich features that are available in the modules that are buried beneath the titles. It often takes research and patience to scan through the hundreds of modules to find the one that provides the functionality that you need. Complex requirements may also take more than one module to provide the functionally you need to address a larger problem. Understanding which modules do what, which modules work well together, and which modules do not work together is often the hardest challenge of building a complex Drupal website.

A recommended exercise is to visit www.drupal.org/project/project_module, select the "Last release" sort option for the "Sort by" field, and then click the Search button. The list displayed will show the latest modules and module updates that have been released to the community. Visit the site every day or two and read through the description of the newest modules that were added or updated on the site. It only takes a couple of minutes a day to quickly build up your understanding of the modules and types of solutions that are available through Drupal's contributed modules.

A great third-party website that helps solve the issue of finding the right modules is http://drupalmodules.com. This site provides a Search with Module Finder feature that makes it easier to look for and find the right module for the right job.

Downloading and Installing a Module

There are three basic approaches for installing a new module on your site: downloading the module files to your server, using the "Install new module" feature on the module administrative interface, or using Drush. I'll cover the first two methods in this chapter and cover using Drush in Chapter 15.

The first step in installing a module is finding the right module to use. As described in the previous section, there are thousands of modules to pick from; finding the right one is often the biggest challenge. For demonstration purposes, let's pick two of the most popular and useful modules: the Google Analytics module and the Display Suite module. First we'll download the Google Analytics module by downloading its files to the server, and then we'll download the Display Suite module using the section approach, via the "Install new module" feature.

Downloading Module Files to Your Server

I'll demonstrate how to install the Google Analytics module by downloading the module file to the module directory on my Drupal 8 site. The steps are as follows:

1. Visit Drupal.org/project/modules and find the module. You can use the Search feature or the filters on the Modules page to locate a module, but knowing that Drupal.org's standard naming convention for the URLs of modules is to use the name of the module as the last element of the URL speeds the search for the Google Analytics module: visit www.drupal.org/project/google_analytics.

2. Scroll down to the Downloads section for the module. You should, in most cases, select the current release for the module that you are installing. The current release should be highlighted with a green background. In some cases, you may need to use a module that is still in development because a stable production version is not yet available. Development versions are typically highlighted with a red background and have a version number that ends in -dev. You should use preproduction (dev) versions with caution, as those modules are not yet fully developed and have not been thoroughly tested. To download a module right-click the tar.gz link for the Drupal 8 version (8.x), and click the Save option provided by your browser in the pop-up menu. If your Drupal 8 installation is

on your local computer, you can save the `tar.gz` file directly in the modules directory of your Drupal installation. If not, use FTP to copy the file to the module directory on your server. The module directory is located in Drupal 8 in the root directory of your site installation.

3. Unzip the file. Depending on your operating system, you may be able to unzip the file by locating it in a file explorer window and double-clicking the file, or from the command line using a tool like `gunzip` to expand the gz file and `tar` to expand the tar file. With the expanded file in your module directory, you should now see a folder with the name `google_analytics` in the modules folder. At this point you are ready to enable the module.

4. To enable the module, click the Manage link on the administrative menu at the top of the page, followed by clicking the Extend link in the secondary menu. Clicking the Extend link takes you to the module administration page where you can now search for the module. Scroll down the page and you should see a section titled Statistics, which should include the Google Analytics module. Check the box next to the module's name and then click the "Save configuration" button at the bottom of the page.

Volia! The Google Analytics module is now enabled and ready to use on your site. You may follow the same process to install any contributed module you wish to add to your site.

Using the Install New Module Feature

A second way of installing a new module is to use the installation feature on the module administration page. This feature provides the ability to download and install a module by simply entering the URL of the install file and clicking a button. This approach does require that you have FTP access to your server, a valid FTP user account, and that the directories are set up with the proper permissions to allow that FTP user with write access. Drupal handles the task of downloading the module's install file, expanding the install file, moving the files to the correct directory, and installing the module. To access the Modules page, where you can download and install a new Drupal module, simply click the Manage link in the top menu, followed by the Extend link in the secondary menu. Drupal will display the module administration page, which at this point shows all of the modules that are shipped as part of Drupal core (see Figure 11-1) plus the Google Analytics module that we just installed and enabled.

From the module administration page, the steps are as follows:

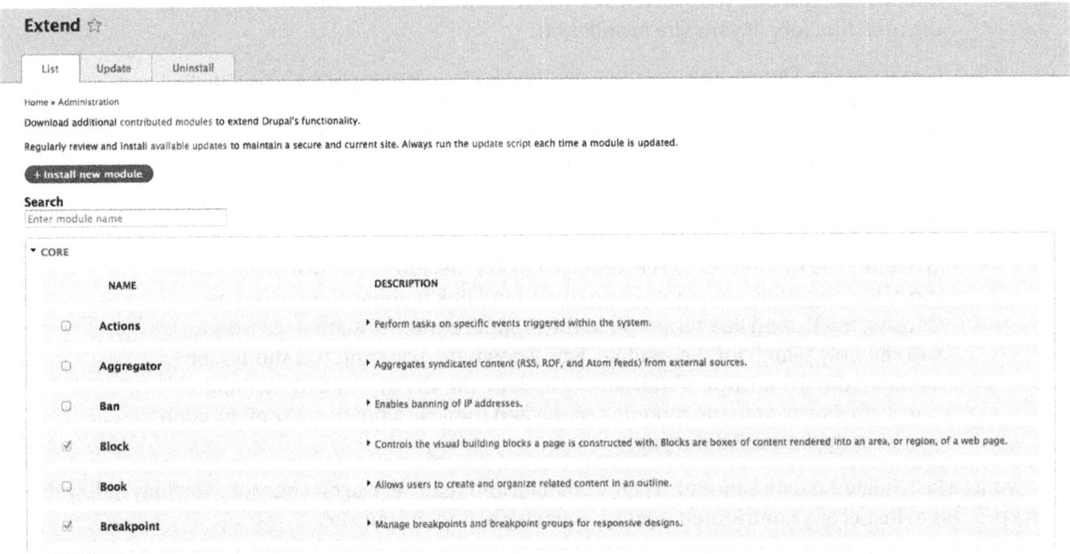

Figure 11-1. Drupal modules

1. To begin the installation process, click the "Install new module" button near the top of the page, which reveals the module installation page, shown in Figure 11-2.

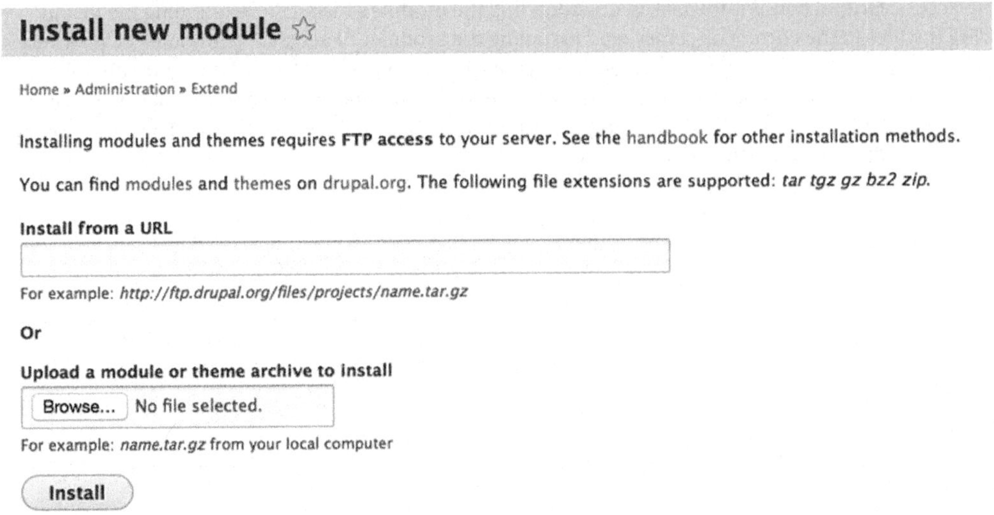

Figure 11-2. The module installation page

2. On the module installation page, either provide the URL for the module's installation file (from Drupal.org) or, in the case where you downloaded the module to your computer, upload the file from your computer to the server using the "Upload a module or theme" feature. To simplify the process, we'll use the first text box to specify the URL of the file that we are going to install, the Display Suite module. To find the URL of the Display Suite module, visit www.drupal.org/project/project_module, choose "8.x" from the "Core compatibility" select list, and enter "Display Suite" in the Search Modules text box. Click the Search button. In the search results, scroll down until you see the Display Suite module in the list, and click the title to display the module's homepage. You should be on the www.drupal.org/project/ds page, where ds is the abbreviation used by the module developer for Display Suite.

3. Scroll down to Downloads section of the Display Suite homepage, where you will find a list of the current versions of the module, as shown in Figure 11-3. In our case, we want the current Drupal 8 version of the module, so locate the 8.x version of the module on the list of available releases.

Downloads

Recommended releases

Version	Download	Date	Links
8.x–2.0–alpha4	gz (106.12 KB) | zip (190.6 KB)	2013–Oct–18	Notes
7.x–2.6	gz (123.69 KB) | zip (172.53 KB)	2013–Sep–04	Notes
6.x–2.3	gz (60.64 KB) | zip (76.62 KB)	2012–Feb–13	Notes

Other releases

Version	Download	Date	Links
7.x–1.9	gz (112.37 KB) | zip (152.39 KB)	2013–Aug–30	Notes

Development releases

Version	Download	Date	Links
8.x–2.x–dev	gz (106.43 KB) | zip (190.82 KB)	2014–Feb–08	Notes
7.x–2.x–dev	gz (125.74 KB) | zip (173.35 KB)	2014–Jan–08	Notes
7.x–1.x–dev	gz (112.41 KB) | zip (152.43 KB)	2013–Sep–30	Notes
6.x–2.x–dev	gz (61.49 KB) | zip (77.42 KB)	2013–Sep–30	Notes

View all releases

Figure 11-3. Available releases for the Display Suite module

4. To capture the URL of the installation file, right-click the Download link for the version you wish to install, and select the appropriate copy link location option from the browser's options menu. Return to the module administration page and paste the URL for the file in the top text box. You are now ready to install the module.

5. To begin the installation process, click the Install button. Drupal will download the installation file from Drupal.org, expand the compressed file, move all of the files and directories associated with the module to the appropriate directories on your server, and then run the installation script associated with your module.

6. The module is now installed but not yet enabled. To use the module, you must enable it by checking the appropriate boxes on the module administration page (see Figure 11-4) and clicking the "Save configuration" button at the bottom of the page. For Display Suite, you will want to enable at minimum the Display Suite and Display Suite UI modules.

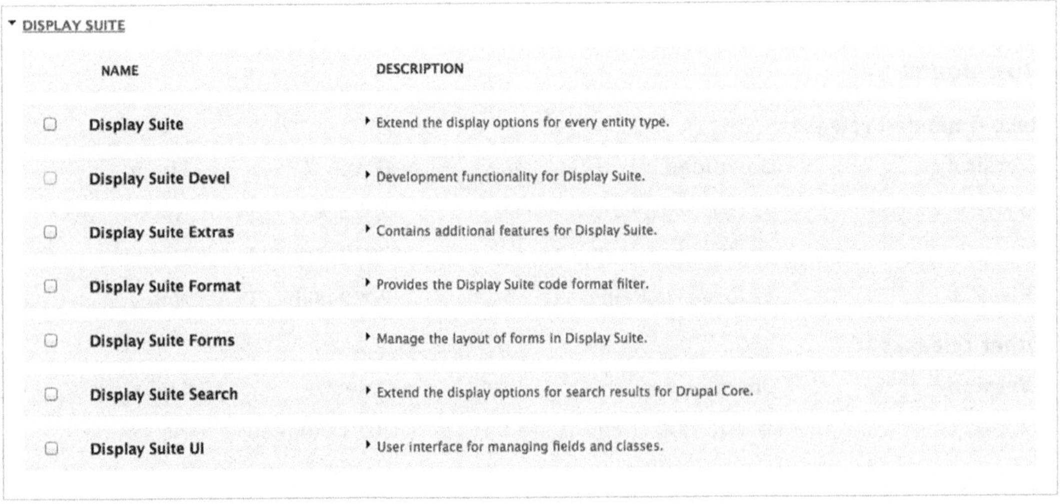

▼ DISPLAY SUITE

	NAME	DESCRIPTION
☐	**Display Suite**	▸ Extend the display options for every entity type.
☐	**Display Suite Devel**	▸ Development functionality for Display Suite.
☐	**Display Suite Extras**	▸ Contains additional features for Display Suite.
☐	**Display Suite Format**	▸ Provides the Display Suite code format filter.
☐	**Display Suite Forms**	▸ Manage the layout of forms in Display Suite.
☐	**Display Suite Search**	▸ Extend the display options for search results for Drupal Core.
☐	**Display Suite UI**	▸ User interface for managing fields and classes.

Figure 11-4. *The module administration page*

At this point the Display Suite module is installed, enabled, and ready to use. You may now follow the same process to install any contributed module you wish to add to your site.

Configuring Modules and Setting Permissions

Some, although not all, modules provide some level of customization and configuration. In many cases the only configuration tasks are to set the permissions of who can use those modules.

To configure the permissions for modules, click the Manage link in the administration menu at the top of the page, followed by the People link in the secondary menu. On the People administration page, click the Permissions tab to view all of the permissions that may be set on the site.

We installed the Google Analytics module in the previous steps and need to set the permissions so that administrators can manage the configuration parameters for the Google Analytics module. Scroll down the list of permissions until you find the module, as shown in Figure 11-5.

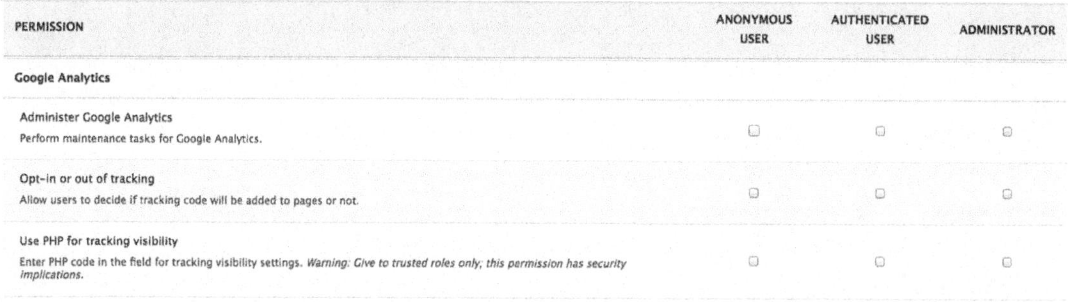

PERMISSION	ANONYMOUS USER	AUTHENTICATED USER	ADMINISTRATOR
Google Analytics			
Administer Google Analytics Perform maintenance tasks for Google Analytics.	☐	☐	☑
Opt-in or out of tracking Allow users to decide if tracking code will be added to pages or not.	☐	☐	☐
Use PHP for tracking visibility Enter PHP code in the field for tracking visibility settings. *Warning: Give to trusted roles only; this permission has security implications.*	☐	☐	☐

Figure 11-5. *Permissions for the Google Analytics module*

To set permissions for the module, check the box under the Administrator column for Administer Google Analytics and click the "Save permissions" button at the bottom of the page. You now have the ability to set the configuration parameters for the Google Analytics module while logged in to an account that has a role assigned as administrator. As you install and enable other modules, remember to review and set the permissions for that module.

Some modules provide the ability to set configuration parameters, such as the Search module (part of Drupal core). To view the configuration parameters for modules, click the Manage link in the admin menu at the top of the page followed by the Configuration link in the secondary menu. The Configuration page lists all of the modules that provide the ability to set configuration options (see Figure 11-6). Not all modules follow this convention. If you do not see a configuration link for the module you are working with, check the module's homepage on Drupal.org for documentation or, alternatively, check the README.txt file in the modules directory on your site.

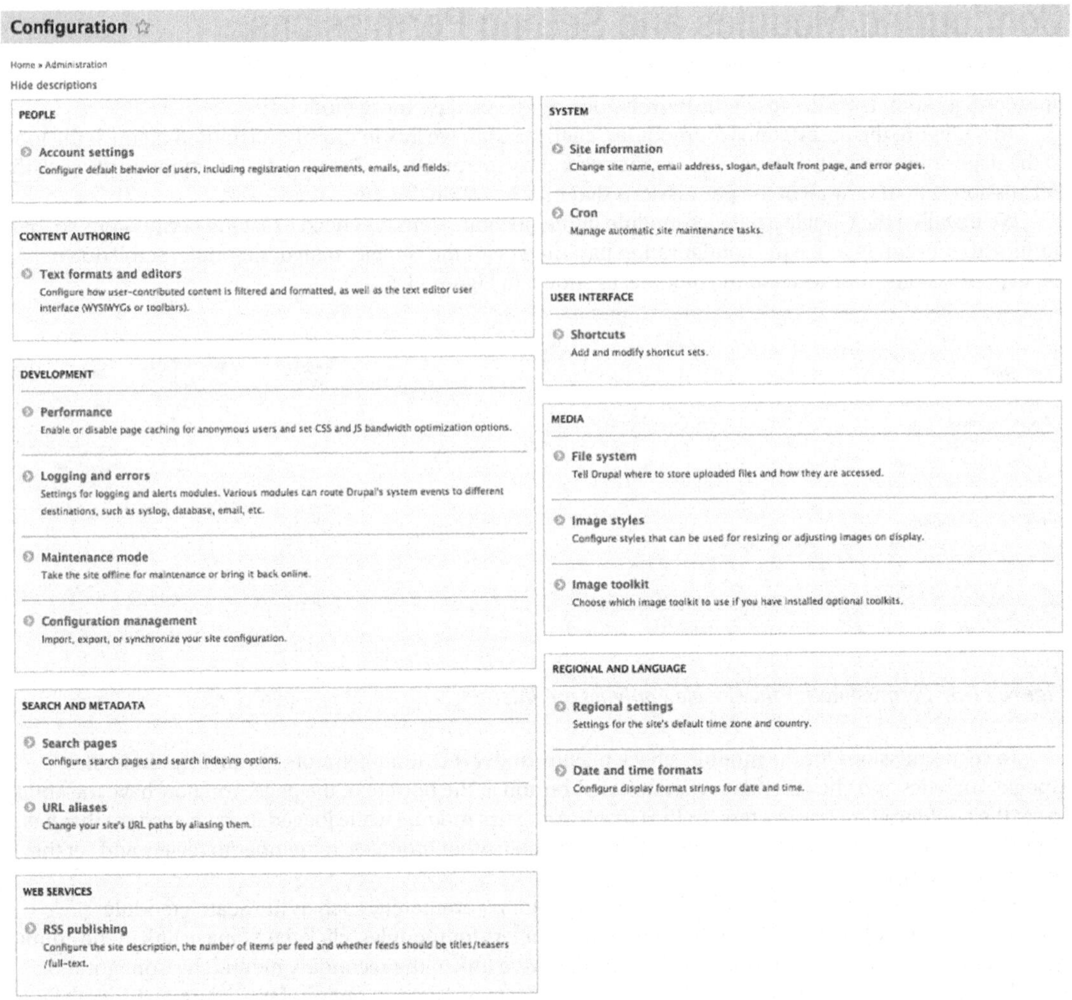

Configuration ☆

Home » Administration

Hide descriptions

PEOPLE

○ **Account settings**
Configure default behavior of users, including registration requirements, emails, and fields.

CONTENT AUTHORING

○ **Text formats and editors**
Configure how user-contributed content is filtered and formatted, as well as the text editor user interface (WYSIWYGs or toolbars).

DEVELOPMENT

○ **Performance**
Enable or disable page caching for anonymous users and set CSS and JS bandwidth optimization options.

○ **Logging and errors**
Settings for logging and alerts modules. Various modules can route Drupal's system events to different destinations, such as syslog, database, email, etc.

○ **Maintenance mode**
Take the site offline for maintenance or bring it back online.

○ **Configuration management**
Import, export, or synchronize your site configuration.

SEARCH AND METADATA

○ **Search pages**
Configure search pages and search indexing options.

○ **URL aliases**
Change your site's URL paths by aliasing them.

WEB SERVICES

○ **RSS publishing**
Configure the site description, the number of items per feed and whether feeds should be titles/teasers /full-text.

SYSTEM

○ **Site information**
Change site name, email address, slogan, default front page, and error pages.

○ **Cron**
Manage automatic site maintenance tasks.

USER INTERFACE

○ **Shortcuts**
Add and modify shortcut sets.

MEDIA

○ **File system**
Tell Drupal where to store uploaded files and how they are accessed.

○ **Image styles**
Configure styles that can be used for resizing or adjusting images on display.

○ **Image toolkit**
Choose which image toolkit to use if you have installed optional toolkits.

REGIONAL AND LANGUAGE

○ **Regional settings**
Settings for the site's default time zone and country.

○ **Date and time formats**
Configure display format strings for date and time.

Figure 11-6. *Configuration page for modules*

When viewing the Module configuration page (see Figure 11-6), you'll see a Search and Metadata section and, in that section, a link for Search settings. Click that link to view the configuration parameters for search (see Figure 11-7).

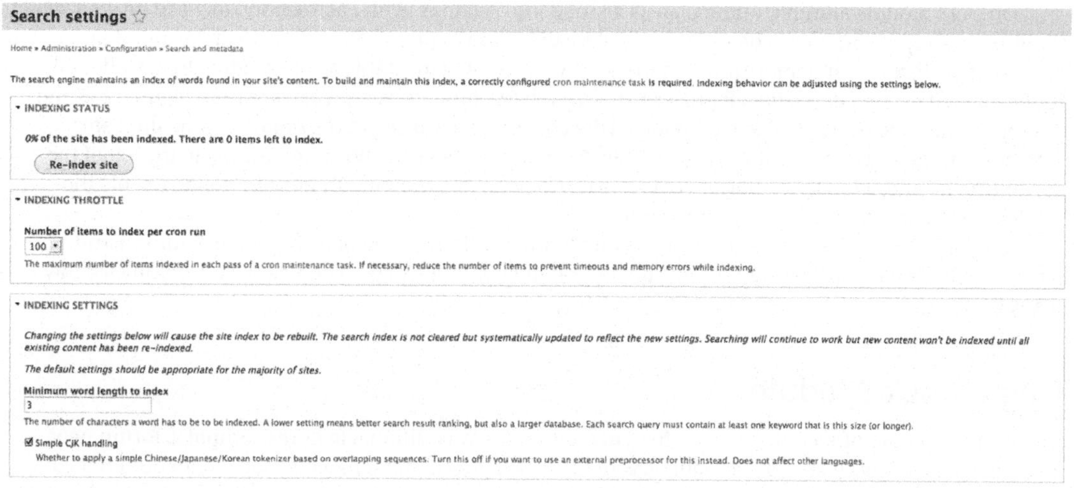

Search settings ☆

Home » Administration » Configuration » Search and metadata

The search engine maintains an index of words found in your site's content. To build and maintain this index, a correctly configured cron maintenance task is required. Indexing behavior can be adjusted using the settings below.

▾ INDEXING STATUS

0% of the site has been indexed. There are 0 items left to index.

(Re-index site)

▾ INDEXING THROTTLE

Number of items to index per cron run
[100 ▾]
The maximum number of items indexed in each pass of a cron maintenance task. If necessary, reduce the number of items to prevent timeouts and memory errors while indexing.

▾ INDEXING SETTINGS

Changing the settings below will cause the site index to be rebuilt. The search index is not cleared but systematically updated to reflect the new settings. Searching will continue to work but new content won't be indexed until all existing content has been re-indexed.

The default settings should be appropriate for the majority of sites.

Minimum word length to index
[3]
The number of characters a word has to be to be indexed. A lower setting means better search result ranking, but also a larger database. Each search query must contain at least one keyword that is this size (or longer).

☑ Simple CJK handling
Whether to apply a simple Chinese/Japanese/Korean tokenizer based on overlapping sequences. Turn this off if you want to use an external preprocessor for this instead. Does not affect other languages.

Figure 11-7. Search module configuration options

Not all modules provide the ability to set configuration parameters; it is dependent on what the module does and whether the module developer determined that configuration options were necessary. It is a good idea to visit the Configuration page and examine the configuration options for all of your installed and enabled modules to ensure that they are set properly.

Enabling Other Modules

You may "inherit" an existing Drupal site, or you may wish to enable other Drupal modules that already exist on your site (e.g., modules that are part of Drupal core but not automatically enabled by the Drupal installation process). To see the list of modules that are available on your site, simply click the Manage link at the top of the page, followed by the Extend link in the secondary menu. Doing so reveals the module administration page shown in Figure 11-8.

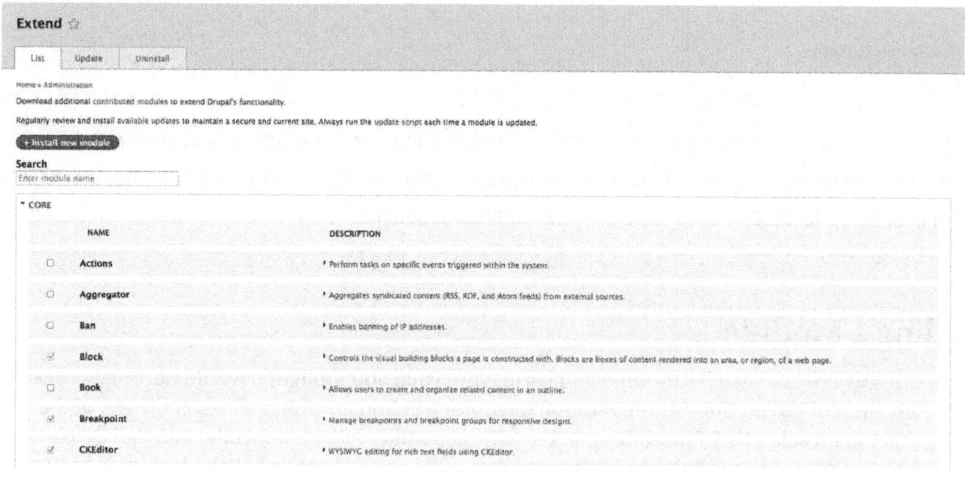

Extend ☆

| List | Update | Uninstall |

Home » Administration

Download additional contributed modules to extend Drupal's functionality.

Regularly review and install available updates to maintain a secure and current site. Always run the update script each time a module is updated.

(+ Install new module)

Search
[Enter module name]

▾ CORE

	NAME	DESCRIPTION
☐	Actions	▸ Perform tasks on specific events triggered within the system.
☐	Aggregator	▸ Aggregates syndicated content (RSS, RDF, and Atom feeds) from external sources.
☐	Ban	▸ Enables banning of IP addresses.
☑	Block	▸ Controls the visual building blocks a page is constructed with. Blocks are boxes of content rendered into an area, or region, of a web page.
☐	Book	▸ Allows users to create and organize related content in an outline.
☑	Breakpoint	▸ Manage breakpoints and breakpoint groups for responsive designs.
☑	CKEditor	▸ WYSIWYG editing for rich text fields using CKEditor.

Figure 11-8. Module administration page

Drupal's module administration page is divided into sections, with each section focused on a particular module or group of modules. The modules that are delivered as part of Drupal core can be found in the Core section of the listing. For demonstration purposes, we are going to enable a core module that, by default, is not enabled by the Drupal install process: the Aggregator module. As you can see from Figure 11-8, the Aggregator module is not checked as enabled (the check box to the left of the module name indicates whether a module is enabled or not). To enable the module, check the box immediately to the left of the module name and scroll to the bottom of the page. Click the "Save configuration" button to enable the module so that it can be used on your new site.

After clicking the Save configuration button, Drupal will then redisplay the module administration page with the "successful configuration" message at the top of the page. The Aggregator module is now ready for use.

Upgrading a Module

Drupal modules are often updated with fixes to bugs and new additional features. Drupal 8, fortunately, tells you when a new version of a module has been released, and provides a mechanism for automatically updating that module to the latest version. To view all of the available updates, simply click the Update tab at the top of the module administration page (see Figure 11-8), or click the Reports link in the secondary menu (under Manage) and click the "Available updates" link (see Figure 11-9).

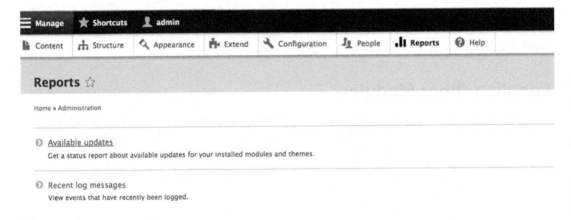

Figure 11-9. *Reports page*

■ **Note**   There may be cases where you don't want to upgrade a module; for example, a case where an upgrade to one module breaks another related module. I suggest that before you perform an update, you review the forums on Drupal.org to check to see if anyone has reported problems.

Uninstalling a Module

There may be cases where you install a module and it's just not what you thought it would be, or it causes problems on your site. On the module administration page you will find an Uninstall tab at the top of the page. Clicking that tab reveals a list of modules that have the capability to automatically uninstall themselves (see Figure 11-10). To uninstall a module check the box next to that module and click the Uninstall button at the bottom of the page.

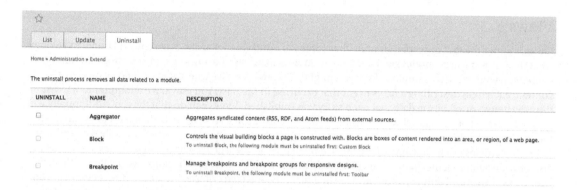

Figure 11-10. The module Uninstall page

■ **Note** Not all modules have the capability to automatically perform an uninstall. It is up to the module developer to create this capability, and not all module developers are kind enough to provide this feature.

In the case where a module does not provide an automatic uninstall feature, the process for removing a module is

1. Navigate to the modules directory on your server.

2. Highlight the folder containing the module and delete the folder.

You should use caution when uninstalling a module, as there are often module dependencies, meaning one module depends on another module to function properly. If you are unsure as to whether a module has dependencies, visit that module's page on Drupal.org and look through the module's description. Modules with dependencies will list those dependencies in the body of their description. Alternatively, check the module's .info.yml file on your server, which lists dependencies, as shown here for the Views module:

```
name: Views
  type: module
  description: 'Create customized lists and queries from your database.'
  package: Core
  # version: VERSION
  # core: 8.x
  dependencies:
    - filter
```

The Top Eleven Modules

There are several modules that seem to make it to everyone's "favorites" list. For those of us who eat, breathe, drink, and live Drupal, these modules represent our standard "tool belt" that we use on nearly every Drupal project. This section provide a brief overview of each. As I mentioned before, please take a few minutes a day to visit hwww.drupal.org/project/project_module and browse through the pages and pages of modules that are available for free!

Views

Views is either the first or second module that comes to mind when you ask experienced Drupal developers what their most favorite module is. The Views module is like a Swiss army knife for selecting and rendering content on your site. An example of how you might use views is a case where you created 50 pieces of content, each item describing a news event that occurred in the past. You may have a requirement to list those 50 items sorted by the date that each story was published. Views can do that for you. Additionally you may want the list of news articles to be listed in tabular format, like an Excel spreadsheet. Views can do that for you. You may also want to provide visitors with a page that lists the news article as a table with the ability to sort the articles by clicking one of the titles in the table view of articles. Views can do that for you. You can also provide a filtering mechanism so visitors can pick a subject, person, or location associated with all of your news stories and only see those articles that meet the selected criteria. Views can do that for you. You may also want to provide an RSS feed of the news articles to visitors who use feed aggregators. Views can do that for you. Views is an amazingly easy-to-use module that is extremely powerful and a "must have" on nearly everyone's list, and the good news is that it's part of Drupal 8 core. Chapter 9 describes in detail how to use Views.

Layout

A close second to Views in popularity is the Layout module. As we placed blocks on pages in Chapter 8, you saw that we were limited to putting blocks into the regions defined by the Bartik theme that we were using. But what if we wanted to divide the content area into rows and columns so that we can create landing pages with lots of elements? The Layout module comes to the rescue. For advanced page layouts, there isn't a tool that is easier to use and more powerful than the Layout module. Chapter 10 describes how to use Layouts.

Rules

The Rules module enables administrators to define conditionally executed actions based on events. For example, if you want to send an e-mail automatically to a content administrator every time a comment is posted to the site, for the administrator's review and approval, you can use Rules to configure that action.

Display Suite

Display Suite gives you a drag-and-drop interface that allows you to take full control over how your content is displayed. Arrange your nodes, views, comments, and user data the way you want without having to walk through dozens of template files.

Nicemenus

Drupal's out-of-the-box menu features provide an easy-to-use mechanism for creating horizontal and vertical menus, where those menus are restricted to a single level. In many cases you'll want to have the ability to create menus that have drop-downs (for horizontal menus) or fly-outs (for vertical menus). Drupal's menuing system provides the ability to assign menu items in a hierarchical fashion; however, it is up to us, Drupal developers, to format menus so that items drop down or fly out when a user hovers over a menu item. Fortunately, we have the Nicemenus module that automatically handles the rendering of drop-downs and fly-outs.

Pathauto

One of the key elements of successful search engine optimization is providing URLs on your site that are meaningful. By default, Drupal 8 out-of-the-box URLs look something like `http://localhost/node/1`. Search engines have no idea what "node/1" means, nor what the content associated with that page may be about, just by looking at the URL. Humans visiting the site may also have a difficult time navigating around to pages that are not linked or accessible by a menu, as `http://localhost/node/2487`, for example, is not very intuitive. Fortunately, we have the Pathauto module, which creates an "alias URL" to the node being created, and the alias URL takes the form of the title of the node with hyphens used to separate words, and all words are made lowercase. Using `http://localhost/node/2487` as an example, if that node has a title of "Special deals of the month," the URL as generated by Pathauto would be `http://localhost/special-deals-month` (Pathauto removes common words like "the" and "of" from titles when generating URLs). The alias URL becomes the primary path used by Drupal when that page is rendered, and is significantly more user- and SEO-friendly than the `http://localhost/node/2487` version.

Webform

The Webform module provides a simple-to-use interface for creating online forms. You can use online forms to capture virtually any type of information you can think of that would come from a form that a site visitor might fill out. Examples of forms could be an employment application, an information request form, or an event registration form. There are virtually no limits as to what types of forms you can create using the Webform module. The module extends beyond its ability to create and render forms by providing a mechanism for e-mailing a predefined person the results when someone enters information on a form, a tool for generating reports against the information that is captured on forms, and a tool for exporting information entered in forms to an Excel spreadsheet.

Backup and Migrate

The Backup and Migrate module automates the task of backing up the information that is stored in your Drupal database based on a schedule that you define (every 12 hours, every 24 hours, and so on). Backup and Migrate also provides the ability to manually back up the database (in real time) by simply clicking a button. You can also restore a backup by selecting a previous backup and by clicking a Restore button. Many Drupal administrators sleep better at night knowing that their site is being backed up automatically.

Date

The Date module provides a set of tools for creating and using dates on your site, such as a pop-up calendar for selecting a date.

Library

The Library module is the common denominator for all modules that integrate with external libraries. While not sexy by any stretch of the word, Library is one of those must-have modules if you use modules that call on, for example, external JavaScript libraries.

Drupal Commerce

If your site has any element of e-commerce (such as selling physical items like shirts or selling virtual items like subscriptions), then there are two primary options: Ubercart, which is the granddaddy of commerce modules in Drupal, or Drupal Commerce. Both solutions provide world-class commerce capabilities and are the de facto standards for conducting e-commerce on a Drupal site.

Summary

In this chapter you learned how to significantly enhance the functionality of your Drupal website through the use of contributed modules. There are literally thousands of free modules to select from, meaning that if there's something you want to do with your Drupal site, there is likely a module that provides the functionality that you need. Coming up next we will look at modules and how they are constructed.

■ ■ ■

## CHAPTER 12

Anatomy of a Module

Although it is possible to build relatively complex Drupal 8 sites without ever having to look at the internals of a module, there may be instances where you'll need to understand some of the inner workings of a module in order to fully take advantage of the features that the module provides. In this chapter I'll take you on a high-level tour of what constitutes a module in Drupal 8 by walking you through the creation of a simple Drupal 8 module.

Your First Drupal 8 Module

Don't worry, we'll keep it simple! Our example module does only one thing, but it does it very well: display the text "Hello Drupal 8 World!" on a page. The result of our efforts in this section will be a page that looks similar to Figure 12-1.

Figure 12-1. *Hello Drupal 8 World!*

Step 1: Create the Module's Directory

The first step is to create a directory where the files that constitute your module will reside. All contributed modules (non-core) reside in the module directory located at the root directory of your Drupal 8 site. If you have installed any modules beyond what comes with Drupal 8 core, you'll see those modules in this directory.

Using your operating system's file manager, or from a terminal window and a command prompt, navigate to the modules directory of your site and create a new directory named custom. Drupal best practices state that custom modules, those not downloaded from Drupal.org, should be stored in a subdirectory named custom. Navigate to the custom directory and within the custom directory create a new directory named hello.

Step 2: Create the Module's info File

The next step is to create a hello.info.yml file. This file tells Drupal about your module and provides the information that appears on the Extend page in the Administration section of your site. Using your favorite text editor, create the hello.info.yml file with the following content:

```
name: Hello
type: module
description: 'My first Drupal 8 module.'
package: Awesome modules
version: 1.0
core: '8.x'
```

The first line specifies the name of the module as it appears on the module page. The second line specifies that we're creating a module. (Themes, for example, would use a value of theme for the type.) The third line captures the description of the module, which also appears on the Extend page. The package field provides a mechanism for grouping modules together. For example, if you visit the Extend page of your site, you'll see a number of modules listed in a box with a title of Core. We'll use something unique for our module and place it in a package called Awesome modules. If you're writing a module that, for example, creates new web services capabilities, you should use the package name of the other modules that create web services, to ensure that a site administrator can easily find your module. Version creates a version number for your module, and core specifies which version of Drupal this module was written for. In our case we wrote this module for Drupal 8.

Step 3: Create the Module File

The module file for our Hello module does one thing: returns the text that will be displayed on the page that our module provides. Module files can do many things, but for our example we'll just focus on the basics.

Using your favorite text editor, create a new file named hello.module with the following text:

```
<?php

use Drupal\Core\Routing\RouteMatchInterface;

function hello_hello_world() {

    return t('Hello Drupal 8 World!');

}
```

The file begins with the opening PHP tag, <?php, as all modules are written in the PHP programming language. The specific elements of our module file are

```
function hello_hello_world () {
```

This defines a PHP function that can be called from other modules. In this case it is a simple function named hello_hello_world(). The first hello is the name of the module, in our case hello. As a Drupal coding standard, all functions should begin with the name of the module, followed by a descriptive function name.

Again, our function does one thing: return a text string to the code that called this function. I've wrapped the text that we are returning in a Drupal function called t(). This function translates any text within the parentheses, if you have multilingual capabilities enabled (see Chapter 13). It is another Drupal coding standard to wrap all text values using the t() function.

Although our module is simple, it demonstrates the basic functionality of what modules do. The module file is the workhorse of any module, and can be as simple as our example module or as complex as needed to meet the functional and technical requirements for your module.

Step 4: Create the Module's Routing File

The foundation of Drupal 8 is Symfony, a PHP framework that simplifies the creation of complex PHP-based applications, like Drupal. The Symfony framework provides the mechanisms for creating a Model-View-Controller (MVC)-based application, where *Model* represents the underlying data that the application operates against, *View* defines the user interface to the application, and *Controller* is the workhorse of the applications, including routing requests from users and returning information back to the view to display to the user. The next step in the process is to create our module's routing file, which defines how a visitor will access the functionality of our module and what returns the values to be displayed.

In the same directory, using your favorite text editor, create the module's routing file. In our case the routing file will be named help.routing.yml. The contents of the file should be

```
hello.content:
  path: '/hello'
  defaults:
    _controller: '\Drupal\hello\Controller\HelloController::sayhello'
  requirements:
    _permission: 'TRUE'
```

The first line of code represents the name of our module (hello). The next line represents the path that an end user would use to access the functionality provided by the module, which is /hello. The defaults section provides the source of the content that will be returned to the end user, which is the sayhello function within the HelloController (more on this in a moment). The requirements section defines what permissions a visitor must have in order to access our module; in this case we just use the word TRUE, as anyone can access this page. Check out the Examples module for details on how modules can restrict access (www.drupal.org/project/examples).

Step 5: Create the Module's Controller

Drupal 8 follows Symfony's and PHP 5's object orientation approach. One of the key concepts that Drupal 8 has adopted is a standard called PSR-4, which defines how code is loaded into memory. One of the issues with previous versions of Drupal is that a lot of code is loaded into memory when it doesn't need to be there. PSR-4 solves that issue, and one of the enablers is something called *namespaces*. In our routing file, the value associated with _content starts with \Drupal\hello\Controller, which is a namespace. PSR-4 defines that a namespace maps directly to the file structure of your application. Symfony requires that all of our namespace directories reside within a directory named src, which resides in the root directory of our module.

So let's get busy and create the directories where the next component of our module will reside, the controller. While in the root directory of our hello module, create a new directory named src, and within the src directory, create a new directory named Controller. Within the Controller directory, we're now ready to create the controller for our application, the "traffic cop" of our application. In your favorite text editor, create a file named HelloController.php. The contents of our controller should be

```php
<?php

namespace Drupal\hello\Controller;

use Drupal\Core\Controller\ControllerBase;

class HelloController extends ControllerBase {

  public function sayhello() {
    return array(
      '#markup' => hello_hello_world(),
    );
  }

}
```

The beginning of our controller file starts with the PHP opening tag, as the controller is written using PHP. The second line defines the namespace that we are using for our controller:

```php
namespace Drupal\hello\Controller;
```

The third line defines that we are going to inherit the ControllerBase class from Drupal core without having to write it all from scratch:

```php
use Drupal\Core\Controller\ControllerBase;
```

Recall from Step 4 that in our module's routing file we called a function that returns the content to display using '\Drupal\hello\Controller\HelloController::sayhello'. The class HelloController is the first part of the HelloController::sayhello:

```php
class HelloController extends ControllerBase {
```

The following line is the last half of the call from our router (HelloController:sayhello). The line of code defines the function that will return the information back to the page that is displayed when the visitor accesses the /hello URL on our site.

```
public function sayhello() {
```

The remaining code simply calls the function we created in our module file hello_hello_world(). This function returns the text "Hello Drupal 8 World!" in a renderable array that Drupal knows how to display on a page, and returns it back to our modules router.

```
return array(
    '#markup' => hello_hello_world(),
);
```

Save this file, and we're ready to enable our new module! Visit the Extend page in the admin section of the site and scroll down until you see the Awesome Modules section (see Figure 12-2).

Figure 12-2. *Our Hello Drupal 8 World! module on the Extend page*

Check the box next to the module's name and click the "Save configuration" button to enable the module. With the module enabled, you're now ready to test your first Drupal 8 module! To execute the module, navigate to your homepage and add /hello to the end of the URL (we defined that path in our module's routing file). You should see the output shown earlier in Figure 12-1.

Other Module Files

Our Hello module is a very simple module, the purpose being to help you past the initial learning curve of how a module is structured in Drupal. Now that you know the very basics, you can look at other contributed modules, or even Drupal core, to see how more complex modules are created and study the files associated with that increased complexity. You can learn about writing more complex modules at www.drupal.org/developing/modules/8. I highly recommend downloading the Examples module from www.drupal.org/project/examples. Within that module you will find several examples that demonstrate how Drupal 8 modules are constructed, a great starting place for creating Drupal 8 modules.

Summary

Congratulations! You have written a Drupal 8 module and earned your first stripe toward becoming a Drupal module developer ninja. The purpose of this chapter was to give you an overview so you would have enough information under your belt to go exploring through other modules. While the learning curve can be steep for Drupal module development, you've taken the first step along that path

CHAPTER 13

■ ■ ■

Multilingual Capabilities

We live in a world where cultural and country boundaries, while still important, are blurred by the Internet's capability to connect two people who are geographically thousands of miles apart and enable them to communicate through text, voice, and video. The visitors who come to our websites may be our next-door neighbors or they may live half a world away. Catering to those who live beyond our region and do not share our native tongue is now more commonplace than ever. Website designers who break through the language barriers on their sites may attract audiences that they never dreamed of having in the past, and Drupal 8 makes that possibility a reality through its built-in multilingual capabilities.

Getting Started with Multilingual

The first step in creating a website with multilingual support is to determine which languages you wish to publish content in. Drupal 8 provides the capability to render your site in nearly any language spoken on the planet. Drupal does not do the actual translation of the content; rather, it facilitates the translation by providing the mechanisms that enable visitors to select which language they wish to see (from the list that you offer), and then rendering content that has been previously translated by humans into that language.

After you determine the list of languages that you wish to support, the next step is to enable the multilingual modules that are part of Drupal 8 core. Visit the module administration page by clicking the Manage link in the admin menu at the top of the page, followed by the Extend link in the secondary menu. Scroll down the page until you see the list of multilingual modules that are part of Drupal 8 (see Figure 13-1).

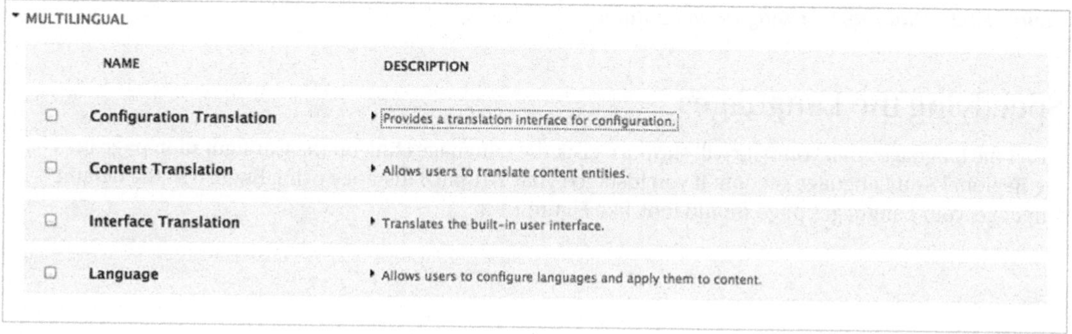

▼ MULTILINGUAL		
	NAME	DESCRIPTION
☐	**Configuration Translation**	▸ Provides a translation interface for configuration.
☐	**Content Translation**	▸ Allows users to translate content entities.
☐	**Interface Translation**	▸ Translates the built-in user interface.
☐	**Language**	▸ Allows users to configure languages and apply them to content.

Figure 13-1. List of multilingual modules

Configuration Translation provides the ability to translate elements of your site such as the site name, vocabularies, menus, blocks, and other configuration related text on your site. The Content Translation module handles all of the content-related text, such as articles. The Interface Translation module provides an easy-to-use interface for translating elements of your site that are static strings, such as form labels, and the Language module is the module that enables the definition of which languages your site supports.

Check all of the modules in the Multilingual category and then click the "Save configuration" button.

Configuring Multilingual Capabilities

The next step in the process is to configure the multilingual capabilities of Drupal 8. Start by navigating to the Configuration page. Click the Manage link in the admin menu, followed by the Configuration link in the secondary menu. On the Configuration page, scroll down until you see the Regional And Language section (see Figure 13-2).

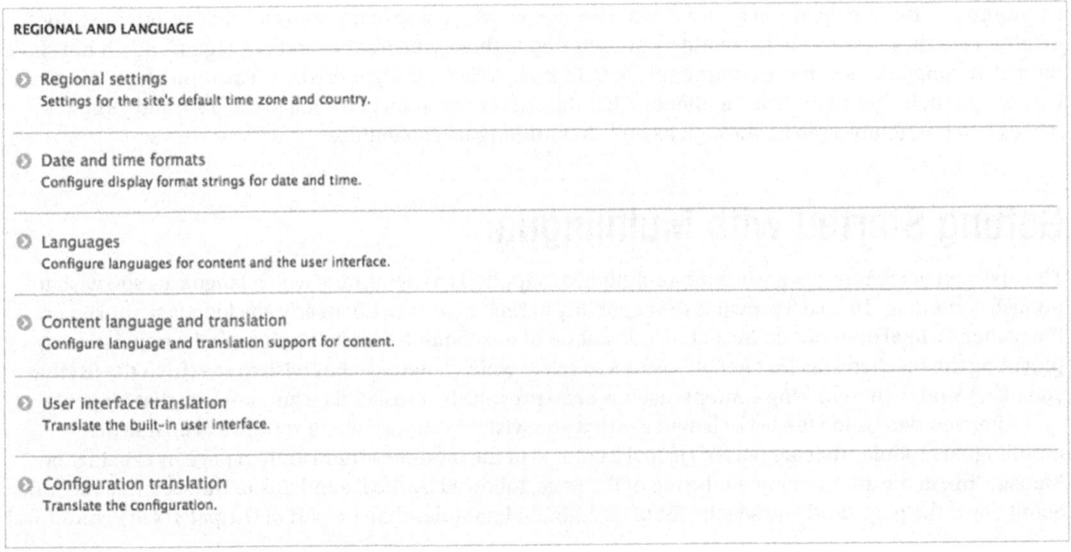

REGIONAL AND LANGUAGE

◎ Regional settings
Settings for the site's default time zone and country.

◎ Date and time formats
Configure display format strings for date and time.

◎ Languages
Configure languages for content and the user interface.

◎ Content language and translation
Configure language and translation support for content.

◎ User interface translation
Translate the built-in user interface.

◎ Configuration translation
Translate the configuration.

Figure 13-2. *Multilingual configuration options*

Specifying the Languages

To set the languages that your site will support, click the Languages link on the Configuration page in the Regional And Language section. If you installed your Drupal 8 instance using English as the default language, your Languages page should look like Figure 13-3.

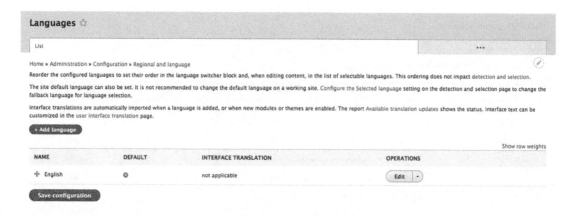

Figure 13-3. *Base language*

To enable a new language, click the "Add language" button and select a language to add to your site from the drop-down list of available language options and click the Add language button (see Figure 13-4).

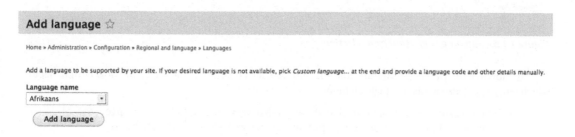

Figure 13-4. *Adding a language*

Configuring Language Activation

After setting the list of languages that you wish to support, the next step is to specify under what conditions Drupal should switch to a different language. At the top of the Languages page, click the Detection and Selection tab to see a list of options to specify when language switching is to occur (see Figure 13-5).

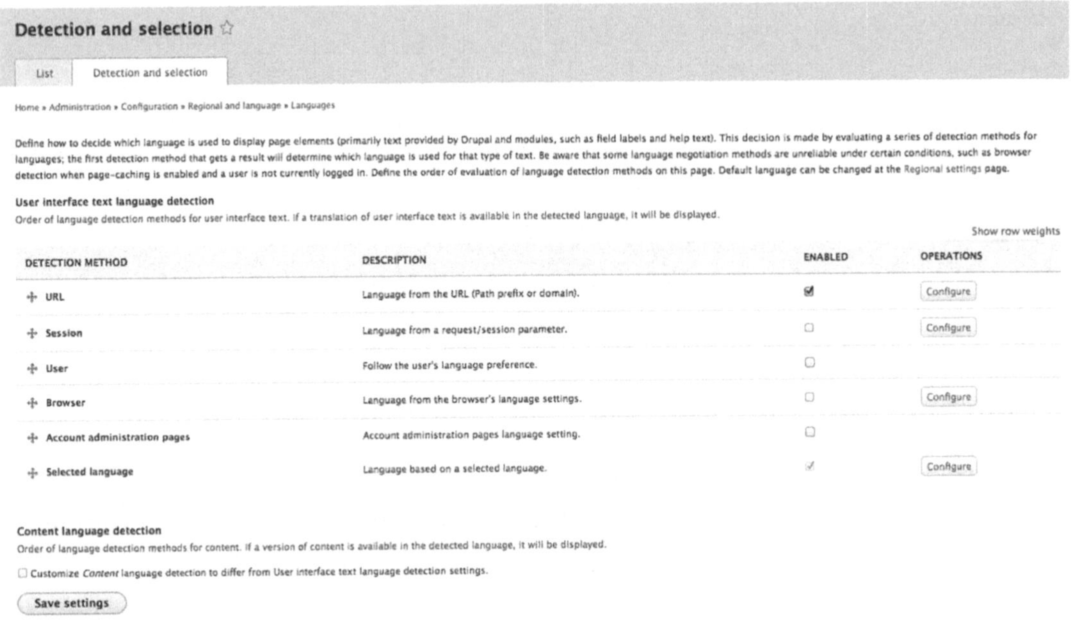

Figure 13-5. *Language detection and selection*

As shown in the Detection Method column, you have several options for specifying how Drupal decides which language to use to display page elements:

- Specify specific URL patterns that apply to languages, such as `http://example.com/en` for the English version and `http://example.com/ru` for the Russian version.

- Session parameters that are set by custom code and stored in a session variable.

- A user's language preference as set on their user profile.

- The browser's default language settings as set in the user's browser preferences.

- Account administration pages allow you to set a different language for the administrative interface and the content portion of your site.

- A user selecting a language from a drop down list or radio buttons in a block on your site. Checking this option enables a block that provides the ability to select the visitors preferred language.

For demonstration purposes check the URL and Selected languages options and click the Save settings button to continue.

Some of the options, such as URL settings, provide the ability to configure the parameters that define how those setting will take effect. Click on the Configure button to see the parameters.

By selecting the Selected languages option we now have access to a block that provides the ability for a user to select which language they prefer. To place that block on a page navigate to the "Block layout" page (Manage ➤ Structure ➤ Block layout) and you'll see in the "Place blocks" list, under the System category, a block named "Language switcher." Click the "Language switcher" link and assign the block to a region provided by your theme. If you are using Bartik, a good choice would be one of the two Sidebar regions. After you select the region, don't forget to click the "Save blocks" button at the bottom of the "Block layout" page. After enabling the "Language switcher" block, your page should look similar to Figure 13-6.

Figure 13-6. Language switcher block

Content Translation Example

With the "Language switcher" block in place, you are now ready to take the next steps of translating content. Return to the Configuration page by clicking the Manage link in the admin menu, followed by clicking the Configuration link on the secondary menu. Click the Languages link on the Configuration page to return to the Languages page. After enabling the languages you want to support, you'll see entries for each in a column titled Interface Translation (see Figure 13-7). For each language, this column shows the number of elements that are already translated (the first number) and total number of elements available to translate, where *elements* are field labels, error messages, or other text strings that are defined in template files and modules. As you can see in Figure 13-7, many elements have already been translated by the Drupal community.

Languages ☆

List   ...

Home » Administration » Configuration » Regional and language

Reorder the configured languages to set their order in the language switcher block and, when editing content, in the list of selectable languages. This ordering does not impact detection and selection.

The site default language can also be set. It is not recommended to change the default language on a working site. Configure the Selected language setting on the detection and selection page to change the fallback language for language selection.

Interface translations are automatically imported when a language is added, or when new modules or themes are enabled. The report Available translation updates shows the status. Interface text can be customized in the user interface translation page.

[+ Add language]

Show row weights

NAME	DEFAULT	INTERFACE TRANSLATION	OPERATIONS
✛ English	⦿	not applicable	[Edit ▾]
✛ French	○	5870/7638 (76.85%)	[Edit ▾]
✛ Hebrew	○	2745/7638 (35.94%)	[Edit ▾]
✛ Spanish	○	7393/7638 (96.79%)	[Edit ▾]

[Save configuration]

Figure 13-7. Interface translation

Clicking any of the values in the Interface Translation column displays the list of elements, with a text box next to each element where the person doing the translation enters the translated text for that text string (see Figure 13-8). To filter the list to only show elements that do not have a translation, click the Search in select list in the Filter translatable strings secton of the page and select Only untranslated strings. Press the Filter button to see the list of items that are missing a translation.

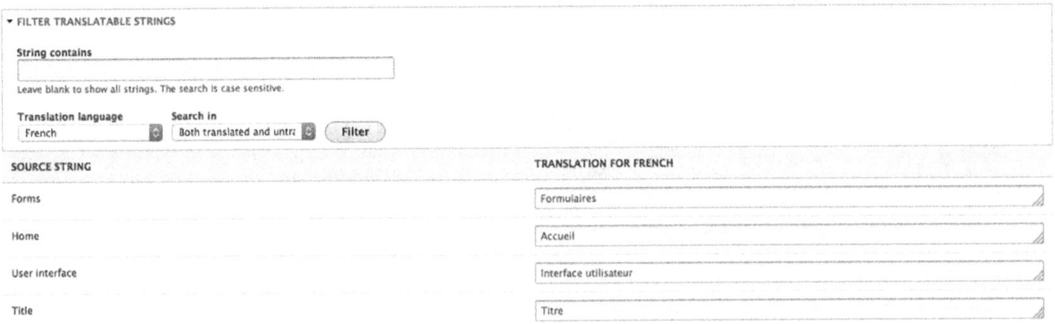

Figure 13-8. *Translation of source strings to alternative language*

After entering values for some or all of the source strings, click the "Save translations" button. Back on the Languages page, the number of strings you have translated will appear in the Interface Translation column, along with the total number of strings and the percentage of strings that have been translated for that language. The total number of strings to be translated may increase as you install new modules, create new forms, or create other features that have interface elements that are translatable. Check this page often to ensure that everything has an associated translation.

Configuring Entities

The next step in the setup of multilingual support on your site is to specify which content types, taxonomy vocabularies, user profiles, or other supported elements are translatable. Return to the Configuration page and click the "Content language and translation" link in the Regional And Language section (refer to Figure 13-2). On this page you will see a list of check boxes related to the types of elements on your site that support translation. Simply check the box next to the elements you wish to provide translation capabilities for. For demonstration purposes, check the boxes for Content, Custom menu link, and Taxonomy term. As you check each box, a list of options appears where you can set the translation capabilities for that element (see Figure 13-9).

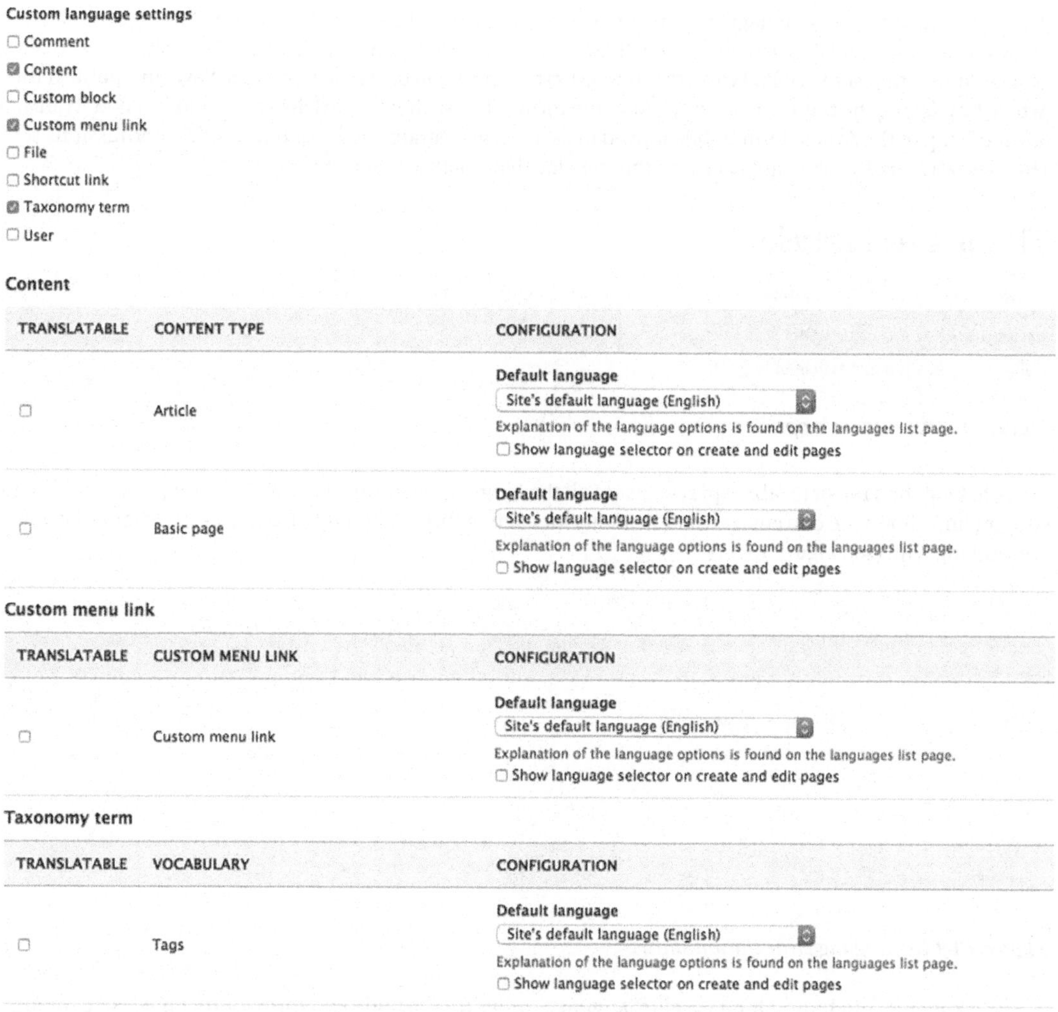

Custom language settings

☐ Comment
☑ Content
☐ Custom block
☑ Custom menu link
☐ File
☐ Shortcut link
☑ Taxonomy term
☐ User

Content

TRANSLATABLE	CONTENT TYPE	CONFIGURATION
☐	Article	**Default language** Site's default language (English) Explanation of the language options is found on the languages list page. ☐ Show language selector on create and edit pages
☐	Basic page	**Default language** Site's default language (English) Explanation of the language options is found on the languages list page. ☐ Show language selector on create and edit pages

Custom menu link

TRANSLATABLE	CUSTOM MENU LINK	CONFIGURATION
☐	Custom menu link	**Default language** Site's default language (English) Explanation of the language options is found on the languages list page. ☐ Show language selector on create and edit pages

Taxonomy term

TRANSLATABLE	VOCABULARY	CONFIGURATION
☐	Tags	**Default language** Site's default language (English) Explanation of the language options is found on the languages list page. ☐ Show language selector on create and edit pages

Figure 13-9. Content language configuration

Checking the box, for example, for the Article content type displays additional details as to which elements of that item are translatable. For the Article content type, this includes the title, body, comment settings, image, and tag fields. For demonstration purposes, check all the boxes for all the elements, followed by clicking the Save button.

Translating Content

With the pieces in place, the next step is to author content in the site's native language and translate it to the various languages that your site has been configured to support. For demonstration purposes, assuming you checked the box for Article in the previous step, create a test article in the native language set for your site. Click the Manage link on the admin menu, the Content link in the secondary menu, and the "Add content" button on the Content page. Select Article as the type of content to create. Note that a new field appears on the "Create article" form, the "Language select" list. For demonstration purposes, select the default language that represents the base language of your site (e.g., if you installed the English version of Drupal 8, select English from the select list). On my Drupal 8 example site, I created an Article in English using "This is a test article" for the title, and "Hello World this is a test article in English." as the body text. Save and publish the Article by clicking the button at the bottom of the form. After saving the article, you'll notice a new Translate tab at the top of the Article form (while logged in as an administrator with content-editing permissions set). The new tab allows you instant access to the translate feature (see Figure 13-10).

This is a test article

| View | Edit | Delete | Translate |

Submitted by admin on Sun, 02/09/2014 - 22:31

Hello World this is a test article in English.

Figure 13-10. Translate option

Clicking the Translate tab displays a list of all the languages you specified while configuring multilingual support and shows the current translation status for each of those languages for the content item that you are working with (see Figure 13-11).

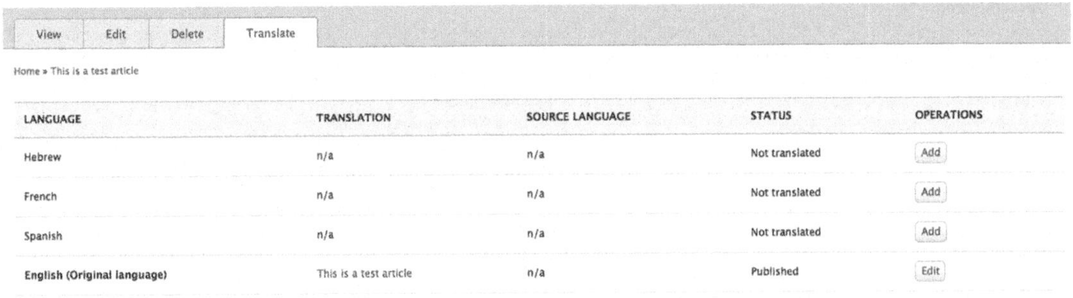

| View | Edit | Delete | Translate |

Home » This is a test article

LANGUAGE	TRANSLATION	SOURCE LANGUAGE	STATUS	OPERATIONS
Hebrew	n/a	n/a	Not translated	Add
French	n/a	n/a	Not translated	Add
Spanish	n/a	n/a	Not translated	Add
English (Original language)	This is a test article	n/a	Published	Edit

Figure 13-11. Language translation status

Clicking the Add button for a specific language brings up the node edit form for that piece of content, allowing you (or another human translator) to see the original-language version of that content item, with the ability to override that version with the translated version. Pick one of your languages from the list and give it a try. Here is my test article being translated into French (see Figure 13-12).

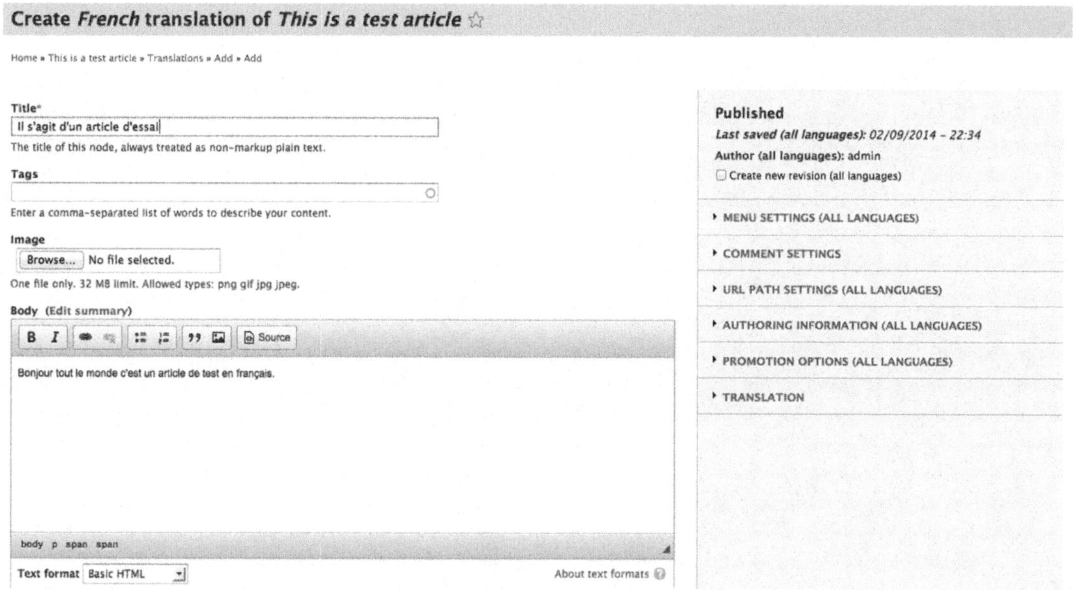

Create *French* translation of *This is a test article* ☆

Home » This is a test article » Translations » Add » Add

Title*

Il s'agit d'un article d'essai

The title of this node, always treated as non-markup plain text.

Tags

Enter a comma-separated list of words to describe your content.

Image

Browse... | No file selected.

One file only. 32 MB limit. Allowed types: png gif jpg jpeg.

Body (Edit summary)

B I ⚭ ⚏ ⋮⋮ ⋮⋮ ⟩⟩ 🖼 ⬒ Source

Bonjour tout le monde c'est un article de test en français.

body p span span

Text format | Basic HTML ▾   About text formats ❓

Published

Last saved (all languages): 02/09/2014 – 22:34

Author (all languages): admin

☐ Create new revision (all languages)

▸ MENU SETTINGS (ALL LANGUAGES)

▸ COMMENT SETTINGS

▸ URL PATH SETTINGS (ALL LANGUAGES)

▸ AUTHORING INFORMATION (ALL LANGUAGES)

▸ PROMOTION OPTIONS (ALL LANGUAGES)

▸ TRANSLATION

Figure 13-12. *Translating an article into French*

After you click the "Save and keep published" button, Drupal will display the article in the language that you just translated it into, highlighting the language in the "Language switcher" block. Try completing the translation in all of the other languages by following the preceding steps, beginning with clicking the Translate tab. After you have translated the Article into all of the languages, test the "Language switcher" block to view the Article in each translation. If you selected a left-to-right language (I chose Hebrew), you'll note that Drupal renders the page a little differently, moving elements such as the "Language switcher" block from the left to the right (assuming you placed the block in the Sidebar First region of the Bartik theme).

If you edit a content item and change any of the fields (e.g., the title or body in an article), remember that the other translations need to be updated to reflect the change.

Summary

In this chapter I demonstrated Drupal 8's capability to handle multilingual content. This is a feature-rich and powerful tool for sites that wish to reach a broader audience than just the native language in which the site is written. Translating your content into multiple languages literally opens the opportunity to reach the world—just one of Drupal 8's powerful features and capabilities.

CHAPTER 14

■ ■ ■

Administering Your Drupal Site

If you have followed along in the previous chapters, you now have enough knowledge to build a Drupal 8-based website. Building your website and releasing it to the world is an exciting experience, and one that often brings with it great pride and joy. Whether your site has two or three pages or hundreds, deploying a website and seeing traffic on it is a rewarding and enriching experience. Deploying your website is just a step along the journey; it is by no means the end. As the proud owner of a website, you must monitor it, nurture it, expand it, and support it, all of which are involved in administering your website.

Administering a Drupal website can be a relatively simple task, depending on the size of your site, the number of users, the number of users who have the ability to author content, and the number of modules that you've installed. Over the past several years, I've created a number of personal "pet" project websites that are up and running, and I rarely do anything other than go out and glimpse at the site logs. There are other sites that I have built that require more attention, and the amount of attention really depends on the criteria I just mentioned.

Typical site administration tasks that you will want to consider performing on a periodic basis include

- Backing up the site so you can restore it should anything disastrous happen.

- Backing up the file system.

- Checking the logs to see if there are any errors that you need to address.

- Checking to see if there are any security patches to modules you have installed.

- Checking to see if there are any module upgrades that make sense to deploy on your site.

- Checking to see if there are any Drupal core updates that you need to deploy.

- Approving requests for new user accounts.

In this chapter, I'll describe in detail each of these administrative tasks.

Backing Up and Restoring Your Site

If you don't do anything else on this list of administrative tasks, at least make sure that your data is safe and recoverable in the case of an unexpected disaster. It's easy to put off backing up your site, as it's likely that you'll rarely need to go back and restore your site from a backup. But speaking from experience, the first time you need to restore your site but don't have a backup is the last time you won't have backups in place from the start. Take it from the voice of experience: the few minutes it takes to set up backups are well spent.

There are three paths to take to address backups on your new site:

- You can use utilities that your hosting provider gives to you to back up your database and directories.

- You can use a Drupal module called Backup and Migrate to automatically back up your site's database on a defined schedule, and, just as important, to easily restore your site from a previous backup.

- You can use Drush to download a copy of your site and database.

All three approaches work equally well, and the Backup and Migrate module is a perfect solution for those who are less inclined to use operating system–level commands to schedule backups and to create the scripts necessary to back up your Drupal site. The first approach is too broad to cover here because it varies widely depending on your hosting provider, so I'll present only the latter two approaches. I'll then show you how to restore a site you've backed up with either method.

Backing Up with the Backup and Restore Module

You will need to install the Backup and Migrate module, because it is not part of Drupal core. You can find details for this module at `www.drupal.org/project/backup_migrate`. To install the module, follow the steps covered in Chapter 11.

To access the Backup and Migrate configuration page, go to `http://localhost/admin/content/backup_migrate` (replacing `http://localhost` with the actual URL where your site resides). After pressing Enter, you will see the configuration panel for the Backup and Migrate module.

The first step in configuring the Backup and Migrate module is to define where backup files will be stored on the server. Click the Destinations tab at the top of the page, revealing the page shown in Figure 14-1. There are two settings for where files will be stored: one for manual backups, where the site administrator clicks a "Backup now" link to perform the backup, and the automatic backup. I'll explain how to set up automatic backups in a minute. You can also set the database that you want backed up. By default, the module automatically detects the database that your site is running on and sets the parameter. You may choose to override the default directories and database that are set during the process of installing the module, or you may, as I do, leave the defaults.

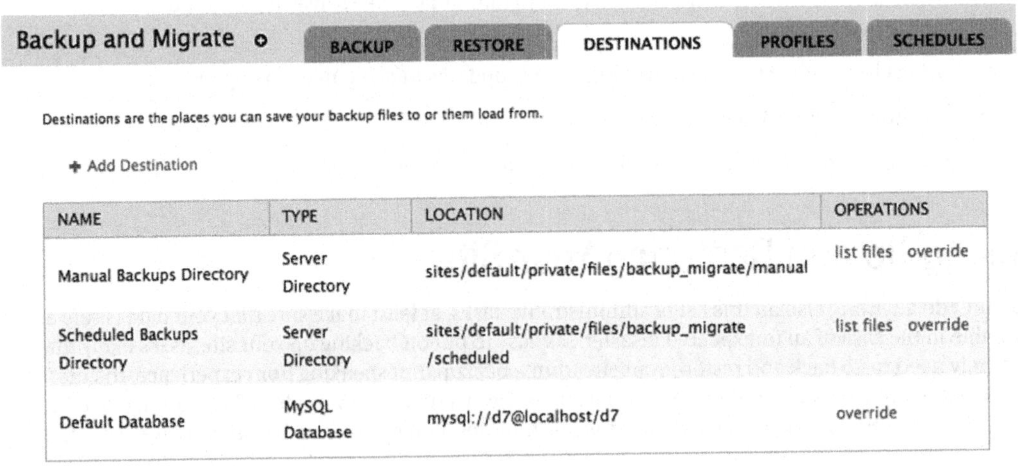

Backup and Migrate ✪   BACKUP   RESTORE   **DESTINATIONS**   PROFILES   SCHEDULES

Destinations are the places you can save your backup files to or them load from.

✚ Add Destination

NAME	TYPE	LOCATION	OPERATIONS
Manual Backups Directory	Server Directory	sites/default/private/files/backup_migrate/manual	list files override
Scheduled Backups Directory	Server Directory	sites/default/private/files/backup_migrate /scheduled	list files override
Default Database	MySQL Database	mysql://d7@localhost/d7	override

Figure 14-1. Setting the destination directories for backups

The next step is to set the schedule for automatic backups. To do so, click the Schedules tab at the top of the page, revealing the configuration options shown in Figure 14-2. If you haven't set a schedule previously, the page will simply display an "Add schedule" link. Click that link to view the parameters that you can set for scheduling backups. First, enter a name for the Schedule. We are going to set the backups to be performed on a daily basis, so enter "Daily Backups" as the name. Next, set the "Backup every" field to 1 Day(s). Finally, set the "Number of Backup files to keep" to 14, meaning Drupal will retain 14 days' of backups before deleting the oldest backup file and storing the newest file. This helps protect you from consuming massive amounts of disk space for old backup files. Set this value carefully. You may have legal requirements in your industry that require that you keep backup files for a certain number of days, weeks, months, or years. Finally, click the "Save schedule" button.

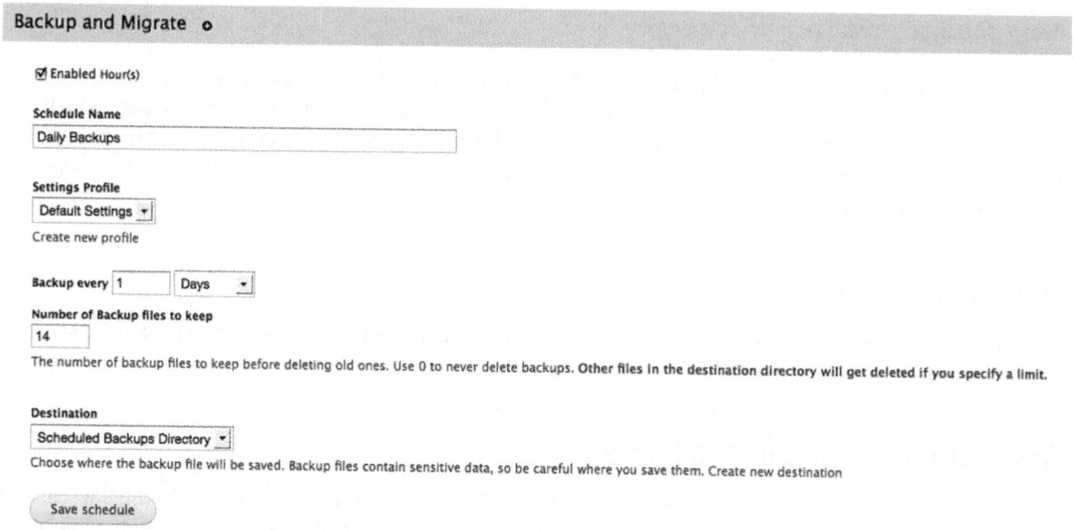

Backup and Migrate ○

☑ Enabled Hour(s)

Schedule Name

Daily Backups

Settings Profile

Default Settings ▾

Create new profile

Backup every 1   Days ▾

Number of Backup files to keep

14

The number of backup files to keep before deleting old ones. Use 0 to never delete backups. Other files in the destination directory will get deleted if you specify a limit.

Destination

Scheduled Backups Directory ▾

Choose where the backup file will be saved. Backup files contain sensitive data, so be careful where you save them. Create new destination

(Save schedule)

Figure 14-2. *Setting up the automatic backup schedule*

Drupal will now automatically back up the site on a daily basis. The last step is to perform a manual backup of your site. To do so, click the Backup tab (see Figure 14-3). On the resulting page, select the Default Database as the database to back up from, set the "to" option to the Manual Backups Directory (you can also select Download, which will download the backup to your local computer), and set the "using" option to Default Settings. Finally, click the "Backup now" button.

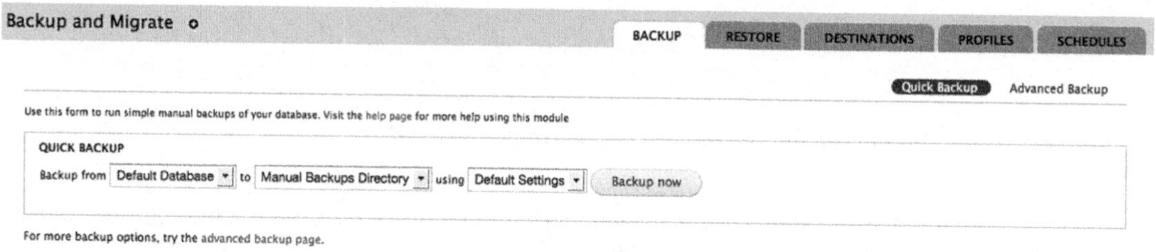

Backup and Migrate ○   BACKUP   RESTORE   DESTINATIONS   PROFILES   SCHEDULES

Quick Backup   Advanced Backup

Use this form to run simple manual backups of your database. Visit the help page for more help using this module

QUICK BACKUP

Backup from Default Database ▾ to Manual Backups Directory ▾ using Default Settings ▾ (Backup now)

For more backup options, try the advanced backup page.

Figure 14-3. *Manually backing up your site*

When the backup is completed, Drupal will redisplay the screen with information including the name of the backup file that was generated, the directory where it was stored, and how long the backup took to execute.

Backing Up with Drush

Using Drush from the command line provides a simple solution for those who are comfortable with the command line. To back up the database only, simply execute the following Drush command from a command prompt while positioned within the directory structure of your site, replacing <filename> with the name of the file you wish to create:

```
drush sql-dump -result-file=<filename>
```

This results in a SQL dump being created and stored in the root directory of your Drupal site. If you wish to back up your entire site, including code, files, and the database, use drush archive-dump, which results in an archive with three files in it, a file for the database, code, and files. In the case of archive-dump, Drush creates a file name for the archive based on date and time and reports where it places that file upon completion of the process.

Restoring a Backup

If, for some reason, you need to restore your system to a previously backed-up state, you can use the same tool that you used to create the backup, as described next.

Restoring with Backup and Migrate

If you need to restore your system from a backup created with Backup and Migrate, return to the Backup and Migrate administration page (http://localhost/admin/content/backup_migrate) and select the backup file to restore. Click the Destinations tab, revealing the list of destination directories where backups are stored. See Figure 14-4.

Backup and Migrate ○		BACKUP RESTORE **DESTINATIONS** PROFILES SCHEDULES	

Destinations are the places you can save your backup files to or them load from.

✦ Add Destination

NAME	TYPE	LOCATION	OPERATIONS
Manual Backups Directory	Server Directory	sites/default/private/files/backup_migrate/manual	list files override
Scheduled Backups Directory	Server Directory	sites/default/private/files/backup_migrate/scheduled	list files override
Default Database	MySQL Database	mysql://d7@localhost/d7	override

Figure 14-4. Listing the backup directories where backup files are stored

Because we backed up our system using the manual backup process, click the "list files" link for Manual Backups Directory, revealing the page shown in Figure 14-5.

<em class="placeholder">Manual Backups Directory</em> Files ○		BACKUP	RESTORE	DESTINATIONS	PROFILES	SCHEDULES

FILENAME	DATE	AGE ▼	SIZE	OPERATIONS		
Drupal7DemoSite-2010-04-09T21-38-52.mysql	Fri, 04/09/2010 – 21:38	5 min	702.81 KB	download	restore	delete

Figure 14-5. The Manual Backups Directory and the file to restore

In this example, we could restore our system to the state it was in at the time we did the manual backup by simply clicking the "restore" link for that backup file. If you have scheduled backups enabled and have not manually backed up your system, the process described would be identical, with the exception of selecting the "list files" link for the Scheduled Backups Directory. Clicking that link would reveal a list of backup files that were automatically created based on the schedule that you set in the previous steps.

Restoring with Drush

Using drush from the command line provides a simple solution for those who are comfortable with the command line. To restore the database only from a backup created using `drush sql-dump` simply execute the following drush command from a command prompt while positioned within the directory structure of your site (replacing `example.sql` with the name of the file you created using the `sql-dump` command):

```
drush sql-connect < example.sql
```

To restore an entire site from an `archive-dump`, use `drush archive-restore <filename>`, where `<filename>` is the name of the archive that contains the code, database, and files.

Backing Up the File System

The Backup and Migrate module only backs up the contents of your Drupal database. The Drupal installation itself, meaning Drupal core, all of the contributed modules you have installed, all of the themes you have installed, any customizations you have made to modules, and any files that users have uploaded, will not be saved by the Backup and Migrate module.

There are several options for backing up the file system:

- Simply copy the entire Drupal directory to another destination (for example, download the site to your local PC if you are running on a hosted server).

- Copy the Drupal directory to a USB/CD/DVD if you are running on your local desktop/laptop.

- In the case of a hosted environment, work with your provider to ensure that your Drupal directory is being backed up often enough to ensure minimal disruption in the case of a disaster.

- Use the command line and create an archive (e.g., tar) of the site.

Whichever scenario you choose, you should back up the file system on a frequent basis if users are uploading and attaching files to content (even daily, just as you do with your Backup and Migrate schedule), and in a case where you do not allow file attachments and uploads, it is still a good idea to back up your file system on at least a weekly basis (due to module updates).

Restoring the File System

To restore the file system copy the backup you created in the previous steps to the root directory of your site on the server. If you used a compression tool such as tar or zip, uncompress the file in the root directory.

Checking the Log Files

With backups in place, the next administrative task is to periodically check the log files to see if there are errors in the system that need to be corrected (for example, "page not found" errors). To view the log files, click the Reports link in the top menu, revealing a list of reports that are available to help you administer your new Drupal site. See Figure 14-6.

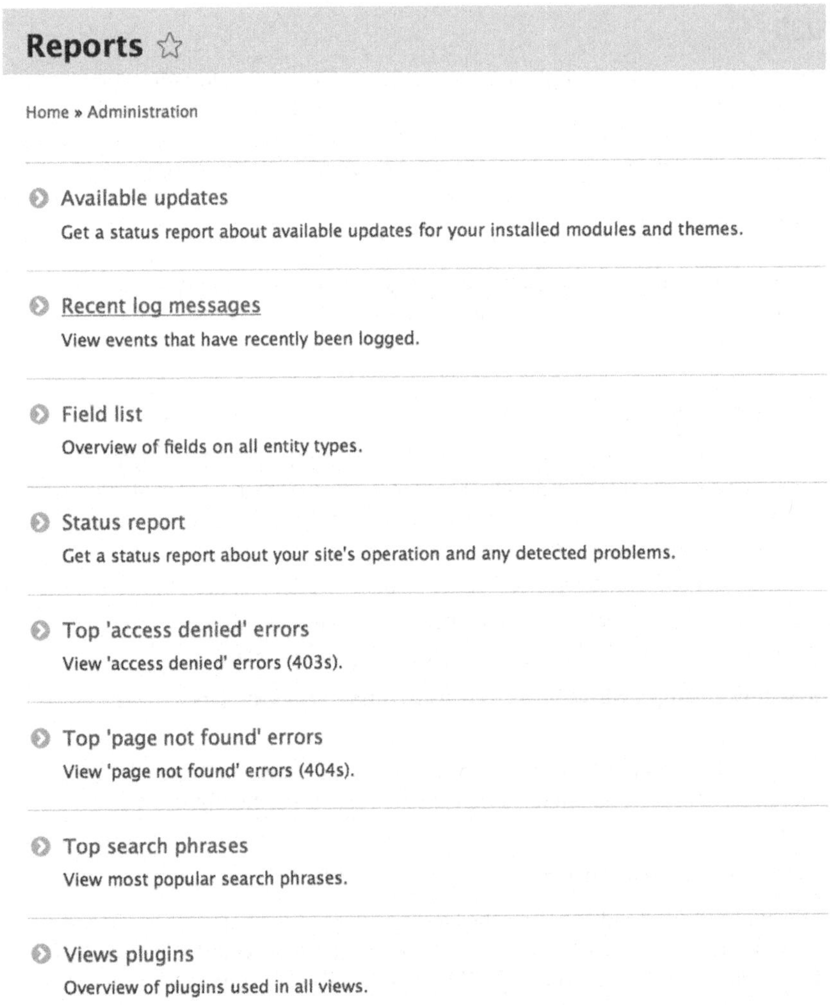

Reports ☆

Home » Administration

⊙ Available updates

Get a status report about available updates for your installed modules and themes.

⊙ Recent log messages

View events that have recently been logged.

⊙ Field list

Overview of fields on all entity types.

⊙ Status report

Get a status report about your site's operation and any detected problems.

⊙ Top 'access denied' errors

View 'access denied' errors (403s).

⊙ Top 'page not found' errors

View 'page not found' errors (404s).

⊙ Top search phrases

View most popular search phrases.

⊙ Views plugins

Overview of plugins used in all views.

Figure 14-6. *List of standard reports*

There are three reports that I will focus on in this section (you can easily view the other reports by simply clicking the links): Recent log messages, Top 'page not found' errors, and Status report. (I'll cover available updates later in this chapter.)

Recent Log Messages

Drupal provides a rich framework for recording events in the system that may be of interest to someone who is administering a Drupal site. Module developers and Drupal core maintainers leverage this capability to log any events that they feel are important enough to warrant an entry in the log file. If you click the "Recent log messages" link, you will see a report that looks similar to Figure 14-7.

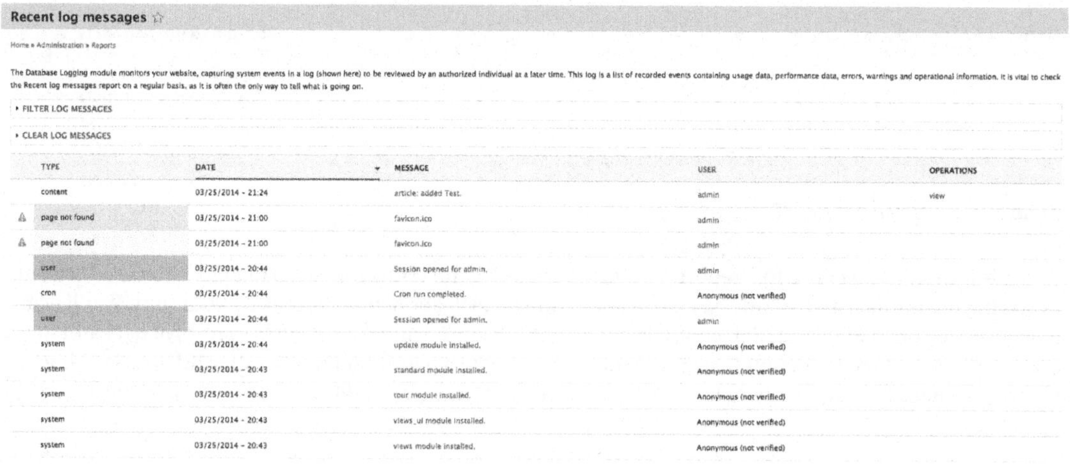

Figure 14-7. *Recent log messages*

Your messages will be different from those shown in Figure 14-7, because the actions you have performed will have been different. This list of messages includes both errors and successful events (for example, a user logging in to the system results in a log entry that shows the date and time of when they logged in). Simply click the message to see whatever details the module or Drupal core developer deemed appropriate to share with a site administrator. The best resource for resolving errors that you may see are the Drupal.org website and the specific module's issue queue that is generating the errors. If you do not find answers on the module's homepage, the next step is to consult the forums on the Drupal.org website. It is highly unlikely that you're the first one to encounter the error, and if you are, posting a request for help in the forum will typically result in a rapid response from someone who knows how to solve the issue.

Top 'Page Not Found' Errors

Returning to the Reports main page and clicking the "Top 'page not found' errors" link reveals a list of "404" errors, or "page not found," errors. See Figure 14-8.

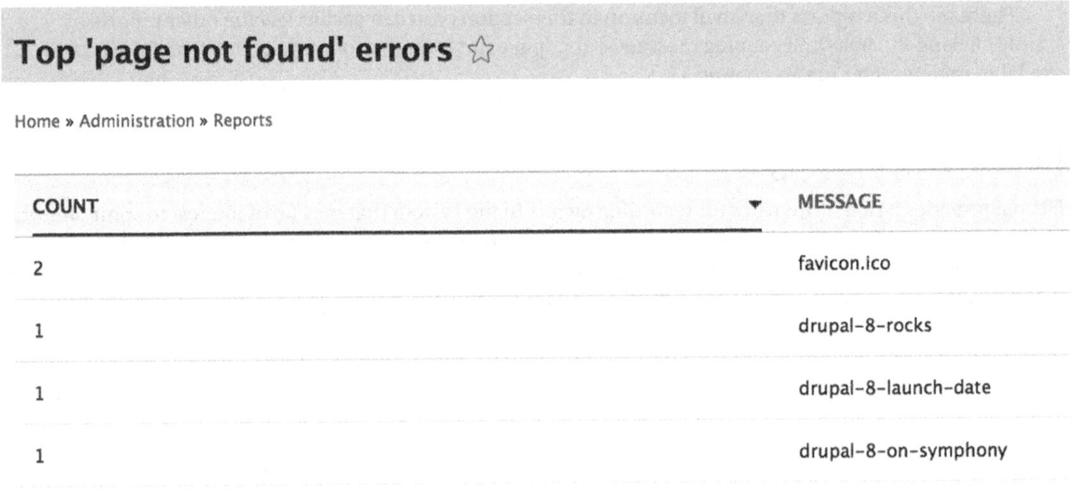

Top 'page not found' errors ☆

Home » Administration » Reports

COUNT ▼	MESSAGE
2	favicon.ico
1	drupal-8-rocks
1	drupal-8-launch-date
1	drupal-8-on-symphony

Figure 14-8. *"Page not found" report*

It is important to check this report periodically to see if site visitors are clicking links that are "broken." Resolving the errors listed on this page may take some investigation and analysis on your part. You'll want to focus on errors that have a high count, as they are likely impacting site visitors. To resolve page not found errors, you have three basic options: ignore the errors, create a page that matches the URL that is being reported as page not found, or create redirect rules in your .htaccess file to redirect those requests to a valid URL.

Status Report

A general "health" report for your site can be accessed from the Reports page by clicking the "Status report" link. Clicking this link reveals a page that highlights key areas of your Drupal installation that are of relatively high importance (see Figure 14-9). Items that are checked when you run this report include whether critical configuration files are protected from unauthorized changes and whether the database is up to date.

In Drupal 8, with the revised approach for installing modules, it's unlikely that the database will become out of date. If it is reported as out of date, run the http://localhost/core/update.php script to synchronize the database with the current state of your modules (replacing http://localhost with the actual URL of where your site resides).

Status report ☆

Home » Administration » Reports

Here you can find a short overview of your site's parameters as well as any problems detected with your installation. It may be useful to copy and paste this information into support requests filed on drupal.org's support forums and project issue queues. Before filing a support request, ensure that your web server meets the system requirements.

Drupal	8.0-dev
Access to update.php	Protected
⊗ Configuration files	Not protected
	The file *sites/default/settings.php* is not protected from modifications and poses a security risk. You must change the file's permissions to be non-writable.
Cron maintenance tasks	Last run 49 min 18 sec ago
	You can run cron manually.
	To run cron from outside the site, go to http://loc.d8/cron/ig1t0LeBdw262MHY8ZTIMaoXM9RWchq2puTwc1D2dYzVCC2FotZ6hOdMZjPGc2gNVGrXthupew
Database system	MySQL, MariaDB, Percona Server, or equivalent
Database system version	5.5.25
Database updates	Up to date

Figure 14-9. *Status report*

You are most likely to see issues regarding the status of Drupal core, contributed modules, and themes. If there is an updated version of Drupal or if a contributed module or theme has been updated on Drupal. org, these items will appear as yellow.

Checking for Updates and Security Patches

If the status report shows that module or theme updates are available, you'll want to check to see which types of updates are available. There are three general categories of updates that you will want to pay attention to both as you develop your new site and once the site is in production:

- Security patches
- Module updates
- Drupal core updates

In most cases you will want to address security updates as soon as possible, whereas you may choose to address module updates and Drupal core updates on a monthly, quarterly, or even less frequent basis. Module and Drupal core updates typically address bugs that were found in a module or Drupal core and/or offer new features that were added to the module or Drupal core. As the site administrator, you will need to determine, by looking at the release notes for each update, whether the update is something you should do immediately (for example, fixing a bug that you have struggled with on your site) or can delay.

To check to see if there are any security patches or updates, click the "Out of date" link on the Status report next to the modules and themes item. The "Out of date" report lists all modules and themes that you have installed on your site that have available updates on Drupal.org. It's a good idea to visit each module's page on Drupal.org to see if there are any critical bugs reported for the new version of the module, before you decide to download and install it. I have experienced cases where a new version of a contributed module that I have installed on one of my sites introduced new bugs that I didn't have on the site prior to the upgrade. It's a good idea to check before upgrading.

To install the updates for a theme or module, simply click the "Download the updates." Drupal will automatically download, install, and enable the updates. See Figure 14-10.

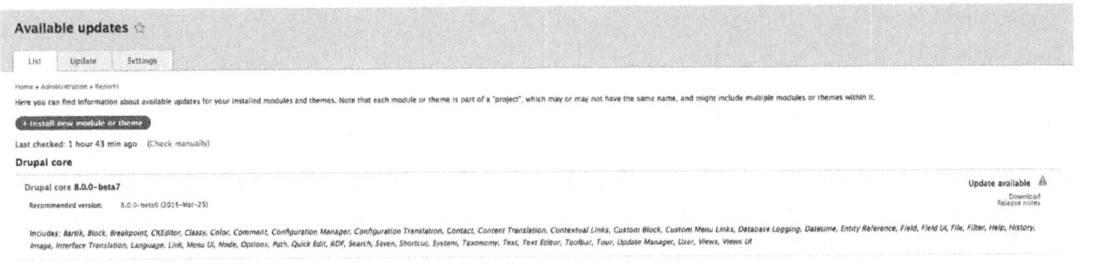

Figure 14-10. *Available module and theme updates*

In a case where Drupal core is updated, the process is slightly more complex. To update Drupal core:

1. Make sure you back up your database!

2. Make sure you back up your entire Drupal directory!

3. Using Drush, run the following command: `drush up drupal`.

4. Test your site.

An alternative approach for updating Drupal core is to first back up the modules, profiles, sites, and themes directories in the root directory of your site, and the `.htaccess` and `web.config` files. Once you have secured copies of those directories, download Drupal core and extract the archive file in the root directory of your site. The extraction process will place Drupal in a subdirectory with a name of the version that you downloaded (e.g., `drupal-8.0.0-beta7`). You'll need to move all of the files from this subdirectory to the root directory of your site. To do so on Linux/OS X, use the following commands:

```
mv * ../
mv .* ../
```

On other operating systems, use the tools available to you to move files and directories.

Once you have moved Drupal into place, proceed with moving the directories and files that you backed up into their respective locations in the root directory of your site.

Approving Requests for User Accounts

Drupal lets you, the site administrator, determine how user accounts are created on your website. You can

-   Allow site visitors to create their own accounts without approval by a site administrator.

-   Allow site visitors to register an account, but require that a site administrator approve it before allowing the visitor to use the account.

-   Restrict account creation to only the site administrator.

The approach you use is completely dependent on whether you allow visitors to have their own accounts. There is no reason to provide this feature if you don't provide interactive features on your site. If you provide limited capabilities for authenticated users (for example, if you don't enable permissions for any administrative features to the generic "authenticated users" category) and you don't want to be bothered with enabling user accounts, then allowing visitors to create accounts without approval is appropriate. If you want control over who has an account, then you will want to configure your site so that visitors can register an account but you must approve their requests before their accounts become active.

To set how your site handles user accounts, click the Configuration link in the top menu, revealing the main Configuration page for your site. On this page, you will see a category of options for "People." Within this category you will see a link for Account Settings. Click the link to reveal the account settings page, shown in Figure 4-11.

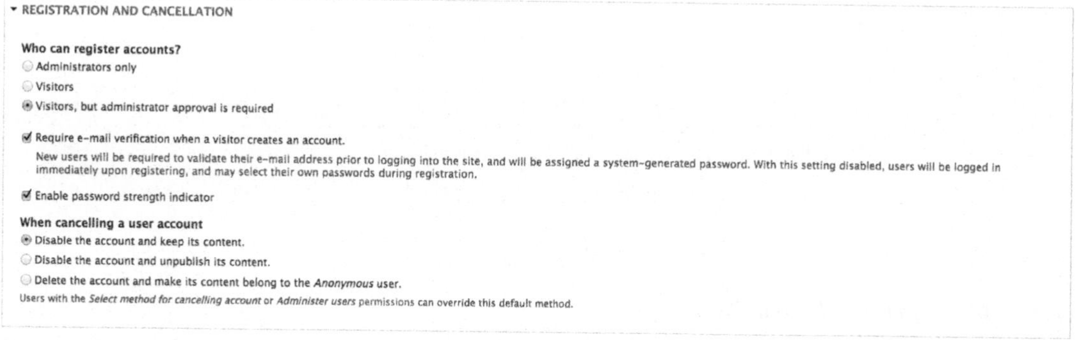

▼ REGISTRATION AND CANCELLATION

Who can register accounts?
◯ Administrators only
◯ Visitors
◉ Visitors, but administrator approval is required

☑ Require e-mail verification when a visitor creates an account.
New users will be required to validate their e-mail address prior to logging into the site, and will be assigned a system-generated password. With this setting disabled, users will be logged in immediately upon registering, and may select their own passwords during registration.

☑ Enable password strength indicator

When cancelling a user account
◉ Disable the account and keep its content.
◯ Disable the account and unpublish its content.
◯ Delete the account and make its content belong to the *Anonymous* user.
Users with the *Select method for cancelling account* or *Administer users* permissions can override this default method.

Figure 14-11. *Account settings page*

On this page, you will find a section titled Registration And Cancellation. In Figure 14-11, the option is set where visitors can register a user account, but administrator approval is required.

To see how this feature works, click the "Log out" link at the top right-hand corner of the page, which will return you to your site's homepage as an anonymous user (not logged into the site).

In the left column, under the login form, there is a link for "Create new account." Click that link to see the form where a new user can request a new account.

The visitor needs to provide a username and a valid e-mail address to create a new account. Once these values have been entered and the visitor has clicked "Create new account," Drupal redisplays your site's homepage with a message that their account is pending approval by the site administrator.

You, as the site administrator, must now enable their account. To do so, click the People link at the top of the page to see the list of users on your site. See Figure 14-12.

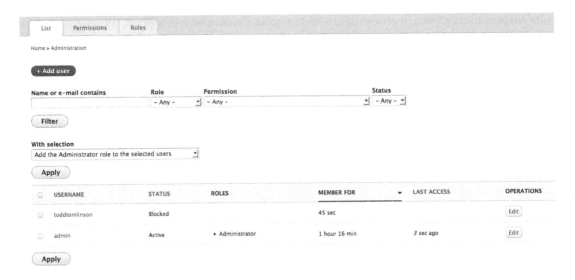

Figure 14-12. *New user listed as Blocked*

In Figure 14-12, you can see that a user account was just created for toddtomlinson, and that the user's status is set to Blocked, meaning the user is blocked from logging into the site.

If your site has several user accounts, you may wish to filter the list to find only those user accounts that are blocked and hence need to be activated. To filter the list, click the Status select list in the fields above the Filter button and select "blocked.

Next, click the Filter button to limit the list of users shown on the page to only those that are blocked and need to be activated. Click the check box next to each of the users that you wish to activate, and make sure that the Update Options select list is set to "Unblock the selected user(s)." Click the Update button.

Once the updates have completed the Status column now shows that our new user, toddtomlinson, is Active. See Figure 14-13.

	USERNAME	STATUS	ROLES	MEMBER FOR ▾	LAST ACCESS	OPERATIONS
☐	toddtomlinson	Active		2 min 43 sec		Edit
☐	admin	Active	• Administrator	1 hour 18 min	2 min 1 sec ago	Edit

Figure 14-13. *All users now set to Active*

Summary

In this chapter, I covered the basics of administering a Drupal website. I explained the key administrative tasks associated with running your new site.

Depending on the complexity of your site and the features you have deployed, there may be other administrative tasks that are specific to those additional features. This list will get you started down the path to ensuring that your site is backed up, error free, and up to date. For additional Drupal administrative topics, visit the Drupal.org website.

Wow, we've covered a lot of information up to this point. You now have the knowledge necessary to build simple to complex websites on Drupal, and you now know how to administer your new site. The next chapter provides an overview of the Drush a tool.

CHAPTER 15

Using Drush

This chapter provides a basic overview of Drush, a command-line tool that greatly simplifies the tasks of building and administering a Drupal 8 website. With Drush, tasks that often require logging onto your site, navigating to a site administration page, and filling out a form can now be performed with a simple command-line interface. Drush also enables you to administer one or several sites remotely, without having to log onto each server and each site to perform routine maintenance tasks. Drush handles most of the tasks associated with managing modules, themes, and user profiles and common administrative tasks like running cron, creating backups, and clearing caches. You can even execute SQL command from Drush.

Installing Drush

Drush is at its core a set of shell scripts (Unix/Linux) or bat scripts (Windows), combined with PHP scripts that handle most of the common tasks of administering a Drupal site. Installing the scripts and PHP is a relatively straightforward process on both Unix/Linux and Windows.

Installing Drush on Unix, Linux, or OS X

To install Drush on Unix, Linux, or OS X, follow these steps:

1. Download Drush from `https://github.com/drush-ops/drush`. In the right column of the Drush landing page on GitHub, you will see a Download ZIP button. If you are familiar with Git (see Chapter 16), you may wish to clone the Git repository so that updates to Drush are easier to manage. For information on cloning repositories, see Chapter 16.

2. Place the uncompressed `drush.zip` file in a directory that is outside of your web root. On most web servers, the webroot will be something like `public_html` or `www_root` or `docroot`. Review your web server's documentation for details on where the web root directory resides. For security purposes, you don't want to place it in your web root, as it would then be available and executable by anyone.

3. Make the `drush` command executable:

   ```
   $ chmod u+x /path/to/drush/drush
   ```

4. Configure your system to recognize where Drush resides. There are three options:

   a. Create a symbolic link to the Drush executable in a directory that is already in your PATH; for example:

      ```
      $ ln -s /path/to/drush/drush /usr/bin/drush
      ```

   b. Explicitly add the Drush executable to the PATH variable, which is defined in the shell configuration file, called .profile, .bash_profile, .bash_aliases, or .bashrc, that is located in your home folder; for example:

      ```
      export PATH="$PATH:/path/to/drush:/usr/local/bin"
      ```

      Your system will search path options from left to right until it finds a result.

   c. Add an alias for Drush; this method can also be handy if you want to use two versions of Drush, such as Drush 5 or 6 (stable) for Drupal 7 development and Drush 7 (master) for Drupal 8 development. To add an alias to your Drush 7 executable, add this to your shell configuration file (see list in previous option):

      ```
      $ alias drush-master=/path/to/drush/drush
      ```

   For options b and c, to apply your changes to your current session, either log out and then log back in again, or reload your bash configuration file as follows:

   ```
   $ source .bashrc
   ```

■ **Note** If you do not follow this step, you will need to (inconveniently) run Drush commands either by using the full path to the executable, /path/to/drush/drush, or by navigating to /path/to/drush and running Drush ./drush. The -r or -l option will be required (see USAGE, below).

---

5. Test that Drush is found by your system:

   ```
   $ which drush
   ```

6. From Drush root, run Composer to fetch dependencies:

   ```
   $ composer install
   ```

For more information about Composer, please visit https://getcomposer.org/doc/00-intro.md.

Installing Drush on Windows

To install Drush on Windows visit https://www.drupal.org/node/594744 for the latest instructions on how to install Drush on Windows. The approach varies for version of Drush and version of Windows.

Drush Commands

Executing Drush commands is relatively simple and straightforward. From a terminal window or other tool that allows you to access the command line of your operating system, navigate to the document root directory of your Drupal site. To give Drush a try, from the command prompt type drush status and press Return. The output returned by Drush should look something like the following:

```
Drupal version         :  8.0-dev
Site URI               :  http://default
Database driver        :  mysql
Database username      :  d8
Database name          :  d8
Database               :  Connected
Drupal bootstrap       :  Successful
Drupal user            :  Anonymous
Default theme          :  bartik
Administration         :  seven
theme
PHP executable         :  /usr/bin/php
PHP configuration      :
PHP OS                 :  Darwin
Drush version          :  7.0-dev
Drush configuration    :
Drush alias files      :
Drupal root            :  /Applications/MAMP/htdocs/d8
Site path              :  sites/default
File directory path    :  sites/default/files
Temporary file         :  /Applications/MAMP/tmp/php
directory path
Active config path     :  sites/default/files/config_1FEpXnCuJgRcTNOkwUlVqp7FAr
                          JU7Cj4s2AbZN9Fg6W22BksQHWkPzhJGqU4cfsOIx2UD7YEqg/active
Staging config path    :  sites/default/files/config_1FEpXnCuJgRcTNOkwUlVqp7FAr
                          JU7Cj4s2AbZN9Fg6W22BksQHWkPzhJGqU4cfsOIx2UD7YEqg/staging
```

The status command returns a list of helpful information about your current Drupal 8 installation. Another key example is to download a module or theme using the drush pm-download command:

```
drush pm-download calendar
```

This command would download the latest production version of the Calendar module to your site. There is also a shortened version of the command, drush dl calendar.

To enable the Calendar module (for example) from the command line, you would execute

```
drush pm-enable calendar
```

or the shortened version, drush en calendar.

To disable the Calendar module, use

```
drush pm-disable calendar
```

or the shortened version, `drush pm calendar`.

If a new version or security patch for the calendar module is released and you're ready to apply the update, run

```
drush pm-update calendar
```

or the shortened version, `drush up calendar`.

As you can see, what may take several clicks through the administrative interface can be done through simple and quick command-line tools.

Table 15-1 represents a comprehensive list of common Drush commands. For a more complete description, visit `http://drush.org`.

Table 15-1. *Core Drush Commands*

Command	Description
archive-dump	Back up your code, files, and database into a single file.
archive-restore	Expand a site archive into a Drupal web site.
cache-clear	Clear a specific cache, or all Drupal caches.
cache-get	Fetch a cached object and display it.
cache-set	Cache an object expressed in JSON or `var_export()` format.
core-config	Edit `drushrc`, site alias, and Drupal `settings.php` files.
core-cron	Run all cron hooks in all active modules for specified site.
core-execute	Execute a shell command. Usually used with a site alias.
core-quick-drupal	Download, install, serve, and log in to Drupal with minimal configuration and dependencies.
core-requirements	Provides information about things that may be wrong in your Drupal installation, if any.
core-rsync	Rsync the Drupal tree to/from another server using SSH.
core-status	Provide a bird's-eye view of the current Drupal installation, if any.
core-topic	Read detailed documentation on a given topic.
drupal-directory	Return path to a given module/theme directory.
help	Print this help message. See `drush help help` for more options.
image-flush	Flush all derived images for a given style.
php-eval	Evaluate arbitrary PHP code after bootstrapping Drupal (if available).
php-script	Run PHP script(s).
queue-list	Return a list of all defined queues.
queue-run	Run a specific queue by name.

(continued)

Table 15-1. (*continued*)

Command	Description
search-index	Index the remaining search items without wiping the index.
search-reindex	Force the search index to be rebuilt.
search-status	Show how many items remain to be indexed out of the total.
self-update	Check to see if there is a newer Drush release available.
shell-alias	Print all known shell alias records.
site-alias	Print site alias records for all known site aliases and local sites.
site-install	Install Drupal along with modules/themes/configuration using the specified install profile.
site-reset	Reset a persistently set site.
site-set	Set a site alias to work on that will persist for the current session.
site-ssh	Connect to a Drupal site's server via SSH for an interactive session or to run a shell command.
test-clean	Clean temporary tables and files.
test-run	Run tests. Note that you must use the --uri option.
updatedb	Apply any database updates required (as with running update.php).
usage-send	Send anonymous Drush usage information to statistics logging site. Usage statistics contain the Drush command name and the Drush option names, but no arguments or option values.
usage-show	Show Drush usage information that has been logged but not sent. Usage statistics contain the Drush command name and the Drush option names, but no arguments or option values.
variable-delete	Delete a variable.
variable-get	Get a list of some or all site variables and values.
variable-set	Set a variable.
version	Show Drush version.
watchdog-delete	Delete watchdog messages.
watchdog-list	Show available message types and severity levels. A prompt will ask for a choice to show watchdog messages.
watchdog-show	Show watchdog messages.

Table 15-2. *Field Commands*

Command	Description
field-clone	Clone a field and all its instances.
field-create	Create fields and instances. Returns URLs for field editing.
field-delete	Delete a field and its instances.
field-info	View information about fields, field types, and widgets.
field-update	Return URL for field editing web page.

Table 15-3. *Project Manger Commands*

Command	Description
pm-disable	Disable one or more extensions (modules or themes).
pm-download	Download projects from Drupal.org or other sources.
pm-enable	Enable one or more extensions (modules or themes).
pm-info	Show detailed info for one or more extensions (modules or themes).
pm-list	Show a list of available extensions (modules and themes).
pm-refresh	Refresh update status information.
pm-releasenotes	Print release notes for given projects.
pm-releases	Print release information for given projects.
pm-uninstall	Uninstall one or more modules.
pm-update	Update Drupal core and contrib projects and apply any pending database updates (same as pm-updatecode + updatedb).
pm-updatecode	Update Drupal core and contrib projects to latest recommended releases.

Table 15-4. *SQL Commands*

Command	Description
sql-cli	Open a SQL command-line interface using Drupal's credentials.
sql-connect	A string for connecting to the database.
sql-create	Create a database.
sql-drop	Drop all tables in a given database.
sql-dump	Export the Drupal DB as SQL using mysqldump or equivalent.
sql-query	Execute a query against the site database.
sql-sync	Copy and import source database to target database. Transfers via rsync.

Table 15-5. User Commands

Command	Description
user-add-role	Add a role to the specified user accounts.
user-block	Block the specified user(s).
user-cancel	Cancel a user account with the specified name.
user-create	Create a user account with the specified name.
user-information	Print information about the specified user(s).
user-login	Display a one-time login link for the given user account (defaults to uid 1).
user-password	(Re)set the password for the user account with the specified name.
user-remove-role	Remove a role from the specified user accounts.
user-unblock	Unblock the specified user(s).

Summary

Drush provides a quick and easy way to administer websites for those who are comfortable at the command line. There are more advanced Drush features, such as building Drush scripts to perform several tasks at once. For more information, visit http://drush.org.

Next up, Chapter 16 explains how to manage your source code in Drupal using Git. If you like Drush, you'll love Git!

CHAPTER 16

■ ■ ■

Using Git

This chapter provides a basic overview of Git, a source code control system adopted by the Drupal community during the creation of Drupal 7. What is a source code control system, you ask? It is any tool that enables developers to manage changes to documents, source code, and other collections of information. If you have ever made changes to a document or a piece of code and then subsequently wished that you could go back in time and undo those changes, a source code control system would have saved the day. That's one of the key features of source code control: the ability to take a snapshot of digital assets at a given point in time and then retrieve that snapshot at a later date to restore the previous state.

Other key aspects of a source code control system include the ability to distribute changes to other developers or systems, and the ability to take a single code base and create copies (or *branches*, the more technically correct term) of that code base so that multiple developers can work on it simultaneously without clobbering each other's work, and then at some point in time merge all of those branches back together with the ability to resolve conflicts where two people made changes to the same elements of a digital asset (e.g., a line of code).

There are several source code control systems in the market. The one selected and adopted by the Drupal community is Git. Linus Torvalds, the creator of the Linux operating system, created Git during the creation of Linux as he was looking for something that was truly open source, fast, and powerful, yet easy to use. In this chapter I'll talk about some of the basic functions of Git that you may wish to use on your new Drupal 8 site.

Installing Git

The first step in using Git is to install it. But before you install it, check to see if it's already installed by typing git at the command prompt in a terminal window and pressing Return. If you see a list of Git commands, congratulations, you already have Git installed. If you see something along the lines of "command not found," then it's time to install Git.

Installing Git on Linux

Installing Git on Linux is a simple one-step process. If you are on a Debian-based distribution like Ubuntu, the command to enter in a terminal window is apt-get install git. If you are on a non-Debian-based Linux system, then you can use yum to install Git by entering yum install git-core at the command prompt in a terminal window. After installing, type git at the command prompt and press return. You should now see a list of Git commands. If you do not, check the helpful documentation on the Git website at http://git-scm.com.

Installing Git on OS X

Installing Git on OS X is accomplished through the graphical installer that is available at `http://sourceforge.net/projects/git-osx-installer`. This simple-to-use tool provides a quick way to successfully install Git on your Mac. Download the `dmg` file, click it to launch the installer, and follow the instructions. Once it's installed, test to ensure that Git is installed by launching a terminal window and typing `git` at the command prompt and pressing Return. You should see a list of Git commands if Git is installed correctly. If you do not see a list of commands, visit `http://git-scm.com` for help.

Installing Git on Windows

To install Git on Windows, download the Git installer exe file from `http://msygit.github.io`. The Windows installer installs Git tools that allow you to execute Git commands from a terminal window and installs a GUI tool for managing your Git repositories. After installing, launch a terminal window, enter `git` at the command line, and press Enter. You should see a list of Git commands. If you do not see a list of commands, visit `http://msygit.github.io` for help.

Using Git

There are several basic Git commands that will propel you along the path of getting hooked on Git. The first step in the process of using Git is to set up a Git repository where all of the items you wish to place under revision control will be stored. Let's use our Drupal 8 installation as our first Git project to place under source control. Using a terminal window, navigate to the root directory of your Drupal 8 installation. In the terminal window, type `git init` and press Return.

■ **Note**   The `git init` command will return an error message if you have already created a Git repository for this site.

You should see something similar to this message:

```
Initialized empty Git repository in /Applications/MAMP/htdocs/drupal8/.git/
```

If the repository was not successfully created visit the Git website for help on your specific errors.

With the repository created, the next step is to add elements to the repository. Since we haven't added any files yet, we will add all files in our Drupal 8 directory to Git. To do so, enter the following command:

```
git add -A.
```

Make sure you enter the period at the end of the command, as that signifies the current directory. If you successfully added all the files to your repository, you should be returned to the command prompt without any messages. If you enter `git status` at the command prompt and press Return, you should see a long list of new files that were added to the repository but not yet committed.

The process of committing the files that were just added provides a snapshot that you can roll back to in the event you make changes in the future that you need to revert to a previous state. How often you add and commit files is up to you or your project team, the key point being that in order to have the ability to roll back to a previous point in time, those files must have been added and committed. So let's commit our Drupal 8 files to our Git repository using the following command:

```
git commit -m "initial commit to the repository"
```

After executing the `commit` command, you should see a long list of messages that new nodes were created in your Git repository, one message per file committed. If you execute the `git status` command, you should see that everything is up to date:

```
# On branch master
nothing to commit, working directory clean
```

At this point we've committed the files and now have the ability to revert files to the state they were in when we committed them a few moments ago. The next step in the process is adding changes to files and committing those changes. Let's make a change to an existing file and add a new file to see how Git responds to both situations. First, create a new file in your `sites/default/files` directory. For demonstration purposes, create a new file named `test.txt` with a few lines of information so we can see Git in action. After creating the file, execute `git status` to verify that Git recognized the new file. You should see output similar to

```
# On branch master
# Untracked files:
#   (use "git add <file>..." to include in what will be committed)
#
#   test.txt
```

So let's follow the instruction and use `git add test.txt` to add the file to Git. After adding the file, use `git status` to check to see that the file was added. You should see output similar to

```
# On branch master
# Changes to be committed:
#   (use "git reset HEAD <file>..." to unstage)
#
#   new file:   test.txt
#
```

where `new file:` was prepended to the file name to indicate that Git is now tracking that file.

Let's commit the new file to the repository so we have the ability to revert to the current state in the future. Use the following to commit the file:

```
git commit -m "committing the initial version of test.txt to the repository"
```

After committing, run `git status` to see that everything is committed. You should see the message stating that there is nothing to commit.

Let's now change the `test.txt` file by adding more information to it to see if Git sees the changes to the file. After adding text to your file, run `git status`. You should see a message similar to

```
# On branch master
# Changes not staged for commit:
#   (use "git add <file>..." to update what will be committed)
#   (use "git checkout -- <file>..." to discard changes in working directory)
#
#       modified:   test.txt
#
```

Git recognized the changes to test.txt. We can now add the modified version of test.txt and commit it using git add test.txt and git commit -m "modified test.txt". After committing, use the git log command to see the history of the commits to your repository. You should see two commits for the file you committed that look similar to the following:

```
commit d4c24ca1854e53676178141be86246b1a3cb0a1a
Author: Todd Tomlinson <todd@radiantmediasolutions.com>
Date:   Wed Mar 19 08:27:10 2014 -0700

    modified test.txt

commit 39b5859fa70d1aafacd5c04d7695e715fdfd6bd6
Author: Todd Tomlinson <todd@radiantmediasolutions.com>
Date:   Wed Mar 19 08:23:04 2014 -0700

    committing the initial version of test.txt to the repository
```

You'll see in the previous listing that there are two different commit IDs. If you needed to revert test.txt to its initial state, you could do so by using the initial commit ID. The command for reverting to a previous commit is git revert <commit id>. To revert my changes to test.txt, I would use the first commit ID, the one ending in bd6:

```
git revert 39b5859fa70d1aafacd5c04d7695e715fdfd6bd6
```

After reverting and checking my test.txt file, I can see that the file is back to its original state before I made changes to it. Whew!

You now have enough basic information to set up your local Git repository and store your changes, but all your changes are stored locally on your laptop, desktop, or server, and often you may want to enable others to view and/or make changes to your repository. There are several solutions for providing access to your Git repository, including one of the more popular solutions, GitHub, which is the one I will introduce you to in this chapter.

Using GitHub

Using GitHub enables you to share your Git repositories with others and facilitates situations where you're doing development on your laptop or desktop and your site resides on a remote server. In either of these scenarios, GitHub provides an environment that is accessible over the Internet, and if you're okay with the general public having access to your repositories, the service is free. For a small monthly fee you can upgrade to a GitHub account that provides private repositories that are only accessible to those who you have granted access rights to. For demonstration purposes, we'll use the free version of GitHub. If you do not already have an account, visit https://github.com and sign up for a new account.

After setting up your account, the first step is to create a repository. On your GitHub landing page (once you've logged on), you'll see one or more links and buttons to create a repository. Click one of the links and you'll see a page similar to Figure 16-1.

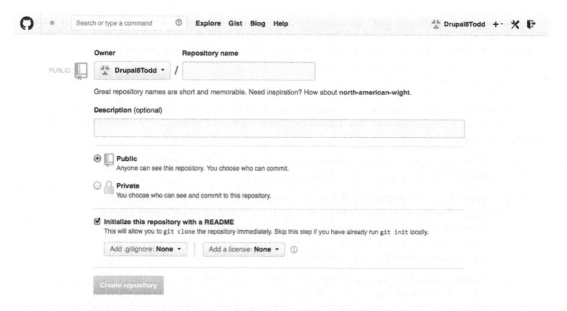

Figure 16-1. *Creating a new GitHub repository*

To create a repository, enter a name in the "Repository name" field, enter a description in the Description field, and in the "Add .gitignore" select list, choose Drupal.

A .gitignore file contains the names of files that you want Git to not track. In the case of Drupal, there are local configuration files such as settings.php that are specific to the local environment where the site is running. By ignoring settings.php you'll save the steps of having to modify items such as the database settings every time you pull from the master repository.

With the repository created on GitHub, the next step is to push your local repository up to GitHub. On the GitHub page for your repository, you'll see a clone URL listed in the right column of the page. Copy that URL, as you are going to need it to push your local repository up to GitHub.

The first step in the process is to set up the GitHub connection on your local machine. From within the root directory of your Drupal 8 site, use the following command to add a reference to your remote GitHub repository, remembering to paste the clone URL in place of <clone url from GitHub>:

```
git remote add origin <clone url from GitHub>
```

Once you've added the remote repository, the next step is to pull down any changes that exist on GitHub that don't exist locally, before attempting to push your local repository to GitHub. If you do try to push changes to GitHub and there are remote changes that don't exist locally, Git will tell you that your branch is behind and you have to first pull down the changes. Since we added a .gitignore file on GitHub, the remote repository does have changes that our local copy of the site does not. So to fix that, use the following:

```
git pull origin master
```

This will pull down any changes that exist on GitHub and will merge them into our local repository. The next step in the process is to push our local repository up to GitHub, as GitHub right now is basically empty. Use the following command to push our Drupal 8 site up to the remote repository:

```
Git push origin master
```

After pushing our changes, both our local and remote repositories will be in sync. As you add files or change files on your local repository, you'll need to push them up to GitHub so that others will have access. The process is relatively straightforward:

1. Using `git status`, check to see which local files have been added to your Drupal 8 instance or what files have been changed.

2. From the list of additions and changes, use `git add <filename>` to add each of the files to Git, replacing `<filename>` with the actual names of the files listed from `git status`. If you have several files in a single directory that were added or changed, you can accomplish the same tasks by adding the directory that the files reside in using `git add <directory>`.

3. Commit your changes locally using `git commit -m "some message that describes the changes you are committing"`. You may commit after each file is added or you may commit once after you've added all the files that were added or changed. It depends on the granularity of what you want to revert to in case of an issue. In most cases, committing after adding a group of files is adequate.

4. After the files have been committed locally, it's time to push them to GitHub. To push the changes, use `git push origin master`. If there are multiple people working on your GitHub repository, you may run into a situation where attempting to push files results in an error stating that your master branch is behind *X* number of commits. Simply execute `git pull` to download and merge those changes and then re-execute `git push origin master`. In situations where you've changed a file that was also changed by someone else, Git will report that there is a merge conflict. Git writes useful information into the file where the merge conflict occurred. Examine the file and resolve the issues. For more information on resolving merge conflicts, visit the Git documentation site at `http://git-scm.com/documentation`.

With your Drupal 8 site uploaded to GitHub, you can now provide other people access to your repository so that they can download and optionally commit changes to your repository. If you have upgraded your GitHub account, you will need to grant access to your repository by following the steps listed on your GitHub repository's landing page. If you have not upgraded your account, you won't need to do anything to grant access because, by default, free accounts are publicly accessible. To clone your GitHub repository on a laptop, desktop, or server, you may either use the `git clone` command or download a zip file of the repository using the Download ZIP button on your repository's landing page. The best approach is to use Git and to clone the repository. To do so, simply copy the HTTPS clone URL listed in the right column of your GitHub repository landing page and execute the following command:

```
git clone <clone URL> <target directory>
```

replacing `<clone URL>` with the actual URL listed on your GitHub repository landing page. For example,

```
git clone https://github.com/Drupal8Todd/drupal8.git drupal8
```

would clone the GitHub repository into a directory named `drupal8`. After cloning I could then use, modify, add to the repository, and optionally commit those changes back to the GitHub repository. There is a great deal of documentation on how to manage a multideveloper Git repository on the Git website, including topics such as creating separate branches where developers may work on changes that are then merged back into the master branch when they are ready to do so.

Using Git on Drupal.org

You can also use Git to clone Drupal itself or modules and themes. While Drush (see Chapter 15) makes downloading and updating modules and themes simple, there may be times when you want to contribute changes back to Drupal core or a contributed module or theme. To do so requires that you use Git and contribute your changes back to Drupal.org, a module's repository, or a theme's repository. Following the steps outlined previously in this chapter for creating a clone of a remote repository, visit `www.drupal.org/project/drupal` and click the "Version control" link near the top of the page. On the resulting page you will see instructions for how to clone the repository. That same "Version control" link appears at the top of each module's or theme's landing page on Drupal.org. You may also clone a module's or theme's repository following the same steps as previously outlined. For guidelines on how to contribute code to the community, visit `www.drupal.org/contribute/development`.

Summary

The first time you're able to revert a file to a previous state will be the day that you fall on your knees and praise those who have created source code control systems like Git. While it's possible to restore files from backups, the reality is that with a few simple keystrokes, you can roll back a file or your entire site to a previous state with relative ease. The second time that you will praise the Git creators is when you have a situation where you have multiple developers working on your site and they all need to jointly contribute code to the project. Spending a few minutes to learn the basics of Git will save you a lifetime of headaches, heartaches, and the occasional all-nighter as you try to restore a site back to a previous state from spotty backups.

CHAPTER 17

■ ■ ■

Putting It All Together

Reading this book has given you the foundation of knowledge on which to continue to build your Drupal skills. If you are new to the concept of a web content management system, you may not be able to jump in and build a highly complex site as your first endeavor with Drupal. But like all things in life, you have to start somewhere, and you now have the tools and knowledge to begin your journey. For those of you who had previous content management experience, hopefully the book helped to cast a light on how Drupal works so you can correlate what you know from other CMS platforms with what Drupal provides.

Now What?

Learning anything new takes practice, and with practice comes comfort, and with comfort comes the ability to do new and exciting things. Learning Drupal takes time, study, practice, and patience. One of the best ways to learn Drupal is to find a real-world opportunity to build a website and do it in Drupal. Whether the site is for your child's sports team, your church, a community group, a nonprofit organization, or anything else under the sun, having a project to focus on that you know will benefit a person or organization gives you incentive to learn, which helps in the learning process. How else can you keep up-to-date with your Drupal knowledge?

Look At Other Drupal-Based Sites for Ideas

Although it's hard to look at a site and immediately detect that it is a Drupal site, there is an excellent resource that will help you find sites that were built on Drupal. Dries Buytaert, the creator of Drupal, maintains a fairly up-to-date list of very high-profile websites that are built on Drupal. You can find that list on his personal website at `http://buytaert.net/tag/drupal-sites`. Dries does an excellent job of capturing a broad spectrum of sites from various industries and sites from all around the world. He updates the list continually, so it is a good idea to bookmark that page and to visit it frequently.

By scanning through the list of sites that Dries has compiled (currently well over 100), you can quickly get a sense for the types of sites that people have successfully built on Drupal. By looking at other sites, you can get inspiration for design (the visual look of the site), layout (how the pages are structured), organization (how content is displayed), and the features and functions that have been deployed. Looking at other sites is a common starting point for many people who are embarking on a new Drupal project.

Keep Tabs on Drupal and Contributed Modules

One of the benefits of using Drupal is that it is a constantly evolving platform. As new concepts are defined on the Web, Drupal is often one of the first content management systems to employ those capabilities. Keeping up with the changes is relatively simple: just check `www.drupal.org/project/project_module` and look at the latest modules and updates posted to the site. (See Figure 17-1.)

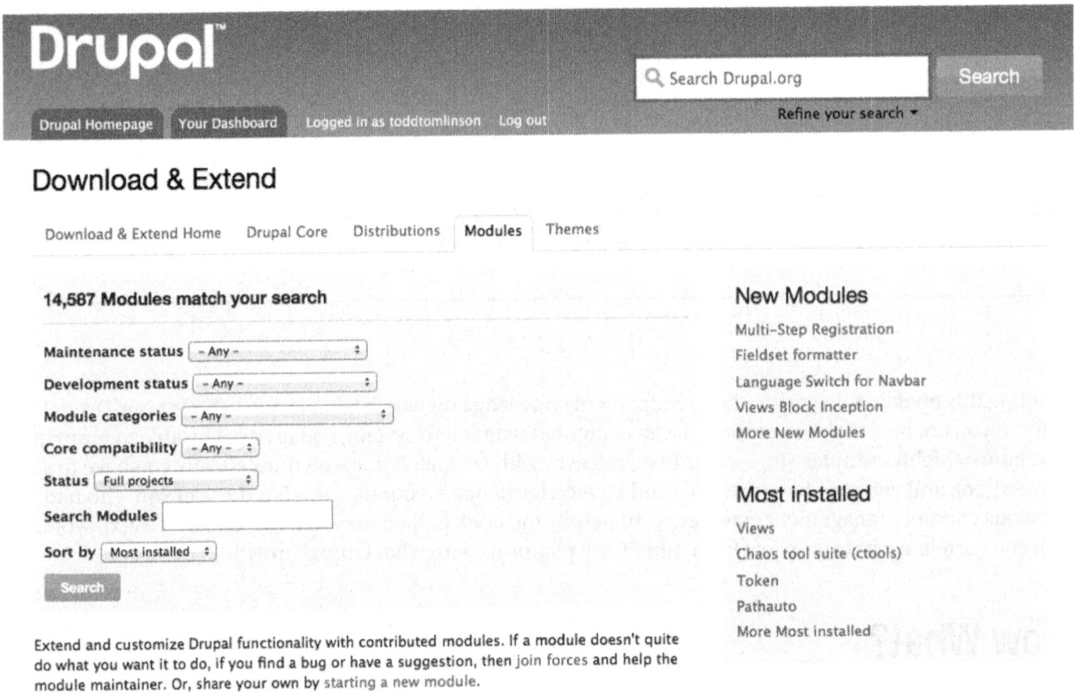

Figure 17-1. *Search filters for finding modules on Drupal.org*

When visiting the page, you'll notice a "Sort by" select list. One of those options is "Last release." Choosing this option and clicking Search sorts the list of modules in date-descending order, with the last modules posted to the site listed first. Depending on how frequently you visit the site, you may only have to spend a minute or two looking through the list of new modules to see what is available.

Get Involved in Your Local Drupal Users Group

There are hundreds of Drupal users groups all around the globe, including regional users groups as well as groups that are focused on specific topics or industries (such as Drupal in Education, Drupal in Libraries, Drupal in Government). Your local Drupal users group is a great place to meet others in your community who are also new to Drupal, and also a great place to learn, as most groups provide training as part of their periodic meetings. To locate a group near you or a group that is focused on an area that you are interested in, visit https://groups.drupal.org.

A Methodology for Building Your Site on Drupal

While there isn't a formal "Drupal Methodology" for building sites on Drupal, there are several industry best practices and processes that you may wish to follow as you embark on the journey of creating a new Drupal website. The process described in Table 17-1 may seem overwhelming and more complex and involved than what you think you need to build your new site, but from experience I've found that it's good to at least think about the steps listed and apply and perform the tasks that I think are appropriate, based on the scope and complexity of the site that I am building.

Table 17-1. *A Methodology for Building Your Drupal Site*

Phase	Task	Activity
I		**Starting Your Project** The seven tasks in this phase are focused on helping you think about and define what your site is going to be. Drupal is a lot like a stack of lumber: you could build virtually any type and style of house with an appropriately sized stack of lumber. However, you wouldn't start picking up boards and nailing them together without first knowing the details of the house that you are going to build. Think of this phase of the project as defining the blueprint of your new site. In this phase, you're documenting key aspects of your site on paper, and not in Drupal. Once you have an understanding of what it is you're going to build, you can embark on the construction activities.
	A	**What is your new website all about?** Write down, in narrative form, what the purpose of your new site is and, in general, describe the audience that you intend to target with your site. Think of this document as your "elevator pitch," meaning if you met someone in an elevator and they asked you what your website was about, you could recite this document verbatim before the two of you left the elevator. This activity forces you to define in concise terms what it is you are building and who is going to view the site.
	B	**Identify who is going to visit and use your website** List the various types of visitors who you intend to target with your new website. Examples of visitor types for a library site might be children, teens, young adults, adults, jobseekers, and senior citizens. A favorite technique is to use a blank piece of paper and on this paper draw a "box" representing a browser window with your website in that browser window. Draw a number of stick figures around the box and label each one with the type of visitor that "person" represents.
	C	**Identify the content that you are going to deliver to your visitors** A common mistake in the website construction process is the "field of dreams" mentality: "if I build it they will come." Well if "they" come to your site, what content are you going to present to "them" so they stay on your site, look around, and bookmark your site for future visits? You may wish to use a blank piece of paper for each visitor type, drawing a stick figure on the left and listing the content that this person would be interested in seeing on your site. There will likely be duplication between various visitor types, and that is okay, but it is important to step into the "shoes" of each visitor type to think about what content you are going to provide each visitor that will make them pay attention and return to your site in the future. Examples of content types might be, for a library website, book reviews, movie reviews, music reviews, recommended reading lists, and a list of upcoming programs at the library.
	D	**Identify the functionality that you are going to deliver to your visitors** Content is typically only one aspect of what constitutes a website; there may be interactive features that you want to deliver, such as blogs, surveys, videos, audio, discussion forums, online forms, e-commerce, RSS feeds, or other interactive features. In this task, list all of the interactive features that you wish to provide to your visitors.

(continued)

Table 17-1. (*continued*)

Phase	Task	Activity
	E	**Define the sites structure** Examine the types of content and functionality documented in the previous steps; you will start to see logical groupings or categories. You may see logical groupings based on a topic or subject, or you may see groupings based on specific visitor types. Using a library site as an example, you might see that there is a logical grouping of content across all visitor types that is focused on book reviews. You might also see a logical grouping of content that is focused on senior citizens and their use of community resources. Each of these logical groupings may, and probably should, become a major page on your website.
	F	**Define custom content types and taxonomy structure** There may be types of content that do not fit the generic Drupal page content type with just a title and body. An example might be that you identified "Events" as a type of content. An Event has a title, a start date, a start time, an end date, an end time, and a location. It might be advantageous to create for events a custom content type that enforces the entry of those additional details, rather than relying on the author to remember to enter those values in the body of a generic page. In this step, you should create a list of custom content types and the attributes (such as start date, start time) associated with each content type. While defining content types, it's also time to think about taxonomy and how you are going to categorize content on your site.
	G	**Define the navigational structure of your website** With an understanding of the visitor types, the content that they will want to see on your site, and the logical groupings or major pages that will make up your site, you can now define the navigation (menus) for your site. If you know that a specific visitor type is a primary visitor of your website, you should make it easy for that visitor to find the information that they are seeking. The typical mechanism for doing that is to provide some form of menu or menus. In this task you would identify all of the links that you wish to provide to your site visitors and how those links should be organized (as menus). Using the library example, you may decide that you want a primary menu at the top of the page that provides links to About the Library, Locations and Hours, and How to Contact the Library. You may decide that you want a secondary menu that links visitors to pages for Books, Movies, Music, and Events. You may decide that you want another menu that helps to direct specific visitor types to pages that are focused on their specific interest areas, such as links for youth, teens, adults, senior citizens, and business owners. You can take the concept to another level of detail by defining drop-down menu items for certain menu links; for example, under the Books menu you may want to provide a link to Recommended Books, What's New, and What's on Order.
II		**Setting Up Your Drupal Environment** Now that you have an understanding of what you're going to build, the next phase is to set up your Drupal environment to begin the construction process.
	A	**Decide where you are going to host your new website** You can easily build your new website on your desktop or laptop and then deploy that site on a hosted environment, or you can choose to build the site in the environment where you are going to host the production version of your website. Either approach works well. However, at some point in the near future you are going to want to deploy your site with a commercially viable hosting provider or your organization's own hosting platforms. To find a list of commercial hosting providers that support Drupal, visit www.drupal.org/hosting.

(*continued*)

Table 17-1. (*continued*)

Phase	Task	Activity
	B	**Install and configure Drupal** Following the step-by-step instructions outlined in Appendix A, install Drupal on either your local desktop/laptop or on your hosting provider's environment.
III		**Visual Design** Picking or designing your Drupal theme is one of those activities that you can choose to do early in the process, midway through the development process, or near the end of your efforts. For most people, having a sense of what the site is going to look like helps to visualize the layout as it will look in its final state. There may be circumstances where you can't pick or design the theme up front, such as the case where the organization you are building the site for doesn't have their branding completed (including logo, colors, iconography, fonts, and so on). In that case it is still possible to continue with the construction activities using a generic theme.
	A	**Look for an existing theme that matches what you are trying to accomplish** Hundreds of themes are available on Drupal.org, and there is likely one that comes close to the layout and design that you would like to use on your site. To see the list of themes, visit www.drupal.org/project/project_theme. If you can't find a theme that matches your requirements, you can use one of the various "starter" themes listed on the Drupal site (such as Zen) as a place to start. Revisit Chapter 6 for detailed instructions on how to download and install a Drupal theme.
	B	**Implement your site's specific design elements** If you pick an off-the-shelf theme from Drupal.org (versus creating one from scratch), you will likely want to change the theme's logo, colors, and so on. The topic of theme development is beyond the scope of this book; however, you can read up on the concepts behind Drupal themes, and discover which files you will want to look in to make changes to customize the theme, at www.drupal.org/documentation/theme.
IV		**Downloading and Installing Contributed Modules** In Task D of Phase I, you documented the functionality that you want to deliver to your site visitors beyond just content (such as blogs, RSS feeds, video, polls, forums, and e-commerce). In this phase you will search for, install, and enable the modules that you need to address the desired functionality.
	A	**Identify the modules required to address the desired functionality** Some of the functionality may be addressed by Drupal 8 core modules (such as the Book module, Forums, and the like) while other functionality may require searching for an appropriate module. To look for modules, visit www.drupal.org/project/project_module. Using the filters available at the top of the page, narrow the search to those modules that are based on the functionality that you wish to fulfill on your site. If you're struggling to find the right module, a good resource to use is the Drupal.org forums. The community is extremely helpful, and posting a quick question asking for advice on which module to use for a specific feature or function may cut down on your research time as well as save you from picking the wrong module for the job.
	B	**Download and install required modules** Once you've identified the right modules to address the required functionality on your site, follow the instructions listed in Chapter 11 for installing, enabling, configuring, and setting permissions for each of the modules.

(*continued*)

Table 17-1. (*continued*)

Phase	Task	Activity
V		**Creating Custom Content Types** If you identified custom content types in Phase I, Task E, now is a good time to create those content types. Using the list of content types and the list of attributes for each type, follow the instructions in Chapter 5 for creating new content types.
VI		**Creating Views** There may be pages on which you want to provide a list or table view of content. Now is a good time to construct those views to support creation of pages in the next step. The process for creating views can be found in Chapter 9.
VII		**Creating the Physical Pages** Use the techniques described in this book to create the actual pages (for example, use the Layouts module to create complex page layouts). Visit Chapter 10 for a description of how to use layouts, and Chapter 8 for a description of using blocks. Create the various pages that you defined in Phase I, Task E
VIII		**Finishing Up the Menus on Your Site** With the pages in place, you're now ready to finalize the menus on your site. Revisit the navigational structure you defined in Phase I, Task F to ensure that you've addressed all of the navigational requirements for your new site. For a description of how to create menus, visit Chapter 7.
IX		**Finalizing the Configuration** At this point, the site should be configured and ready to go. In this phase, make sure that you have created all of the user roles, have assigned the appropriate permissions to those roles, and have configured how users accounts will be created. Visit Chapter 3 for a description of how to define roles and assign permissions.
X		**Creating Content** Now that you have the site configured, content types created, views defined, panels created, and user roles and permissions defined, it's the time to create content on your site.
X		**Testing Your Site** With your site nearly ready for production, now is the time to test to make sure that everything works as you expect it to work. Make sure you test the site, as an anonymous user (not logged into the site). It is also a good idea to create test accounts for each of the user roles that you have defined and to visit the site while logged into each account to ensure that the roles and permissions are working as you had envisioned.
XI		**Deploying to Production** It's now time to deploy your site to your production-hosting environment.
	A	If you created your site on your desktop or laptop, you'll need to copy the entire Drupal directory to your production web server, and you'll need to back up your database and restore the database on your hosting environment. For additional details on this process, please see Chapter 14.
	B	If you created your site on a hosting provider's platform, you are already there and don't need to move your site.
XII		**Administering Your Site** As described in Chapter 14, monitor and manage your new Drupal website.

Summary

In this chapter I covered the methodology for creating a new Drupal site, linking the methodology back to the steps that I covered throughout the rest of the book. Although every website is different, the steps outlined in the methodology work for virtually any type of website. It's important to think through everything described in the methodology, and in fact I would suggest that you find a quiet corner and walk through the methodology before starting to build your new site. The methodology forces you to think about what you are trying to accomplish before you build it, minimizing the risk of creating your website and then finding out that you missed the boat completely.

The next chapter focuses on building Drupal sites that are responsive, meaning making your site display in a form that works well on smart phones, tablets, laptops, desktops, and other emerging devices like watches.

CHAPTER 18

■ ■ ■

Creating a Responsive Site

Just a few short years ago, smartphones and tablets didn't exist, yet here we are today living in a world where analysts predict that web traffic from these devices will surpass that of laptops and desktops in 2014. We live in a mobile world, and as Drupal site builders, it's important to address the growing usage of smartphones and tablets and begin to think about mobile first as we build new sites. If the majority of users visiting our sites are on smaller screens, it would be wise for us to deliver an amazing user experience regardless of the device they are using.

Fortunately for us, Drupal 8 addresses many of the challenges of rendering our sites on a variety of screen widths (phones, phablets, tablets, laptops, desktops, televisions), and in this chapter we will look at leveraging Drupal 8's responsive tools and responsive themes, as well as stepping into basic CSS theming to address responsiveness.

Responsive Defined

You hear all of this talk about "responsive" and "mobile friendly," but what does it really mean for a website to be responsive? Simply stated, *responsive* means that your site is viewable and usable on a variety of devices with different screen widths, without having to scroll great distances, and that the content is still large enough to read on smaller devices. *Responsive* also means that the user experience on your site is tailored to best fit the device that the user is accessing your site on. For example, if certain elements on your site don't display well on smaller devices, you may choose not to display those elements to visitors using smaller devices, but still display them to visitors viewing your site on a laptop or desktop. *Responsive* may also mean leveraging a device's capabilities, such as gestures or swiping, to navigate through your site instead of requiring more traditional point-and-click interfaces. Regardless of the definition that you choose, the fundamental concept of responsive design is to make your site usable across all devices.

How Responsive Web Design Works

Responsive web design works through a combination of detecting the width of the screen that the site visitor is using and leveraging CSS that defines how elements are displayed on the page based on the width of the screen. Take for example a page that has three equal-width columns that are each 33% of the width of the screen. If you view the page on a laptop with a 15-inch screen at a resolution of 1,680 pixels, each column is approximately 560 pixels wide and the site looks great (see Figure 18-1).

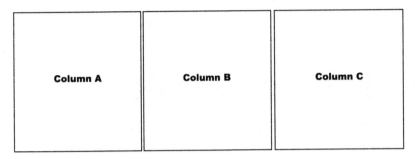

Figure 18-1. *Normal laptop screen resolution*

Open that same page on an iPhone and the columns shrink to 33% of 320 pixels, or approximately 106 pixels. The columns become narrow and long, and the text within the columns becomes unreadable—or at best the viewer has to scroll left and right to see very small columns of very small text and images (see Figure 18-2).

33% @ 320px Wide

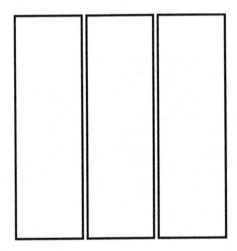

Figure 18-2. *Normal iPhone 4 screen resolution*

A better approach would be to detect that the user is viewing the site on a device that is 320 pixels wide and, instead of offering three columns horizontally spread across the page, make each column 320 pixels wide (or 100% of the width) and stack the columns on top of each other. At 320 pixels wide, each column is nearly as wide as viewing that column on a 15-inch laptop screen, still very readable on an iPhone 4 (see Figure 18-3).

100% @ 320px

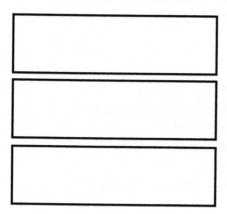

Figure 18-3. *Stacked columns*

Media Queries is a CSS tool that, in conjunction with the browser reporting the width of the screen, allows you to write CSS specifically for devices of a given width. The general format of a media query is

```
@media (max-width: 600px) {

    .body {
        font-size: .9em;
    }

}
```

The query begins with @media and max-width: 600px specifies that the CSS within the { } should only be applied when the width of the browser window is 600px or smaller. You can also specify ranges of widths within your query, such as:

```
@media (min-width: 321px) and (max-width: 599px) {

    .body {
        font-size: .7em;
    }

}
```

In this case any device with a screen width of 321px or greater and less than or equal to 599px will have the CSS contained within the { } applied. In the previous two examples, any body text on a device that is up to 600px wide will have a font size of .9em, whereas devices that are between 321px and 599px will have a font size of .7em (em units are explained in the section "Common CSS Changes to Address Responsiveness" later in the chapter).

As you look at the various devices in the market, you'll see that you may have to use several media queries within your CSS files to address how your site renders on various devices. The number of media queries is dependent on how much change needs to occur in the format of the content and structure of your pages as the screen shrinks. If your site is a single-column design, then you may be able to get away with not using any media queries; however, most sites have more than one column, and even a single-column site still needs the display to be adjusted for things like horizontal menus.

Making Your Site Responsive

There are three basic options for making your Drupal 8 site responsive:

- Pick an off-the-shelf theme from Drupal.org that has the media queries defined in the theme's style sheets and includes CSS that works across devices.

- Pick a starter theme, such as Zen, from Drupal.org that has the responsive framework in place to build upon.

- Take a nonresponsive theme and add the media queries and the width-specific CSS to make the site render properly at each width.

Each approach has its merits and depending on your level of comfort with CSS and your ability to identify that elements on the page need to change based on the screen width that visitors will use to view your site.

The solution I use the most is the second option, starting with a Zen subtheme and customizing it to address the needs of my clients. Regardless of the approach you choose, it is well worth purchasing *Beginning Responsive Web Design with HTML5 and CSS3* by Jonathan Fielding (Apress, 2014) to guide you along the path.

Browser Tools to Help You Test Your Responsive Theme

After you select and install the desired theme, it's a good idea to download a browser plug-in that makes it easy for you to see your site in various device widths (unless you are wealthy enough to afford one of every device in the market). Chrome has an excellent tool called the Responsive Web Design Tester. It's a free plug-in available from the Google Store that provides a drop-down list of commonly used devices. Click the tools icon in the toolbar and you'll see a list of devices (see Figure 18-4). Select from that list, and a new Chrome window will open displaying your site as it would appear on that device. Firefox and Safari both have similar plug-ins that work equally as well.

Figure 18-4. Chrome's Responsive Web Design Tester plug-in

With the browser tool in place, the next step is to look at your site in the various screen widths and answer the following questions:

1. Which elements on the page require resizing to appear properly (for example, columns, images, and font sizes)?

2. For smaller screens, which elements should be removed from the page? The focus should be on the content that is most likely to be of importance to users on smaller screens.

3. Which navigational elements need to be changed to make navigation easier for those on small devices without a mouse to point and click?

It is likely that you'll find several elements at various screen widths that need to change in order to be usable at smaller screen widths. To enable the ability to change how elements are displayed you'll need to find your theme's style sheets (typically found in the themes/<themename>/css folder) and add the media queries that are required to enable adjusting CSS. The following is a recommended list of media queries that address most screen widths in the market today:

```
/* Smartphones (portrait and landscape) ----------- */
@media only screen  and (min-device-width : 320px)  and (max-device-width : 480px)
{ /* Styles */ }

/* Smartphones (landscape) ----------- */
@media only screen  and (min-width : 321px) { /* Styles */ }

/* Smartphones (portrait) ----------- */
@media only screen  and (max-width : 320px) { /* Styles */ }

/* iPads (portrait and landscape) ----------- */
@media only screen  and (min-device-width : 768px)  and (max-device-width : 1024px)
{ /* Styles */ }

/* iPads (landscape) ----------- */
@media only screen  and (min-device-width : 768px)  and (max-device-width : 1024px)  and
(orientation : landscape) { /* Styles */ }

/* iPads (portrait) ----------- */
@media only screen  and (min-device-width : 768px)  and (max-device-width : 1024px)  and
(orientation : portrait) { /* Styles */ }

/* Desktops and laptops ----------- */
@media only screen  and (min-width : 1224px) { /* Styles */ }

/* Large screens ----------- */
@media only screen  and (min-width : 1824px) { /* Styles */ }

/* iPhone 4 ----------- */
@media only screen and (-webkit-min-device-pixel-ratio : 1.5), only screen and
(min-device-pixel-ratio : 1.5) { /* Styles */ }
```

You'll note that some of the media queries specify the orientation of the device being used, portrait or landscape. This is just another tool to help narrow which CSS will be applied to a given device.

Depending on the theme you are using, the media queries will often be placed at the end of the style.css or layout.css files. If you are using a theme that already supports responsiveness through media queries, it's a good idea to build on what's already there. In the case of the Bartik theme, looking at the css directory, you'll see three CSS files: layout.css, style.css, and colors.css. If you examine the layout.css file, you'll see that the theme's creator already has two media queries in the CSS file:

```
@media all and (min-width: 560px) and (max-width: 850px)
@media all and (min-width: 851px)
```

Both media queries contain a number of CSS overrides to elements that appear on the various pages of a site built using that theme. The two media queries address most of the cases where elements on the page need to be adjusted to be usable on most devices, but there may be cases where you may want to address specific elements for iPhone 4. In that case, adding the following media query and associated CSS entries would address the changes specific to devices with iPhone 4 or smaller screens:

```
@media all and (max-width: 320px)
```

Common elements that you may want to adjust are column widths, font sizes, and image sizes. Viewing the site using one of the browser responsive web design tools will help you to identify which elements need to change.

Common CSS Changes to Address Responsiveness

One of the first things to think about when designing a responsive website is the need to change from fixed pixel widths and point-based font sizes. For years we've been designing sites to be pixel perfect, but with responsive design we need to shift our thinking from exact pixels to percentages and ems. If you're an experienced designer and CSS developer, this may be one of the hardest aspects of changing how you think about design and the CSS that enables that design. Once you've made the transition, the process will be relatively simple—but to begin with, we need to think about the size of elements on the page in perspective of the percentage of the display width that they are going to consume. If you stay with fixed pixel widths, the results will be that your visitors on small-screen devices will have to scroll horizontally to see the full width of your website. Check out whitehouse.gov on your smartphone as an example. It unfortunately isn't responsive (as of early 2015) and requires that you use your finger to scroll to the right to see the full width of the site.

One of the first things to examine are any elements on the page that, when viewed on a smaller screen, result in either your site shrinking down to fit within the window or requiring you to scroll right to view the full width of your page. Typical elements on a Drupal site that often require adjustment include regions, blocks, panel panes, and views. These elements are typically set to a fixed pixel width and, to become responsive, need to be set to percentage widths.

To identify which CSS elements to change, using the Google Chrome Responsive Web Design Tester, simply right-click an element you wish to change and select the Inspect Element option (see Figure 18-5).

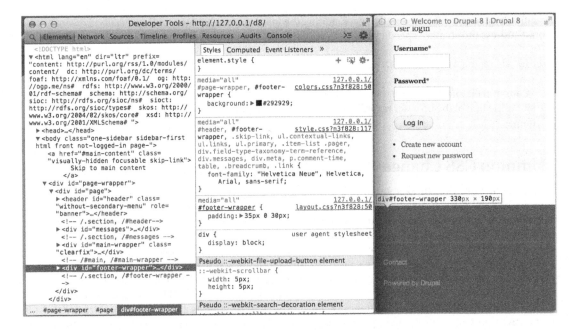

Figure 18-5. *Using Chrome's Inspect Element tool*

Responsive theming becomes a relatively easy task with the combination of media queries, a browser's responsive design tool like Chrome's Responsive Web Design Tester, and the ability to right-click an item and identify which CSS element you wish to change. The only thing left is adding that CSS selector within the brackets of your media query and changing the CSS attribute, such as width, to an appropriate value. The browser does all the rest.

There is a learning curve to responsive design and getting things to appear appropriately across device widths. The journey starts with the first step, and you now have enough knowledge to step out with gusto!

Summary

In today's mobile world, building a website that is not responsive to mobile devices ensures that a large percentage of your site visitors will be frustrated with the user experience. Take the time to add a few media queries and CSS overrides to your CSS files, and your site visitors will be happier. While it's impossible to please all the people all the time, it's a good idea to at least attempt to address the devices that your site visitors will be using. And as you've seen in this chapter, it really isn't that hard and can actually be fun!

CHAPTER 19

■ ■ ■

Creating a Blog Site

Blogs, blogs, and more blogs. As of April 2015 there were approximately 229.7 million blogs on Tumblr, 75.8 million blogs on WordPress, and millions of other blogs on Blogger and other platforms like Drupal. Conservatively, that's a nearly a third of a billion websites dedicated to blogging, or roughly 33% of all websites on the Internet (currently hovering around 923,000,000 according to www.internetlivestats.com). When you couple the sheer number of blog sites with the average number of blog posts published per day, 3 million (Technorati), the numbers are staggering. A Drupal site builder could stay very busy just building blog sites!

In this chapter I'll walk you through the process of building a blog-centric website using just Drupal 8 core. To demonstrate the ease of building a blog site on Drupal, I'll create a site that is focused on learning Drupal 8. I'll assume that you are building the site along with me as a learning exercise, but you are welcome to use the example presented here as a guide to create your own blog site. Get ready to get your blog on!

Identifying Requirements for a Blog Site

As discussed in previous chapters, the place to start when creating any website is to identify the requirements for the site. Requirements for the blog site in our example include

1. The capability to create blog posts using a simple content type with title, subject, and featured image.

2. The capability to easily categorize and browse through content by major topics, including Contributed Modules, Hosting, Installing Drupal 8, Module Development, Performance, Security, Site Administration, Site Building, and Theming.

3. An easy-to-use editorial tool for authoring content, preferably a WYSIWYG editor.

4. The capability to list blog posts by date posted, with the newest blog posts at the top of the page.

5. The capability to browse through blog posts by category.

6. The capability for site visitors to comment on blog posts.

With these requirements in hand, we can then identify how we're going to meet those requirements with Drupal. The solutions corresponding to the requirements in the previous list are as follows:

1. Using the Article content type as the foundation for a Blog content type, which addresses all the requirements for a Blog content type. Articles have a title, body, and image field.

2. Use taxonomy to categorize content by topic. We'll need to create a vocabulary, assign the topics as terms in that vocabulary, and update our Article content type to include a term reference field that provides the capability to select a topic.

3. Drupal 8 provides a WYSIWYG editor as part of core.

4. Create a view that renders a teaser list of blog posts, sorted in descending order by date posted.

5. Create a view that lists the taxonomy terms in the Topic vocabulary, using a block as the format, and add links to the taxonomy listing pages for each term.

6. The Article content type has commenting enabled by default.

Installing Drupal

After identifying the requirements and how to meet those requirements, the next step in creating the blog site is to install Drupal. Follow the steps outlined in Appendix A to install Drupal either locally, on your server, on shared hosting, through a service such as Pantheon or Acquia.

Installing and Creating a Theme

After installing Drupal, the next step is to pick a theme. You have several choices:

*   Create your own theme from scratch.

*   Start with one of the Drupal starter themes and customize it to meet your needs.

*   Find a theme on www.drupal.org/project/project_theme that is close to what you want, and modify the CSS and layout to meet your specific needs.

*   Find a theme on www.drupal.org/project/project_theme that meets your needs without modification.

*   Find and pay for a theme on one of the Drupal commercial theme sites.

*   Convert a theme from another CMS, such as WordPress, into a Drupal 8 theme.

*   Use one of the standard Drupal 8 core themes.

For our blog project, we'll focus on the fourth option in the list. Visit www.drupal.org/project/ project_theme, filter your search by core compatibility of Drupal 8.x, and click Search. Searching through the list of themes, the one that most closely fits what we are trying to achieve on our example blog site is Gratis. Using the process described in Chapter 6, download, install, and set Gratis as the default theme for our new blog site. After setting Gratis as the default theme, our new blog site is ready (see Figure 19-1) to begin the site-building process.

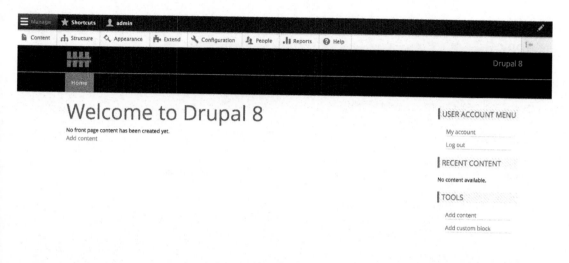

Figure 19-1. *Gratis theme installed*

The next step in configuring a theme is to set the logo and site name and remove the standard blocks that are enabled by default when you install Drupal 8. To change the logo, click the Appearance link in the secondary admin menu and click the Settings link next to the theme you selected and installed (Gratis in our example). Uncheck the "Use the default logo supplied by theme" check box, upload your logo, and click the "Save configuration" button.

To update the site name, click the Configuration link in the secondary admin menu and the "Site information" link on the Configuration page. Since the site that we are building is focused on learning Drupal 8, enter an appropriate title in the "Site name" field, followed by clicking the "Save configuration" button.

The last step in cleaning up the site before launching into site building is to remove the blocks that appear by default when installing Drupal 8. Click the Structure link on the secondary admin menu and click the "Block layout" link. Remove all of the blocks that are set to display automatically by changing all of their Region column settings to None. Click the "Save blocks" button at the bottom of the page when finished. At this point the site is ready for us to proceed with the next step, categorizing content by topic.

Creating Taxonomy

Our blog is focused on learning Drupal 8, and one of the requirements we previously identified is the capability to browse content by topic. To enable this capability, we'll create a new taxonomy vocabulary called Topics and assign the terms listed in requirement 2 (Contributed Modules, Hosting, Installing Drupal 8, Module Development, Performance, Security, Site Administration, Site Building, and Theming). To create the vocabulary, click the Structure link in the secondary admin menu followed by the Taxonomy link on the Structure page. Click the "Add vocabulary" button to create the new container for topic terms, and name the vocabulary "Topics." Add each of the terms listed in requirement 2 to the vocabulary in preparation for assigning the vocabulary to the Article content type. After creating the vocabulary and terms, the listing page for the Topics vocabulary should appear as shown in Figure 19-2.

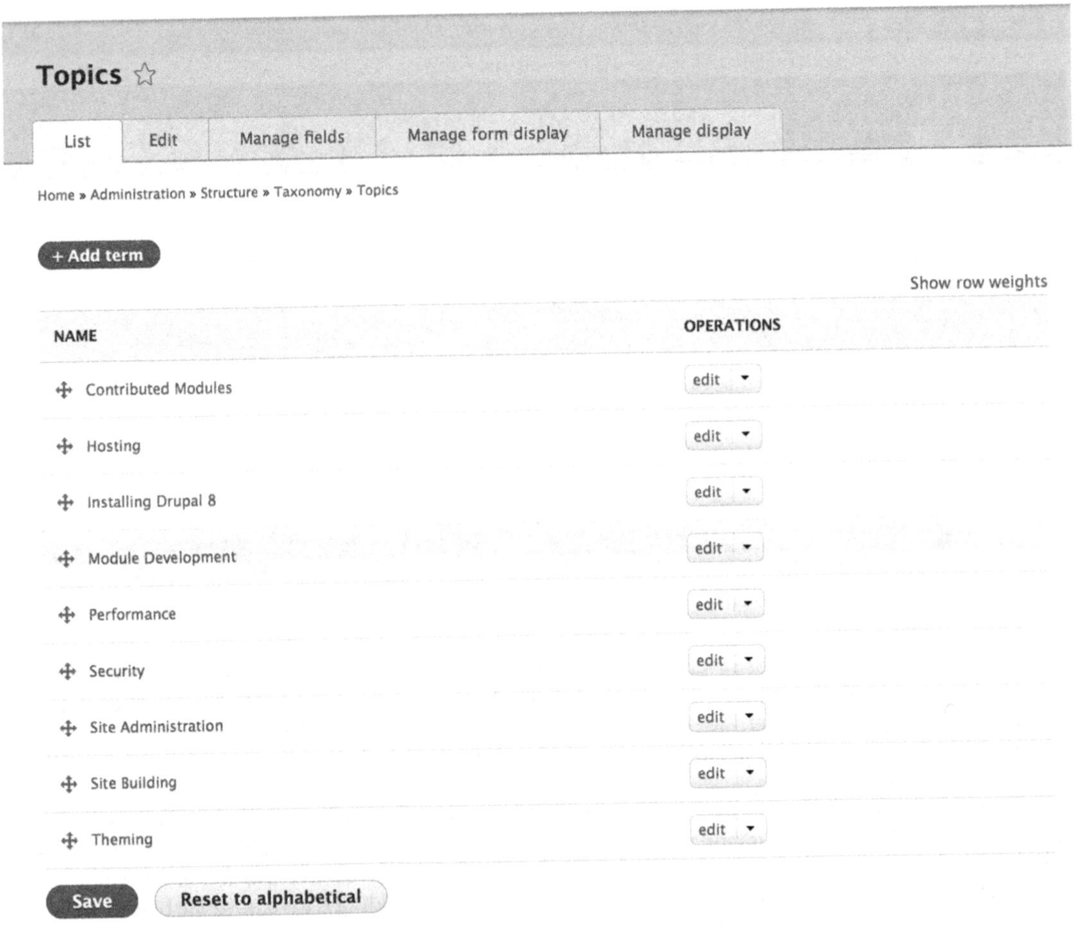

Figure 19-2. *The Topics vocabulary*

Updating the Article Content Type

The next step is to create a new field on the Article content type for capturing the topic of the blog posting. To create the field, navigate to Structure ➤ Content types and click the "Manage fields" link for the Article content type and create a new field of type "Term reference," using the Topics vocabulary as the basis of the values to be selected for this field. For details on adding fields, refer to Chapter 5. After adding the field to the Article content type, creating a new Article should appear similar to Figure 19-3 with the terms listed from the Topics vocabulary.

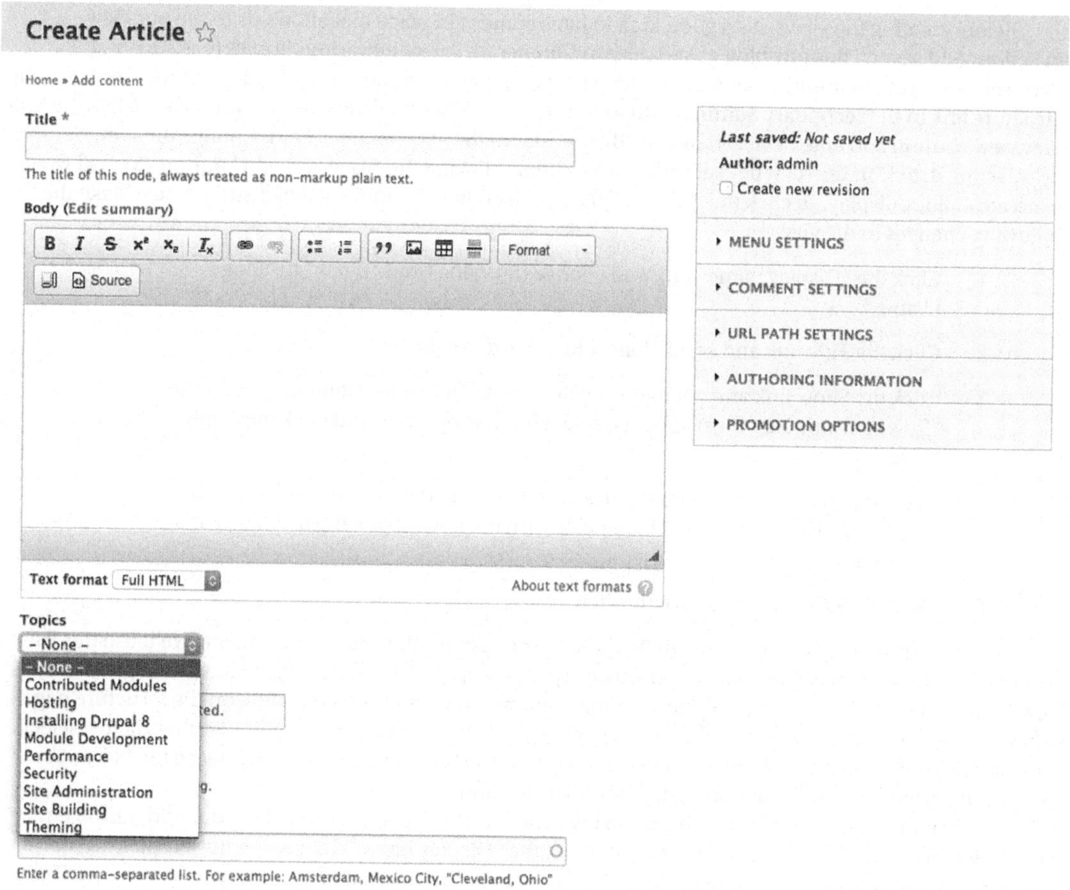

Create Article ☆

Home » Add content

Title *

The title of this node, always treated as non-markup plain text.

Body (Edit summary)

Text format Full HTML

About text formats

Topics

– None –

– None –
Contributed Modules
Hosting
Installing Drupal 8
Module Development
Performance
Security
Site Administration
Site Building
Theming

Enter a comma–separated list. For example: Amsterdam, Mexico City, "Cleveland, Ohio"

Last saved: Not saved yet
Author: admin
Create new revision

▸ MENU SETTINGS

▸ COMMENT SETTINGS

▸ URL PATH SETTINGS

▸ AUTHORING INFORMATION

▸ PROMOTION OPTIONS

Figure 19-3. *Topics added to the Article content type*

Another change that we'll want to make to the Article content type is to turn off the option to automatically post new blog entries to the front page of the site. We want to control what is displayed through the view that we'll create in the next steps. To turn off the automatic publishing to the front page feature, click the Edit tab at the top of the "Edit Article content type" page and select "Publishing options" from the vertical tabs at the bottom of the form. Uncheck the "Promoted to front page" option and click the "Save content type" button. We're now ready to use the Article content type to author blog postings.

Creating Views

The next step in the site-building process is to create the views that will be used to render content on the site. We'll need two views:

- A teaser listing sorted in descending order based on post date, showing the newest blog post at the top of the page

- A list of taxonomy terms in the Topics vocabulary, providing an easy way for site visitors to browse through postings based on topic of interest

205

Before creating the views, it's a good idea to have content in place that allows us to see our view in action. Add several dummy blog posts (refer to Chapter 2), selecting various Topics (e.g., Hosting, Performance, and Theming). After creating blog posts, it's time to create the main view for the site. Click the Structure link in the secondary admin menu followed by the Views link on the Structure page. Click the "Add new view" button and enter a view name of "Blog posts" in the "View name" field. Change the View Settings by selecting Article in the "of type" select list, followed by clicking the "Save and edit" button. We will want to create a Block display, so click the Add button and select Block from the list of display types. Make the following changes to the view:

1. Click the "Display name" link and change the value from "Block" to "Blog Listing."

2. Click the Title link and enter "Latest Blog Posts" as the title.

3. Click the Show link and change the value from "Fields" to "Content." When the "Row style options" form appears, select the Teaser mode and click the Apply button.

4. The Sort Criteria section should already be set to sort descending on post date, which will give us a listing of blog posts with the newest posting displayed at the top of the list.

5. Click the Save button to save the view.

The second view that we need to create is the list of terms in the Topics vocabulary. We'll use this list of terms as a menu to navigate to taxonomy listing pages that show all of the blog postings assigned to that topic. Click the Structure link in the secondary admin menu and the Views link on the Structure page. Click the "Add new view" button and enter a view name of "Blog Topics." In the View Settings fields, select "Taxonomy terms" from the Show select list, Topics from the "of type" select list, and leave the "sorted by" field as Unsorted. Click the "Save and edit" button to continue.

We want the view to display as a block, so create a new Block display by clicking the Add button and selecting Block from the list of display options. Click the "Display name" field and enter "Topics Menu" in the "Administrative name" field and click the Apply button. Click the Title link and enter "Browse by Topic" in the Title field, followed by clicking the "Apply (all displays)" button. The view is now ready to save.

Now that we have all the views we need to address the requirements of our site, the next step is to place the views on the page.

Assigning Blocks

With the views complete, we're ready to assign to the page the blocks we created. Click the Structure link in the secondary menu followed by the "Block layout" link. Click the Blog Posts: Blog Listing link in the "Place blocks" box on the right and select Content as the region to display the list. We want to restrict this view so that it appears only on the front page of our site (and not on every page that we visit), so select the Pages tab in the vertical menu at the bottom of the block configuration page and select "Show for the listed pages" from the "Show block on specific pages" form. In the text box, enter <front>, which is a shortcut that Drupal uses to represent the front page of a site, and then click the "Save block" button.

Next, select the Blog Topics: Topics Menu block from the "Place blocks" box and place it in one of the sidebars provided by your theme. Since commenting is enabled, we'll want to display a list of the most recent comments on our site. Drupal 8 provides a block that does just that by default. Select the "Recent comments" block from the "Place blocks" box and place that block in the same sidebar as the Topics menu. Your block layout should look similar to Figure 19-4. Save your blocks before exiting the "Blocks layout" page.

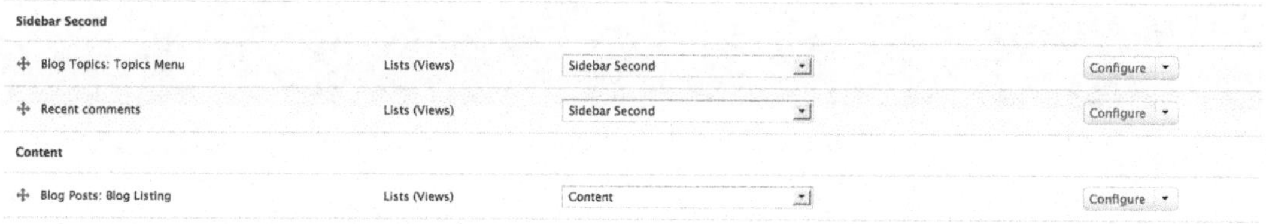

Sidebar Second				
✛ Blog Topics: Topics Menu	Lists (Views)	Sidebar Second ▾		Configure ▾
✛ Recent comments	Lists (Views)	Sidebar Second ▾		Configure ▾
Content				
✛ Blog Posts: Blog Listing	Lists (Views)	Content ▾		Configure ▾

Figure 19-4. *Blocks assigned to regions*

After creating test blog posts, sample comments, and assigning blocks to the layout of the site, the final product looks great! (See Figure 19-5).

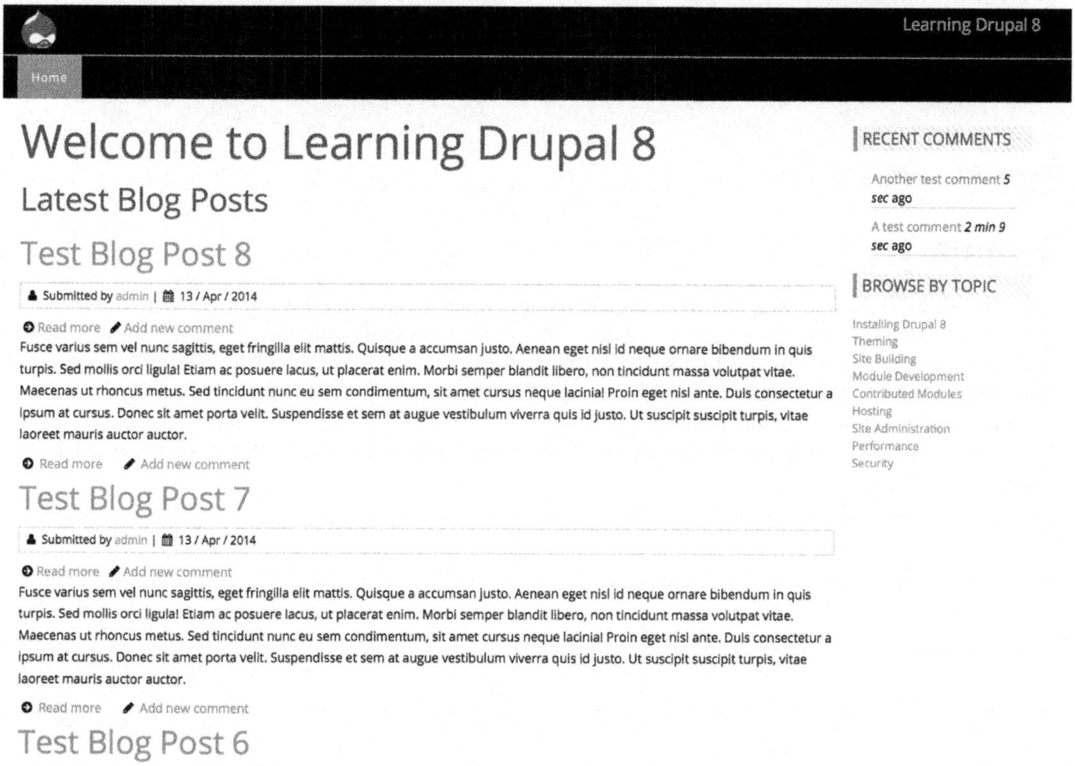

Welcome to Learning Drupal 8

Latest Blog Posts

Test Blog Post 8

👤 Submitted by admin | 📅 13 / Apr / 2014

⊕ Read more ✏ Add new comment

Fusce varius sem vel nunc sagittis, eget fringilla elit mattis. Quisque a accumsan justo. Aenean eget nisl id neque ornare bibendum in quis turpis. Sed mollis orci ligula! Etiam ac posuere lacus, ut placerat enim. Morbi semper blandit libero, non tincidunt massa volutpat vitae. Maecenas ut rhoncus metus. Sed tincidunt nunc eu sem condimentum, sit amet cursus neque lacinia! Proin eget nisl ante. Duis consectetur a ipsum at cursus. Donec sit amet porta velit. Suspendisse et sem at augue vestibulum viverra quis id justo. Ut suscipit suscipit turpis, vitae laoreet mauris auctor auctor.

⊕ Read more ✏ Add new comment

Test Blog Post 7

👤 Submitted by admin | 📅 13 / Apr / 2014

⊕ Read more ✏ Add new comment

Fusce varius sem vel nunc sagittis, eget fringilla elit mattis. Quisque a accumsan justo. Aenean eget nisl id neque ornare bibendum in quis turpis. Sed mollis orci ligula! Etiam ac posuere lacus, ut placerat enim. Morbi semper blandit libero, non tincidunt massa volutpat vitae. Maecenas ut rhoncus metus. Sed tincidunt nunc eu sem condimentum, sit amet cursus neque lacinia! Proin eget nisl ante. Duis consectetur a ipsum at cursus. Donec sit amet porta velit. Suspendisse et sem at augue vestibulum viverra quis id justo. Ut suscipit suscipit turpis, vitae laoreet mauris auctor auctor.

⊕ Read more ✏ Add new comment

Test Blog Post 6

RECENT COMMENTS

Another test comment *5 sec ago*

A test comment *2 min 9 sec ago*

BROWSE BY TOPIC

Installing Drupal 8
Theming
Site Building
Module Development
Contributed Modules
Hosting
Site Administration
Performance
Security

Figure 19-5. *The final product*

Clicking any of the blog post titles or the "Read more" links takes you to the detail page for a single blog posting, and clicking any of the Browse By Topic links in the sidebar takes you to a page that lists all of the blog posts assigned to the topic that was selected, with the page title set to the taxonomy term selected, as shown in Figure 19-6. It's a powerful yet simple solution for filtering content by taxonomy term!

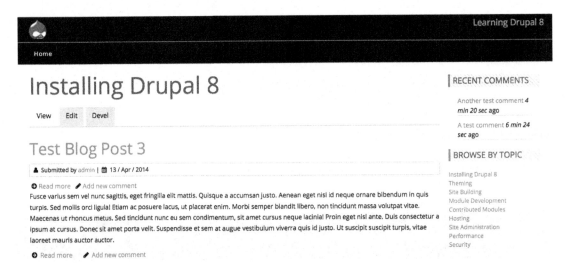

Figure 19-6. *Topic landing page*

Summary

With a few simple steps we created a blogging site using only Drupal 8 core. While it's a great foundation, there are other features that you could create using the solution created in this chapter as the starting point, such as a view that shows blog postings segregated by month, a forum that allows site visitors to interact with each other, or other features that you may dream up. With Drupal you're only limited by your imagination, your skills, and the time it takes to create a solution.

In the next chapter we'll expand the solution to encompass the typical features required to build a corporate website on Drupal.

■ ■ ■

## CHAPTER 20

Building a Company Site

In a relatively short time span, the Internet has changed everything about the way business is conducted. What was once a novelty, having a website on the Web, has now become essential for all companies large and small, regardless of industry. In the eyes of the customer, a company that doesn't have a website is often perceived as possibly being illegitimate. Fortunately, Drupal 8 is an excellent platform for quickly and effectively creating an organization's online presence.

In this chapter we'll build on the concepts covered previously in this book, with a focus on building a marketing-centric website that is functional for a wide variety of companies. To demonstrate the ease of building a company site on Drupal, I'll create a marketing-focused site for a company that provides general business consulting services. I'll assume that you are building the site along with me as a learning exercise, but you are welcome to use the example presented here as a guide to create your own company site.

Identifying Requirements for a Company Site

As stated several times in this book, the place to start when creating any website is to identify the requirements for the site.

Requirements for the company site in our example include

1. An overview of the company in the form of an About Us page.

2. A portfolio of client projects.

3. An overview of the services offered by the company and the capability to link client project information to each service offering.

4. A section that highlights key staff members.

5. The capability to author and publish news articles.

6. The capability to pull news feeds from various sources on the topic of general business.

7. The capability for select staff to blog.

8. A contact form.

9. A main navigational menu that links to the main sections of the site.

10. A footer that lists key pages on the site, the company address, and contact information.

11. A corporate-looking theme.

With the preceding requirements in hand, we can then identify how we're going to meet those requirements with Drupal. The solutions corresponding to the requirements listed are as follows:

1.   Use the Basic page content type to create a page that describes the company.

2.   Use a custom content type for client projects.

3.   Use the Article content type tagged as a Service Offering, and an entity reference field to link selected client projects.

4.   Expand the standard Drupal user profile to include biographical information for staff, and add a view to display a page of staff profiles.

5.   Create a taxonomy vocabulary called Article Type, add vocabulary terms (e.g., News, Blog Posts, Service Offering), and add a view to display news articles in chronological order (descending by post date, with the newest article at the top of the list).

6.   Use the Aggregator module to pull and display news feeds from identified sources on the Web.

7.   Use the Article content type with the Article Type taxonomy term of Blog Post. We will also add a view to display blog posts in chronological order (descending by post date, with the newest blog post at the top of the list).

8.   Use the Contact module and the contact form that is provided by that module.

9.   Use blocks and menus.

10.   Use a theme from Drupal.org.

Installing Drupal

After identifying the requirements and how to meet those requirements, the next step in creating the corporate site is to install Drupal. Follow the steps outlined in Appendix A to install Drupal either locally, on your server, on shared hosting, or a solution such as Pantheon or Acquia.

Installing and Creating a Theme

After installing Drupal, the next step is to pick a theme. You have many choices:

- Create your own theme from scratch.

- Start with one of the Drupal starter themes and customize it to meet your needs.

- Find a theme on www.drupal.org/project/project_theme that is close to what you want, and modify the CSS and layout to meet your specific needs.

- Find a theme on www.drupal.org/project/project_theme that meets your needs without modification.

- Find and pay for a theme on one of the Drupal commercial theme sites.

- Convert a theme from another CMS, such as WordPress, into a Drupal 8 theme.

- Use one of the standard Drupal 8 core themes.

For our corporate website project, we'll focus on the second option, using a starter theme. A starter theme provides the foundation for creating a theme that addresses the specific design requirements for a site. A starter theme is typically fairly stark from a design perspective, which is purposeful in that the focus of starter themes is on the foundation, not the visual design.

Visit www.drupal.org/project/project_theme, filter your search by core compatibility of Drupal 8x, and click Search. In the list of results, look for themes identified as starter themes. Some of the widely installed starter themes are Zen, Omega, Adaptive, Basic, Bootstrap, and NineSixty. For this project we'll use Basic, as it provides a nice set of options and an easy-to-understand structure. Download Basic and follow the instructions in the README.txt file, including renaming the theme to acme_co, the name of the fictitious consulting company for whom we are going to create a website. Also set the "Site name" field to ACME Co on the "Site information" page (Manage ➤ Configuration ➤ Site information).

The next step is to install the theme and set it as the default theme for the site (choose Manage ➤ Appearance and click "Install and set as default" in the Uninstalled Themes section). After setting the new theme to the default theme and changing the default logo to the ACME Company logo (on the Appearance page, click the Settings link to find the field to upload a new logo), I made a few quick changes to a few elements in the theme's primary style sheet (styles.css) and reloaded the homepage, revealing the start of the new corporate website (see Figure 20-1).

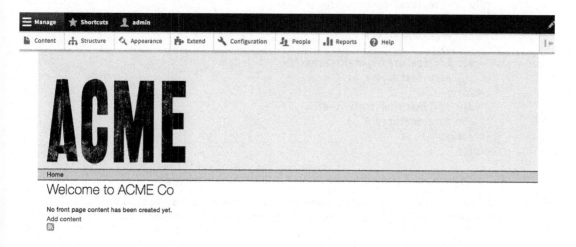

Figure 20-1. *Basic starter theme installed*

The next step in the site build is to change the logo. Click the Appearance link in the secondary admin menu and click the Settings link next to the theme you selected and installed. Uncheck the "Use the default logo supplied by theme" check box, upload your logo, and click the "Save configuration" button.

The last step in cleaning up the site before launching into site building is to remove the blocks that appear by default when installing Drupal 8. Click the Structure link on the secondary admin menu and click the "Block layout" link. Remove the blocks that are set to display automatically, with the exception of the "Main page content" block, by changing all of their Region column settings to None. Click the "Save blocks" button at the bottom of the page when finished.

The design for our homepage calls for a list of the latest blog posts, a list of the latest news articles, and a list of aggregated news feeds. While we could place all of those items into the Content area of our homepage, a more preferred approach is to drop each of those into a separate region at the bottom of the page. The Basic starter theme doesn't provide regions for that, so we'll add those to our version of the theme. There are three quick steps to adding new regions to a theme:

1. In the theme's `.info.yml` file (`acme_co.info.yml` for the sample site; yours may be different if you chose a different name for your version of the Basic starter theme), add three regions to the list of existing regions:

    ```
    featured_1: 'Featured First'
    featured_2: 'Featured Second'
    featured_3: 'Featured Third'
    ```

2. Display the three new regions on a page. I'll update the `page.html.twig` file, located in the `templates` subfolder of the theme, to incorporate those regions into the page. I want the regions to display below the Content area, so immediately following the closing `div` tag for the `content-area`, I'll add the following:

    ```
    <div id="featured-content-area">
      <div id="featured-content-area-1">
        {{ page.featured_1 }}
      </div>
      <div id="featured-content-area-2">
        {{ page.featured_2 }}
      </div>
      <div id="featured-content-area-3">
        {{ page.featured_3 }}
      </div>
    </div>
    ```

    The `{{ page.xxxxxx }}` items print the content of the regions to the page.

3. Create the CSS in the `css/style.css` style sheet to render the regions as 33% of the width of the page, floating each of the regions next to each other:

    ```
    #featured-content-area {
      border-top: #676767 2px solid;
      padding-top: 20px;
    }

    #featured-content-area-1,
    #featured-content-area-2,
    #featured-content-area-3 {
      width: 33%;
      float: left;
      padding: 10px;
    }
    ```

With the changes to the theme in place, we are ready to start laying the foundation and building the site.

Creating Taxonomy

The corporate site utilizes the Article content type for a variety of purposes, including for news articles, blog posts, and service offerings. To enable this capability, we'll create a new taxonomy vocabulary called Article Type and create terms for Blog Post, News, and Service Offering.

To create the vocabulary, navigate to Structure ➤ Taxonomy and click the "Add vocabulary" button to create the new container for topic terms, and name the vocabulary "Article Type". Add each of the terms in preparation for assigning the vocabulary to the Article content type. After creating the vocabulary and terms, the listing page for the Article Type vocabulary should appear as shown in Figure 20-2.

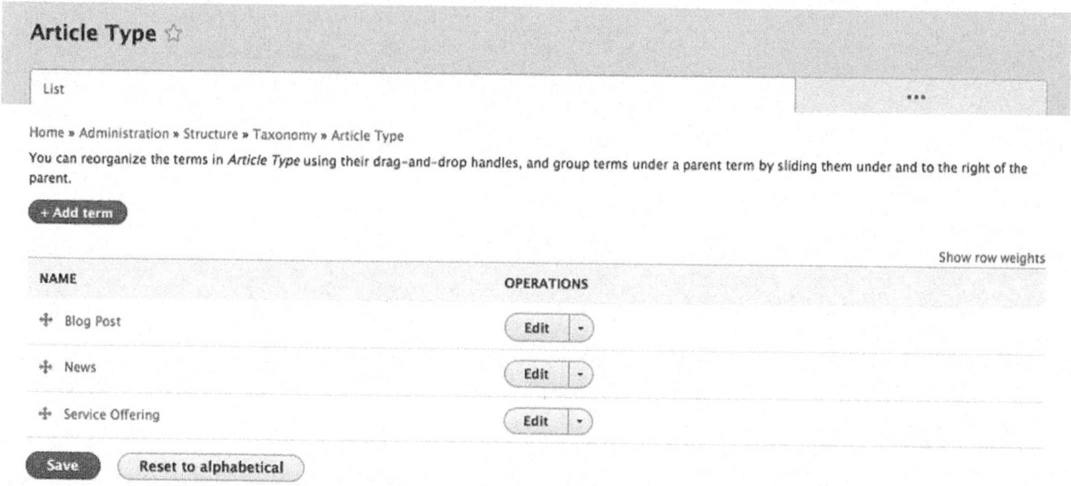

Figure 20-2. *The Article Type vocabulary*

Updating the Article Content Type

The next step is to create a new field on the Article content type for capturing the type of article being created (Blog Post, News, or Service Offering). To create the field, click the Structure link on the secondary admin menu, followed by the "Content types" link on the Structure page. Click the "Manage fields" link for the Article content type and create a new field of type "Term reference," using the Article Type vocabulary as the basis of the values to be selected for this field. For details on adding fields, refer to Chapter 5. After adding the field to the Article content type, creating a new article should appear similar to Figure 20-3 with the terms listed from the Article Type vocabulary.

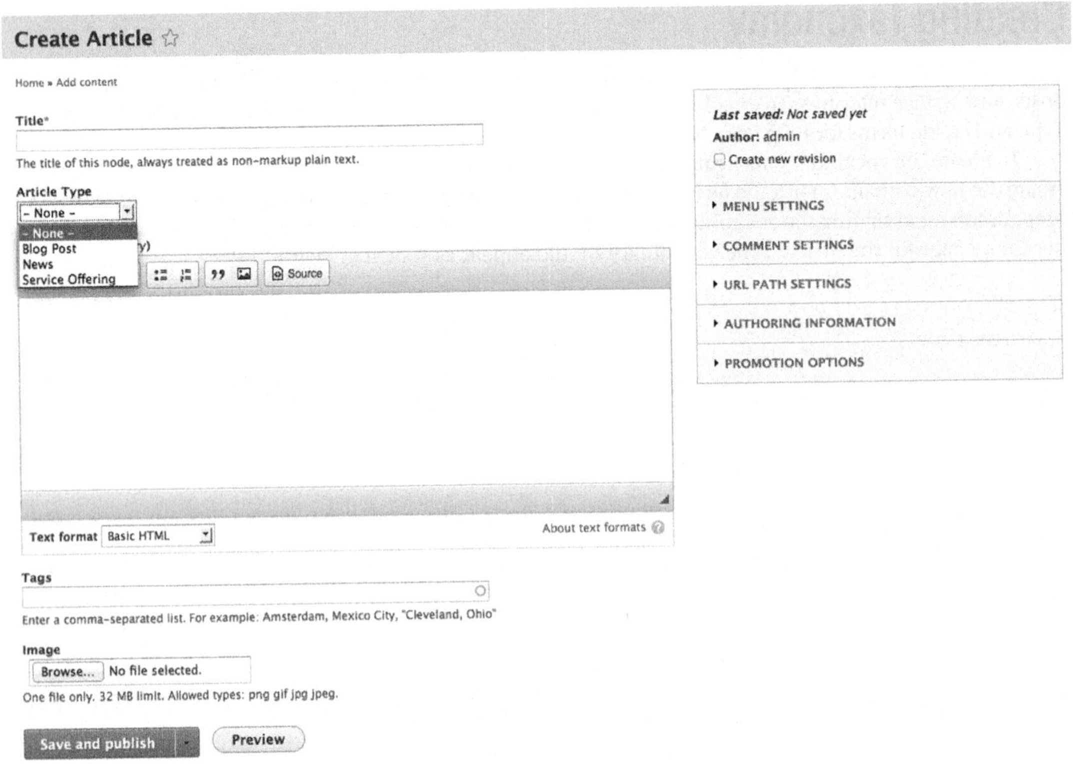

Figure 20-3. *Article Type added to the Article content type*

Another change that we'll want to make to the Article content type is to turn off the option to automatically post new articles to the front page of the site. We want to control what is displayed through the view that we'll create in the next steps. To turn off the automatic publishing to the front page feature, click the Edit tab at the top of the "Edit Article content type" page and select "Publishing options" from the vertical tabs at the bottom of the form. Uncheck the "Promoted to front page" option and click the "Save content type" button. We're now ready to use the Article content type to author content.

Creating the Client Portfolio Content Type

We will create a Client Portfolio content type to capture and display information about client projects. The following fields are associated with this content type:

- *Project Title*: The name of the project

- *Client*: The name of the client

- *Types of Services*: An entity reference to the types of services performed on this project. The values represented by this field will come from the articles that were written with a taxonomy term of Service Offering selected as the Article Type.

- *Key Staff*: A reference to the key staff members who participated on this project (entity reference to a user entity)

- *Description*: A description of the project (using the Body field as the basis of the description, changing the label to Description from the default value of body)

214

To create the new content type, return to the "Content types" page and click the "Add content type" button. Follow the steps that were outlined in Chapter 5 to create the fields. When creating the entity reference field for Types of Services, select Views as the Type of item to reference and create a new view that lists all articles that have the taxonomy term of Service Offering. This will provide you with a list of service offerings to select from. You may create the view before starting the creation of the content type by following the steps outlined in Chapter 9. The difference in this view as compared to what we created in Chapter 9 is that the display type is Entity Reference and the Settings for the Entity Reference List format requires that you pick a field that the editor will use to search for content to connect to the article they are writing. I'll use the standard title field and update the label for that field to Project Title. The view that supports the requirements is as shown in Figure 20-4.

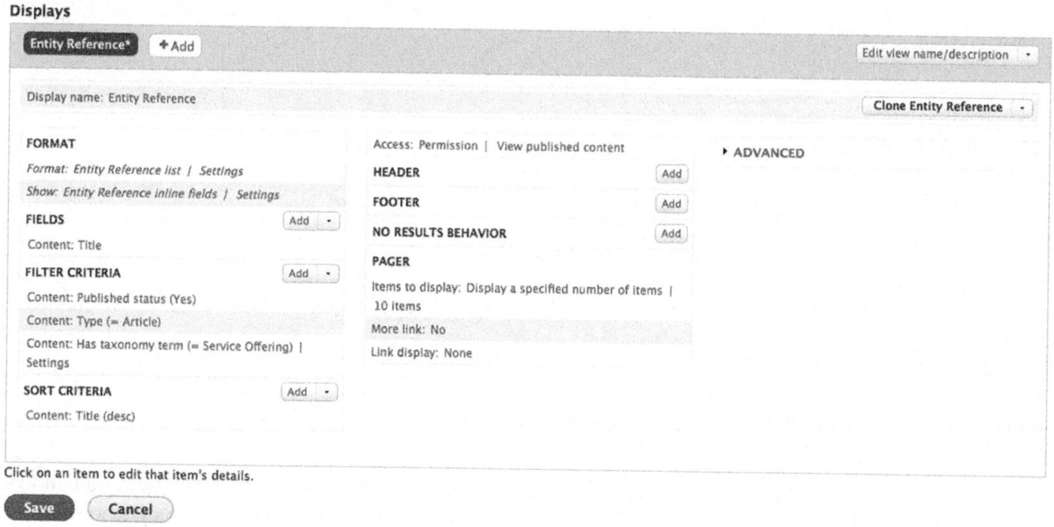

Displays

Entity Reference* | +Add | Edit view name/description | ▾

Display name: Entity Reference | Clone Entity Reference | ▾

FORMAT
Format: Entity Reference list | Settings
Show: Entity Reference inline fields | Settings

FIELDS | Add | ▾
Content: Title

FILTER CRITERIA | Add | ▾
Content: Published status (Yes)
Content: Type (= Article)
Content: Has taxonomy term (= Service Offering) | Settings

SORT CRITERIA | Add | ▾
Content: Title (desc)

Access: Permission | View published content
HEADER | Add
FOOTER | Add
NO RESULTS BEHAVIOR | Add
PAGER
Items to display: Display a specified number of items | 10 items
More link: No
Link display: None

▸ **ADVANCED**

Click on an item to edit that item's details.

Save | Cancel

Figure 20-4. *Entity Reference view for Service Offering*

After creating the view, we can now add the entity reference field to the Client Portfolio content type. Figure 20-5 demonstrates setting the Reference Type fields to Views and assigning the Service Offerings view as the source of the content to be reference.

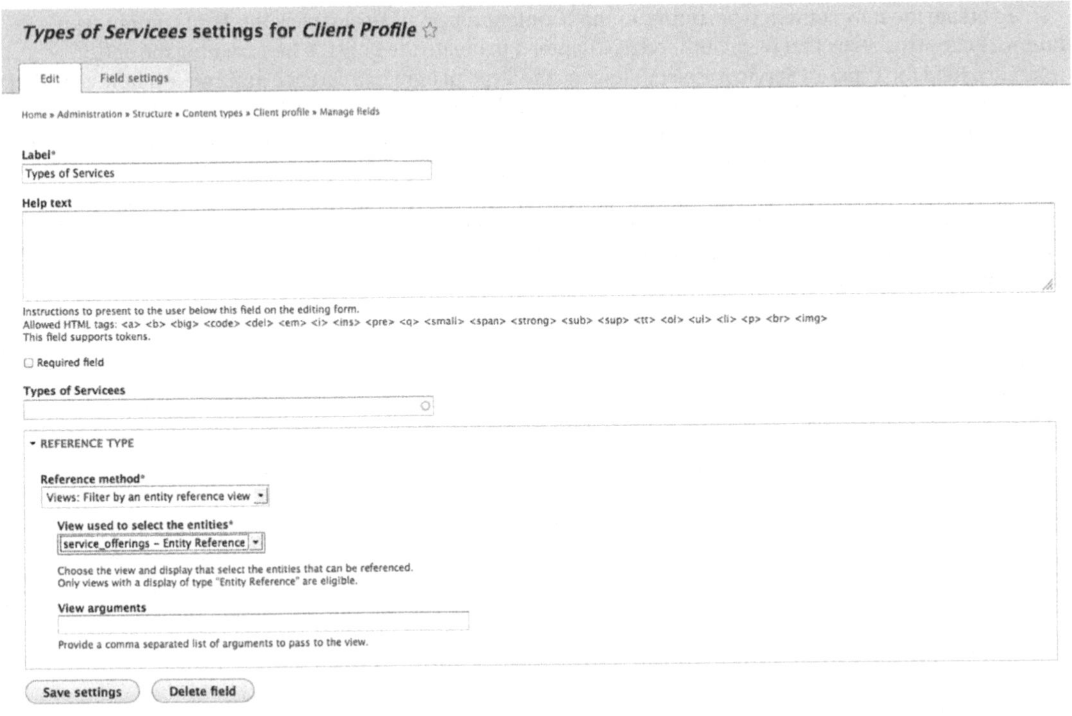

Types of Servicees settings for Client Profile ☆

| Edit | Field settings |

Home » Administration » Structure » Content types » Client profile » Manage fields

Label*

Types of Services

Help text

Instructions to present to the user below this field on the editing form.
Allowed HTML tags: <a> <b> <big> <code> <del> <em> <i> <ins> <pre> <q> <small> <span> <strong> <sub> <sup> <tt> <ol> <ul> <li> <p>
 <img>
This field supports tokens.

☐ Required field

Types of Servicees

▼ REFERENCE TYPE

Reference method*

Views: Filter by an entity reference view ▾

View used to select the entities*

service_offerings – Entity Reference ▾

Choose the view and display that select the entities that can be referenced.
Only views with a display of type "Entity Reference" are eligible.

View arguments

Provide a comma separated list of arguments to pass to the view.

(Save settings)   (Delete field)

Figure 20-5. *Service Offerings entity reference field details*

The final field required for our Client Portfolio content type is another entity reference field that allows an editor to reference staff members (Drupal users) who worked on the project. Follow the same steps as when creating the Service Offerings entity reference field, but instead of selecting Content as the type of item to reference, select User. For Reference Type, leave the Reference method as the default, sorted by Name. After saving the fields, the editorial interface for creating a new client profile should look like the form shown in Figure 20-6.

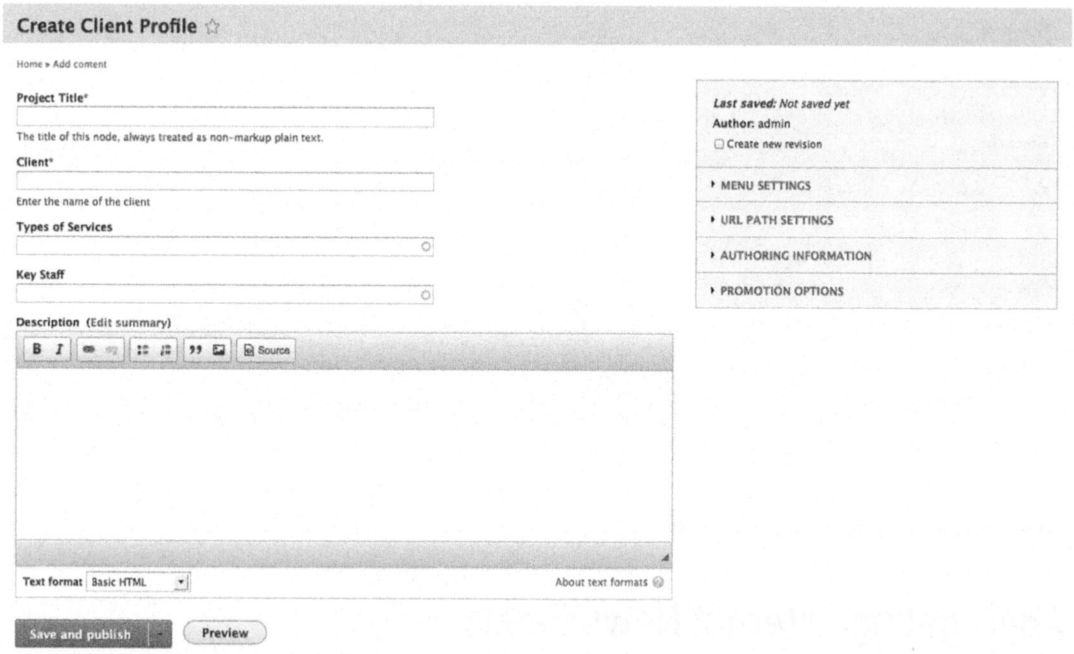

Create Client Profile ☆

Home » Add content

Project Title*

_____

The title of this node, always treated as non-markup plain text.

Client*

_____

Enter the name of the client

Types of Services

_____ ○

Key Staff

_____ ○

Description (Edit summary)

| B | _I_ | ∞ | ⟨⟩ | ⋮⋮ | ⋮⋮ | ⟩⟩ | 🖼 | 🖹 Source |

Text format Basic HTML ▾   About text formats ⓘ

[Save and publish ▾] (Preview)

Last saved: *Not saved yet*
Author: admin
☐ Create new revision

▸ MENU SETTINGS

▸ URL PATH SETTINGS

▸ AUTHORING INFORMATION

▸ PROMOTION OPTIONS

Figure 20-6. *Create Client Profile content item*

Expanding Drupal's User Profile

We are using the standard Drupal 8 user as the basis for collecting and displaying biographical information for key staff members. If you visit the standard Drupal user profile, you'll see that there are fields for entering a username, e-mail address, password, user role, and a picture. For the website, we also need a Biography field to describe our staff members' experience and expertise, as well as fields for their first and last names. To add new fields to the standard Drupal 8 user, click the Configuration link in the secondary menu and the "Account settings" link in the People section of the Configuration page. At the top of the "Account settings" page, you'll find a "Manage fields" tab. You may add fields for Biography, First Name, and Last Name using the same approach as you used to create fields on a content type:

1. Create a new Biography field, selecting text (formatted long) as the field type.

2. Create a new First Name field, selecting text as the field type.

3. Create a new Last Name field, selecting text as the field type.

After adding the fields and saving the changes to the user entity, return to the "Add user" form (People ➤ Add user). You should now see the three new fields on the "Add user" page (see Figure 20-7). Add several staff members to your site.

217

First Name

Last Name

Biography

| B | *I* | | | | | | " | | Source |

Text format Basic HTML

About text formats

Figure 20-7. *User profile with new fields*

Aggregating External News Feeds

One of the requirements we identified earlier in the chapter is the capability to collect news articles from external websites and aggregate those articles into lists on the corporate website. The Aggregator module is part of Drupal core and is a great solution. By default, the Aggregator module is disabled and may be enabled by visiting the Extend page. Click the Extend link in the secondary menu and check the box next to the Aggregator module. Click the "Save configuration" button to enable the Aggregator module.

The next step is to define from which sources we will pull information. On the Configuration page, search for and click the "Feed aggregator" link (Web Services section). On the "Feed aggregator" page, click the "Add feed" button to configure a news feed. For demonstration purposes, we'll use the Reuters Business News RSS feed as the source of content for our news feed by entering "Latest Business News" in the Title field and by copying and pasting the URL from Reuters into the URL field (`http://feeds.reuters.com/reuters/businessNews`). Leave the update interval set to 1 hour, which is how often Drupal will query Reuters for new news articles. After saving the news feed, run cron to pull the content from Reuters (Configuration ➤ Cron). After running cron, return to the Feed aggregator configuration page and click the feed's title to view the latest news (see Figure 20-8).

Home

Home » Feed aggregator » Sources

Latest Business News

| View | Configure |

1   2   next ›   last »

Former e-commerce executive pleads guilty in eBay insider case

2 hours 29 min ago

(Reuters) - A former executive at an e-commerce company that was acquired in 2011 by online retailer eBay Inc pleaded guilty on Friday to insider trading in connection with the takeover.

Deutsche Telekom seeks breakup fee of more than $1 billion on T-Mobile-Sprint deal: WSJ

2 hours 40 min ago

(Reuters) - Deutsche Telekom AG wants to be compensated by Sprint Corp in the event its planned merger with the German firm's T-Mobile US Inc does not win regulatory approval, the Wall Street Journal reported, citing people familiar with the matter.

Figure 20-8. *The latest news from Reuters*

Contact Form

Another requirement for our corporate site is to have a contact form where site visitors can submit requests for information. Drupal 8 ships with a Contact module that provides functionality that meets the requirements of most Contact Us forms. To configure the contact form, click Structure in the secondary menu, followed by the "Contact form" categories link on the Structure page. The Contact module offers a "Website feedback" form that is great for general contact requests. Click the Edit link for the "Website feedback" form and, on the Edit tab, enter the e-mail addresses of the recipients of contact requests from the website. If you would like to send a response to the visitor who submitted the request, enter a message in the Auto-reply text area.

Next, click the Manage Form Display tab to see the fields that appear by default on the contact form. The default fields are for the sender's name, e-mail address, a subject, a message, and a check box that allows the user to request that a copy of the message be sent to their e-mail address. You may add new fields by clicking the Manage Fields tab. For demonstration purposes, we will use the standard fields, as they address all of our corporate website needs.

Assembling the Site

With the foundational elements in place, it is time to start assembling the rest of the site. We'll walk through the requirements, building each section of the site using the tools that were assembled in the previous steps.

The About US Page

The first requirement is to provide an About Us page. We'll use the "Basic page" content type to fulfill that requirement. To create a new Basic page, click the Content link in the secondary menu and click the "Add content" button. Select the "Basic page" content type and proceed to fill out the title (About Us) and the body. Add the new Basic page to the "Main navigation" menu so that visitors have an easy path for getting to the About Us page. After authoring the content and saving the About Us page, it appears in the Main navigation menu and the content appears on the site (see Figure 20-9).

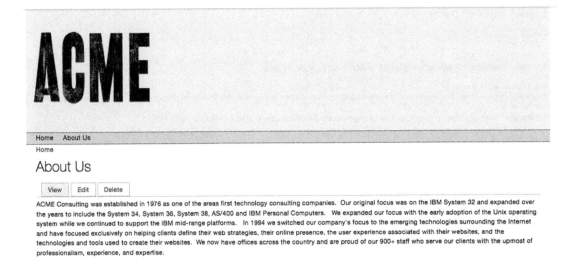

Figure 20-9. *The About Us page*

The Client Portfolio Page

The Client Portfolio page will be constructed using a view that displays a list of client profile content items, sorted in date published, descending, as teasers. We will also create a featured Client Project view, randomly selecting one of the published content items and displaying that Client Portfolio content item as a full article.

The first step is to create several client profile content items so that we have content to work with when creating the views. Each client profile links to one or more service offerings and one or more staff members. We'll first create several service offering content items using the Article content type, selecting "Service offering" as the Article Type being created. We'll also create several Drupal user accounts for featured staff members. To create the service offerings, click the Content link in the secondary menu followed by the "Create content" button. To create new users, click the People link in the secondary menu followed by the "Add user" button.

After creating service offerings and users, create the first client profile, as shown in Figure 20-10. The Type Of Services reference field works like a search filter. I typed in the first few letters of the service, and the view I created returned a list of service offering content items that have titles that start with the letters that I typed. The same approach works with the Key Staff field.

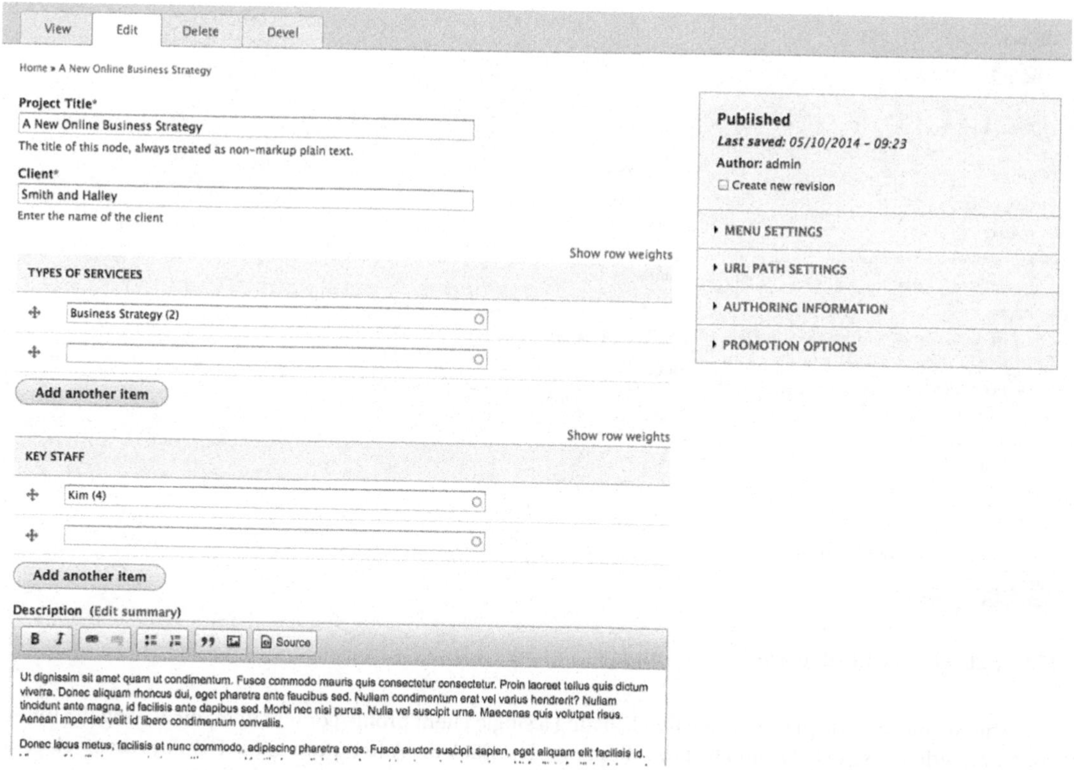

Figure 20-10. *A client profile content item*

After creating a number of client profile content items, we're ready to create the view that will be used on the Client Portfolio page. We'll create a generic view that is tied to the client profile content type and add various view displays to accomplish the goals and requirements of the site. The first display that we will create is a Page. For the page view, follow the steps outlined in Chapter 9, adding a URL in the Path field, linking the page to the Main navigation menu, and showing content as a teaser (see Figure 20-11).

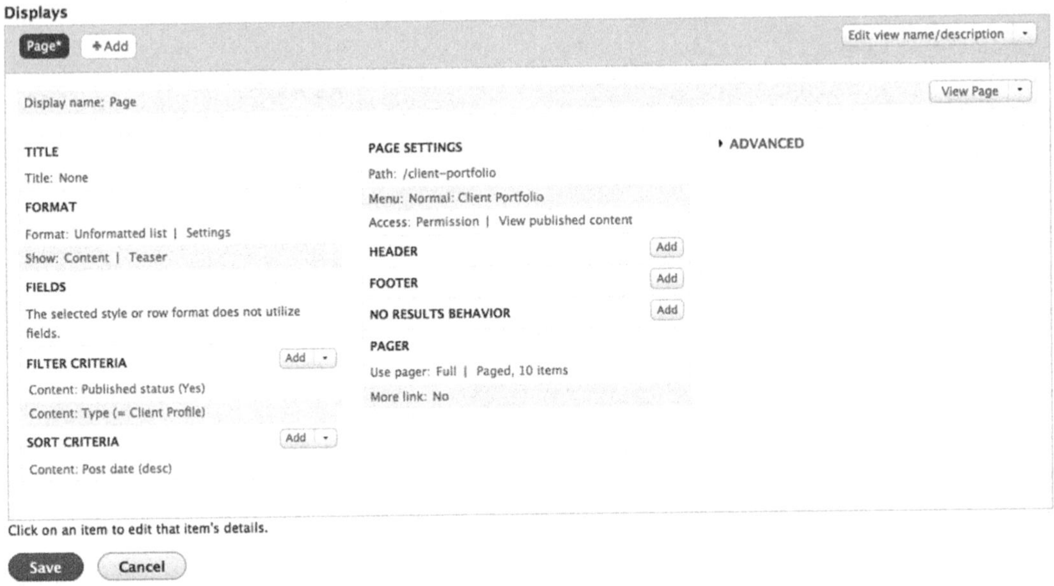

Figure 20-11. *The Client portfolio view display*

The second view display will be a Block, listing a single client profile content item, displaying the full content, randomly selected from all of the client profiles. Click the Add button in the Displays area, select Block, and make the following changes to the display:

1. Change the "Display name" field from Block to Featured.

2. Change the Title field to "Featured Client Project," and add a Title to the page display using Client Portfolio (see Chapter 9 for details on how to change the title).

3. Change the value for Show in the Format section so that it shows the Default display instead of the Teaser.

4. Change the Sort Criteria settings, removing the sort by Post date adding a Random sort.

5. Change the Pager setting to display a single item.

6. Save the view.

The end result of making those changes is that there is now a Block display for the featured client profile that we can then add to the Sidebar Second region through the "Block layout" page (see Chapter 8). On the "Block layout" page, select the Client Profile: Featured block from the "Place blocks" box and set the Region to "Sidebar second." Also set the block to display only on the Client Portfolio page. After making those changes, the new Client Portfolio page looks awesome (see Figure 20-12).

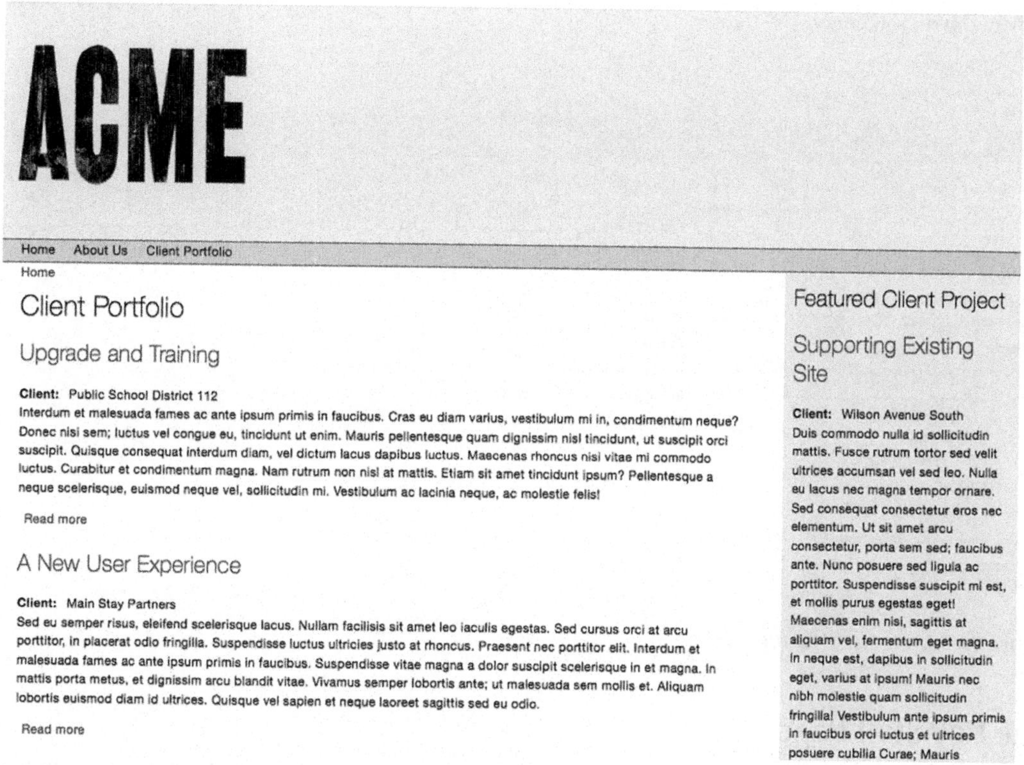

ACME

Home   About Us   Client Portfolio

Home

Client Portfolio

Upgrade and Training

Client: Public School District 112

Interdum et malesuada fames ac ante ipsum primis in faucibus. Cras eu diam varius, vestibulum mi in, condimentum neque? Donec nisi sem; luctus vel congue eu, tincidunt ut enim. Mauris pellentesque quam dignissim nisl tincidunt, ut suscipit orci suscipit. Quisque consequat interdum diam, vel dictum lacus dapibus luctus. Maecenas rhoncus nisi vitae mi commodo luctus. Curabitur et condimentum magna. Nam rutrum non nisl at mattis. Etiam sit amet tincidunt ipsum? Pellentesque a neque scelerisque, euismod neque vel, sollicitudin mi. Vestibulum ac lacinia neque, ac molestie felis!

Read more

A New User Experience

Client: Main Stay Partners

Sed eu semper risus, eleifend scelerisque lacus. Nullam facilisis sit amet leo iaculis egestas. Sed cursus orci at arcu porttitor, in placerat odio fringilla. Suspendisse luctus ultricies justo at rhoncus. Praesent nec porttitor elit. Interdum et malesuada fames ac ante ipsum primis in faucibus. Suspendisse vitae magna a dolor suscipit scelerisque in et magna. In mattis porta metus, et dignissim arcu blandit vitae. Vivamus semper lobortis ante; ut malesuada sem mollis et. Aliquam lobortis euismod diam id ultrices. Quisque vel sapien et neque laoreet sagittis sed eu odio.

Read more

Featured Client Project

Supporting Existing Site

Client: Wilson Avenue South

Duis commodo nulla id sollicitudin mattis. Fusce rutrum tortor sed velit ultrices accumsan vel sed leo. Nulla eu lacus nec magna tempor ornare. Sed consequat consectetur eros nec elementum. Ut sit amet arcu consectetur, porta sem sed; faucibus ante. Nunc posuere sed ligula ac porttitor. Suspendisse suscipit mi est, et mollis purus egestas eget! Maecenas enim nisi, sagittis at aliquam vel, fermentum eget magna. In neque est, dapibus in sollicitudin eget, varius at ipsum! Mauris nec nibh molestie quam sollicitudin fringilla! Vestibulum ante ipsum primis in faucibus orci luctus et ultrices posuere cubilia Curae; Mauris

Figure 20-12. *The Client Portfolio page*

The Service Offerings Page

Create the Service Offerings page by using a view that creates a Page display, displaying teasers of all Article content items that have the taxonomy term of Service Offering. Add a path to the view (service-offerings) and add it to the Main navigation menu so that site visitors have easy access to the page. The view as it is set up should look something similar to Figure 20-13.

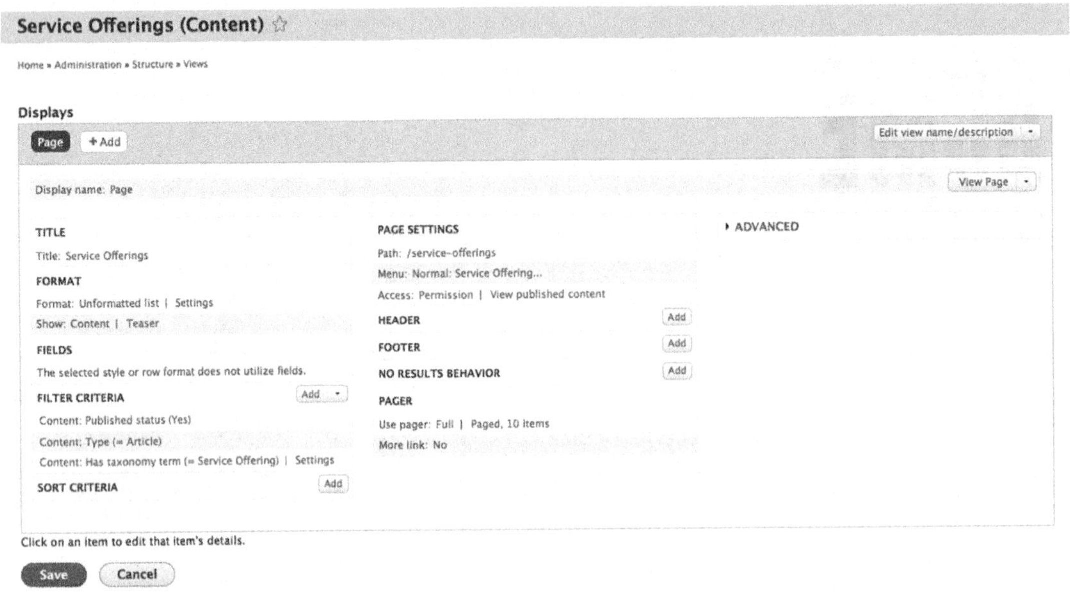

Service Offerings (Content) ☆

Home » Administration » Structure » Views

Displays

[Page] [+ Add]   [Edit view name/description ▾]

Display name: Page   [View Page ▾]

TITLE   **PAGE SETTINGS**   ▸ ADVANCED

Title: Service Offerings   Path: /service-offerings

FORMAT   Menu: Normal: Service Offering...

Format: Unformatted list | Settings   Access: Permission | View published content

Show: Content | Teaser   **HEADER** [Add]

FIELDS   **FOOTER** [Add]

The selected style or row format does not utilize fields.   **NO RESULTS BEHAVIOR** [Add]

FILTER CRITERIA [Add ▾]   **PAGER**

Content: Published status (Yes)   Use pager: Full | Paged, 10 Items

Content: Type (= Article)   More link: No

Content: Has taxonomy term (= Service Offering) | Settings

SORT CRITERIA [Add]

Click on an item to edit that item's details.

[Save] [Cancel]

Figure 20-13. Service Offerings view

The Key Staff Page

We'll follow the same approach for creating the Key Staff page, using views as the mechanism for displaying user profile information on a page. To make it easier to distinguish staff members, we'll add a new user role called Staff and assign each staff member to that role.

To create a new role, click the People link in the secondary menu, followed by clicking the Roles tab at the top of the screen. Click the "Add role" button and enter a new role called Staff. Click the List tab to return to the list of users. We will use a feature called Views bulk operations to assign all user accounts that are staff to the Staff role. As shown in Figure 20-14, check the box next to each user that you want to assign as staff and select "Add the Staff role to the selected users" from the "With selection" drop-down list.

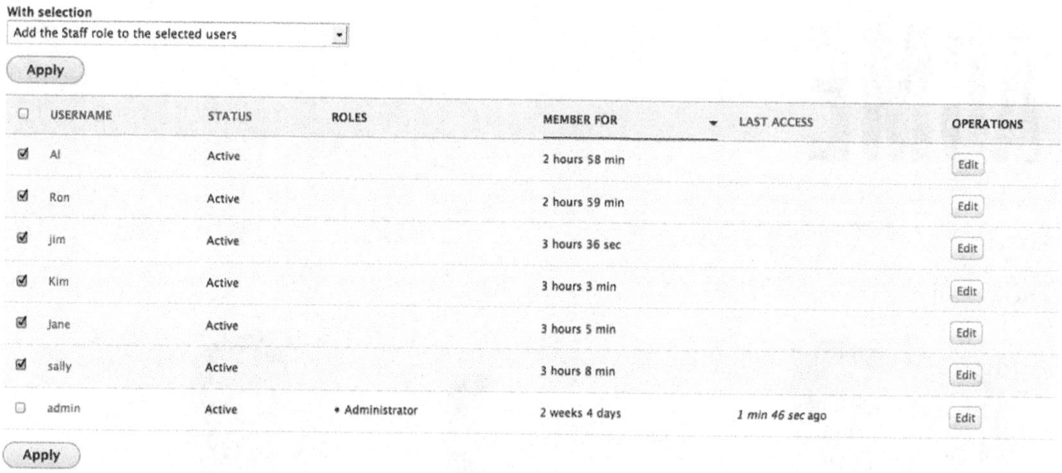

With selection

| Add the Staff role to the selected users | ▾ |

Apply

	USERNAME	STATUS	ROLES	MEMBER FOR	▾	LAST ACCESS	OPERATIONS
☑	Al	Active		2 hours 58 min			Edit
☑	Ron	Active		2 hours 59 min			Edit
☑	Jim	Active		3 hours 36 sec			Edit
☑	Kim	Active		3 hours 3 min			Edit
☑	Jane	Active		3 hours 5 min			Edit
☑	sally	Active		3 hours 8 min			Edit
☐	admin	Active	• Administrator	2 weeks 4 days		1 min 46 sec ago	Edit

Apply

Figure 20-14. *Assigning users to the Staff role*

Click the Apply button, and all of the user roles that we checked are now assigned as Staff, making it easy to use views to extract the list of user accounts to display as key staff members on the site.

To create the view, select Users from the Show select list in the View Settings area of the "Add new view" page, followed by clicking "Save and edit." Add a Page display, use "staff" as the URL in the Path field, and add the page to the Main navigation menu via the Menu field. Add a Title to the view, set the Format to Grid, and display 3 users per row in the grid's settings. Unlike the content views that we've created previously in this chapter, we are going to use specific fields to construct a gallery of staff. The three fields that we'll add to the view are the User's picture, First Name, and Biography. Remove the Name field that is added by default. Also trim the user's biography to the first 300 characters by clicking on the rewrite results section of the field configuration form and selecting Trim this field to a maximum number of characters, entering 300 as the value in the Maximum number of characters field. Add a Filter to only show users who are assigned to the role of Staff. After making those changes, we are ready to save the view and examine the page (see Figure 20-15).

Home   About Us   Key Staff   Service Offerings   Client Portfolio
Home

Key Staff

Al

Donec eget consectetur erat. Nullam eget
pellentesque sapien. Etiam lacinia sem at hendrerit
accumsan. Curabitur lorem mi, rutrum sed neque a,
tristique consequat sapien. Etiam at neque eu nulla
scelerisque sollicitudin. Praesent laoreet bibendum
massa, ac tincidunt libero commodo eget.

Jane

Aliquam euismod dolor et dictum dictum. Duis
condimentum rutrum arcu, et sodales purus
fermentum nec? Maecenas a est sodales, sollicitudin
ipsum ut, tristique ante. Donec interdum lorem lacus.
Sed facilisis, lectus vel ultricies blandit, nunc mi
volutpat augue, non malesuada enim arcu nec felis.

Jim

Aliquam nec dapibus quam. Nullam pharetra, dui
placerat accumsan pulvinar, nulla enim laoreet est,
vel venenatis orci enim ac lorem. Cras urna mauris,
eleifend rutrum imperdiet sed, accumsan aliquet
augue? Morbi in eros porta, congue dolor in,
convallis eros.

Figure 20-15. *The Key Staff page*

I made a few minor modifications to effect the look I wanted for the page. I added a few CSS attributes to the `style.css` style sheet, specifically making the name bold and slightly bigger than normal text and adding padding to the view columns. I also created a new image style (Configuration ➤ Image styles) called Profile. I created an effect of scaling and cropping the images uploaded by the user to 250px wide and 225px high. I edited the view and assigned the new image format to the picture. I also updated the image attributes on the user profile to accept larger pictures. I removed the restrictions placed by Drupal 8 by blanking out the values found on the Picture settings for User (Configuration ➤ Account settings ➤ Manage fields). The end result of the minor modifications is what is shown in Figure 20-15.

The News Page

Earlier we added a taxonomy term for News to the Article Type taxonomy vocabulary, providing the capability to use the Article content type as the template for authoring news. To follow the example, create a few sample News articles to have as material to test out our view. Create a new view for News, creating a Page display that provides a link to the News page. This view will list Articles that are filtered by the taxonomy term News, sorted by post date in descending order so that the newest item is always at the top. Use Teasers as the format for the output, and set the Title of the Page display to "Latest News." Also create a Block view display that lists only the latest five news article titles and publish dates. Use this block on the homepage. After creating the view, the output of our News page is as shown in Figure 20-16.

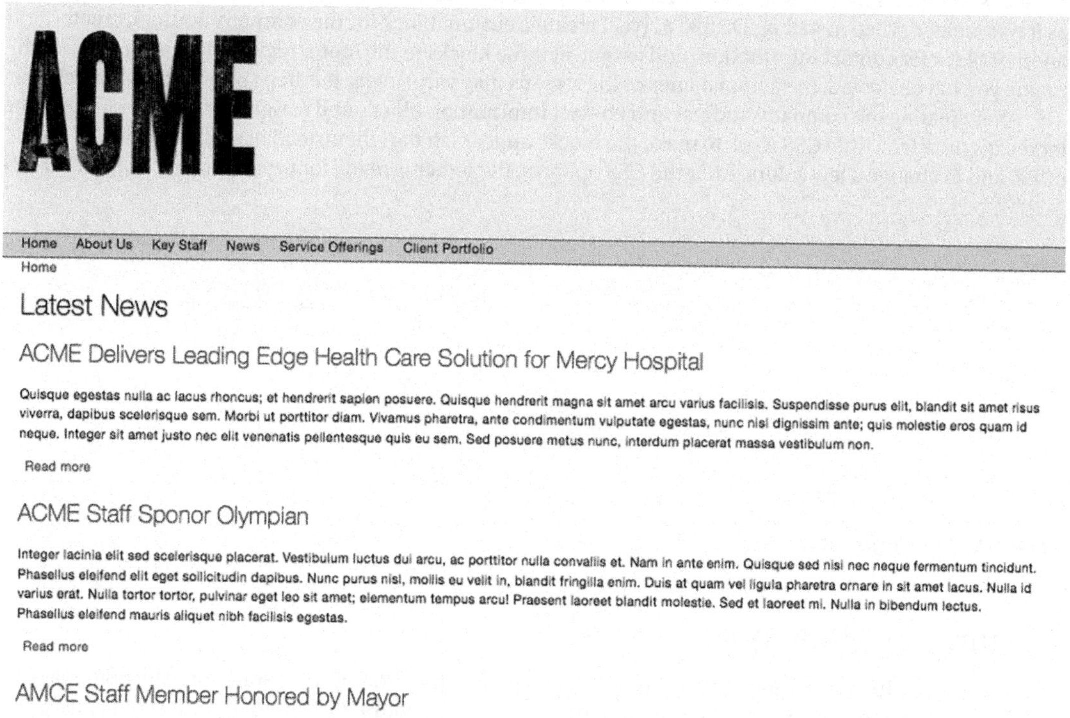

Figure 20-16. *The News page*

The Staff Blog Page

One of the requirements is that staff should have the capability to blog. When we created the Article Type taxonomy vocabulary, we included a term named Blog Post. That term is available on the Article content type, which is the template that we'll use for staff to blog. Each staff will have the ability to log onto the site and author Article content, selecting Blog Post from the Article Type. Go ahead and author a few blog posts so that you can create and test a view to display Blogs.

Follow the same pattern for Blogs as we used for News, a page displaying all blog posts as well as a block for displaying the latest blog posts on the homepage. Set the Path for the Page display to "blogs" and add the view to the Main navigation menu. Also create a Block display that lists the latest five blog posts, showing only the title and the date the blog post was posted.

Adding the Contact Form to the Main Menu

The next step is to add the contact form to the Main navigation menu (Structure ➤ Menus ➤ Main navigation). Edit the menu, click the "Add link" button, and add a new menu item with a "Menu link title" of "Contact Us" and a Path of "contact." Refer to Chapter 7 for more information about managing menus.

Creating the Footer

The footer will display the Main navigation menu, company address, and contact information. All three elements will be displayed using blocks via the Block layout. The Main navigation menu block already exists, as it was created when installing Drupal 8. We'll create a custom block for the company address, create another block for contact information, and assign all three blocks to the footer region (depending on which theme you have selected, the actual names of the regions may vary) using the steps outlined in Chapter 10.

After creating the company address and contact information blocks and assigning all three blocks to the footer, it's time for a little CSS work to make the blocks appear left to right instead of stacked on top of each other, and to change a few colors. After the CSS updates, the footer is ready for production (see Figure 20-17).

Figure 20-17. *Site footer*

Creating the Homepage

The final step in the site-building process is to create the homepage for our corporate site. The homepage will consist of a simple introductory paragraph that describes the company, a list of the latest blog posts, latest news items, and the news feed created by the aggregator.

First, visit the "Block layout" page and assign the News: Homepage News block to the Featured First region, remembering to only show the block on the homepage (by using <front> as the value entered in the "Show for the listed pages" text area). Assign the Blog: Homepage Blog Posts block to the Featured Second region, also setting the block visibility to only show on the homepage. Assign the Aggregator feed block to the Featured Third region, also setting block visibility to only show on the homepage, overriding the default title to "Latest Business News," and setting the number of items to display to 5.

The last item to add to the homepage is the introductory paragraph that describes ACME Co. Use a standard Article as the source of information about ACME. To force the article to appear on the homepage, check the "Promoted to front page" option in the "Promotion options" section of the Article edit form. The last step is to update the standard off-the-shelf Frontpage view to display the default view of content instead of the teaser.

The result of all of the work is a great start to a corporate website, as shown in Figure 20-18.

ACME

Home About Us Blogs Contact Key Staff News Service Offerings Client Portfolio

ACME Co. The Trusted Source

Submitted by admin on Sat, 05/10/2014 - 18:38

Pellentesque ut sem eget magna volutpat consequat eget id tortor! Quisque sagittis urna eu enim sodales, ut rhoncus justo faucibus. Fusce dictum tristique lectus, quis tristique ipsum egestas eu! Pellentesque et elit augue. Quisque at pretium est. Nunc id tincidunt odio. Pellentesque habitant morbi tristique senectus et netus et malesuada fames ac turpis egestas. Proin dapibus quis turpis in sollicitudin. Praesent euismod odio et justo sagittis tempor.

Donec vitae congue ante; eget auctor risus. Donec lobortis scelerisque magna sed imperdiet. In vel pellentesque ipsum, eu tempor sem. Integer erat odio, accumsan a elit et, lacinia commodo urna. Proin at gravida tortor. Aliquam erat volutpat. Fusce tempus, orci eu scelerisque sodales, libero urna vulputate quam, id laoreet enim magna ac sem. Aenean in magna sollicitudin, luctus leo vel, accumsan arcu. Morbi non est a orci bibendum dapibus ac et enim. Pellentesque habitant morbi tristique senectus et netus et malesuada fames ac turpis egestas. Duis rutrum et augue ut congue. Curabitur viverra magna a diam tempus, sed eleifend diam molestie.

Aliquam vulputate mattis pretium. Aliquam sodales eget tellus eget dignissim. Fusce vulputate elit eu orci porttitor interdum! Cras vel venenatis elit, id iaculis dui. Etiam aliquet sit amet mi vitae congue. Sed porta tellus id metus adipiscing cursus? Aliquam tempus, nisl non tincidunt tempus, quam nunc condimentum turpis, eu vulputate lorem nibh interdum dolor.

Latest News

ACME Delivers Leading Edge Health Care Solution for Mercy Hospital
Sat, 05/10/2014 - 13:32
ACME Staff Sponor Olympian
Sat, 05/10/2014 - 13:32
AMCE Staff Member Honored by Mayor
Sat, 05/10/2014 - 13:32
ACME Receives Award
Sat, 05/10/2014 - 13:31
ACME Opens New Office
Sat, 05/10/2014 - 13:31

Our Latest Blog Postings

Is a Balanced Life a Myth?
Sat, 05/10/2014 - 13:51
What Worked, What Failed
Sat, 05/10/2014 - 13:50
Content Strategy 101
Sat, 05/10/2014 - 13:50
Can Agile Succeed on All Projects?
Sat, 05/10/2014 - 13:49
User Experience Best Practices for Mobile Devices
Sat, 05/10/2014 - 13:48

Latest Business News

- Under fire, Pfizer hits back as it weighs next Astra move
- Murdoch reported to be moving to consolidate European pay-TV holdings
- Lonmin expects mass return at strike-hit South Africa platinum mines
- Venezuela's Polar finds temporary solution to currency hurdle
- Merkel says German government would support Siemens-Alstom tie-up

More

Home
About Us
Blogs
Contact
Key Staff
News
Service Offerings
Client Portfolio

ACME Co.
555 West Main Street
Suite 102
Anytown, CA 95123

Phone: 415-555-1212
Fax: 415-555-1313
Email: info@acmeco.com

Figure 20-18. *The homepage*

Summary

In this chapter I covered the methodology for creating a new corporate website using Drupal 8, linking the methodology back to the steps covered throughout the rest of the book. The site created in this chapter may be the end-all website for a company, or it might represent the starting point for something much bigger. With Drupal, all things are possible and you are only limited by your imagination and the amount of time required to build your dreams.

In the next chapter we'll look at how to build a different kind of Drupal 8–based website, a community-based website using an off-the-shelf Drupal distribution, Drupal Commons.

■ ■ ■

## CHAPTER 21

Building a Community Site

The ability for people to assemble in online communities has exploded over the past several years. There are online communities for nearly everything you can think of—from technology (think Drupal!), sports (e.g., fans of a soccer club), and entertainment (e.g., enthusiasts of a particular music genre), to food, nutrition, boating, flying, hiking, endangered animals, and thousands of other topics for which there are groups of people who gather in a virtual community to share ideas, ask questions, set up events, and connect. There are online communities focused around individual products, groups of products, and companies. There are also online communities sponsored by companies to help guide and direct those who purchase their goods and services. The opportunities are limitless; all it takes is two or more people and an idea to launch an online community.

Drupal is an excellent platform for building an online community, and the Drupal Commons distribution (`www.drupal.org/project/commons`) provides an off-the-shelf solution that fulfills a vast majority of the functional requirements for online communities. In this chapter I'll create an online community site focused on those who want to learn about Drupal. You can follow along and build the same site as a learning exercise, or you can use the example as a guide to create your own community site.

Requirements for a Community Site

As always, the place to start when creating any website is to identify the requirements for the site. The requirements for a community site are relatively common across all types of online communities:

1. The capability to grow and create new subgroups organically within the community site.

2. The capability to publish content.

3. The capability to create and manage a wiki.

4. The capability to author and publish information about events.

5. The capability for users to create relationships and follow each other.

Drupal Commons provides all of these capabilities as part of the base distribution.

Installing Drupal Commons

The first step in creating the corporate site is to install Drupal Commons. You can download the Drupal Commons distribution from `www.drupal.org/project/commons`. As with previous examples of installing Drupal, you'll need to expand the tar or zip file in the appropriate directory on your web server (check your web server's documentation for the directory in which a site should reside on your web server platform).

After expanding the archive file, you'll note that what you have is a top-level directory named something like `commons-8.x-3.12`. You will need to move all of the files up one directory to keep from having to enter `example.com/commons-8.x-3.12` to get to your site. On Linux or OS X, you can move the files by navigating to the `commons-8.x-3.12` directory (note your directory will likely be named something different depending on the version that you've downloaded) and using the following commands:

```
mv * ../
mv .* ../
```

It's important to note that using `mv * ../` does not move key files like `.htaccess`. The second move command does move those hidden files up a level.

After moving all the files, you are free to delete the distribution directory that was created when you expanded the Drupal Commons archive file. While working with the files, you'll also need to create a `settings.php` file. Navigate to your site's `site/default` directory and copy the `default.settings.php` file to `settings.php`. You also need to create a `files` directory. For both of these items, you'll also need to set the permissions so that the web server can read and write to the file and directory.

After getting the files in place, it's time to create a new empty database, database user ID, and password, and assign the rights to the user so that they can modify the content and structure of the database. Check with your hosting provider's documentation or, if you're installing the site locally, the LAMP, MAMP, or WAMP stack provider's documentation on how to create a new MySQL database and create users (e.g., using PHPMyAdmin).

After performing the preliminary setup tasks, it's time to install Drupal Commons. The installation process for Commons begins the same as with Drupal 8 core, visiting the URL of where the site is installed.

You may encounter an error stating that the PHP Max Execution Time value is too low. If you are using a typical MAMP, LAMP, or WAMP stack, the PHP Max Execution Time is often set to 30 seconds. Due to long-running jobs that are associated with the tasks performed on a Drupal Commons site, that value will need to be increased to 120 seconds. You can make that change through several venues, but the easiest is to add the following line of code to the bottom of your `sites/default/settings.php` file:

```
ini_set('max_execution_time', 120);
```

The first form that appears in the installation process is the standard Drupal 8 installation form for setting database information (Set up the database). Enter the appropriate values in the Database name, Database username, and Database password fields and click the "Save and continue" button.

The next form is the standard Drupal 8 site information configuration form (Configure site). Enter the appropriate values for the Site name, Site e-mail address, Site maintenance account, Default country, and Timezone. The Site maintenance account is equivalent to the standard Drupal 8 administrator's account but with a larger role in managing the community as a whole.

The next step is to pick the color palette for the site (Choose site color palette). This is the first major deviation from the standard Drupal 8 core installation process. Pick the palette and save it to continue to the next step.

Next you are prompted to enter the welcome text for the homepage (see Figure 21-1). On this page you are prompted to enter a Welcome headline, Welcome body text, and determine whether to install the example content. For demonstration purposes, I'm going to install the example content, but when you are creating a new site, if you don't want to try out Commons with content, uncheck the "Install example content" check box.

Home

✓ Verify requirements

✓ Set up database

✓ Install profile

✓ Configure site

✓ Choose site color palette

▶ **Enter Homepage welcome text**

Create the first group

Finished

Homepage welcome text

Below, enter text that will be shown on your community's homepage to help new visitors understand what your community is about and why they should join. The image below shows an example of how this text will appear. You can always change this text later.

Welcome headline *

Welcome to Learning about Drupal

A short description of the community that visitors can understand at a glance.

Welcome body text *

Learning Drupal 8 is fun, especially when you're doing it with a group of friends. Join our community and learn, share, teach.

Enter a couple of sentences elaborating about your community.

☑ Install example content

Install Commons with example content so that you can get a sense of what your site will look like once it becomes more active. Example content includes a group, a few users and content for that group. Example content can be modified or deleted like normal content.

Save and continue

Figure 21-1. *Creating the homepage welcome text*

The next step in the process is to create the first community by providing a Group name and a Group description. The first group on the example Learning Drupal community site will be named "New to Drupal," geared toward those who haven't worked with Drupal in the past (see Figure 21-2). Click "Save and continue" to complete the installation.

Create the first group in your new community.

Commons uses groups to collect community members and content related to a particular interest, working goal or geographic area.

✓ Verify requirements

✓ Set up database

✓ Install profile

✓ Configure site

✓ Choose site color palette

✓ Enter Homepage welcome text

▶ **Create the first group**

Finished

Group name *

New to Drupal

For example: "Boston food lovers" or "Engineering team."

Group description *

A group focused on those who are new to the Drupal platform.

This text will appear on the group's homepage and helps new contributors to become familiar with the purpose of the group. You can always change this text or add another group later.

(Save and continue)

Figure 21-2. *Setting up the first group*

After Drupal completes the installation process, you are directed back to the homepage and the site is ready to go. Figure 21-3 shows the sample site with sample content.

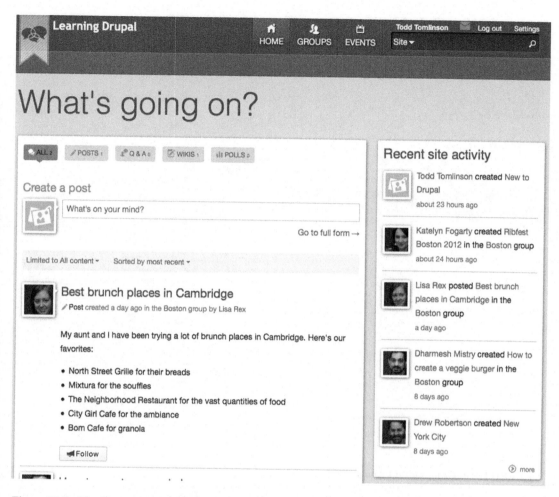

Figure 21-3. *The Community Site with sample content*

The homepage displays a summary of activities performed on the site by the various groups and members of those groups who are contained within the sample community site. Clicking the Groups link at the top of the page displays the landing page that lists all of the groups on the site, and an overview of each group (see Figure 21-4).

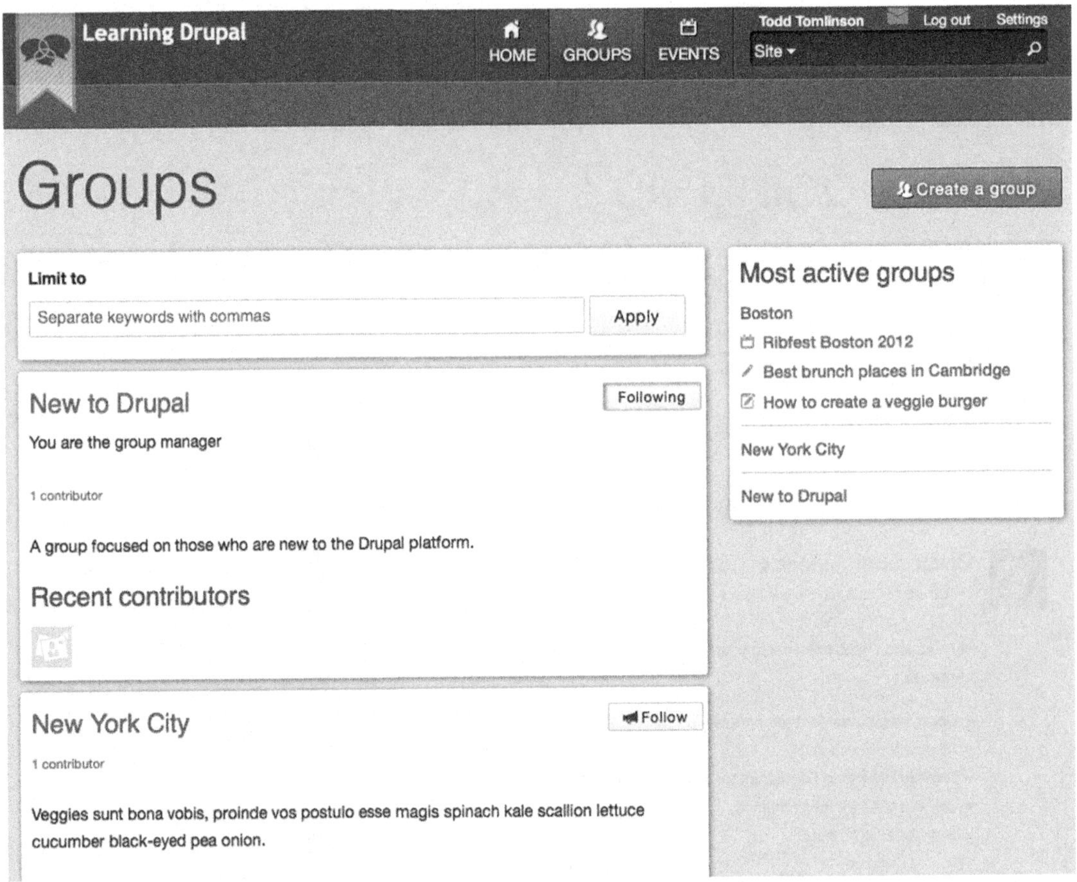

Figure 21-4. *The Groups landing page*

Clicking a group's name takes you to the landing page for that group, displaying all of the posts that have been made on the group, who the group contributors are, as well as other elements that the group deems as appropriate for their landing page (e.g., list of upcoming events). Figure 21-5 shows the New to Drupal group landing page.

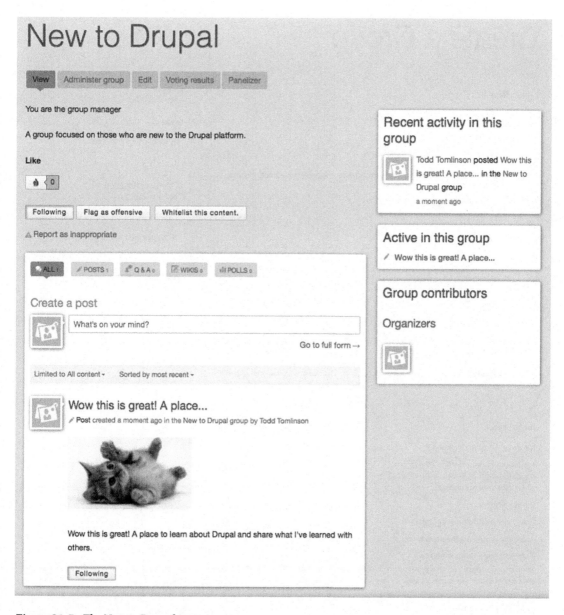

Figure 21-5. *The New to Drupal group page*

Creating New Groups

We created the New to Drupal group during the installation process of the site, but what if we wanted to add a new group? Drupal Commons provides the capability to add and manage groups through the Content page. Click Content in the admin menu, and on the Content page click the Add Content button. Select Group as the content type that you wish to create, and on the Create a Group page, enter the details for the new group (see Figure 21-6).

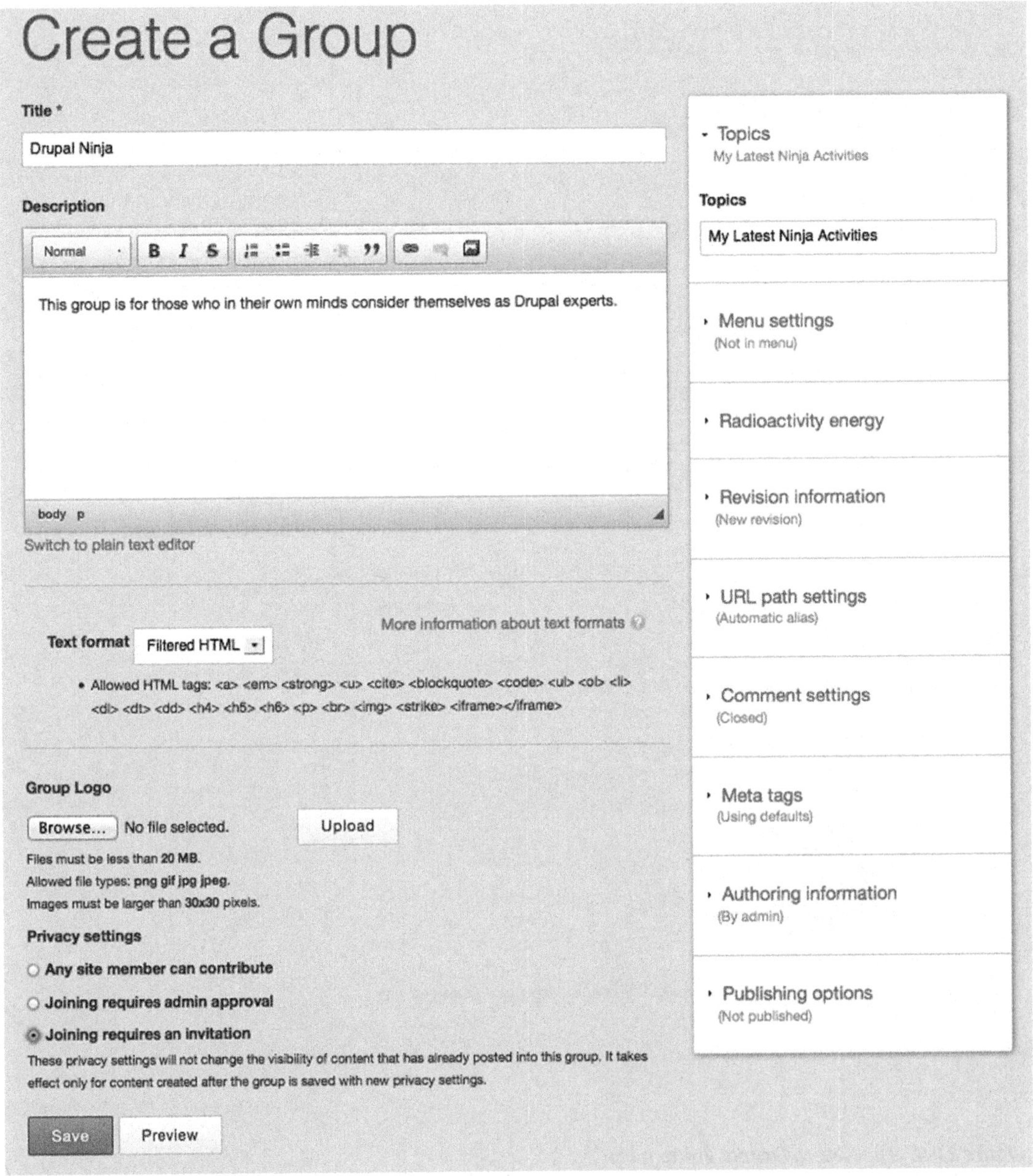

Create a Group

Title *

> Drupal Ninja

Description

| Normal · | **B** *I* S̶ | ☰ ☷ ⁀ ⁀ ❞ | 🔗 🔗 🖼 |

> This group is for those who in their own minds consider themselves as Drupal experts.

body p

Switch to plain text editor

More information about text formats ⓘ

Text format   Filtered HTML ▾

- Allowed HTML tags: <a> <em> <strong> <u> <cite> <blockquote> <code> <ul> <ol> <li>
  <dl> <dt> <dd> <h4> <h5> <h6> <p>
 <img> <strike> <iframe></iframe>

Group Logo

[Browse...] No file selected.   [Upload]

Files must be less than 20 MB.
Allowed file types: png gif jpg jpeg.
Images must be larger than 30x30 pixels.

Privacy settings

○ Any site member can contribute

○ Joining requires admin approval

◉ Joining requires an invitation

These privacy settings will not change the visibility of content that has already posted into this group. It takes
effect only for content created after the group is saved with new privacy settings.

[Save]   [Preview]

▾ Topics
My Latest Ninja Activities

Topics

> My Latest Ninja Activities

▸ Menu settings
(Not in menu)

▸ Radioactivity energy

▸ Revision information
(New revision)

▸ URL path settings
(Automatic alias)

▸ Comment settings
(Closed)

▸ Meta tags
(Using defaults)

▸ Authoring information
(By admin)

▸ Publishing options
(Not published)

Figure 21-6. Creating a new group

In the example, I'm creating a new group for Drupal Ninjas. I've provided a Title for the group, entered a Description of the group, set the Privacy settings so that only people I choose to invite can be a member of the group (after all, Drupal Ninjas are a rare breed), and created the first topic for discussion in the Topics field. Clicking the Save button adds the new group, at which point it's ready to receive new members. Since the group is restricted, it will not appear on the public side of the site unless the person logs in and is a member of the Ninjas.

Adding Events

Drupal Commons provides a great tool for creating and listing events on the site. To create a new event, click the Content link in the admin menu followed by the "Add content" link on the Content page. Select Event from the list of content types and fill out the details for the event. The Event content type provides fields for the Title of the event, the Description of the event, a URL for more information about the event, the groups associated with the event, the date and location of the event, and other information such as whether registration is required and how many people can attend the meeting. After adding an event, it automatically appears on the list of events, found by clicking the Events link in the primary navigation menu.

Creating Posts

One of the most common uses of groups is to share information with other members. The primary mechanism for posting status information is through the Posts feature. To create a new post, visit the group's landing page enter content in the Create a post field. You can enter the post directly on the Group landing page or, for more detailed information, after clicking the "Create a post" link then click the "Go to full form" mode by clicking on at the bottom right of the Create a post text field. Posts automatically show up on the Group landing page, sorted in "date created" descending order (newest post first).

Creating Wikis

The other form of content for groups is a wiki, where a wiki is defined as content in which the entire community has the permission to add, change, and delete content. To create a wiki for a group, click the Content link in the admin menu followed by the "Create content" link. Select Wiki from the list of content types and enter the Title, Body, and the group associated with the wiki. After you create the wiki, it will appear in the "river of content" that appears on the landing page of the group that is associated with the wiki. Members of the group can then edit the wiki, organically growing the content contained within the document.

Managing Groups

As a manager of a group, you have access to a set of tools that helps you administer your group. Click the Administer Group button near the top of the group's landing page (assuming you are logged in and assigned as the administrator for the group). The Administer Group landing page lists links for adding people to the group, managing the people who are in the group, assigning permissions to those who are assigned to the group, and managing roles. Each group has its own set of user permissions and own set of roles, making each group responsible for managing who has access to what.

Additional Capabilities

There are many additional capabilities that you can use on your Drupal Commons–based site, including these examples:

- *Radioactivity*: The capability to model popularity of content on the site.

- *Follow*: The capability to follow users, content, and groups on the site, similar to Facebook

- *Like*: The capability to "like" a piece of content on the site

- *Social sharing*: The capability to share content on the site with other social media sites

- *Trusted contacts and private messaging*: The capability to connect with other users on the site and message each other

- *Multilingual*: The capability to support multilingual content on a community site

Since Drupal Commons is built on Drupal core, you also can install and enable virtually any other Drupal contributed module on the site.

Summary

Building a community-focused site in Drupal is relatively easy using the Drupal Commons distribution as the starting point for the site. The hardest part of building the site is defining the logistics around who can create a group, who can manage a group, and who can post content. The physical activities of building the site is easy using Drupal Commons.

In the next chapter we'll look at how to build a commerce-based website using an off-the-shelf Drupal distribution, Drupal Commerce.

CHAPTER 22

■ ■ ■

Building a Commerce Site

In a relatively short 20 years, the concept of selling goods and services on the Internet has gone from a novelty to the mainstay of business. If you are a business and don't provide an online channel to sell to your target customers, you are missing out on a tremendous opportunity to increase revenue, market share, and profitability. Drupal Commerce provides a robust and full-featured solution for building online storefronts, and in this chapter I'll walk you through the process of creating a commerce site. To demonstrate the ease of building a commerce site on Drupal, I'll create a site that is focused on selling Drupal T-shirts, coffee cups, and hats. The concepts can be expanded on to sell any physical or virtual goods, so you are welcome to either follow along and build the Drupal commerce site or use the example presented as a guide to create your own commerce site.

Identifying Requirements for a Commerce Site

As you've read several times in this book, the place to start with any website is to identify the requirements for the site.

Requirements for the example commerce site presented in this chapter are common to many commerce sites and include

1. The capability to display products for sale on the site.

2. The capability to sell products that have specific attributes such as size.

3. The capability for shoppers to put items into a shopping cart and manage that shopping cart.

4. The capability for shoppers to check out and pay, including providing a credit card and selecting a shipping method.

5. The capability for shoppers to visit the site and examine previous orders.

With requirements in hand, we can then identify how we're going to meet those requirements with Drupal. Using Drupal Commerce Kickstart as the distribution to build the storefront upon. Commerce Kickstart provides a preconfigured solution that meets many of the requirements right out of the box, including:

- Product templates for creating and displaying products on the site, including products that have attributes such as size

- A shopping cart the provides the capabilities for visitors to put items into a cart and manage those products through the shopping experience, including the checkout process with various payment methods and selecting the method to ship the products (physical goods)

- Customer interface for reviewing previous orders

As a Drupal distribution, the Commerce Kickstart distribution was assembled by a team that has already done all the hard work of putting all the contributed modules in place, making it simple to get your storefront up and running quickly with the least amount of effort. You can also follow the same path that the Commerce Kickstart team did and find all of the related modules and install them individually. I've done it both ways, and I found that using Kickstart is significantly faster and easier, so I'll take the road of least resistance for the demonstration site and start with Commerce Kickstart.

Installing Drupal Commerce Kickstart

The process for installing Drupal Commerce Kickstart is nearly identical to that of installing Drupal 8 core, with the exception of a customized installation interface. Follow the steps for downloading Drupal Commerce Kickstart (`www.drupal.org/project/commerce_kickstart`) into a directory on your web server, performing the same basic steps as installing Drupal core. Create the database and database user and launch the site in your web browser to begin the installation process.

The first step in the process is to accept the Privacy Policy and User Agreement. This differs from installing Drupal 8 core, as there are third-party libraries included in the distribution that require acceptance of the Privacy Policy and User Agreement (see Figure 22-1). If you agree with the terms, click the Let's Get Started! button.

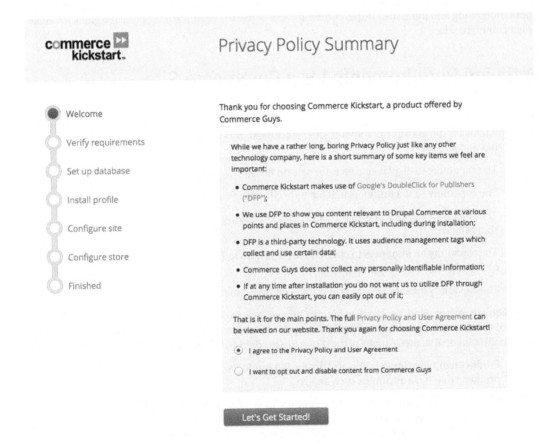

Figure 22-1. *Acknowledging acceptance of the Privacy Policy and User Agreement*

The next step in the process is to verify the requirements for the installation to continue. If you haven't done so already, create the /sites/default/files directory and the settings.php file. These steps are identical to installing Drupal 8 core. Navigate to the file system and create both.

After completing the verification of system requirements, the next step is to specify the Database type, Database name, Database username, and Database password. This is identical to installing Drupal 8 core, with the exception of a slightly different interface (see Figure 22-2). You'll need to create the database either through your hosting provider's administrative interface, MySQL at the command line, or through a tool like PHPMyAdmin.

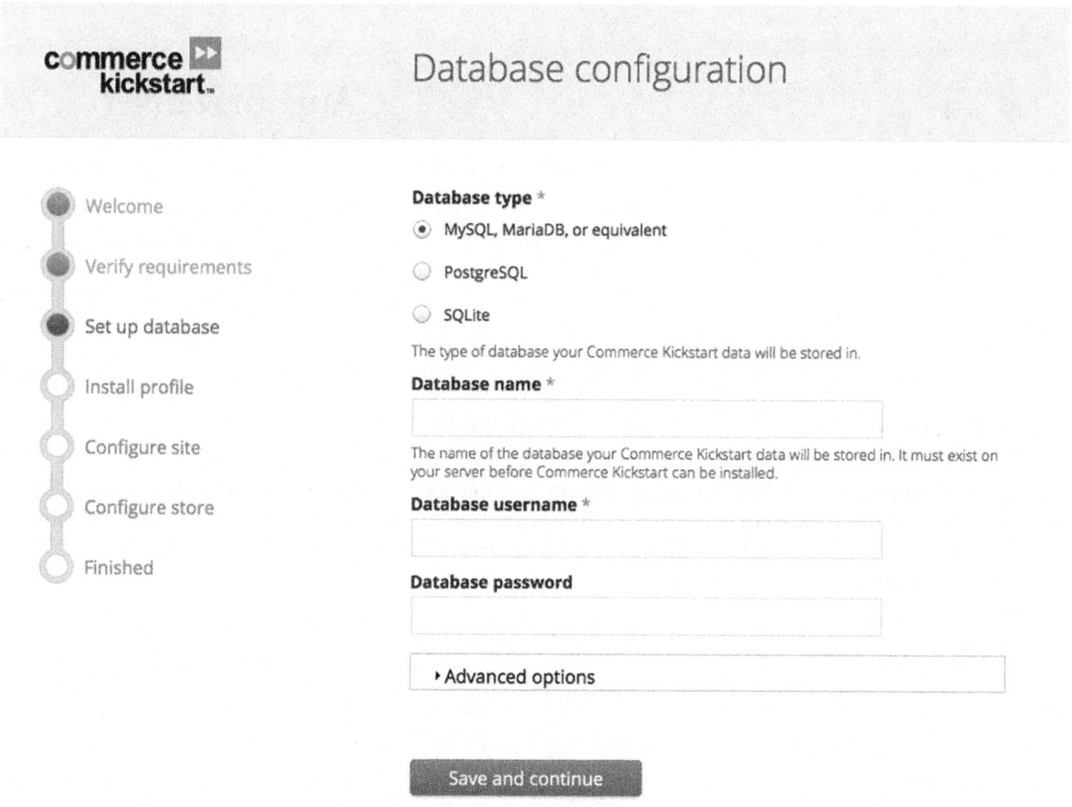

Figure 22-2. *Database settings*

After you enter the database settings and click "Save and continue," Drupal Commerce will create the required tables in the database and run through the enabling and installation steps for the Drupal 8 core and contributed modules associated with a Drupal Commerce–based implementation. Figure 22-3 shows the installation progress.

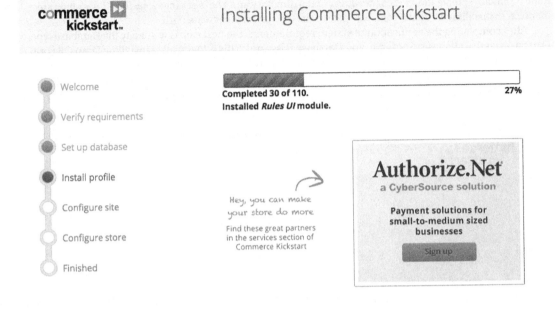

Figure 22-3. *Creating the database tables and enabling modules*

The next step in the process is to enter basic information about your site, specifically the name of the site, the e-mail address of the store, the username and password of the store's administrator, and the store's country and time zone information (see Figure 22-4). After entering the store's information, click the "Save and continue" button.

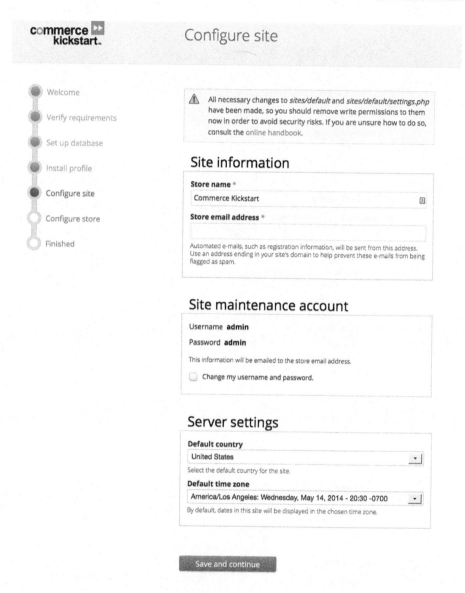

Figure 22-4. *The site configuration parameters*

The final step in the process is to indicate whether you want to start with the demonstration store, whether you want to translate content on the site into multiple languages, what the base currency of the site is, and what types of tax rates, if any, are required for your storefront (see Figure 22-5). For purposes of demonstrating how to build a commerce site, I'll not install the demo store, but I will enable all of the additional functionality to jumpstart the process of creating the new store and I'll enable the US tax rates.

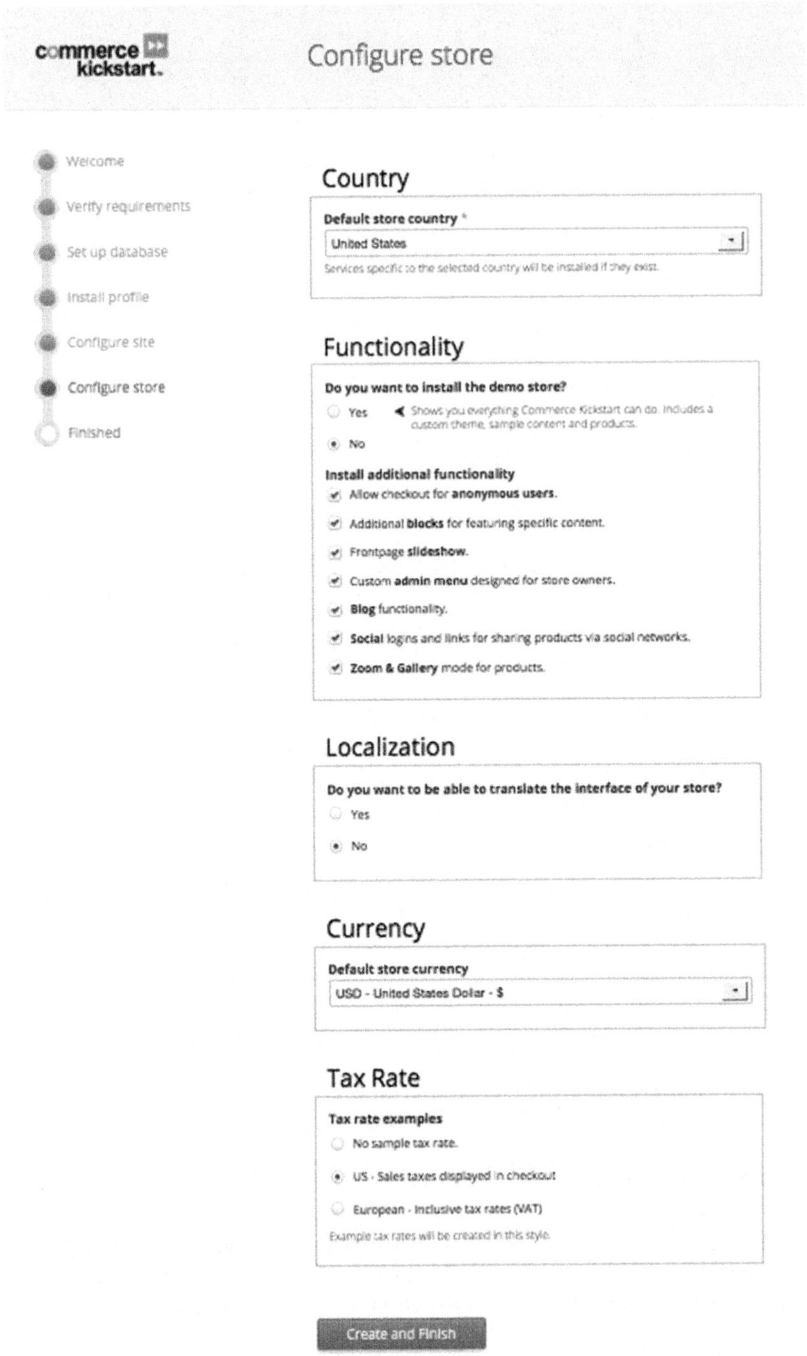

***Figure 22-5.** Configuring the store*

Click the Create and Finish button, and Drupal Commerce will install the additional functionality and finish the installation process. Visiting the homepage of the site, you will see a "Getting Started" pop-up window that provides you with a wealth of information about setting up your site. I suggest taking the time to read through it. Closing the pop-up displays the default homepage, similar to Figure 22-6.

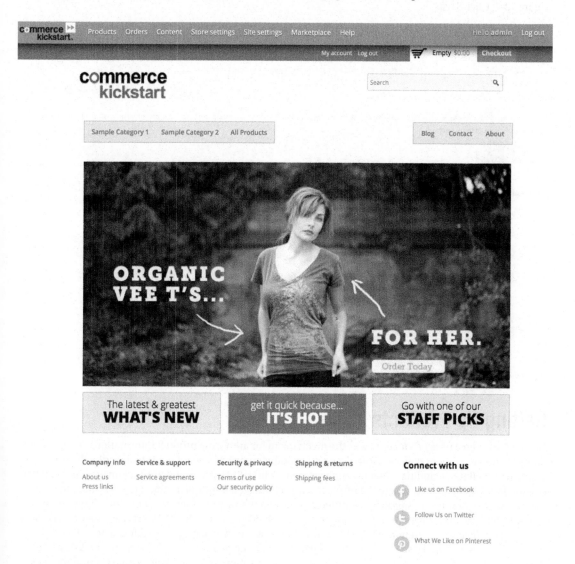

Figure 22-6. *The new storefront*

Setting Up Product Categories

Commerce Kickstart provides a mechanism for grouping products into categories so that site visitors can browse products by the categories that you define. After installing Kickstart, you'll see at the top of the page links for Sample Category 1 and Sample Category 2. For our example site, we are going to change those categories to Cups and Shirts, and add a third category, Hats.

To manage categories, click the Products link in the admin menu and click Categories in the drop-down menu. On the Categories page, click the List terms link for "Product category" and edit Sample Category 1, changing it to Shirts, and then change Sample Category 2 to Cups. Click "Add term" to add a new category for Hats. After making the changes and adding the Hats category, the list of categories should look like Figure 22-7. Click Save.

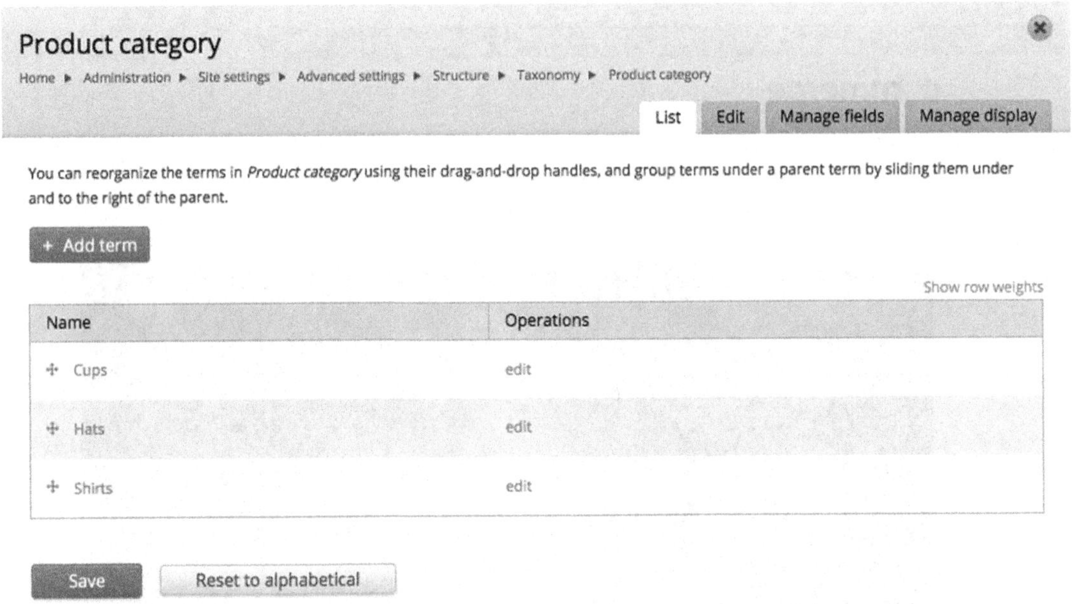

Figure 22-7. *Product categories*

Setting Up Products

Drupal Commerce uses *product types* as the mechanism for authoring product information. Think of product types as content types in Drupal 8 core. A product type has a set of fields to describe the products that you are selling, including elements such as product title, SKU, price, and product images. You can have one to many product types, where the primary reason for having multiple product types is that the fields that describe a product are significantly different between the various items that you are selling. As an example, let's say that you sell T-shirts and movies. The fields that describe a T-shirt (e.g., material, color, size) are significantly different from the fields that describe a movie (e.g., genre, rating, actors, length). In that case, it would make sense to create a separate product type for movies. Commerce Kickstart uses the term *variations* as the label for product types (whereas straight-off-the-shelf Drupal Commerce uses *product types*).

To view variations in Commerce Kickstart, click the "Store settings" link on the admin menu and then click "Variation types" in the drop-down menu. The "Variation types" page (see Figure 22-8) lists all the product variations that are defined on the site. Clicking the "manage fields" link for a variation displays all of the fields for the product variation using the same interface as content types in Drupal 8 core. You can add fields, rearrange fields, and control the display of products.

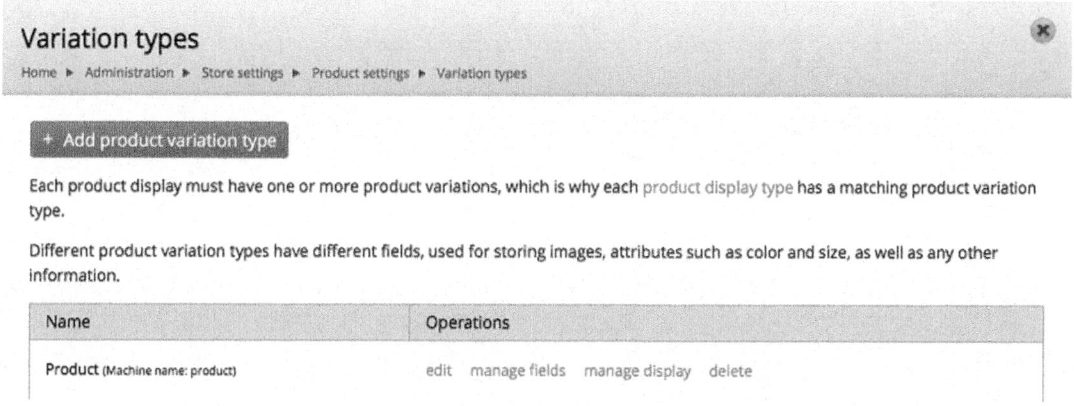

Variation types

+ Add product variation type

Each product display must have one or more product variations, which is why each product display type has a matching product variation type.

Different product variation types have different fields, used for storing images, attributes such as color and size, as well as any other information.

Name	Operations
Product (Machine name: product)	edit manage fields manage display delete

Figure 22-8. *Product variations*

The off-the-shelf product variation provides fields for title, SKU, price, and images. While this works well for the coffee cups that we'll be selling on the site, it doesn't work quite as well for T-shirts, as we need the ability to specify color and size, and for hats we need to specify color but not size. The solution is to create two new product variations, one for hats and one for shirts.

To create a new product variation, click the "Add product variation type" button on the "Variation types" page (see Figure 22-8) and give it a name of "shirts." Leave checked both the "Default product variations of this type to be saved as new revisions when edited" and "Create matching product display type" check boxes.

■ **Note**   A matching product display type is actually a content type that is used to display a product in the store. By convention Drupal Commerce separates the presentation of products (merchandising) from the storage of information about the product. What this means is that in order to view a product, you need to have both a product variation and a content type that displays the product. Commerce Kickstart makes the process a little easier in that by checking the "Create matching product display type" check box, Drupal will create the content type to display the product automatically.

After clicking "Save and add fields," the only thing we need to do is to add an image field, a select list for color, and a select list for size on the Manage fields page as shown in Figure 22-9. Kickstart comes with a preconfigured image field, so just pick that field from the Select and existing field select list in the "Add existing field" area. To add the Color select list, create a new "List (text)" field to enable selecting a color. After giving the field a name (Color) and selecting the "List (text)" field type, set the Widget column to "Select list." Click the Save button, and then enter the list of available options for color as a name-value pair (e.g., white|White). Click the "Save field" settings button, and on the final configuration form for this field, check the "Enable this field to function as an attribute field on Add to Cart form" check box so that shoppers can specify the color when adding the product to their shopping cart. Finish the Color field by clicking the "Save settings" button. Follow the same steps for creating the Size field. After adding the fields, the shirts product type should look like Figure 22-9.

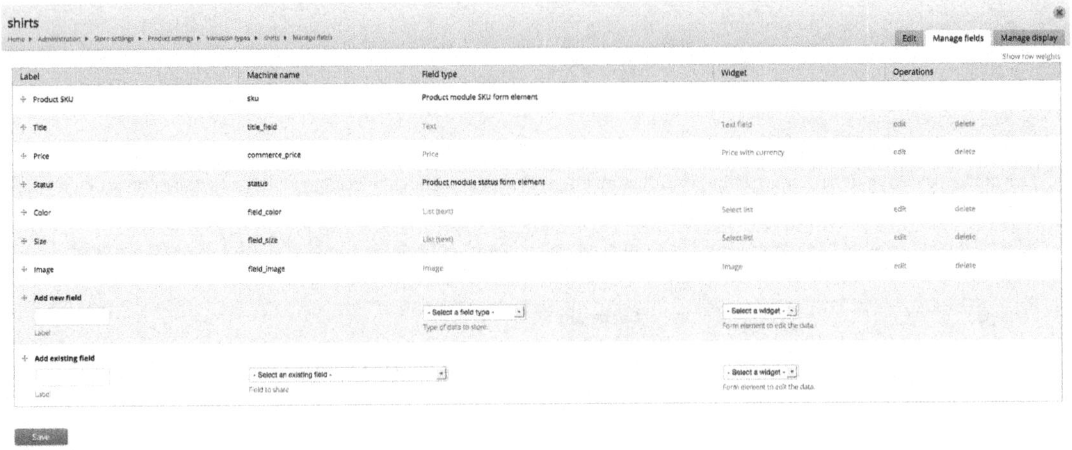

Figure 22-9. *The shirts content type*

After adding the fields, there are a few other tasks to perform. The first is to clean up the display of the shirts variation. Click the "Manage display" tab at the top of the screen and hide the label for the Image field. Click the "Add to cart confirmation" link near the top of the page to set what values will appear on the "Cart confirmation" page. Add the title, size, and color to the display so that the shopper has a more complete picture of what's in their cart. Do the same for the Product in cart, Line item, and Node: Teaser displays.

We also need to make a few modifications to the content type that was automatically created to display shirts. Click "Site settings," and in the drop-down menu, click the Structure link. On the Structure page, click the "Content types" link to see the list of content types created for the store. From the list, click the "edit" link for the shirts content type and make the following changes:

1. Click the "Comment settings" tab and set "Default comment setting for new content" to Hidden, as we don't want customers posting comments about the shirts.

2. Click the "Manage fields" tab at the top of the page (see Figure 22-9). We need to add two fields to the content type, a Body field and a "Product category" field. These fields are used for merchandising the products on our example site, and belong here instead of on the product. Fortunately, both fields exist as part of the default Kickstart implementation, so all we have to do is use the "Add existing field" settings to add both.

3. Click the "Manage display" tab at the top of the page to make a few changes to how the shirts appear:

   a. Ensure the Label column for Title is set to Hidden.

   b. Move the Product: Title field to the Hidden section of the list, as we already have a Title field.

   c. Move Product Price to the second position in the list.

   d. Move Body to the third position and hide the label.

   e. Move Product: Color, Product: Size, and Product category fields to the Hidden area, as color and size already appear as part of the Product variations display.

   f. Save the changes.

250

4. Make the following changes to the Teaser display by clicking the Teaser link near the top of the page:

    a. Move all of the fields except for Title, Product: Price, Product variations, and Product: Image to the Hidden area.

    b. Move the Product: Image field to the first position.

    c. Hide the label for Product variations.

    d. Save the changes.

5. Update the Product list display on the Manage display tab as follows:

    a. Move the Product: Image field to the first display position.

    b. Move the Product: Title to the Hidden area, as we already have the Title field.

    c. Move Price to the last position in the fields to be displayed.

    d. Save the changes.

Following the same steps as for shirts and cups, also add a hats product variation, with the exception of the Size field, as hats only come in one size.

Creating a Product

After creating the product variations for shirts and hats, it's time to test them to make sure they function as desired. I'll start by creating a new shirt, the Drupal Flys T-shirt. To follow along with the example, click the Product link on the main menu and click "Add a product" in the drop-down menu. Select "shirts" from the list of Actions and enter "Drupal Flys" in the Title field. Here's where the fun begins; we need to add a variation for every combination of color and size that we want to sell. For example, we want to sell white T-shirts in all four sizes, so we need to select White from the Color drop-down menu and, for each size, select one size from the Size select list. Enter a SKU for that combination of color and size, select Shirts in the Category drop-down menu, set a price, and add an image. For purposes of this demonstration, the images all show blue shirts. After filling out the values for the first variation, the form should look like Figure 22-10.

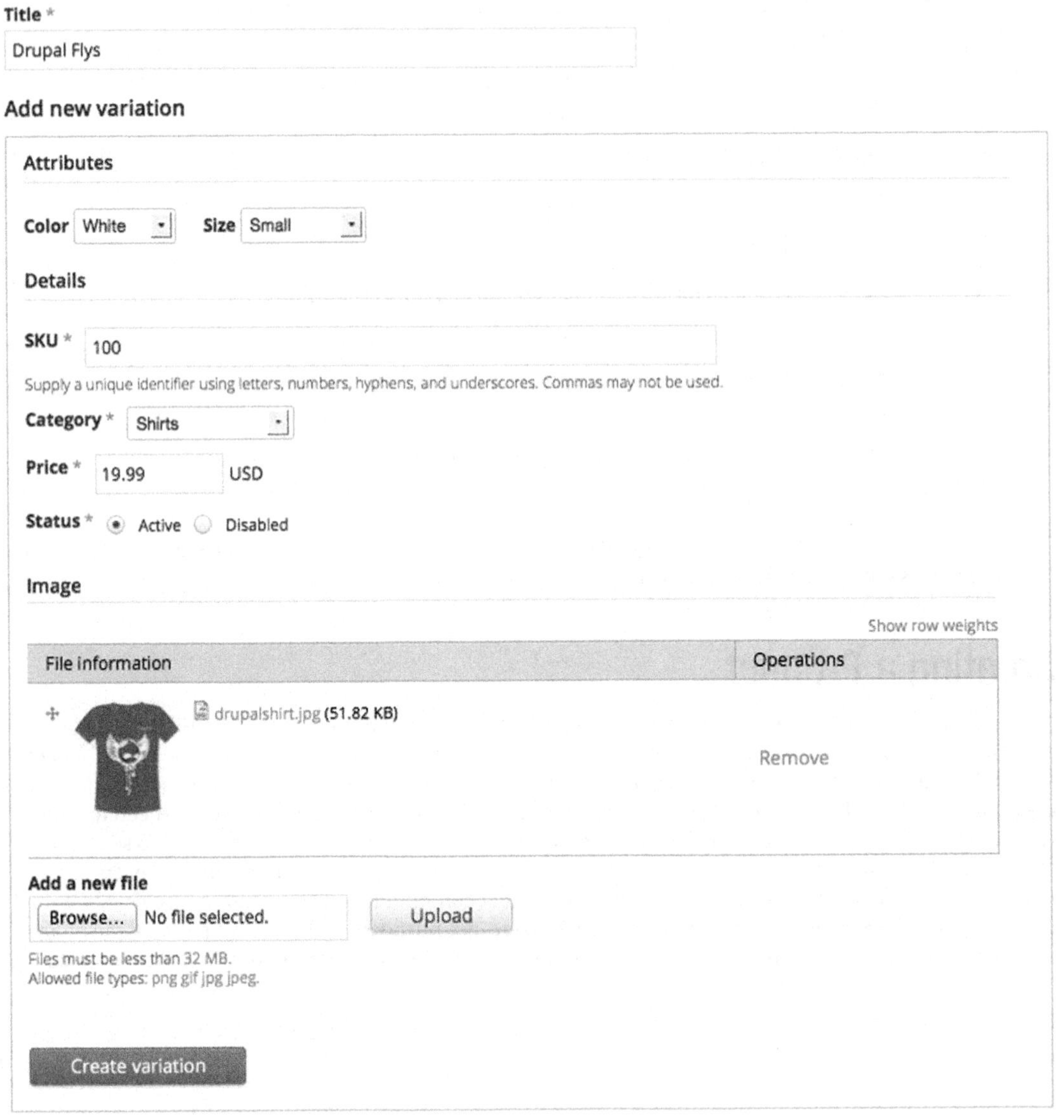

Title *

Drupal Flys

Add new variation

Attributes

Color White ▾   **Size** Small ▾

Details

SKU * 100

Supply a unique identifier using letters, numbers, hyphens, and underscores. Commas may not be used.

Category * Shirts ▾

Price * 19.99   USD

Status * ⦿ Active ◯ Disabled

Image

Show row weights

File information	Operations
✛ drupalshirt.jpg **(51.82 KB)**	Remove

Add a new file

Browse... No file selected.   Upload

Files must be less than 32 MB.
Allowed file types: png gif jpg jpeg.

Create variation

Figure 22-10. *Creating a product variation*

After filling out the first variation fields, click the "Create variation" button. The next step is to create all of the variations that we wish to sell, selecting the color and size and setting a unique SKU for each combination of color and size. Start the process by clicking the "Add new variation button," and then create a new variation for every color and size combination by following the steps in the previous paragraph. The end result is a long list of variations, a partial list of which is shown in Figure 22-11.

⊹		Small	Blue	Will be auto-generated when the form is saved.	112	$19.99	Active	Edit Remove
⊹		Medium	Blue	Will be auto-generated when the form is saved.	113	$19.99	Active	Edit Remove
⊹		Large	Blue	Will be auto-generated when the form is saved.	114	$19.99	Active	Edit Remove
⊹		Extra Large	Blue	Will be auto-generated when the form is saved.	115	$19.99	Active	Edit Remove
⊹		Small	Gray	Will be auto-generated when the form is saved.	116	$19.99	Active	Edit Remove

Figure 22-11. *The list of product variations*

After saving the Drupal Flys T-shirt, the customer-facing view of that product is as shown in Figure 22-12.

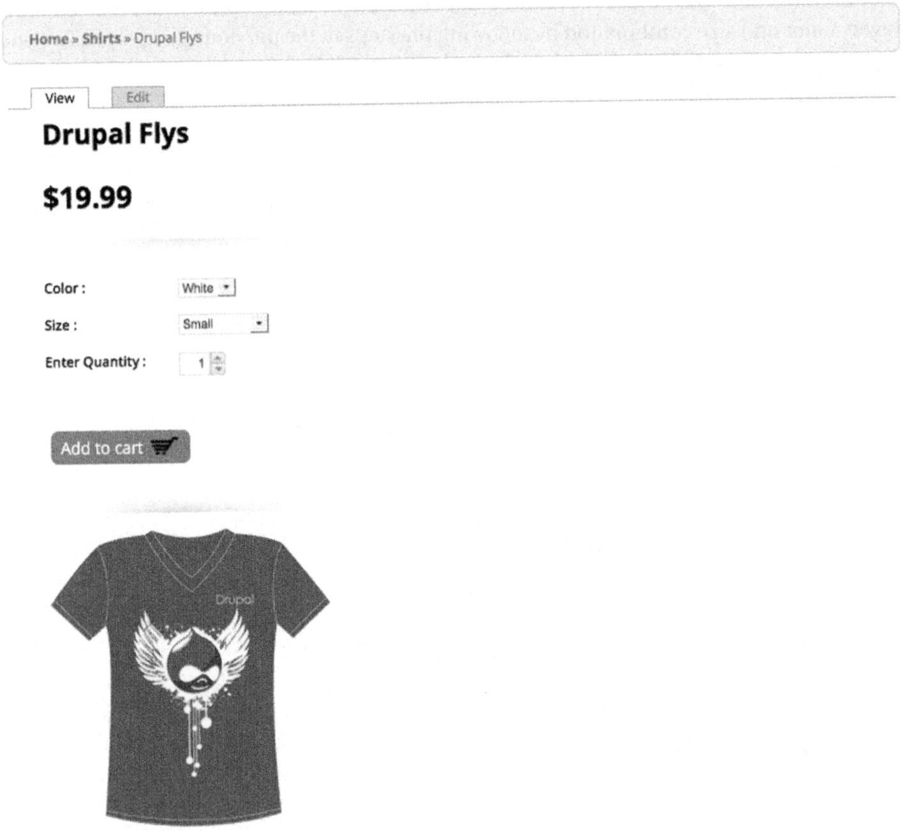

Figure 22-12. *The Drupal Flys T-shirt*

Adding a small white Drupal Flys T-shirt to my shopping cart causes Kickstart to display the item in the shopping cart as I defined it to appear when setting up the product variation template for shirts (see Figure 22-13).

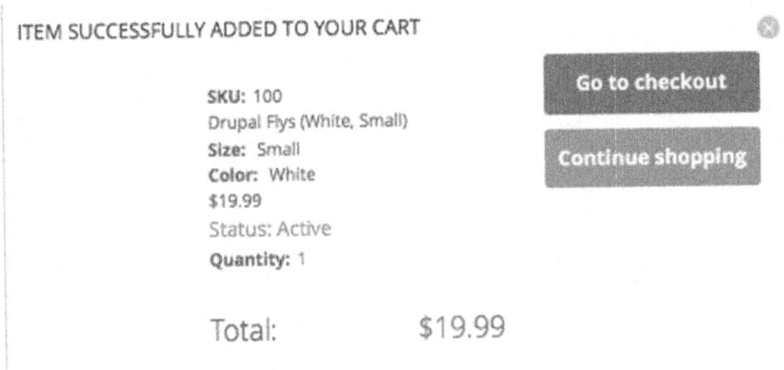

Figure 22-13. *Item added to cart*

To continue building the example commerce site, create an example hat and an example coffee cup following the same process as for the Drupal Flys T-shirt, with the only exception being that hats only come in colors, not sizes, and coffee cups are available in only one color and one size. I'll use the hats product variation to create a hat and use the generic "Product display" to create a cup.

If I now click the category links at the top of the page, clicking Cups displays the one cup that I created, clicking Shirts displays the Drupal Flys shirt, and clicking Hats displays the hat that I created.

Displaying Products

There are many things you can do to display products on your storefront. You can place links to individual products on menus or as embedded links in content; you can use the taxonomy listing approach as demonstrated on the example site by clicking the categories near the top of the page; or you can create views to display products based on the criteria and filtering mechanisms you employ in your view. As an example, I'll create a product listing view for all products on my site, sorted and grouped by category. To follow along, hover over the "Site settings" link on the admin menu and then click the Views link in the drop-down menu. Click the "Add new view" button on the Views page, and on the "Add new view" page (see Figure 22-14), do the following:

1. Give the view a name; in this case I'll call it Product.

2. Select Commerce Product from the Show select list to indicate what to show in the view.

3. Leave All as the type of product to display, as we want to show all product types.

4. Leave the view as Unsorted.

5. Click the "Continue & edit" button.

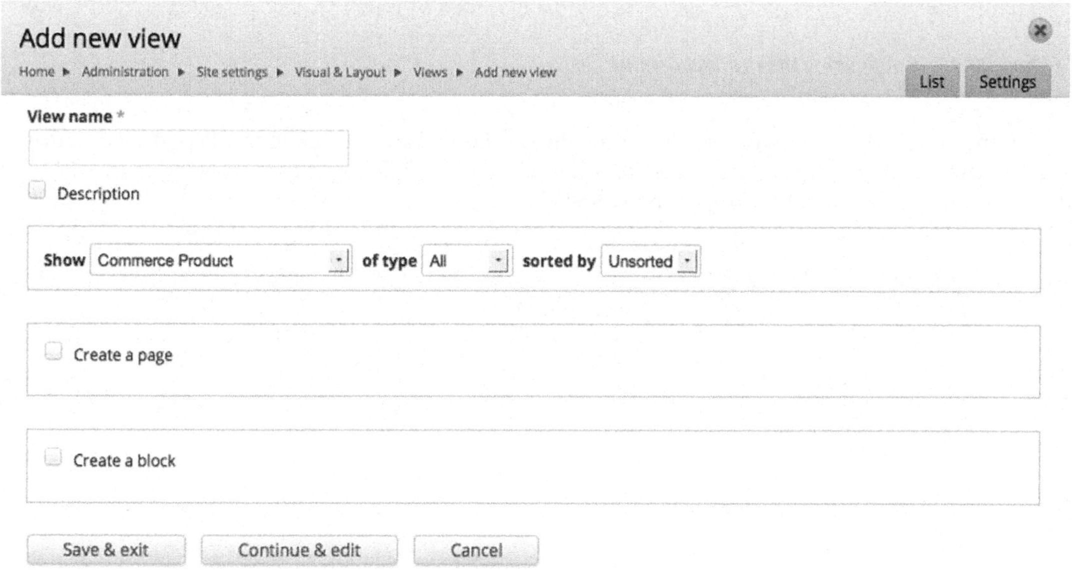

Figure 22-14. *Creating a Product view*

On the view's configuration page, I followed the basic steps of creating a view using fields from the Commerce Product, including a specialized field named "Add to Cart form" that allows a visitor to add an item to their shopping cart by simply clicking an Add to Cart button. Figure 22-15 demonstrates the basic setup that I did to create the view.

Displays

Master + Add

Edit View Name/description ▾

▾ **Master details**

TITLE

Title: Drupal Catalog

FORMAT

Format: Table | Settings

◎ **FIELDS** Add ▾

Commerce Product: Type

Field: Image

Commerce Product: SKU (SKU)

Field: Title (Product)

Commerce Product: Size (Size)

Commerce Product: Color (Color)

Commerce Product: Price (Price)

Commerce Product: Add to Cart form

◎ **FILTER CRITERIA** Add

◎ **SORT CRITERIA** Add ▾

Commerce Product: Type (asc)

Access: None ▸ Advanced

◎ **HEADER** Add

◎ **FOOTER** Add

PAGER

Use pager: Full | Paged, 10 items

More link: No

Figure 22-15. Configuring the Product display view

Depending on how I wish to use this view on the site, I would add a Block and/or Page display so that I could place the product listing on a page or provide a link to the view from a menu (page). Figure 22-16 demonstrates how the view would appear on the site.

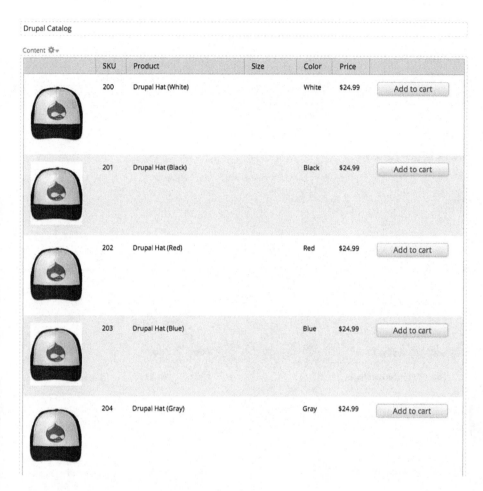

Figure 22-16. *The Product listing view*

Another suggestion is to add filtering to your view so that customers can quickly find the products that they are looking for. Using views filters is a great way to provide that functionality. I've added an exposed filter for Product Type, Product Color, and Product Size to my view, making it easy for customers to narrow the list of products displayed to the specific criteria that they are looking for (e.g., shirts that are black and size medium). See Figure 22-17 for details on the Filter Criteria and the resulting filters that appear at the top of the view.

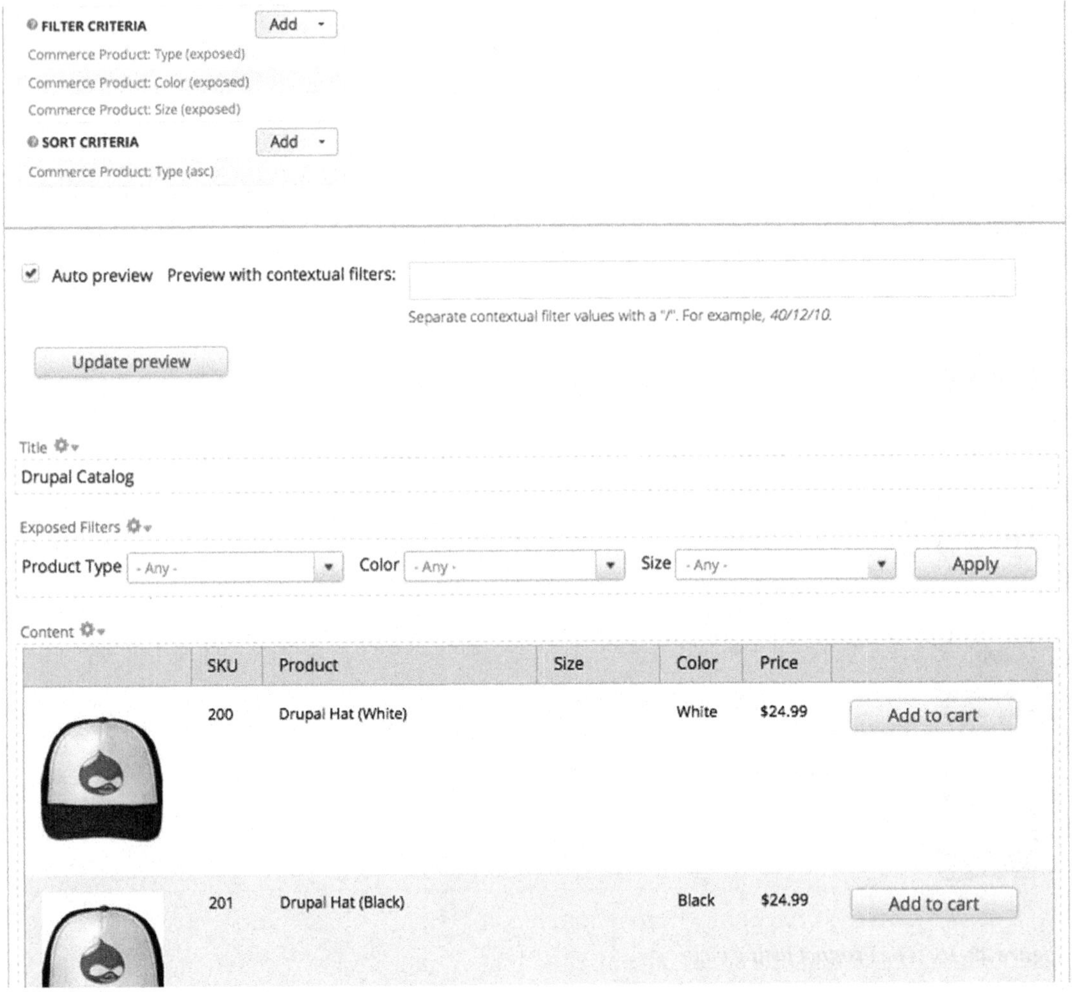

Figure 22-17. *Product filters*

Shipping, Taxes, Payment, and Other Features

There are a number of features that can be implemented on a Drupal Commerce store, including standard items like providing shipping quotes to shoppers, calculating any value added taxes (VAT), taking various forms of payment, providing coupons for discounts, and more. For demonstration purposes, Kickstart comes preconfigured with several features already enabled.

Shipping

There are several Commerce contributed modules that assist in the process of providing shipping options through various carriers such as UPS, USPS, and others. If you visit www.drupal.org/project/commerce_shipping, you'll find that there are modules that provide flat rate shipping, UPS, FedEx, USPS, Canada Post, ConnectShip, and Kiala. There are also developer APIs that provide the capability to create new shipping methods if your desired method isn't found in the list of modules.

Kickstart comes with free shipping enabled; however, for demonstration purposes, I want to charge customers for shipping, and I'll use the Commerce Flat Rate module that is enabled by default with Kickstart. To enable and configure flat rate shipping, hover on the "Store settings" admin menu item and select Shipping from the drop-down menu. On the Shipping administration page, click the "Add a flat rate service" button near the top left of the page. On the "Add a flat rate service" configuration page (see Figure 22-18), give the shipping service a Title, a Display title that will appear in the checkout process, and a Base rate that will be applied to all orders. For the demonstration, I'll charge a flat rate of $10 per shipment for shipping and handling.

Other shipping modules, such as UPS, USPS, and FedEx, all calculate the actual shipping rates based on the number of boxes and the weight of the shipment. When using methods like UPS, USPS, and FedEx, you'll need to do a little extra work by adding dimensions to each product, the weight of each product, and the standard box size that you use to ship products in. Each of those modules does a best guess at how many items will fit in a box to determine how many boxes and what the total rate should be. You may also use calculation rules to mark up the rates returned from UPS, USPS, FedEx, or other shipping services. Check the documentation on Drupal.org for details on how to add other shipping methods, configure those methods, and create and apply calculation rules.

After setting up the flat rate shipping, delete the "Free shipping" method from the list of Shipping services to provide only the option for flat rate. On the "Shipping services" screen (Store settings ➤ Shipping), click the "delete" link to the right of the "Free shipping" option.

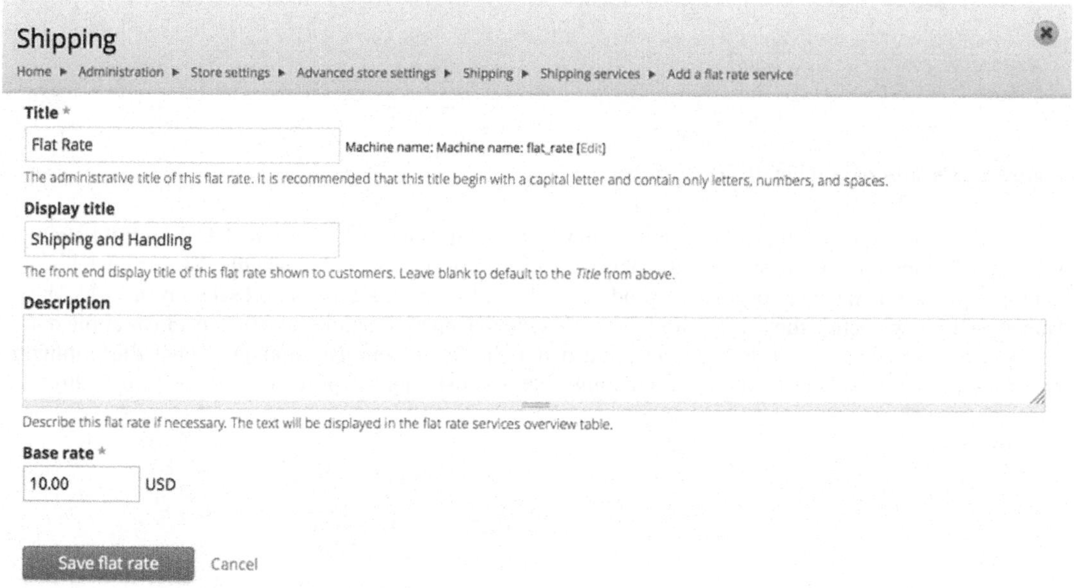

Figure 22-18. *Setting up a flat rate shipping method*

Taxes

Drupal Commerce supports sales and value added taxes (VAT). To configure taxes, hover over the "Store settings" menu item and click Taxes in the drop-down menu. Kickstart comes preconfigured with a sample sales tax rate for the state of Michigan. To see how taxes are configured, click the "edit" link for Michigan Sales Tax and note the fields and their values (see Figure 22-19).

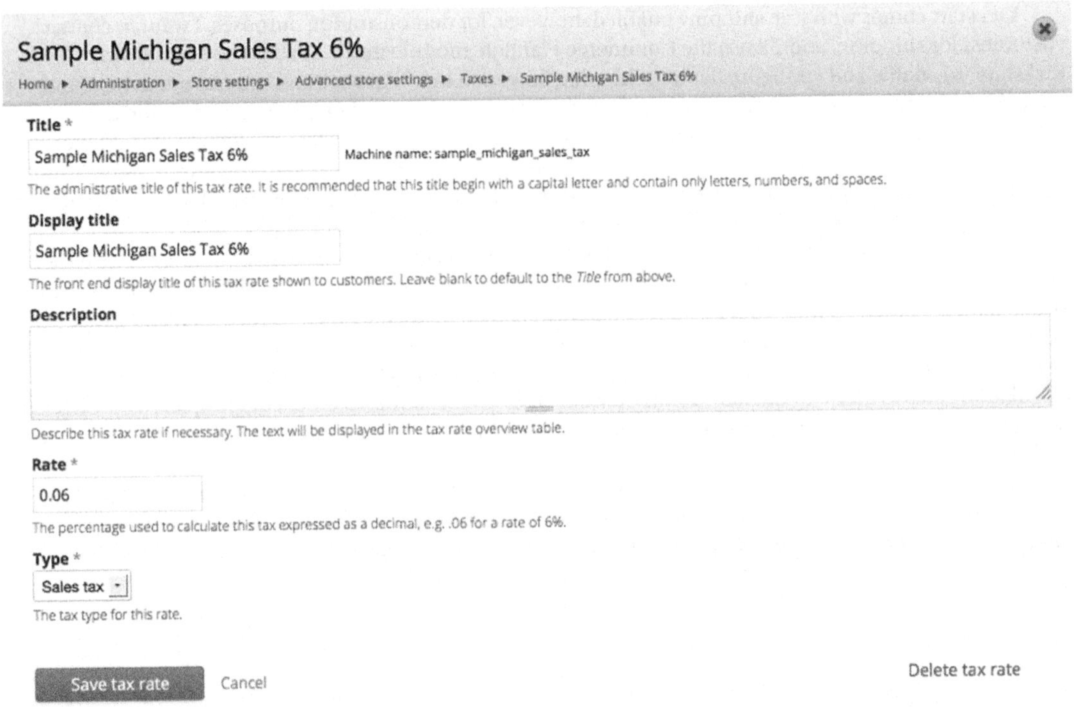

Figure 22-19. *Sample Michigan Sales Tax page*

As shown in Figure 22-19, when defining a new tax, you must give it a Title, which is the administrative title that will appear on the administration pages, a Display title, which is what will display during the checkout process, a Rate to apply to each product on the order, and the Type of tax (Sales tax or VAT). The values on this page define the tax rate, and there is a second step that defines how the tax rate is applied. If you click the "Save tax rate" button, you'll be returned to the Taxes administration page. Click the "configure component" link to see how to apply taxes to items that the customer has purchased (see Figure 22-20).

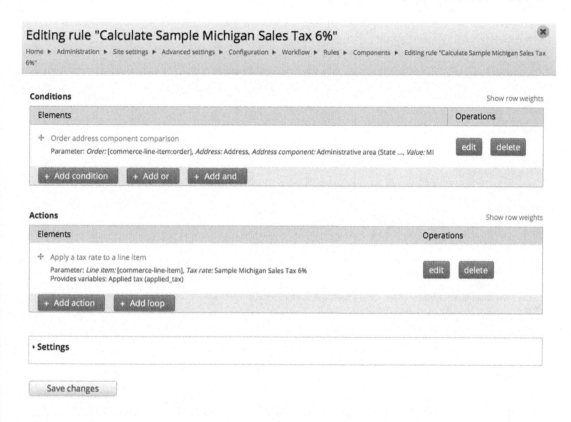

Figure 22-20. *Configuring tax rules*

There are two components to the tax rules configuration, a Condition that must be met for the tax to be applied and an Action that will be performed when the Condition is met. In the case of the Michigan sales tax, the Condition is that the value in the State field for the order is set to MI. To see the details of how this is configured, click the "edit" link next to the Condition. On the Condition configuration form (see Figure 22-21), you'll find a "Data selector" field that defines what value the Condition is based on, in this case a commerce-line-item:order. The Address field allows you to pick whether the sales tax is based on the ship-to address or bill-to address. For US taxes, the rates are based on the bill-to address. The "Address component" field allows you to pick which field is used for the comparison, and since we're dealing with state sales taxes, the field that we select is the "Administrative area (State/Province)." The Operator that we want to use to compare the value of the Administrative area is "equals," and the final element is the Value that we wish to compare, in this case MI.

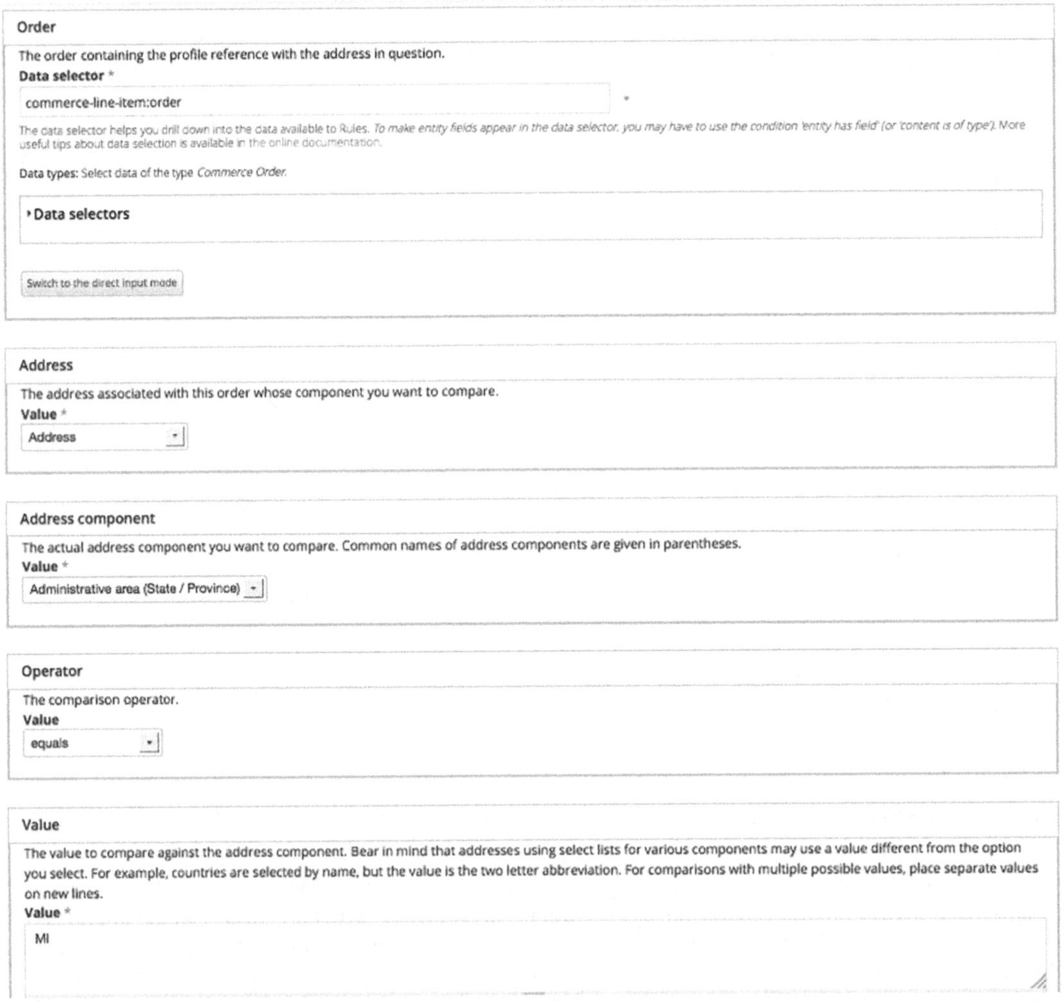

Order

The order containing the profile reference with the address in question.

Data selector *

commerce-line-item:order

The data selector helps you drill down into the data available to Rules. To make entity fields appear in the data selector, you may have to use the condition 'entity has field' (or 'content is of type'). More useful tips about data selection is available in the online documentation.

Data types: Select data of the type *Commerce Order.*

▸ **Data selectors**

Switch to the direct input mode

Address

The address associated with this order whose component you want to compare.

Value *

Address

Address component

The actual address component you want to compare. Common names of address components are given in parentheses.

Value *

Administrative area (State / Province)

Operator

The comparison operator.

Value

equals

Value

The value to compare against the address component. Bear in mind that addresses using select lists for various components may use a value different from the option you select. For example, countries are selected by name, but the value is the two letter abbreviation. For comparisons with multiple possible values, place separate values on new lines.

Value *

MI

Figure 22-21. Configuring the tax rule

In cases where you have county or city taxes, you could use the same approach as outlined for the state tax, selecting either the county or the city as the basis for the comparison, using the name of the county or city as the value. To add new taxes, simply follow the Michigan example to create a new tax rate. You may have several tax rates on your site based on which states you ship to and where your company has operations. Check with your state's regulations for collecting and reporting sales taxes.

Payments

Drupal Commerce provides several methods for collecting payments from customers, including credit cards, PayPal, Amazon, and other methods. For credit cards, you have several options for payment services, such as: Authorize.net, American Express, CyberSource, FirstData, Commerce SagePay, Commerce Cielo, Adyen, ePay, MoIP, Ogone, Pagamento, PageSeguro, PayEx, Payflow Link, PayLeap, PayPal, SagePay, and Sermepa. Each payment service has its own configurable parameters; please review the documentation for the module associated with each service for details on installation and configuration.

For purposes of the demonstration site, I'll use the Example payment method that is enabled by default with Kickstart. You can examine the configuration parameters by navigating to the "Payment methods" administration page. To get there, hover over the "Store settings" link in the admin menu and click the "Payment methods" link in the drop-down menu. On the "Editing reaction rule" page for "Example Payment," you'll see that, like shipping, payments are governed by Events and Actions. You can review the Events and Actions to see the general approach for applying payment methods.

With products available for purchase, shipping configured, taxes enabled, and payments configured, it's time to place an order. To select an item to place in your shopping cart, click one of the product types listed in the menu near the top of the page, and from that list click the name of the product and select the attributes, for example color and size, if applicable to that product, and how many you wish to add to your cart. After adding the item to your cart, you should see a pop-up notification that the item was added to your cart (refer to Figure 22-13). On the pop-up notification, click the "Go to checkout" button to begin the checkout process (see Figure 22-22).

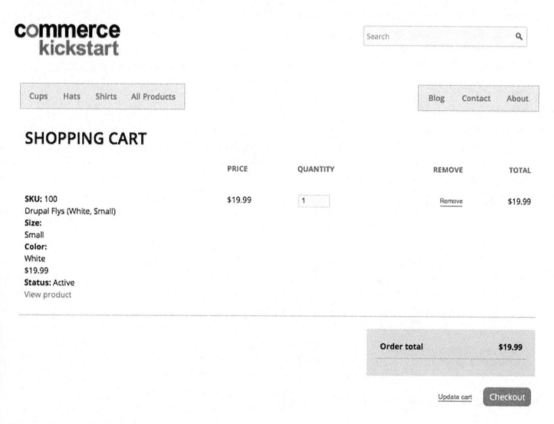

Figure 22-22. *The Shopping Cart*

If the items and quantities in the shopping cart look correct, then click the Checkout button to enter the billing and shipping information. A shipping address and billing address are required for all orders (and can be the same address). If you are a returning customer to the site and have logged in, Drupal Commerce Addressbook module will prepopulate the values from any of the addresses that you have on file in the address book that is created as part of the order processing workflow (see Figure 22-23).

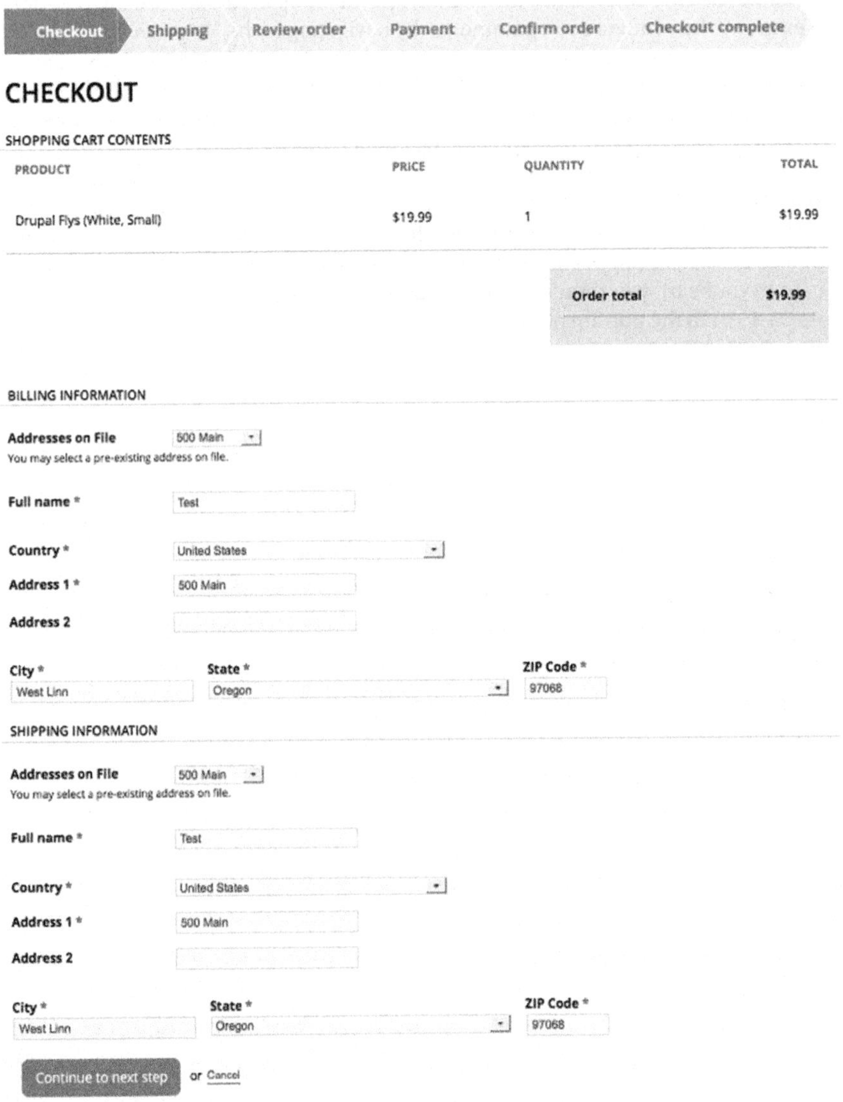

| Checkout | Shipping | Review order | Payment | Confirm order | Checkout complete |

CHECKOUT

SHOPPING CART CONTENTS

PRODUCT	PRICE	QUANTITY	TOTAL
Drupal Flys (White, Small)	$19.99	1	$19.99

	Order total	$19.99

BILLING INFORMATION

Addresses on File   500 Main ▾
You may select a pre-existing address on file.

Full name *   Test

Country *   United States ▾

Address 1 *   500 Main

Address 2

City *   West Linn   **State ***   Oregon ▾   **ZIP Code ***   97068

SHIPPING INFORMATION

Addresses on File   500 Main ▾
You may select a pre-existing address on file.

Full name *   Test

Country *   United States ▾

Address 1 *   500 Main

Address 2

City *   West Linn   **State ***   Oregon ▾   **ZIP Code ***   97068

Continue to next step   or Cancel

Figure 22-23. *Setting the bill-to and ship-to addresses*

Clicking the "Continue to next step" button displays the Shipping step in the checkout process. Since we only have a flat rate shipping method implemented, there isn't much to do on this page. If you've implemented UPS, USPS, FedEx, or other shipping services and have enabled multiple shipping options (e.g., standard ground, next day air, 2-day air), the shopper will be presented with the options and the costs that are pulled from the carriers' pricing systems. The shipping costs are calculated based on the number of packages and the weight of the order.

After selecting the shipping method, the next step is to review the order and enter the payment information. Using the example shipping method from Kickstart prepopulates a sample credit card number and expiration date. If you have another payment method, you may have other options to enter. The next step is to process the payment and complete the order. A Checkout Complete message will be displayed, including the order number for the shopper's reference.

You can modify the checkout flow through the administrative interface. Hover over the "Store settings" item in the admin menu and click the "Checkout settings" link. You'll see a list of the checkout steps and where they appear in the flow (see Figure 22-24). You may rearrange the items, but be cautious if you do so, as some items need to appear in order for the functionality to work (e.g., setting the shipping option after the payment processing happens would cause shipping costs not to be included in the customer's payment).

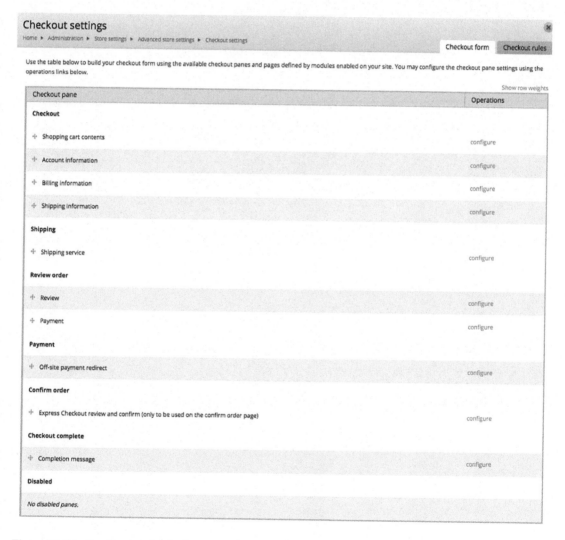

Figure 22-24. *Configuring the checkout workflow*

Summary

In this chapter I covered the basic processes for installing Drupal Commerce and configuring a storefront. There are many additional modules and techniques for building and operating a Drupal Commerce–based website. I suggest spending time on Drupal.org and reviewing the dozens of YouTube videos that are focused on setting up and operating a Drupal Commerce storefront.

At this point you've completed the book. Congratulations! Your journey has only just begun, and I look forward to seeing your work as you progress through your Drupal learning experiences. I hope to see you at an upcoming DrupalCon or DrupalCamp.

APPENDIX A

■ ■ ■

Installing Drupal

If you are hosting your Drupal site on a commercial web-hosting provider, it is likely that it has a tool that installs Drupal for you. If that's the case, you can bypass this appendix and follow the directions provided to you by your web-hosting provider. But if you need to install Drupal on your laptop, desktop, or server, then this appendix is for you.

In the sections that follow, I will walk you through the step-by-step process of installing foundational components such as PHP, MySQL, and Apache, as well as the steps for downloading and installing Drupal 8. At the end of this appendix, you will have installed Drupal and will be ready to work through the main body of the book.

The Foundation Required to Install Drupal

Before installing Drupal, you must have access to the operating system on the platform on which you wish to install Drupal. That platform, whether it's a desktop, laptop, or server, must have several pieces of software installed and configured in order to support the foundational elements required to run Drupal (MySQL, PHP, and Apache/IIS). The type of operating system and hardward that you choose is purely a matter of personal preference. You can install and configure Drupal on Windows-, OS X-, or Linux-based platforms. The hardware can be a local machine (your desktop, laptop, or a server that you have physical access to) or a hosted server (shared or dedicated, hosted by an organization such as Pantheon).

You will need to have the following components loaded, configured, and running on the platform before you begin the Drupal installation process:

- *A web server*: Either Apache, nginx/lighttpd, or Microsoft's Internet Information Services (IIS)). For the purposes of this book, I will focus on an Apache-based solution, because Apache runs on all of the platforms that Drupal supports. For information on installing and configuring IIS, please consult www.microsoft.com.

- *PHP*: The programming language used by Drupal.

- *A relational database server*: Either MySQL or PostgreSQL. For the purposes of simplifying the installation process, I will focus on MySQL. For details on installing and configuring PostgreSQL please consult www.postgresql.org.

- *FTP (File Transfer Protocol)*: Used for uploading files to the server.

- *Various libraries*: For image handling, secure connections, and mail routing.

If your intent is to run your new Drupal site in a hosted environment, the work of setting up the foundational components has already been done for you by the hosting company. If you are using a hosting company, you can skip to the "Installing Drupal" section. If your intention is to develop your site on a desktop or laptop and then deploy your site to a server, you will need to install and configure the components required to support Drupal on your laptop or desktop, as described in the next section.

Setting Up your Platform in Preparation for Drupal

Before you install Drupal, you need three basic components in place: the platform itself (hardware and operating system), a web server (the software, such as Apache), and a database server (such as MySQL). If you are building your site on a commercial hosting company's platform, you can skip to the "Installing Drupal" section, as everything you need is typically installed by default.

Depending on the operating system on your platform, you may already have a few of the required components installed (for example, OS X comes with Apache and PHP already installed). However, getting all of the components to work together may be more of a challenge than most people want to undertake. Fortunately, a group of very talented people at www.apachefriends.org created an "all-in-one" software package called XAMPP (XAMPP stands for Apache, MySQL, PHP, and Python) that is very simple for even the least technical person to install and configure. There is an XAMPP distribution for Windows, OS X, Linux, and Solaris.

The components included in XAMPP that are critical for Drupal are

- *Apache*: The web server software package that handles requests for content residing on your server and returns the results to whoever made the requests.

- *MySQL*: The relational database where Drupal stores all of its content.

- *PHP & PEAR*: PHP, the programming language used by the developers who created and maintain Drupal, and PEAR (PHP Extension and Application Repository), a structured library of open-source code for PHP developers.

- *PHPMyAdmin*: An invaluable tool for creating and managing databases, tables, and data stored in your MySQL database.

There are detailed instructions for installing XAMPP on each of the supported platforms on the www.apachefriends.org website. There are alternatives to XAMPP, such as MAMP for OS X. For a list of alternatives, conduct a Google search for "Apache AND MySQL AND PHP stacks."

Installing Drupal

Now that you have the underlying server components installed, you are ready to install Drupal. There are eight basic steps associated with installing Drupal on your server, regardless of whether you are running your Drupal site on a Windows, OS X, Linux, or shared-hosting-based server.

1. Download the current Drupal 8 installation package from http://drupal.org/ project/drupal to your computer.

2. Decompress the Drupal installation tar.gz or zip file.

3. Move the files from within the expanded installation file to your web server's root directory, or to a subdirectory if you wish to run more than one site on your server (e.g., www-root/drupal8 or htdocs/drupal8).

4. Create the settings.php file.

5. Create the files directory.

6. Create the database that you will be using for your new Drupal website.

7. Create the database user account.

8. Launch the Drupal installation script and configure your site.

These steps are described in more detail in the sections that follow.

Downloading Drupal

Downloading Drupal is a simple matter of visiting www.drupal.org/project/drupal and picking the latest version and language (such as English or French) of Drupal to download from the homepage. Drupal version numbers change over time, but it is safe to pick the latest version listed on the homepage as the version to download, install, and configure. Alternatively, and significantly easier, is to download Drupal via Drush. Please see Chapter 15 for details.

To download Drupal, simply right-click the version and format that you wish to install. The compressed file (tar.gz or zip) will automatically download to your computer into the folder you have configured for receiving downloads from the Internet.

Decompressing the Drupal Installation Package

The file downloaded from Drupal.org is a compressed file that has all of the directories and files required to set up and run Drupal 8 on your server. You will need to decompress the tar.gz or zip file into its individual elements, either by double-clicking the file (this works on OS X and Linux) or by opening the file in a decompression utility. Double-clicking the file will result in a folder being created on your computer with all of the directories and files expanded to their original, pre-compressed state.

■ **Note** Depending on your operating system and your setting for your operating system's file manager, you may or may not see the .htaccess file, as it is classified as a "hidden" file in Linux and OS X. This is a critical file and must be moved in the next step. If you do not see the .htaccess file, please update your file browser's settings to allow you to see hidden files before proceeding to the next step. Other operating systems may have similar files, such as web.config on IIS.

Moving the Drupal Distribution to the Root Directory of Your Web Server

The next step is to move the contents of the Drupal folder that you just decompressed in the previous step, to the "root" directory of your web server. If you are using XAMPP, the "root" directory is the folder marked as htdocs in the directory where XAMPP is installed. If you are installing Drupal on a hosted platform, the root directory will be that specified by your hosting company (for example, the hosting company that I use names the root directory public_html). You should check with your hosting company if you are unsure where to put your Drupal files.

With all of the files in place, you're ready to take the next step.

Creating the settings.php File

Drupal uses a file named settings.php to store configuration parameters for your site, such as the name of the database and the userID and password used to access that database. Drupal ships with a default settings.php file that we will use as the starting point for our site's settings.php file. Navigate to the sites/default directory in the location where you copied the Drupal directories and files to in the previous step. In that directory you will find a default.settings.php file. Copy that file and rename the copied version to settings.php.

Next, set the permissions on the settings.php file so that anyone can read and update the file. Drupal must have the ability to update this file during the update process. Check your operating system's directions for setting permissions if you're unsure about how to do this.

Creating the files Directory

Drupal stores all uploaded files and images in a directory on the server. The standard name for that directory is files and the location is in the sites/default directory. Create a new directory, named files, and set the permissions so that the web server can write to that directory.

Creating the Drupal Database

Creating the database is a relatively simple process. If you are using XAMPP or a hosting provider, you should have access to the phpMyAdmin administrator's tool. To access the admin tool on your laptop or desktop, visit the http://localhost/xampp page (if you are using XAMPP) or the appropriate dashboard URL for the AMP stack that you have installed. In the Tools section, you will see a link to "phpMyAdmin." Please click that link to launch the phpMyAdmin administrator's page.

On this page, locate the text box that is right below the "Create database" label. In this text box, type in a name that is easy for you to remember and is representative of what your website is about (using this approach makes it easier in the future to figure out which database goes with which website, especially when you have multiple Drupal sites running on your server). MySQL is extremely flexible, and you can name your databases anything that you wish; however, there are generally accepted standards that you may want to follow:

- Only use lowercase characters.
- Separate words with underscores.
- Keep the database name shorter than 64 characters (a MySQL restriction).

For demonstration purposes, I have created a new database named "drupal8testsite." After entering the database name, click the Create button. See Figure A-1.

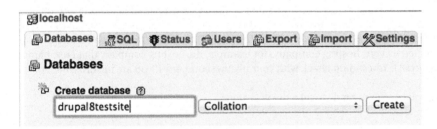

Figure A-1. *Creating a new MySQL database*

The next screen that appears shows that the database was created. We don't have to create any tables, which is what this screen can be used for, because Drupal will create the tables for us as part of the installation script.

Creating a Database User Account

The next step is to create a MySQL user who will be associated with the database that we just created. You can use the "root" account that is created automatically when MySQL is installed. However, for security purposes, it is a better practice to create a user account that can only access this database. To access the user account creation screens, simply click the Privileges tab. This screen lists all existing user accounts. Click the "Add user" link at the bottom of the page.

There are four fields on the "Add user" screen that we need to fill to create our new user account (see Figure A-2):

- *User name*: This is the unique value that represents our database user and will be used by Drupal to log onto the database. For our example enter "drupal8."

- *Host*: This field provides the ability to restrict which system the user can log in from. For security purposes, we want to set this value to "localhost" by selecting the Local option from the drop-down list. Localhost is your web server; we don't want that user to have the ability to log in from any system other than the server.

- *Password*: Create a password and enter that same password in the Re-type field.

- *Database for user*: Leave the default option, which is None.

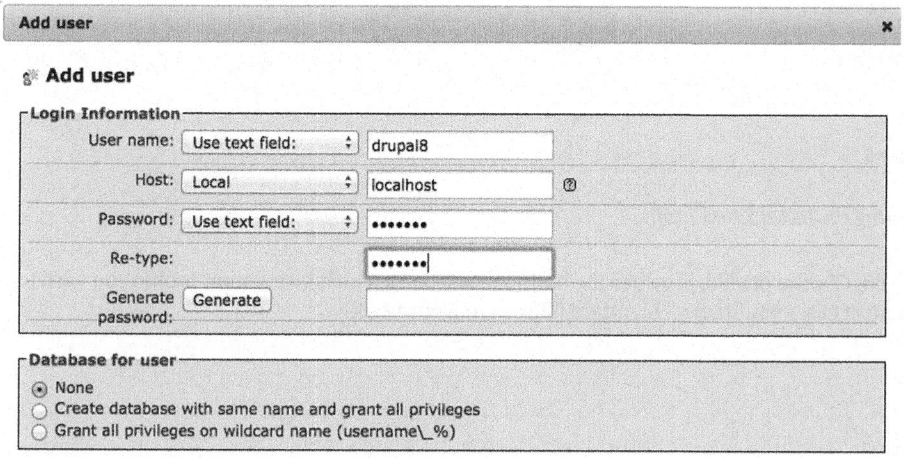

Figure A-2. *Creating a new database user*

One you click the Go button, phpMyAdmin creates your user account. The last step is to assign the user you just created to the database and grant the user the required privileges to use your new database. To assign the user, click the person and pencil icon for the user you just created and scroll down to the section titled "Database-specific privileges." Select the name of the database you created from the drop-down list and click the Go button within that section. You will then be presented with a list of privileges that you can grant to your user on the database you created. Click the Check All link near the top of the list and click the Go button. You are now ready to start the Drupal configuration process.

Configuring Drupal

To start the configuration process, simply open a web browser and type "http://localhost" in the address bar. If you installed Drupal 8 in a subdirectory you'll need to add the subdirectory to the URL path. The first page lists the languages that are available for your site (see Figure A-3). I'll select English. Click "Save and continue." The next step in the installation process allows you to pick which installation profile you wish to install. The Standard option installs the complete version of Drupal with all of the core modules that I describe and use throughout this book. The Minimal profile installs a bare-bones version of Drupal, without many of the core modules that I describe elsewhere in this book. For a vast majority of Drupal site owners, the Standard version is the correct one to select. If you're developing a custom platform (your own distribution profile with specific modules), you may wish to start with the Minimal profile. For our case, select the Standard option and click "Save and continue."

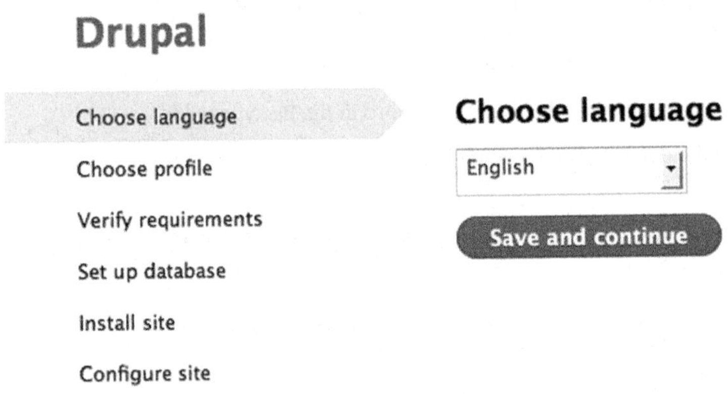

Figure A-3. *Selecting the installation profile*

The next screen, Choose profile, provides the option of selecting which installation profile you wish to proceed with. In most cases you'll select Standard (shown in Figure A-4).

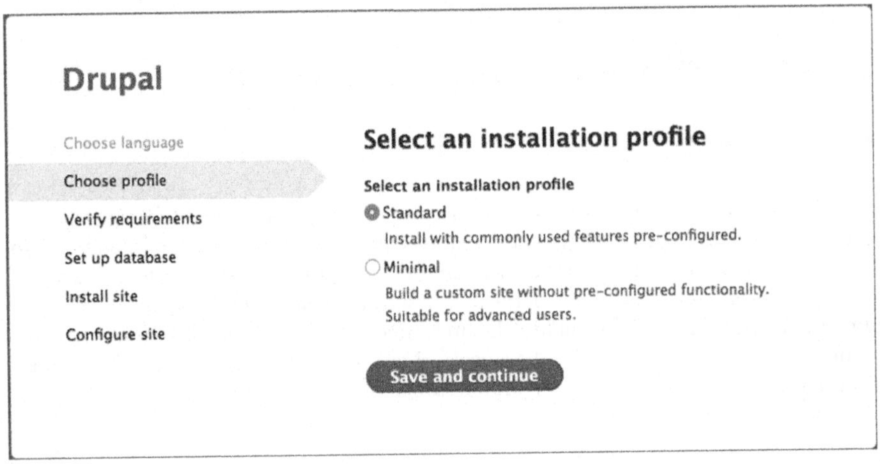

Figure A-4.

The next screen in the process asks for the details of the database that you created in the create database process. On this screen (shown in Figure A-5), complete the following fields:

- *Database name*: Enter the name you used when you created the database ("drupal8testsite" in the example).

- *Database username*: Enter the username you used when you created the new user ("drupal8" in the example).

- *Database password*: Enter the password you used when you created the new user.

Drupal

Choose language

Choose profile

Verify requirements

Set up database

Install site

Configure site

Database configuration

Database type *
- ◉ MySQL, MariaDB, Percona Server, or equivalent
- ○ PostgreSQL
- ○ SQLite

Database name *

Database username *

Database password

▸ ADVANCED OPTIONS

Save and continue

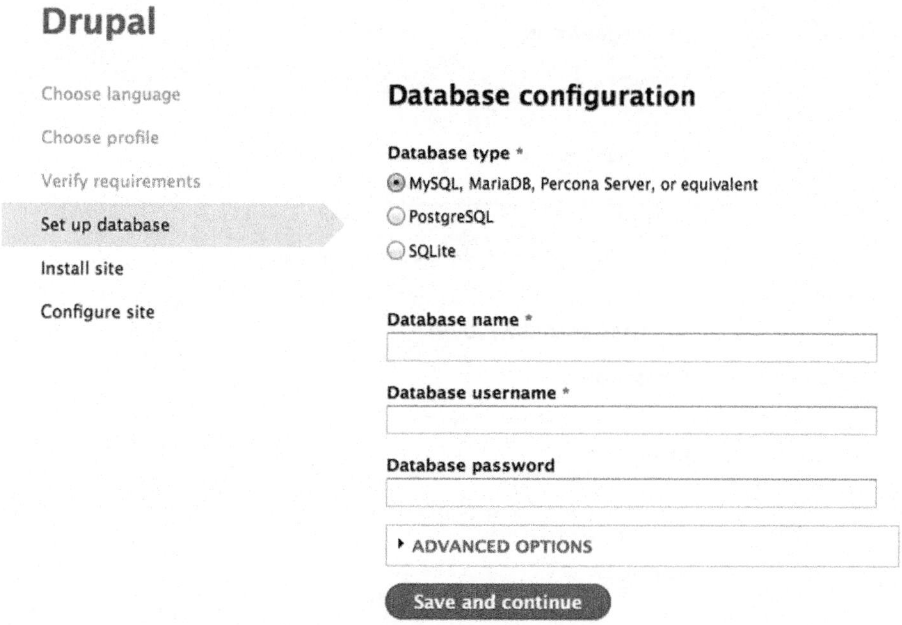

***Figure A-5.** Setting the database parameters*

If you've forgotten what you used for any of the preceding values, you can look them up through phpMyAdmin.

If you entered the correct values, Drupal will run the installation scripts. After Drupal creates the database tables required to support your new site, you're ready to set a few simple configuration parameters (see Figure A-6).

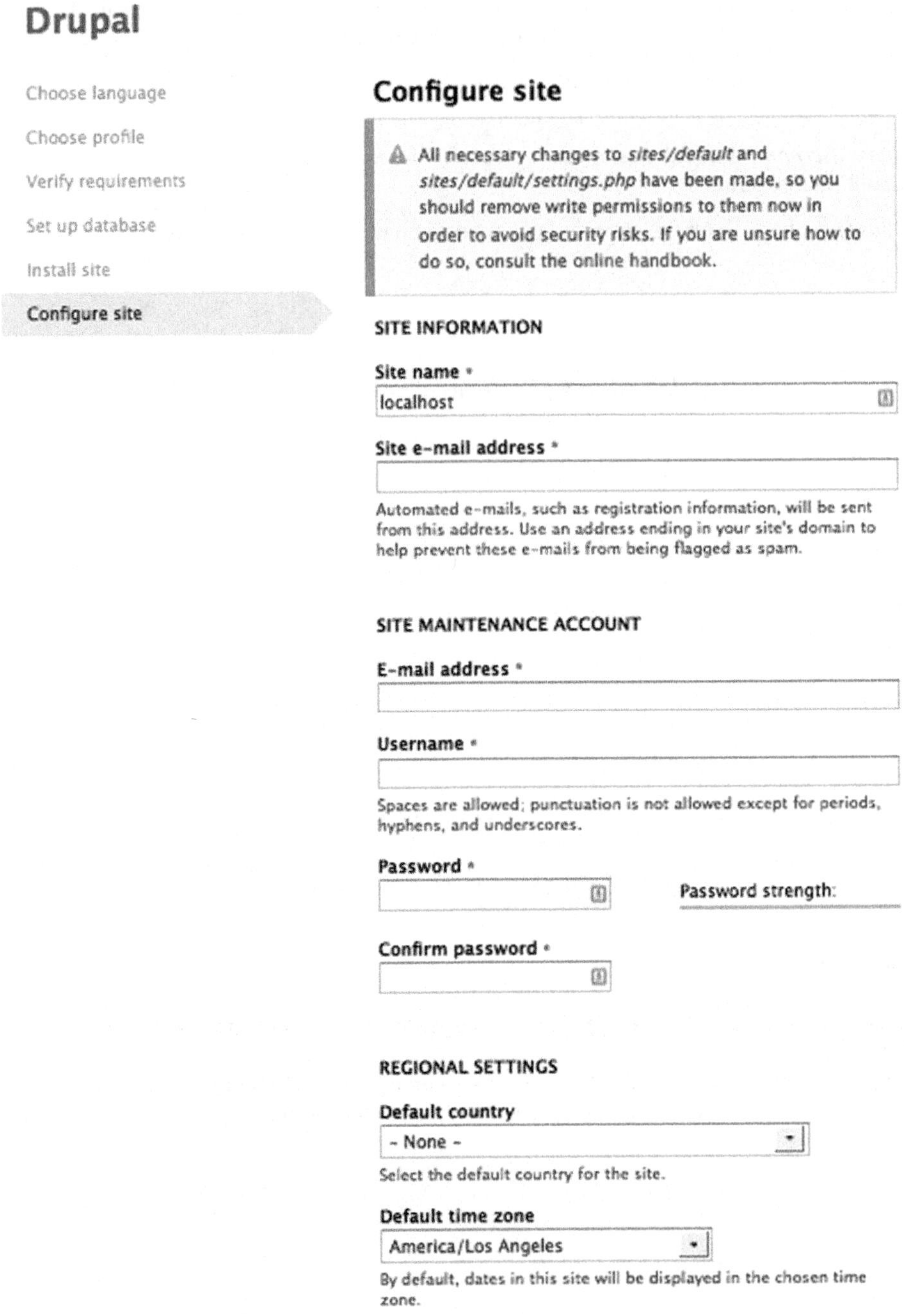

Drupal

Choose language

Choose profile

Verify requirements

Set up database

Install site

Configure site

Configure site

> ⚠ All necessary changes to *sites/default* and *sites/default/settings.php* have been made, so you should remove write permissions to them now in order to avoid security risks. If you are unsure how to do so, consult the online handbook.

SITE INFORMATION

Site name *

```
localhost
```

Site e-mail address *

Automated e-mails, such as registration information, will be sent from this address. Use an address ending in your site's domain to help prevent these e-mails from being flagged as spam.

SITE MAINTENANCE ACCOUNT

E-mail address *

Username *

Spaces are allowed; punctuation is not allowed except for periods, hyphens, and underscores.

Password *

Password strength:

Confirm password *

REGIONAL SETTINGS

Default country

```
– None –
```

Select the default country for the site.

Default time zone

```
America/Los Angeles
```

By default, dates in this site will be displayed in the chosen time zone.

Figure A-6. *The site configuration form*

274

On this form enter the following values:

- **Site Information**

  Site name: The name or title of your site.
  Site e-mail address: This is the default e-mail address that will be used by Drupal for any outbound e-mails generated by the system.

- **Site Maintenance Account**

  E-mail address: The e-mail address to which administrator-related e-mails will be sent.
  Username: This is the username of the administrator's account for your new website. Use something that is easy for you to remember.
  Password: Enter the password for the administrator's account.
  Confirm password: Re-enter the password you entered in the Password field.

- **Regional Settings**

  Default country: The country where you reside (or leave the None value if you do not want to specify the default country; this is an optional field).
  Default time zone: Select the appropriate time zone for your website.

- **Update Notifications**

  Check for updates automatically: If checked, this feature looks for updates to Drupal core and any contributed modules you have installed, and highlights cases where a new version or a security patch has been released. It's a good idea to check this, as it makes the task of tracking updates to modules much easier than having to manually check each module's status.
  Receive e-mail notifications: If checked, this directs Drupal to send an e-mail to the administrator when new versions of modules are detected.
  Once you've updated the values, simply click the "Save and continue" button.
  The result of clicking that button should be a screen that indicates that you have successfully installed Drupal! After the installation finishes, you will be automatically taken to the homepage of your new site.

Summary

In this appendix, I covered the process for setting up the server and installing Drupal. You're now ready to begin the journey of creating an incredible website using the Drupal 8 platform!

■ ■ ■

Additional Resources

As you begin (and continue) your journey of learning Drupal, there will likely be times when you'll need to find a Drupal module, a Drupal theme, additional details about specific Drupal technologies (such as theming), and operating system–level commands (for tasks such as backing up the site from the command line). This appendix points you to recommended websites where you can find additional resources to help you along your journey.

Drupal Modules

The primary site for finding modules is the Drupal.org website (`www.drupal.org/project/project_module`). Every Drupal contributed module has its own "homepage" that describes the module, provides links for downloading the various versions of the module, and, in most cases, links to additional documentation and examples.

Drupal Themes

The primary source of Drupal themes is the Drupal.org website (`www.drupal.org/project/project_theme`). You can browse through dozens of themes, see screenshots of each, and download the themes you like from Drupal.org.

Drupal Documentation

The Drupal community has assembled a number of online guides (`www.drupal.org/documentation`) that are chock-full of information about Drupal. You will find the following guides under the designated categories:

- User and Builder Guides
  - Understanding Drupal
  - Installation Guide
  - Administration & Security Guide
  - Structure Guide
  - Site Building Guide
  - Multilingual Guide

- Theming Guide
- Mobile Guide
- Developer Guides
- Develop for Drupal
- API Reference
- Examples for Developers
- Git documentation
- Other Information
- Glossary
- Code snippets
- Troubleshooting
- FAQs
- Tutorials and recipes
- Resource guides

Where to Go When You Have Problems

One of the best sources for Drupal help is the Community Forum on the Drupal.org website (`www.drupal.org/forum`). There are hundreds of thousands of postings on just about every conceivable topic. If you run into an issue, you're likely to find that the solution to your problem is already documented in the forum. If you can't find a solution, you can post a question to the forum and you'll often receive a solution to your problem within hours of posting the issue. Another great resource is Drupal Answers at Stack Exchange (`http://drupal.stackexchange.com`). When I'm looking for an example, Stack Exchange is my second stop along the journey of finding a solution.

Where to Host Your Drupal Site

If you are looking for a place to host your website, an excellent resource is the Drupal.org site (`www.drupal.org/hosting`). The Hosting page lists a number of companies that are known to support Drupal.

Where to Go to Learn HTML and CSS

A great resource to help you learn HTML and CSS is the W3Schools website (`www.w3schools.com`). You'll find easy-to-understand tutorials and excellent examples. Other alternatives exist, such as the Code School (`www.codeschool.com`), which has several free tutorials on HTML and CSS.

Video Tutorials

There are thousands of YouTube (`www.youtube.com`) videos that cover a wide variety of Drupal topics. It is a great source for learning various aspects of Drupal. Enter "Drupal" in YouTube's search box and you'll see a very long list of Drupal-related videos. There are also excellent paid training sites, such as Drupalize. Me (`https://drupalize.me`) and BuildAModule (`http://buildamodule.com`).

Drupal Podcasts

Another great source for learning Drupal is podcasts. There are a number podcasts that cover Drupal on iTunes.

Index

Get the eBook for only $5!

Why limit yourself?

Now you can take the weightless companion with you wherever you go and access your content on your PC, phone, tablet, or reader.

Since you've purchased this print book, we're happy to offer you the eBook in all 3 formats for just $5.

Convenient and fully searchable, the PDF version enables you to easily find and copy code—or perform examples by quickly toggling between instructions and applications. The MOBI format is ideal for your Kindle, while the ePUB can be utilized on a variety of mobile devices.

To learn more, go to www.apress.com/companion or contact support@apress.com.

21982318307885

CPSIA information can be obtained
at www.ICGtesting.com
Printed in the USA
LVOW04s1924130717
541269LV00007B/129/P

9 781430 265801